THE
PRACTICAL
PEDIATRICIAN

Dr. Howard Markel (right) and Dr. Frank A. Oski (left) and a few of their favorite patients.

THE PRACTICAL PEDIATRICIAN

The A to Z Guide to
Your Child's Health,
Behavior, and Safety

Howard Markel

Frank A. Oski

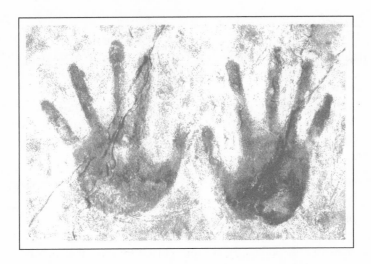

W. H. Freeman and Company
New York

Cover photo © 1995 Barnaby Hall/Photonica.
Cover and interior design: Victoria Tomaselli

Library of Congress Cataloging–in–Publication Data

Markel, Howard.
    The practical pediatrician : the A to Z guide to your child's
health, behavior and safety / Howard Markel, Frank A. Oski.
        p.   cm.
Includes index.
ISBN 0-7167-2897-4 (hardcover).—ISBN 0-7167-2896-6 (softcover)
1. Pediatrics—Popular works.   2. Children—Health and hygiene.
3. Children—Diseases.   I. Oski, Frank A.   II. Title.
RJ61.M392   1996
618.92—dc20   96-17604
                                           CIP

Printed in the United States of America.

First printing 1996, HAM

We dedicate this book to the men and women who have dedicated their creative and professional energies as interns, residents, and fellows of the Harriet Lane Home and Pediatrics Service at the Johns Hopkins Hospital.

CONTENTS

PREFACE

The Many Do's (and the Relatively Few Don'ts) of Parenting

You have the good fortune to be new parents. Too often, the joys of having a baby are dampened by concerns about the things you *"shouldn't"* do with and for your child. But you may take heart from knowing that the things you *should* do as parents far outnumber those you "should not." Most children do grow up to be healthy and productive adults despite a wide variety of parenting techniques or philosophies. One smart aleck expressed this phenomenon more cynically: "No matter how you raise your child, he will ultimately grow up to remind you what you did wrong."

Pediatricians, child-care experts, child-care advice books, and parents add to this confusion by changing their advice about child care from one generation to the next. What may have been an acceptable practice during your mother or grandmother's day may not be as widely practiced today— although you never know. In the pages of this book, we will, from time to time, discuss some of the relatively few "don'ts" of child rearing—such as *"Don't* smoke in a home where a child lives and plays," or *"Don't* insult or physically injure your child." But all told, most of the advice we offer focuses upon what you should *do.* The message of this book is that you can be an excellent parent, and the only way to achieve this goal is to learn "on the job."

The problems that parents and pediatricians face are markedly different from what they were just a generation or two ago. Only a century back, pediatricians spent a great deal of time diagnosing and treating infectious diseases such as whooping cough, diphtheria, measles, and other now-preventable problems. This book was written for the parents of the 1990s. Today, for instance, a pediatrician is much more likely to spend the day discussing such issues as accident and injury prevention, day care, working parents, television, video games and movies, and other issues, along with the more traditional topics of childhood.

The Practical Pediatrician focuses upon the health, behavioral, and safety needs of the child from birth to about eight ears of age. We have based the advice offered in these pages on our experiences as pediatricians who work daily with parents and children and with other physicians, child psychologists, nurses, and health-care professionals at the University of Michigan Medical Center and the Johns Hopkins Hospital. The book has been arranged alphabetically, like a dictionary or encyclopedia, so that you can look up the topic you need most quickly. A more complete index is available at the end of the book, and cross-references to similar or related topics are interspersed throughout. In this way, you may acquaint yourself with the issues discussed in the book by reading it at your leisure or as a particular question arises. We have tried to make the book gender-neutral by using the pronouns "she" and "he" alternatively when speaking of babies and children. We have also included charts and checklists to help you record your child's immunizations, growth, development, and other aspects of the well-child pediatric examination schedule. Thus you may use the book to record important information about your child as she or he grows.

Please note that we use the plural term parents, meaning *both* the mother and the father. Just as marriage is a partnership built upon the foundations of trust, love, and friendship, so should you look at your new roles as parents. Many times both parents are in agreement over child-rearing issues; sometimes, however, you will not agree on a particular matter. Feel free to use this book and other sources of information to help sort out your views. Above all, both parents need to discuss, discuss, and rediscuss these issues together to reach mutual understanding and a plan that works. Remember, there are relatively few "don'ts" in child rearing, and all parents make mistakes. The wonderful thing about parenting is the strength and resilience of the child. Oftentimes the baby or child is stronger than both the parents and the pediatrician put together!

As an introduction to child rearing, we would like to offer some tested and true observations on what you can do to begin to maximize your pleasure and to minimize the anxiety surrounding your new parental responsibilities.

• *Do* trust your instincts. Have confidence in your ability to make correct judgments and choices when it comes to taking care of your baby.

• *Do* allow yourself to ask questions about your child and feel comfortable requesting help when you are puzzled about a particular parental issue or you simply need a break.

• *Do* love your child, and love your child unconditionally. Love your child when he cries, love your child when she doesn't eat, love your child when he makes a mess, love your child when she doesn't obey, love your child when he is sick, and love your child even when she tells you—and someday she will—that she doesn't like you.

• *Do* be consistent. *Do* set limits and make certain that those limits are the same from day to day and parent to parent. Nothing frustrates a child more and produces more misunderstanding and disobedience than a lack of consistency in setting limits. For example, it is difficult for a child to learn about the dangers of smoking when his parent is a cigarette smoker! Be a good role model for your child. Children are wonderful imitators of their parents' behaviors—and that includes the negative behaviors as well as the positive ones.

• *Do* get to know your child and pay attention to her daily habits and personality. Learn to become a good observer. Become familiar with his sleeping and waking patterns, her dietary habits, the food he likes or dislikes, her stool habits, when she gets tired, and his other patterns of behavior. A change in the way your baby or child acts, is far more important than her temperature when you must judge whether she is sick or well. Nobody will know your baby better than you do. Good doctors have all learned to believe parents when they say that their child is not well.

In short, focus on the many *do's* of parenting. Remember that raising an infant and child should be a positive, pleasurable experience. You can do it, and do it well.

ACKNOWLEDGMENTS

Perhaps the most enjoyable part of writing a book is the task of recording the acknowledgments. In composing *The Practical Pediatrician*, we were most fortunate in obtaining help, consultations, and advice from many of our colleagues, patients, and, of course, their parents. We are delighted to take the opportunity to thank them publicly.

This book began as a series of conversations with our long-time publisher, John J. Hanley of Scientific American. We were also fortunate in allying our efforts with Susan Finnemore Brennan and Diane Cimino Maass, our editors, and Robert Biewen, president of W. H. Freeman and Company.

We work with many talented and dedicated physicians and health-care professionals at our home institutions, the University of Michigan Medical Center and the Johns Hopkins Hospital. They generously donated their time and expertise to reviewing the contents of this book. These include Dr. Eileen Mollen (Child Psychology), Dr. Barbara Felt (Behavioral Pediatrics), Dr. Ronald Holmes (Gastroenterology and General Pediatrics), Dr. Robert P. Kelch (Endocrinology), Dr. Thomas Shope (Infectious Diseases and General Pediatrics), Dr. Lawrence Boxer (Hematology and Oncology), Dr. Janet Gilsdorf (Infectious Diseases), Susan Nehring, R.N. (Lactation Consultant), Dr. E. Albert Tzeel (General Pediatrics), Dr. Steven Stryk (Allergy and Immunology), Dr. Elizabeth Quint (Pediatric Gynecology), Dr. Thomas Schwenk (Family Practice), Dr. Andrew Metinko (Critical Care Medicine), Dr. Catherine DeAngelis (General Pediatrics), Dr. Modena Wilson (General Pediatrics), Dr. Julia McMillan (Infectious Diseases and General Pediatrics), Judy Vogelhut, R.N. (Lactation Consultant), and Dr. William T. Zempsky (Emergency Medicine and Pediatric Cardiology). We were also fortunate in having several parents review this book, including Leslie Carr; Lisa L. Mann, R.N., M.N., P.N.P.; Tracy M. McPeake; and Jody Stadler. Critical secretarial help was provided by Janice Williams, Darleen Blackmer, Julie Adams, and Leslie Burke. Technical advice on computer issues was provided by Fred J. Shapiro.

Much of the material in *The Practical Pediatrician* was tested over the past ten years in what we pediatricians call "the court of appeals"—our outpatient general pediatrics clinics at Michigan and Johns Hopkins. We appreciate the invaluable feedback we received from our many patients and their parents as well as from our medical students, interns, and residents. We hope that the result of these efforts provides parents with a useful and enjoyable guide to their child's health, safety, and behavior.

Howard Markel, M.D., Ph.D.
Frank A. Oski, M.D.

A Note to Our Readers

Every situation in your child's life is unique. While the authors of this book and the editors at W. H. Freeman and Company have conscientiously reviewed this book for accuracy, it is not meant to be used for diagnosis or treatment in place of a health-care provider. Only you and your doctor can know the complete circumstances surrounding a problem behavior, injury, or illness. This book is only a general guide. You, as parents, know your child best, and you should not hesitate to contact your health-care provider; no book can replace the advice of a good physician. With that in mind, we trust that our advice will serve you well.

ABDOMINAL PAIN

One of the most common problems in early childhood, the "tummyache," can be caused by more than a hundred different medical, emotional, or psychological conditions.

The appearance of abdominal discomfort during the first two months of life, where the baby cries for hours and draws his legs to his chest, is called colic and is described later in this book.

In the older child, the most common cause of abdominal discomfort is constipation. Other causes of severe abdominal pain include torsion of the testicle (a condition in which a boy's testicle twists upon itself, cutting off blood flow to that testicle); appendicitis; intussception, a urinary tract infection; pneumonia; and even strep throat. These topics are all described elsewhere in this book. There also exist emotional or psychological conditions that present themselves in the form of a "bellyache."

Rather than explain each of these problems here, we would like to review the types of signs and symptoms that you need to worry about and those you need not.

What Type of Abdominal Pain Constitutes an Emergency?

Some medical conditions that cause severe abdominal pain demand immediate medical attention. You need to gauge the severity of your child's belly complaints (this, obviously, can be extremely difficult in the baby or infant who cannot yet talk). Here are a few questions that may help:

1. How much pain does your child appear to be in?

2. What makes him more comfortable?

3. What makes his belly pain worse?

4. Is the belly pain associated with vomiting or fever?

5. Have any new foods been introduced, or have you any grounds to suspect food poisoning (e.g., ingestion of tainted or raw meat, shellfish, and so forth)?

Other symptoms that suggest severe belly pain include:

- Your baby or child appears quite ill
- Extreme irritability and discomfort
- Severe diarrhea (more than 8 diarrheal stools in 8 hours)
- Severe constipation (no bowel movement for more than 3 days)
- Severe fever (above 102°F), with chills
- Exhaustion, lethargy, difficulty in arousing your child from sleep
- Rapid heartbeat, clammy skin
- Severe nausea and vomiting (your child cannot hold liquids or solids down)
- Bloating of the abdomen
- A sudden and unexplainable refusal to eat

If you notice these symptoms in your child, it is a good idea to discuss them with your pediatrician in order to assess the need for medical attention. A quick telephone call can often help the parent and pediatrician decide which problems demand immediate attention and which may simply require an office visit the following day or, better still, parental reassurance.

Recurrent Abdominal Pain

The overwhelming majority (90 percent) of children over the age of three years of age who complain of abdominal pain are *not* experiencing medical conditions or diseases that injure the organs of the abdomen. Their belly pain may be classified as psychosomatic. Much like the stress headache many an adult complains of at the end of a long day at work, recurrent abdominal pain in the child may signify a deeper problem related to school, how he is getting along with friends or family, or other emotional issues. Rather than dismiss this vexing problem as "being in the kid's head," acknowledge to your child that you believe he is experiencing pain and try to discuss what may be bothering him in his emotional life. Try and explore the feelings he is experiencing. Is something going on at school that may be troubling your child? Has he recently had a fight with a best friend or sibling? Think about what is going on at home—is there marital discord that may be affecting the child? It may seem like detective work, but you need to find out what is going on in your child's world that may be troubling him. Sometimes your using an example from your own childhood of similar things that may have scared or bothered you at the same age can help your child better express his own feelings.

We rarely recommend medication for recurrent abdominal pain since it is not caused by a physical disease. Laxatives, stomach remedies, and the like are best left alone. There are times when simple distraction of your child's attention away from his belly and onto something more enjoyable, such as a story or a favorite activity, will help relieve the problem. It is always worthwhile to try reassuring your child during such an episode. Soothing and comforting actions such as cuddling, holding, storytelling, belly-rubbing, rocking, and a nice cup of peppermint or chamomile tea (for the child older than three years who can handle a cup) go much farther than any medication we could think of!

There are some children who experience a problem called irritable bowel syndrome, distinguished by mild abdominal pain accompanied by mushy or loose stools. Adding more dietary fiber in the form of oatmeal, bran, and similar products can help clear this problem up. It generally resolves by the age of two or three years of age *[see Appendicitis; Colic; Constipation; Intussusseption; Pyloric Stenosis; Urinary Tract Problems]*.

ACNE OF THE NEWBORN *[See Newborn appearance]*

AGGRESSION (When your child fights, bites, or hits)

Aggression is a common behavior seen during different periods of child development, particularly during the toddler years. Common types of aggression that tend not to be acceptable for most parents include tantrums, hitting, biting, kicking, and fighting. Obviously children under the age of two or three years may have more trouble understanding the consequences of their aggressive acts than their older counterparts. But if you want it to stop, you need to interrupt aggressive behavior in your children as it occurs. Fighting, biting, and the like are simply not to be tolerated, and you need to say "No!" to these displays in no uncertain terms *[see Negotiating with Your Child]*. Here are some more practical tips.

• Children, especially toddlers, may react with aggressive behaviors to stressors, such as being hungry, being tired, another playmate who is especially aggressive, and so on. Try to reduce thee stressors as much as possible.

• Try not to let your child play with other children who engage in especially aggressive games.

• When you witness your child in an aggressive act such as hitting or biting, a mandatory "time out" is indicated. Briefly isolate your child from the activity he was engaged in and explain to him why you are doing so. The time-out need only be a few minutes, but it needs to be strict and consistent. If you condone aggressive acts, they will be repeated.

• Limit your child's television and video watching to nonviolent shows or movies. Don't purchase toy weapons or arsenals for your children. Explore productive games, toys, and activities where the ultimate aim is fun rather than "annihilating one's enemy" *[see Computers and the Internet; Television; Video Games and VCRs]*.

• Hitting your child rarely yields any consistent behavioral changes. In the case of saying "No" to aggression, it probably reinforces the child's aggressive behavior. Hitting is never acceptable either by child or parent *[see Bites]*.

• It will be easier to discuss the negative aspects of aggressive behavior with children over the age of four than with your two-year-old. The techniques in "Negotiating with Your Child" will be of help.

AIDS (Acquired Immune Deficiency Syndrome)

AIDS, a life-threatening infectious disease, gradually destroys a person's immune system, making him extremely susceptible to serious and overwhelming infections. Caused by a virus called the Human Immunodeficiency Virus (HIV), AIDS is spread in a rather specific manner, either by sexual activity or by introducing the blood of a person with HIV into one who does not (e.g., blood transfusions, etc.). The disease is relatively rare among small children. The majority of babies with AIDS contract the virus from their mothers, infected either before or during the pregnancy. Of those babies born to mothers who are HIV-positive, less than 10 percent will actually go on to develop AIDS. For mothers who are HIV-positive, we do not recommend breastfeeding, since the virus may be transmitted during nursing. To date, no child has contracted HIV/AIDS from activities related to day care, school, or simple childhood play. Nor has any child (or adult) contracted HIV/AIDS from kissing, hugging, playing together, or insect bites *[see Bites]*.

Another group of children with AIDS are those who have hemophilia—a rare blood disorder that interferes with the blood's ability to clot. These children receive hundreds of doses of clotting factors and similar blood products during their lives. For those hemophiliacs who were receiving these products before 1985, when the nation's blood supply began to be scrutinized for HIV, the chances are great that they, too, have been infected with the HIV virus. Currently, blood products in the United States are carefully monitored for HIV (and similar viruses, such as hepatitis, that may be passed via blood), rendering accidental infection through blood products a less than a one-in-a-million chance.

For adults who are thinking about having children, prevention remains the key response to HIV. Avoid high-risk sexual practices (unsafe sex), intravenous drug use (because of the risk of dirty needles), and make sure you are HIV-negative *before* conceiving a child. People with HIV rarely have any symptoms or health problems until the disease has progressed for many years. Generally we recommend that anyone, whether an adult or a child, who feels he or she may have been exposed, should undergo an HIV test, followed by a second test six months later.

For the latest updates on AIDS information, treatments, and advice:

National HIV/AIDS Hotline
Centers for Disease Control and Prevention
(800) 342-AIDS
In Spanish: (800) 344-7432
For the hearing impaired: (800) 243-7889

Allergies

Allergies refer to the broad range of symptoms experienced when a particular substance is inhaled or eaten by a susceptible person. Not all people are allergic to the same substances (allergens), and most people are not allergic to any particular substance at all. Although allergic symptoms may not appear upon the susceptible child's first exposure to a given allergen, the body quickly becomes sensitive with repeated exposures, which leads to a hypersensitivity reaction. The body's mast cells release histamine, antibodies, and a number of other substances that can cause itchiness, localized swelling, inflamed or tender skin, runny nose, watery eyes, low blood pressure, and spasms of the muscles surrounding the lungs, airways, and gastrointestinal tract (gut).

Allergic Rhinitis (Hay fever)

Poets have traditionally identified the return of spring as the rebirth of nature. People with hay fever, or allergic rhinitis, have a far more direct means of detecting the time of year: sneezing; nasal itching; runny nose; sniffling; postnasal drip; red, itchy, watery eyes; bags under the eyes (allergic shiners); and sinus congestion. Some children will complain of being tired or "not feeling great." Allergic rhinitis tends to run in families; if one or both parents suffer from this problem, there is a good chance that their child may, too.

Causes of hay fever

Environmental allergens may be seasonal or they may be present all year round. It depends on the child and what specific allergen causes his hay fever. Listed below are some of the most common culprits and the months when they cause the most problems in North America:

- Tree pollens—April to May
- Grass pollens—May to July
- Weeds, including ragweed—mid-August until the first frost
- Pet danders and saliva—all year round
- Bird feathers—all year round
- Dust mites—all year round
- Cockroaches (and the droppings they leave behind)—all year round
- Molds (which can be found in damp basements, bathrooms, and barns, the woods, and other outdoor areas where it is frequently damp)—all year round

 Since the symptoms of hay fever are so similar to those of a common cold, how do I tell which is going on in my child?

This may be difficult the first time it occurs. Generally hay fever, despite its fiery name, is not associated with actual fever. The child's temperature is normal. Hay fever does not

spread from family member to family member, as a cold often does. Finally, colds go away in a few days. The child with hay fever will exhibit symptoms as often as he is exposed to an allergen.

Prevention

If your child is developing frequent runny noses, watery eyes, or some of the other allergic symptoms discussed above and they are not associated with a cold *[see Upper Respiratory Tract Infections],* you need to do some detective work in order to figure out what the child is allergic to. This is often a difficult task that may require a consultation with an allergist—a physician who specializes in treating allergies. Once you discover what the offending allergen is, the best method of treatment is to avoid it. Here are a few plans of attack:

Pets: The dander, fur, and saliva of animals are among the most common causes of allergic rhinitis symptoms in children and adults. In general, it is wise not to bring a pet into the home that has a new baby or a young child *[see Bites, Animal].* If you have pets and young children in the same household, you should consider keeping the pet outside as much as possible. Cats are the leading offenders of sensitive noses and eyes; more than a third of all people with hay fever react to cats. Because animal allergens are microscopically small substances, they easily move about the house regardless of your restricting the pet in question to one room or floor. Weekly baths for your pet may help somewhat. Pets such as fish, reptiles, and amphibians are less likely to cause allergic symptoms. Thorough handwashing after handling pets is always a good idea in terms of hygiene and health maintenance.

Environmental allergens and irritants such as cigarette, pipe, or cigar smoke; pollens; and air pollution: On breezy spring and summer days, it is wise to keep the windows and doors closed in order to prevent pollen from entering your home. Air conditioning is helpful since it filters incoming air. Home air filtering and humidifying devices may also help, provided that you keep their filters scrupulously clean. Cigarette smoking should always be done *outside* of the home and *away* from your child. Passive smoking can inflame nasal passages and airways, increase the risk of asthma in your child and is probably related to other lung problems *[see Smoking].* Finally, check your local newspaper or television weather service for information on your area's daily pollen count as well as the air quality indexes. This readily available information will help you to decide when it is best to simply keep your allergic child inside an air-conditioned home on a particularly "bad" day.

Dust mites: These almost ubiquitous, microscopic insects live in carpeting, mattresses, pillows, furniture cushions, stuffed animals, and similar household objects. Dust mites live and feed on human skin cells that have been shed. They require a room temperature of at least 65 to 70° F and a relative humidity of at least 50 percent to survive. Dust mites thrive in the warmth and humidity of summer. If your child is found to have an allergy to dust mites, you can begin by removing all of the stuffed animals from his room. The child's mattress, box spring, and pillows should be encased in watertight vinyl or plastic cases, readily available at most department stores. Buy pillows stuffed with something other than feathers or down. The child's bedroom needs to be frequently dusted with a damp cloth. Simple wood floors with washable rugs are preferable to thick wall-to-wall carpeting. Avoid large plants and cool-mist humidifiers in the allergic child's bedroom, since they provide a comfortable environment for dust mites.

Molds: Mold exposure can be reduced in a number of ways. The first is to reduce the humidity of your home as much as possible. Avoid home humidifiers, except in the special cases where they are necessary *[see Croup, Asthma, Upper Respiratory Tract Infections]*. Humidifiers are breeding grounds for molds; if you use one, make sure that you clean it daily with a bleach-containing cleanser. Keep the bathrooms and basement clean and dry: bleach-containing, antifungal cleansers are readily available at your local grocery store. Other locations where molds like to grow include barns or places where there is wet or damp, mold-infested hay (hence the term "hay fever"). Events to reconsider include hayrides, rodeos, visits to petting farms, and similar activities.

Treatments

There are a number of medications that can help to alleviate, though not cure, the symptoms of hay fever. They may be in pill or syrup form or they may be topical. Major classes of allergy medications are listed below.

• Antihistamines help prevent the release of histamine from mast cells in the body in order to reduce the allergic response. These medications can make some children sleepy as a side effect; in other children, they may have the opposite side effect, making them particularly alert and overactive.

• Decongestants help to relieve nasal congestion, but their many potential side effects include restlessness, insomnia, and a decrease in appetite.

• Topical steroid nose drops help reduce inflammation but need to be taken regularly before the allergic response has begun in order to work most effectively.

• Cromylyn sodium helps prevent allergic responses before they happen by stabilizing mast cells and preventing them from releasing histamine, provided the medication has been taken regularly *before* the allergic response occurs.

For severe allergic rhinitis that does not appear to resolve with these medications, more specific allergy testing is needed. Your doctor may prescribe "allergy shots," which help to decrease the body's sensitivity level to these specific allergens. You should discuss all of these options with your pediatrician, who will prescribe and monitor these preventive actions and medications.

[See Asthma and Wheezing; Eyes, Allergic reactions of; Eyes, "Bags" or Dark Circles Under the Eyes; Hives; Sinusitis]

Food Allergies

Food allergies refer to the allergic reaction that may happen when a susceptible person ingests a particular food. These foods enter the bloodstream and tissues, causing the mast cells to release histamine, immunoglobulins (such as IgE), and other allergy-symptom producing substances. The severity of the allergic reaction depends on many factors, including which food was ingested, the amount of food, and the extent of the body's chemical response to that food. Food allergies tend to run in families. If both parents have a food allergy, the chances are great that their child will have one, too.

What are some of the symptoms of a food allergy?

Symptoms typically begin anywhere from immediately to several hours after ingesting the offending food. They include:

- *Gastrointestinal symptoms such as bloating, cramping, vomiting, and diarrhea*
- *Skin symptoms including hives **[see Hives],** rashes, itchy skin, and (rarely) mouth and tongue swelling*
- *Lung symptoms including wheezing, chest tightness, and pain*
- *Rarely, a severe food allergy may generate an anaphylactic reaction, resulting in severe breathing and swallowing difficulties, shock, and even death*

How common are food allergies, and which foods are responsible?

Not as common as you may think. Frequent polls show that most American adults believe that childhood food allergies occur in about 25 to 35 percent of all children; in reality, less than 2 to 4 percent of all children have a true food allergy. Another 10 percent of the population may experience discomfort after eating specific foods, but this is not a true food allergy; instead, it is referred to as a food intolerance. The most common example of this problem is lactose intolerance; lactose is a digestive enzyme that breaks down milk sugar and is absent in about 10 percent of all Americans. Lactose-deficient people can develop bloating and cramping after eating dairy foods.

Common culprits of food allergies include seafood and shellfish; cow's milk; wheat products; soybeans or soy-based products; nuts; and eggs. Foods such as chocolate, strawberries, and tomatoes are often accused of causing food allergies but rarely do.

Many children outgrow their food allergies by the age of three years. Removing the food allergen from the diet for several years reduces allergic reactions in a third of these children when the food is subsequently reintroduced into their diet. The one exception to "outgrowing" food allergies are those to nuts, shellfish, and seafood; these reactions rarely disappear, and the foods that cause them should be removed from that child's diet permanently.

Are there any steps I can take to prevent food allergies from developing in my baby?

Unless your pediatrician recommends differently, it is wise to hold off on introducing solid foods until the baby is at least four to six months of age. Babies under one year should not *be given whole cow's milk or eggs. Breastfed babies tend to develop food allergies far less frequently than bottlefed babies—an important consideration, especially if food allergies run in your family. Other helpful measures include delaying the introduction of such foods as shellfish, nuts, and eggs until the child is at least three years old.*

Too frequently, a baby's artificial formula (whether it is based on cow's milk or soy products) is blamed for causing a baby's food allergy or belly discomfort after a meal. This often leads to parents' complicated and futile switching among many different formulas. This game of infant-formula "musical chairs" is best avoided. Keep in mind that food allergies are quite rare; the overwhelming majority of babies using artificial formulas do just fine. If you do notice the symptoms described above after introducing a new food to your child, write them down and feel free to discuss this record with your pediatrician. Your pediatrician will examine the food diary and may suggest a consultation with a physician who specializes in treating allergies.

Anaphylactic Reactions

The most serious allergic response is called an anaphylactic reaction. It is severe and effects the entire body. Anaphylactic reactions can be triggered by medications, foods, insect bites or stings, and, at times, unknown causes.

Signs and symptoms of an anaphylactic reaction

Symptoms of this severe allergic reaction typically occur thirty minutes after being exposed to the offending allergen in question. The symptoms, from least to most severe, include:

• Itching
• Thickened or swollen tongue, lips, and swelling of the soft tissues of the throat and airway
• Hives (urticarial rash)
• Difficulty breathing
• Low blood pressure, dizziness, fainting
• Shock (and possible death)

Common allergens associated with anaphylactic reactions

• Foods such as shellfish and seafood; nuts, legumes, eggs, celery, milk
• Medications, including penicillin, chemotherapeutic agents, muscle relaxants, biological agents, and blood products
• Bites or stings by bees, wasps, hornets, deerflies, fire ants, kissing bugs
• Food additives such as metabisulfite, monosodium glutamate, aspartame

Prevention and Treatment

The best treatment is to avoid such episodes entirely by helping your child avoid his allergens. Once you discover that your child has an allergy to one of the foods noted, you need to make sure that he does not consume it, either in its natural form or in products that may contain it. Peanuts are especially difficult to avoid, since they can appear in candy, cakes, snacks, and (as peanut oil) a wide variety of foodstuffs. Read product labels, since they usually list all ingredients. Avoid food products that do not list their ingredients! If your child is allergic to a specific type of insect bite or sting, take precautions to make sure that such an event does not occur. For information on avoiding and treating insect bites and stings, see "Bites."

If your child does experience an anaphylactic reaction, you need to call the Emergency Service (911) immediately. An emergency needs to be handled by health-care professionals. In order to prevent subsequent episodes, your pediatrician will prescribe a penlike syringe device containing epinephrine, (called the EPIPEN® or the ANA-KIT®), a common antidote that prevents future anaphylactic reactions from occurring. This should be carried by you (and the child) at all times. In the event of a repeat episode of anaphylaxis associated with an insect sting or the unexpected ingestion of a particular food, you should give the epinephrine as directed, followed by a dose of antihistamines, such as Benedryl® or diphenhydramine, and call 911 (Emergency Services).

Any child at risk for anaphylactic reactions ought to wear a medical alert medallion or bracelet, which can be purchased at your local drug store. This identification helps greatly in those emergency situations where a parent may not be available for consultation.

For further information on allergies you may call or write:

The Asthma and Allergy Foundation of America
1125 15th Street, N.W., Room #502
Washington D.C. 20005
(202) 466-7643

ANTIBIOTICS *[see Medicines]*

APPENDICITIS

The appendix is a small outgrowth of the large intestine or colon. In some children (and adults) the appendix can become inflamed and infected. This condition is called appendicitis, or inflammation of the vermiform appendix. One common cause is a piece of hardened stool that becomes lodged in the appendix. A particular danger of appendicitis is the rupture and bursting of the inflamed appendix; this causes a serious medical problem called peritonitis, which is a bacterial infection of the abdomen. Although appendicitis is rare before the age of two or three years, it remains a common problem of childhood—one of every five hundred children in the United States develops appendicitis. The most common treatment for this potentially life-threatening condition is a surgical operation called an appendectomy.

Symptoms of Appendicitis

- Belly (abdominal) pain that may be mild at first but gradually intensifies over a twenty-four-to-forty-eight-hour period. The belly pain eventually becomes non-stop and may cause the child to walk in a "hunched over" manner. The child may simply want to lie in bed, typically guarding the right leg or right side of the body.

- Fever without any other clear source of infection

- Nausea, diarrhea, vomiting

- The child cannot or will not move because of severe belly pain

 How can I distinguish between a "stomach ache" and a more serious problem such as appendicitis?

This is not an easy question to answer and one that often confuses doctors as well as parents. Specifically, we look at the severity of the symptoms. A child with appendicitis is much sicker than a child with recurrent abdominal pain. The ill child will refuse food, will abstain from favorite activities and, in the case of appendicitis, be in extreme pain. Assess each situation based on your knowledge of how your child reacts to different situations; try to piece things together. Your pediatrician will be happy to help you in this form of detective work, and you should feel free to call with questions. Above all, trust your own instincts. If your child appears ill to you, you are probably correct [see Abdominal Pain; Intussesseption; Pyloric Stenosis].

Asthma and Wheezing

Childhood asthma is one of the most common reasons for admission to a children's hospital in the United States. Although the disease is quite variable among different children and even between "attacks" in the same child, it can be an extremely dangerous condition, especially if its symptoms and warning signs are ignored.

The lungs are the major organs for breathing. They are composed of tiny air sacs called *alveoli* and breathing passages called *bronchii* and *bronchioles*. These airways become progressively smaller as they reach the farthest sections of lung tissue. Around each breathing passage is a layer of smooth muscle that can constrict and tighten the airway. Many things can trigger this muscle tightening (*bronchospasm*), but people with asthma are more prone to its occurrence. Another cause of asthma is the increase of secretions (e.g., phleghm) in the airways.

The hallmark symptom of asthma is wheezing, a high-pitched sound that is emitted upon exhaling (breathing out). It's similar to what happens when you pinch a drinking straw and breathe through it. As the wheezing becomes more severe, however, you may also see symptoms such as retractions (the moving of chest wall, neck, and abdominal muscles in an attempt to simply move air). Other common symptoms include coughing, shortness of breath, and chest congestion. Even more serious are symptoms such as blue-tinged lips or fingernails, both of

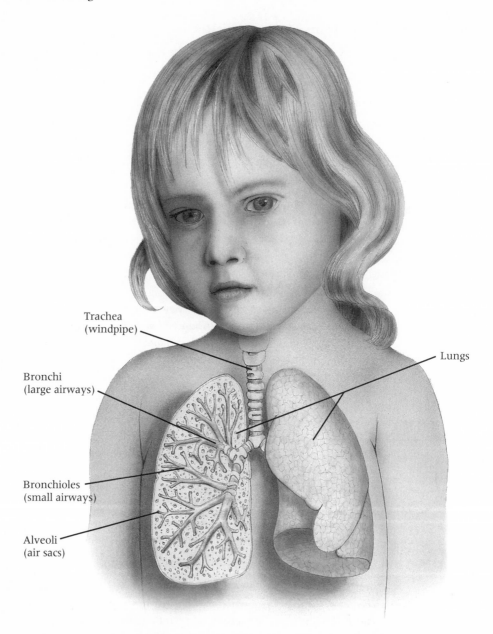

Trachea
(windpipe)

Lungs

Bronchi
(large airways)

Bronchioles
(small airways)

Alveoli
(air sacs)

which indicate that the child is not getting enough oxygen into his lungs. Other upper airway conditions can mimic this "wheezing" sound, such as the barking cough of croup and upper respiratory tract infections ("colds"), which cause a collection of phlegm in the air passages and can make breathing uncomfortable or difficult in a normal child. In a child with asthma, colds can set off a serious "attack" of reactive airway disease.

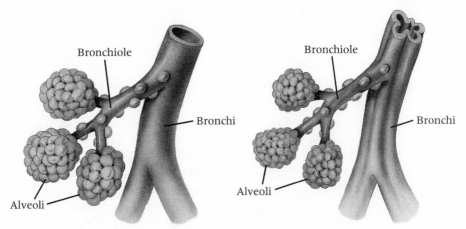

Bronchiole

Bronchiole

Bronchi

Bronchi

Alveoli

Alveoli

A close up of a section of the respiratory system. Normally, airways are open and breathing is easy. However, during an asthma attack airways tighten up, making breathing difficult.

How is Asthma Treated?

The most important thing is to prevent the smooth muscles surrounding the air passages from tightening and hindering the amount of air the child can breathe into his lungs. Different children have different triggers, ranging from allergies to weather changes. Your job is to be an excellent detective and try to identify some of the triggering agents for your child.

Common Triggers

Smoke from cigarettes, cigars, pipes
Mold from wet carpets, basements, or air conditioners
Upper respiratory tract infections *[see **Upper Respiratory Tract Infections and Colds**]*
Ear infections
Dust around the home
Stuffed animals
Mattresses
Pollen from trees or plants
Feathers
Food allergies
Paint fumes
Changes in the weather (hot to cold or cold to hot)
Breathing in cold air
Household sprays
Exercise: Exercise-induced asthma is one of the more common and easily treated forms of asthma; it does not mean that your child cannot exercise and

play. Many great athletes have exercise-induced asthma. Typically, they are treated with a medication just before beginning the exercise. You should discuss such a plan with your physician.

Some Tips Regarding Environmental Triggers

If you discover that a particular environmental allergen is irritating your child's asthma, you must do your best to try and remove that trigger from his environment *[see Allergies].* As best you can, eliminate dust, pollen, grass, and weeds, from the home environment; avoid smoking cigarettes, cigars, or pipes in the house where an asthmatic child lives; avoid owning pets whose fur or dander might irritate the breathing passages of your child; keep the filters of heaters, air conditioners, humidifiers, and similar appliances scrupulously clean.

Other things you can do to make your child's room "allergen-free" include removing stuffed animals and avoiding cluttered and dusty closet shelves, using hypoallergenic pillows and plastic covers on the child's mattress, keeping the floors bare (dense carpet can be a haven for dust), and closing window treatments that prevent the entry of dust, pollen, and other allergens from outside.

Asthma can usually be easily treated if the child in question comes for medical intervention early rather than late in the course of the problem. Frequently the child with reactive airway disease will be placed on specific medications, either to take in the event of an asthma attack or to prevent episodes entirely. The key to these preventive methods is to use the medications regularly and immediately upon developing the symptom of wheezing. These medications come as syrups, tablets, and inhaler devices. Each child's individual medical plan depends upon a great many factors, including which ones he or she best responds to and which ones are best tolerated. As a parent of a child with asthma, you must be responsible not only for making sure that your child takes her medicine but also that there is a steady supply of the medicine in the house or with you, in the event of travel.

Major Categories of Asthma Medications

1. Bronchodilators. These agents relax the bronchial smooth muscle that may be tightened or in bronchospasm. This release causes the airways to open wider and makes it easier to breathe. A side effect of these medications is that one feels a bit shaky or nervous when beginning to take them. For most children, this diminishes with time. If it remains a problem, discuss this with your doctor.

2. Steroids. These medications help reduce inflammation in the tightened airways, making it easier to breathe. Such steroids are completely different from the type abused by some athletes; nevertheless, they need to be carefully prescribed and monitored by your physician. Common side effects include increased appetite and increased energy levels.

3. Cromyln Sodium preparations. This medicine is novel in that its use helps prevent asthma attacks. It does little during an acute episode of reactive airway disease. Basically, it makes the child less sensitive to the environmental triggers that can set off an asthma attack. Since this medication makes your child less liable to a future asthma attack, it must be taken regularly, even when the child feels well, in order to work.

Early Warning Signs of an Asthma Attack

Every child's "warning signs" for an asthma attack are likely to be different. Both the parent and the child need to work together to learn to react to these early warning signs. With your pediatrician, you should work out specific plans of medication for when your child is not experiencing any symptoms, when your child is experiencing mild symptoms of asthma, and, of course, for those periods when your child actually experiences an asthma attack. Further, you need to prepare a plan for those serious asthma attacks that do not get better with the medications you have at home and that therefore require a visit to the physician, emergency room, or hospital for more intensive therapy.

As you get better at assessing your child's asthma attacks you will be better able to judge how serious they are. If your child has any of the following symptoms, however, or you are simply concerned, do not hesitate to call your physician. Asthma is a potentially serious illness. Most pediatricians would prefer to be awakened during the night to prevent an attack from worsening.

Here are a few of the more common serious warning signs to consider:

Coughing or night coughing (when the child is lying down)
Looking pale
Bluish tinge to the lips or nails
Difficulty breathing; retractions
Feeling not quite oneself ("spaced out")
Not being able to sleep
Not being able to finish a sentence without stopping to breathe
Decreased activity
Nervous or irritable behavior
Complaints of feeling short of breath
Complaints of feeling tired

 My five-year-old son has asthma. We are managing it well with a variety of medications, but I wonder if he will ever "outgrow" it, as I did?

Many children do, indeed, outgrow their asthma by the teenage years. It is difficult to make such a prediction without knowing the individual course and causes of your child's reactive airway disease. Some children, however, remain at risk for this condition into adulthood.

My daughter always becomes especially "jumpy" when I give her asthma medications. She is doing beautifully in terms of her breathing, but she is a bit hard to take while the medicine is in her. What can I do?

Many asthma medications, especially preparations of drugs called beta-2 agonists, which open up the airways, can cause hyperactivity, sleeplessness, irritability and—in the event of an overdose—serious cardiac and nervous system problems. If you are concerned with the side effects of any medication your physician prescribes for your child, you should document them carefully by writing the side effects down and discussing them with your doctor. An alternative medication that does not cause the undesired effect but still prevents the asthma attack may be available.

There are a number of books and pamphlets available on asthma and related problems. We recommend that you call or write the following two centers for the most up-to-date information:

The American Lung Association
1740 Broadway
New York, NY 10019-4374
(212) 315-8700

The Asthma and Allergy Foundation of America
1125 15th Street, N.W., Room #502
Washington D.C. 20005
(202) 466-7643

ATTENTION DEFICIT DISORDER (ADD), ATTENTION DEFICIT WITH HYPERACTIVITY DISORDER (ADHD), AND A FEW WORDS ON LEARNING DISABILITIES

Most adults are astounded by the level of energy their children display. Indeed, excess energy may be the principle product of extreme youth; most children are naturally high-spirited and energetic. There are, however, some syndromes where this excess energy is beyond that normally displayed. In these children, high energy and recklessness can become part of a persistent and maladaptive pattern that hinders their learning, friendships, and general development.

Attention Deficit Disorder (ADD) and Attention Deficit Hyperactivity Disorder (ADHD) are broad terms for a complex variety of problems that involve a limited attention span (ADD) and, in the case of ADHD, persistent hyperactive and impulsive behaviors. Physicians and psychologists continue to work on outlining the symptoms, causes, and treatments for these syndromes, but the reality of the matter is that not all children with these problems are exactly alike.

ADD and ADHD appear in about 5 percent of all children, more often in boys than girls. In 50 to 70 percent of these children, the disorders may be associated with a learning disorder and, to a lesser extent, a mood disorder such as depression. No one is quite clear as to their cause, although they are related to imma- ture brain development or neurochemical transmission resulting in poor self-con- trol, inattention, and impulsivity. Both disorders demand greater structure on the part of parents, the school, and the child's immediate community. They may be hereditary disorders, but they are clearly no one's fault and, as medical-psycho- logical problems, need to be tended to like any other. Listed below are the major characteristics of both ADD and ADHD as defined by American Psychiatric Associ- ation in its manual, *Diagnostic and Statistical Manual of Mental Disorders, Fourth Edi- tion* (Washington D.C.: American Psychiatric Association, 1994).

The problems described below generally appear before the age of seven. (ADD and ADHD may be obvious in some children as young as toddlers and preschool- ers. For other children, the problem does not become clear until they are chal- lenged by structured and routine activities such as school.)

ADD

The child exhibits six or more of the following features of inattention, which per- sisted for at least six months; these features contribute to the child acting less highly developed than what one would expect for the child's age:

- Frequently has trouble maintaining attention to assigned tasks or sustained play activities
- May not appear to listen when spoken to directly
- Often fails to pay close attention to details or makes careless mistakes in his schoolwork, home chores, or similar activities
- Commonly fails to complete assigned tasks such as homework or chores, but not because he does not want to or cannot understand the material; instead, he simply loses interest
- Often has a difficult time organizing his work assignments or chores
- Frequently loses things that are necessary for his schoolwork or assigned tasks, such as writing supplies, books, or homework
- Easily distracted by extraneous stimuli such as music playing in another room, other children talking to one another, something going on outside of a classroom window, and so on
- Forgetful in other activities besides school or chores

ADHD

The child exhibits symptoms of inattention as listed above, but also displays six or more of the following features of *hyperactivity and impulsivity* which persist for at least 6 months; these behaviors are maladaptive and are inconsistent with other children at his developmental level. (The behavioral features listed below are al- most exclusively associated with ADHD.)

Hyperactivity

• Frequently fidgets with his hands or squirms in his seat (teenagers may describe this feeling as simply feeling restless)

• Has difficulty remaining seated when asked to do so, such as in a classroom setting

• Often displays bursts of energy by climbing or running about excessively, particularly in places where this behavior is not appropriate

• Frequently has difficulty playing quietly

• Always "on the move," as if a motor of activity is running inside him

• Often talks incessantly (this may result in your child having difficulty making friends)

Impulsivity

• Has difficulty awaiting his turn in group games or activities

• Frequently blurts out the answers to questions before the question has been completed

• Frequently and impulsively interrupts others, butts into other children's games, or blurts out the answers in class

Determining Whether Your Child has ADD or ADHD

If you notice this constellation of behavioral symptoms or suspect that your child has an attention deficit disorder, with or without hyperactivity, discuss the symptoms with your pediatrician and try to keep a journal or diary of your child's activities to better document them.

Your pediatrician should perform a careful physical examination, a review of your child's birth and medical history, and an assessment of his or her development, behavior, social relationships, and academic performance. Although there is no single laboratory or clinical test that will confirm the diagnosis, this evaluation in concert with neuropsychological testing, a careful activity history, discussions with parents, teachers, and others who observe his activities, can usually diagnose most cases of ADHD. If your child is felt to have ADHD, a management plan that includes both behavioral and medication options is often discussed.

Tips for Parents with ADD or ADHD Children

If your child has been diagnosed with attention deficit disorder, you need to take a moment and digest this information. Feel free to talk about it with your friends and family as well as physicians and psychologists. Read about it so you can understand your child's problem. The support group CHADD (Children and Adults with Attention Deficit Disorders) is available on a local and national level to help parents deal with this problem.

ADD and ADHD are not a result of your parenting skills nor the fault of the child. They are medical problems that require extra attention and care. Moreover, children with attention deficit disorders (as well as other behavioral or learning disabilities) are not "dumb"; indeed, many are quite bright. Our job, then, as parents and children's health-care providers is to help these children live up to their potential and learn to cope successfully with these problems.

Be patient and acknowledge that the child is not acting up on purpose. Many parents have a great deal of difficulty believing this, since these kids get into troublesome situations so often. But it is important to remember that they are not "bad" children; rather, their impulsivity lands them in the middle of difficult situations. Unfortunately, they act *before* they consider any consequences of their actions. Physical punishment does not make ADD or ADHD go away. It will only serve to lower the child's self-esteem. Be especially vigilant in keeping your child out of potentially dangerous situations such as crossing the street without looking. Children with attention deficit and hyperactivity disorders tend to get into more accidents than others.

Some of the most fruitful research in the field of attention deficit disorders has been focused on techniques of behavior management that help both you and your child adjust and improve his style of thinking, reacting, and playing. Here are a few techniques that we find particularly useful.

Accept what your child can and cannot do: This is, perhaps, the most difficult task for parents. The most important element in this phrase is focusing on what your child *can* do. Be sure to notice when your child exhibits good behaviors. Tell him he did a good job, or show him with a warm smile, a hug, and reassuring words of congratulations. This positive approach helps increase the child's self-esteem and promotes improvement in his behavioral skills. Sometimes difficulties arise when there is another child in the family who does not have an attention deficit disorder. Parents commonly compare one child's behaviors to others in the family: "Why can't Billy settle down and pay attention like his sister?" This often prompts a futile search for a nonexistent answer. Your child has an attention deficit disorder and will consequently be more active, more energetic, and less attentionally focused than other children.

Keep your child's home life and routine structured and organized: Since ADD and ADHD children have difficulty in focusing their attention and are easily distracted, they require even more structure than other children. Try to keep your home and daily life organized. Try to stick to a schedule of activities. Mealtimes should be set and so should other daily activities such as naps, playtime, and bedtime. Keep the home free of extraneous noise (such as stereo or television blaring away in the background), since these add to the child's distractibility. Remember, as your child conforms to a predictable routine at home, he is likely to react in a more predictable manner.

Be firm (but not physical) in disciplining your child: Your child may test your patience and is, by all accounts, a handful. You need to maintain firm rules of behavior for your child and apply them *consistently*, especially to prevent him from harming himself or others by aggressive or destructive play. When introducing new rules of conduct, it is wise to offer only one or two at a time (usually in their order of importance) so that the child does not become confused, overwhelmed, or in "time out" all day *[see Discipline]*. Discuss these rules with your child and agree on the consequences if they are broken. To get and keep a child's attention, place your hand on his shoulder and make eye-to-eye contact during your discussion. Have your child repeat the directions or instructions you just gave. Some children have success by visualizing the task at hand, such as imagining going up the stairs, going into his bedroom, and hanging up his jacket. You should also try making a chart of your child's progress. Be sure to put it in a prominent place in the kitchen or family room, so that your child can actually observe his progress. Household rules, incidentally, need to apply on a consistent basis to all family members. Efforts to calm an ADD or ADHD child down by means of punishment or yelling will only make both your lives miserable. Accept his problem and learn to work with it. Be patient, be loving, be patient!

Stop aggressive behavior when it occurs: Whenever your child displays aggressive behavior (whether he has ADHD or not), such as hitting, biting, pushing, you must stop it. Instead of yelling "No!" or "Don't!", try a more positive approach. Get up from your chair, get close to your child so you can look eye-to-eye, and explain why such a behavior is unacceptable. Remember to consistently back up your reasonable edicts (e.g., "don't push your brother off the porch") with predictable punishments. An aggressive child needs to be calmly placed in "time-out" or some equivalent situation *[see Aggression; Discipline; Negotiating with Your Child]*.

Make sure your child is allowed to "burn off" excess energy in a parent-acceptable manner: One of our favorite ADHD patients, a delightful 8-year-old boy, explained this technique as "Mommy letting me get my Ya-Ya's out of the house." Let's face it, kids generally have a lot of excess energy; kids with ADHD have even more! It is important to allow a predictable and daily means of energy release for your child. Athletic activities, playing in the yard or playground, walks, and outdoor games are a good place to start. During winter or inclement weather, you still need to be sure your ADHD child has some source of energy release. Indoor swimming pools, gymnasiums, or a basement recreation room are good alternatives. Remember, there is a difference between running about or playing hard (getting one's "ya-ya's" out) and destructive, aggressive, or rowdy behaviors. You need to supervise these activities to prevent the unacceptable energy-releasing behaviors.

Know your child's behaviors and cues: Children with ADD or ADHD will display predictable behaviors. You need to learn their cures to prevent social embarrassments or battles. For example, a tired ADD or ADHD child is more likely to have difficulty in maintaining his self-control. He may then be more likely to engage in maladaptive behaviors. Regular naps, clear bedtimes, and good observation of your child are great ways to start. Similarly, think in advance about the suitability of a particular activity for your child. For example, a huge block party with dozens of people, loud music, street entertainers, and so on might be a difficult place to take such a child. Shopping trips may also be a struggle, so plan accordingly *[see Surviving Shopping with Your Child]*.

Remember, your neighbors are not likely to be understanding of your child's problems: Try to explain your child's attention deficit disorder and its manifestations to those neighbors your child may interact with (e.g., parents of his playmates, teachers, and so forth). Your child is not a "bad kid," nor should he be labeled by others as such. Education goes a long way, but not always far enough. Don't let the opinions of outsiders infiltrate the home. Your job is to encourage, love, and support your child.

Find out about the special programs in your community or schools: Public schools are obliged by law to provide for the educational needs of children with ADD or ADHD. School-sponsored programs may include smaller, different learning techniques, self-esteem instruction, and more involvement of the child in classroom activities, although many school districts provide considerably less. You need to call your local board of education to find out what services are available. And always, always, always keep in close contact with your child's teacher. Remember, all of you are investing a great deal in your child's success. It is essential to work together.

Enhance your child's attention span: Your child with ADD or ADHD needs to learn some techniques to better direct and sustain his attention. You can help this process by breaking down the different components of your child's daily tasks into manageable units; then, slowly, increase the level of difficulty. The key to this behavior management, of course, is praise and support. When your child succeeds, tell him he did a great job! And then tell him again. When he fails, however, check to see if your expectations were too high; then explain to him what went awry. Try to show or elicit from him the means of making it better. This technique works far better than the reverse: ignoring the successes and yelling about the predictable errors.

Spend significant time with your child in structured activities: Begin by reading simple picture books and stories to your child; this helps to enhance her listening skills. As your child grows older and can take on more complex activities, encourage her to draw and practice coloring (ADHD kids are notorious for not being able to color *inside* the lines). More complicated games that enhance one's attention span include puzzles, card games, and games of visual recognition. If your child appears restless or tired after trying a new attention-enhancing activity, give her a break and start anew later. Avoid activities that are almost guaranteed to frustrate the child and, perhaps, instigate some of the other behaviors of ADD and ADHD: for example, computer or video games are best avoided. Think about how rattling and jarring your average video game is—a high-tech media frenzy of high-tech sounds, graphics, and repetitive motions. Remember all of the features of ADD and ADHD and consider how difficult it is for a child with attention difficulties to focus on this activity. Finally, a calm, pleasant environment can help the child keep his focus and avoid some of the negative behaviors of ADD or ADHD.

The child should do her homework in a quiet room with good lighting and no outside distractions such as a television set or stereo.

Medications may be used in conjunction with behavioral management: There is no magic pill that will instantly cure your child of attention deficit disorder. You need to apply the behavioral techniques discussed above in a consistent, loving manner. There do exist some medications that can help these children to focus their attention (e.g., Ritalin® or methylphenidate, dextroamphetamine, pemoline, and other agents such as antidepressants). After the professional evaluations have been performed, a diagnosis of an attention deficit disorder has been made, *and* an individualized educational plan has been applied to your child, you may want to discuss these medication options with your pediatrician. Generally, we like to try the behavioral options first. In the event of little improvement with these options, a medication may be added to the treatment program.

A Few Words on Other Learning Disabilities

We define learning disabilities as problems the child may have in processing information, such as difficulty with reading comprehension, mathematics, or other similar school tasks. Each learning disability has its own pattern of problems and responses. For example, children with *dyslexia* have difficulties associating the sounds of words with their symbolic meaning and may struggle to sound out even simple words; they also have problems with reading comprehension and may transpose letters and words.

When one considers how important basic tasks like reading and writing are to the school-aged child, one begins to get a sense of how devastating learning disabilities can be if left undiagnosed. Other children in the class may call your child "dumb"—something that rarely adds to anyone's self-esteem. Or the child who doesn't follow all that is going on in class may become bored and distracted. These children may simply drift off or act out and disrupt the classroom's activities. Children with learning disabilities generally have normal levels of intelligence and are not lazy. They must, however, learn some techniques and skills to overcome the information-processing problems that result in their difficulties. Fortunately, some (though not all) schools now have specialized programs to treat learning disabilities. If you notice that your school-aged child is having predictable problems with his reading, homework, writing, figuring out math problems, and so on, you need to discuss these issues with his teacher and consider testing. See what programs are available in your area.

Even if your child does not have a learning disability, it is *always* a good idea to help your child with his or her homework. In addition to the opportunity to see how your child is progressing, it is an excellent way to spend quality time together. More important, study after study shows that children whose parents spend time helping them with their homework do significantly better in school performance. Incidentally, this has little to do with the parent's ability to actually know how to complete the homework!

Further reading about ADD and ADHD

For parents and teachers:

Fowler, M.C. *Maybe You Know My Kid: A Parent's Guide to Identifying, Understanding, and Helping Your Child With Attention Deficit Hyperactivity Disorder.* (New York: Birch Lane Press, 1990).

Ingersoll, B. *Your Hyperactive Child.* (New York: Doubleday, 1988.)

Parker, H. *Attention Deficit Disorders: A Parent and Teacher Workbook.* (Plantation, FL: CHADD Press, 1988).

Wender, P. *The Hyperactive child, Adolescent, and Adult.* (New York: Oxford University Press, 1987).

For children with ADHD:

Galvin, M. *Otto Learns About His Medicine.* (New York: Magination Press, 1988).

Moss, D. *Shelly the Hyperactive Turtle.* (New York: Woodbine House, 1989).

Gehret, M.A. Eagle Eyes: A Child's Guide to Paying Attention. (Fairmont, N.Y.: Verbal Images Press, 1991).

For informational packets, write to:

Children and Adults with Attention Deficit Disorders
C.H.A.D.D.
499 Northwest 70th Avenue, Suite 109
Plantation, FL 33317
(305) 587-3700

Further reading on learning disabilities

Bloom, Jill. *Help Me To Help My Child: A Sourcebook for Parents of Learning Disabled Children.* (Boston: Little, Brown, 1989).

Smith, Sally. *No Easy Answers: The Learning Disabled at Home and at School.* (New York: Bantam Books, 1981).

For informational packets, write to:

National Center for Learning Disabilities
381 Park Avenue South, Suite 1420
New York, NY 10016
(212) 545-7510

Learning Disabilities Association of America
4156 Library Road
Pittsburgh, PA 15234
(412) 341-8077

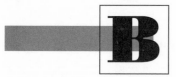

Bathing your baby

Parents should bathe their infant whenever the baby needs it! Your baby's bathing preferences, of course, should dictate the schedule, rather than these pages. Bathing should be good, clean fun for both baby and parent.

During the first days of life when the baby's umbilical stump has not yet fallen off, you should either give the baby sponge baths or make sure to keep the water level in the tub far below the level of the baby's navel. Too much water on the stump can cause an infection or interfere with the process of the stump's drying out and falling off. If a little water does happen to get on the umbilical stump during the bath—and it will—don't worry: simply and gently pat dry *[see Umbilical Cord Care]*.

We recommend using ordinary tap water to bathe your infant. Drying soaps (such as Ivory) are to be avoided, as they irritate a newborn baby's sensitive skin. It is always best to wash the baby's cleanest spots first, proceeding to the dirtier spots. Use a washcloth to bathe the infant. Make sure to wash the baby's face to remove dried milk, which can lead to a rash. You should also wash the genital area, but be careful not to use soap. Plain water will prevent irritation. You should clean the genital and rectal area front to back, winding up at the rectal area; this helps prevent urinary tract infections *[see Circumcision; Urinary Tract Problems]*.

Safety Tips Related to Bathing and the Prevention of Drowning

It is also important to mention the real risk of an unattended baby in a bath or near water. Babies can drown easily and within minutes, even in shallow levels of water. All it takes is for the baby to fall face first in a bathtub. This, of course, need never happen. Simply make sure to *always* pay attention when bathing a baby or small child; *never* leave her to her own resources. The child of five or older is ready to bathe herself *[see Drown-proofing the Home]*.

Hair, Cradle Cap, and Hair Loss

When washing the baby's hair (once or twice a week is sufficient), make sure to use a specially formulated baby shampoo that does not cause eye-stinging. Al-

When bathing your baby, place the baby's bathtub right in your bathroom sink. Fill the baby's tub with one or two inches of water. Make sure that the water is not too warm and not too cold; dip your finger into the water to check. It is a good idea to have all the towels, sponges, and other bathing materials at the ready before you actually bathe the baby. In order to prevent the baby from getting too cold before the bath begins, make sure you unclothe him only when you are all set to begin the bath.

ways rinse well with water to make sure all the shampoo is out of the baby's hair. Remember, gently wash the baby's entire scalp, including the "soft spot" or fontanelle *[see Newborn Appearance]*. This will not hurt the baby as long as you do it with care.

Some babies develop a scaly, crusty rash called cradle cap. It is not contagious and is easily treated by washing the baby's hair once a day with a gentle anti-dandruff shampoo called Sebulex®. Simply lather the shampoo into the baby's hair and massage the scalp with a washcloth. Again, remember to wash the entire scalp, including the baby's soft spot. If the scaly rash does not resolve within two weeks of this treatment, or if the rash becomes red and irritated, you should consult your pediatrician. Many times this can be cleared up by using a mild hydrocortisone cream.

Some small babies rub the back of their head from side to side against the mattress as they sleep. Since babies spend so much time sleeping, this can cause a mild hair loss at the site of most intense rubbing. This is not a problem; as the baby grows—and spends less time on his back—the hair will grow back. Other babies begin to lose some of their "baby" hair during the first six months of life. As this hair falls out, more mature hair grows in.

Nails

It is a good idea to trim the baby's nails with a nail clipper every week or so, after a bath. The warm water will soften the baby's nails and make them easier to cut. The reason it's useful to clip the baby's nails is to prevent her from scratching herself or developing ingrown toenails.

After Diapering

Although there is no need to bathe your baby each time she soils a diaper, it is a good idea to gently rinse the baby's genital and rectal areas (front to back), and pat dry with a towel before putting on the new diaper *[see Diaper Rash]*.

 Do you recommend any type of special baby lotion or powder after bathing?

Most babies have moist, supple skin; it does not need extra oil or grease. Frequently these lotions can clog the sweat glands in a baby's skin and cause a pimple-like rash. If you notice the baby's skin becoming dry or cracked, on the other hand, daily rubbing with a baby-safe

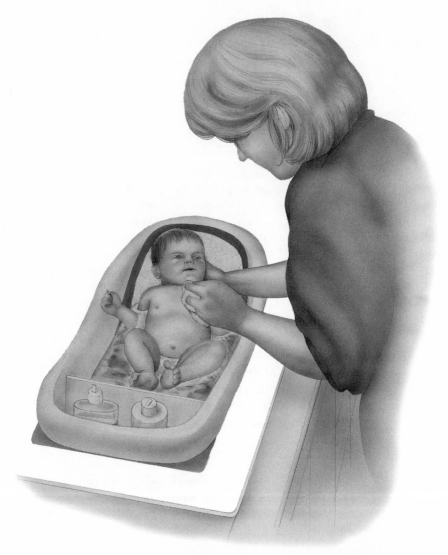

Place the baby, carefully, on her back or in a seated position in the tub, and bathe as directed.

moisturizing lotion or A and D ointment (a petroleum jelly base containing vitamins A and D, which promote skin healing) can be of help.

What about baby powders?

Generally, we do not recommend any baby powder that contains, talc. This substance, when breathed into the baby's lungs, can cause serious irritation or pneumonitis. Many a mother, on the other hand, swears by cornstarch as useful aid for diaper rashes, since it helps reduce the friction of diapers against sensitive skin.

BEDWETTING (Enuresis)

Bedwetting (or, as physicians refer to it, nighttime enuresis) is an all-too-common experience of early childhood. While most of us can recall personal experiences of "accidents," enuresis is defined as unwanted or involuntary urination during sleep at least once or more a month. But before making a diagnosis of abnormal bedwetting, look at the child's age. More than half of all toddlers under the age of three wet their beds, with the numbers decreasing to 40 percent of all four-year-olds, 20 percent of all five-year-olds, 10 percent of all six-year-olds, 7 percent of all eight-year-olds, and about 1 to 5 percent of children between 9 and 18-years-old. Clearly it is the older or school-aged child that has the greatest problems dealing with bedwetting, and it is they who most frequently come to a physician's attention. Most experts do not consider bedwetting in a child under the age of six to be abnormal. Instead, for younger children bedwetting should be expected as a normal and temporary part of growth, development, and maturity of thought and control. One helpful way for both parents and child to think about the problem is to acknowledge the difference between the child's body actually being able to hold his urine and the child's (or the parent's) desire to be dry. Smaller children, especially those under the age of four, are going to bedwet occasionally. Therefore, both the parent and the child need to understand that the accident is "okay" and that, with time, success will be achieved.

The Good News about Most Cases of Bedwetting

The overwhelming majority of bedwetters do not have abnormal urinary tracts or an organic disease process as a cause. Moreover, the majority of bedwetters can learn to control their nighttime misadventures, provided they are encouraged and helped by the parents in a nonjudgmental manner. While bedwetting is not "caused" by traumatic psychological events, it can certainly be exacerbated by insensitivity, family disruption, and stress. Finally, the overwhelming majority of even chronic bedwetters "cure" themselves of this problem by age 8 to 10. One way of predicting when this time will come is to try to recall if one of the child's parents was a bedwetter. Frequently, parents who were once bedwetters beget children who are bedwetters; typically, the children stop their bedwetting at the approximate age that the bedwetting parent stopped. Because even the more resistant bedwetters eventually stop, the relative mildness of the disorder in physical (though not emotional) terms and the side effects of medicines suggested for the prevention of bedwetting lead us to prescribe, in these pages, the most gentle and least invasive of initial approaches to the problem.

Physical Causes of Bedwetting

First, let's review the few conditions or symptoms of bedwetting that are caused by a physical or "organic" disease process. Although underlying physical conditions rarely cause bedwetting, they can be serious, and it is worthwhile to dispense with these situations now.

1. One of the most important distinctions pediatricians try to make when evaluating a child with bedwetting is, when does the wetting actually take place? A child who wets him or herself during the day *and* the night is far more likely to have a physical or anatomical cause of bedwetting than the child who wets exclusively at night. The exclusively daytime wetter also needs to be examined and evaluated by a pediatrician, particularly for behavioral problems.

2. Another "red flag" to organic causes of bedwetting is the sudden onset of the problem in a child who had previously not had a problem with bedwetting.

3. When a child, no matter what his age, complains of *pain* or *burning* with urination, a urinary tract infection may exist. You need to have a physician examine your child and, if necessary, prescribe an antibiotic. Because urinary tract infections can be extremely dangerous in the young child because of a more aggressive invasion of their developing kidneys than is seen in adults, prompt action is important *[see Urinary Tract Problems]*.

4. If you or your child notices blood in her urine, a visit to the physician is warranted. You should call your physician, upon discovering this symptom, to assess the urgency of the situation. Again, a variety of problems—some relatively harmless and others quite serious—can be at the root of this symptom *[see Urinary Tract Problems]*.

5. Three other situations that are best followed up with a visit to your healthcare provider are

• The child with a weak or "drippy" urine stream who may have an anatomical cause of poor urinary control

• The child who is always thirsty and consumes a huge amount of fluids

• The child who is older than ten and is *still* bedwetting

A Plan that Requires a Partnership

Now let's discuss a plan of treatment for that majority of youngsters who experience occasional, and *normal*, episodes of enuresis.

1. All plans need a good foundation, and the foundation of any plan to conquer bedwetting is firmly rooted in some simple principles: Bedwetting is a problem that will take some time to correct. It is an embarrassing problem for your child. Be gentle and try to help your child through it. He needs encouragement, sympathy, and support. With these simple parental elements, the vast majority of bedwetting can be cured in the home.

2. Do not give your child a lot to drink just before he goes to bed. No one is quite clear why bedwetting occurs in some children over the age of six, given that most children learn to master their urinary tract muscles and control urinary habits rather well by that age. Perhaps these children have smaller bladders than their nonbedwetting peers. Possibly these children are exceptionally deep sleepers and do not arise to the neurological signal that their bladders are full. In all cases, these children have *no* defect in their kidney or bladder function, so exact mechanisms of the problem are difficult to prove. A good rule of thumb is to limit the child's nighttime intake to about 2 to 3 ounces of fluid during the period *after* dinner and two hours *before* your child's bedtime. Don't worry about exact rations; if your child is really thirsty before bedtime, don't begrudge a few sips of water or an ice chip or two. That doesn't mean having the child sit down to a tall glass of milk or whatever beverage he prefers. You cannot attack a problem like bedwetting on a full bladder any more than one can begin a diet inside an ice-cream parlor.

3. Conversely, you should encourage your child to drink fluids during the daytime hours. When he is awake he will be more likely to acknowledge the signals to his brain indicating a full bladder and to learn the cues that are part of all of our bladder- and bowel-emptying regimens.

4. During the day, gently encourage your child to "hold" his urine and delay going to the bathroom in order to strengthen the bladder muscles and other muscles that control urination. The more the child can be taught not to respond to his first impulse to urinate, the better control can be taught. The exercise also strengthens muscles that help one hold his urine. Again, the key word is *gentle*. Start with a few minutes and let the child work his way up to a period of ten to fifteen minutes. Draconian time limits are not necessary.

5. Explain to your child the importance of getting up during the nighttime to go to the bathroom. Leave a light, or a nightlight, on in the bathroom, so the child doesn't feel scared about walking in the dark. Encourage him, if he feels the urge, to simply get out of bed and try! This is not a subtle point, given the emphasis most parents place upon bedtime and the sanctity of staying put once lights are out.

6. For those children who wet the bed more frequently, a few precautions can both help stop the bedwetting and keep the child and his bed fairly clean. The bed itself can be protected by purchasing a plastic protector sheet that fits around the mattress. You can add to this protection by having your child wear thick underwear and pajamas to absorb the urine. Most developmental pediatricians advise against the use of diapers in the child over the age of four; there, do, on the other hand, exist new products such as "disposable" underwear for precisely such a child. This underwear is made of the same absorbent material as the diaper products, but is shaped and fashioned to look like underpants. We advise you to consult your child first before insisting on such gear. If the child feels uncomfortable with them or feels they are "babyish," don't belabor the point.

A specific routine needs to be worked out between the child and parent as to what to do with wet bedding and pajamas. For sanitary and practical reasons such a routine is necessary for the frequent bedwetter. Cloth soiled with urine smells, and it can be stained and ruined. Therefore, on the morning after, we suggest a routine where the child is instructed to take his wet pajamas to the bathroom sink and rinse them with cool water until the odor is gone. He should then be instructed where to put the now-wetter pajamas. A hamper with a removable plastic liner is a handy receptacle to have in these circumstances. The child then needs to bathe or shower before school to avoid smelling of urine. The job of laundering bed linens can be worked out as you see fit.

7. Always praise your child for his successful nights. There is no human being on earth who doesn't do anything better with some encouragement. Children especially need it. Constructing a chart where you can monitor progress with "gold stars" or other stickers, goals for a certain period of "dry nights," and even tangible rewards can certainly aid in this process. Remember, the child needs to be an integral and active part in the process. If he is not focused on monitoring his own progress, controlling his intake of fluids, doing the bladder-strengthening exercises and other techniques, immediate success is unlikely. Ultimately most children outgrow this condition, but this time period may seem like an eternity for the child who continues to resist learning bladder control after the age of four.

8. Just as importantly, be understanding and low-keyed in your response to the "wet nights." Ridicule, harsh comments, or sarcasm are precisely what your child *doesn't* need in such a situation. He can get enough of that, sadly, from his school-mates and his siblings. You should encourage brothers and sisters of the bedwetter not to make fun of him. Learn how to empathize with your child. Punishment and other forms of negative reinforcement are doomed to failure and, indeed, may exacerbate the problem or worsen it by adding emotional dimensions.

9. Plan with the child that, if he feels wetness during the night, he should get up and immediately go to the bathroom. Once there, he can either finish urinating or, in the case of an accident, clean himself, change pajamas, and change the bed. The sheets do not necessarily need to be changed, but placing a dry towel over any damp areas is a good idea. Such encouragement helps a child to better recognize signals that his bladder is full, even while asleep, and awaken more quickly.

10. Don't wake your child up yourself during the night to insure dryness. If you wake him up, there is no reason for him to learn how to awaken to signals of a full bladder.

Okay, Doctor, None of These Methods Worked!

More intensive measures—alarm devices that awaken the child at the first hint of moisture, and various drugs—have been advocated by some behavioral pediatricians and psychologists for the child who still bedwets after the age of eight years and has tried the previous recommendations without success. As stated at the onset of this discussion, we prefer the more gentle methods described above. However, there are those children who are not responsive to these techniques and require extra help.

Bedwetting alarms

There exist several alarm devices that can be used to help the child learn to awaken to the message of a full bladder. Although the concept of a buzzer sounds somewhat like a high-school science fair project, this has one of the highest "cure rates" of the available methods—approximately 70 percent—and is useful for the deep sleeper with a small bladder who just can't seem to awaken when necessary. Briefly, the devices work by a moisture sensor that activates an alarm at the first few drops of urine. The child thereupon wakes up and goes to the bathroom until he can learn to do the same thing on his own.

Because the alarms require some degree of behavior modification, you may want to discuss this plan with your pediatrician. Again, the child has to be intimately involved and understand that the alarm is not an absolute solution to the problem. The alarm only works when used in concert with the child's control of fluid intake, bladder exercises, and concerted efforts to awaken himself during the night (usually with an alarm clock) to get up and go to the bathroom.

Companies that offer bedwetter alarms:

Wet Stop Alarm/Palco Industries and Laboratories
8030 Soquel Road
Santa Cruz, CA 95062
(800) 346-4488

Koregon Enterprises (Night Trainer Alarm)
9735 West Sunshine Ct.
Beaverton, OR 97005
(800) 544-4240

Drugs to treat bedwetting

It is important to note that all the drugs currently used to "treat" bedwetting should be used as a last resort. One drug, DDAVP (a nasal spray containing an analogue of a naturally occurring hormone that diminishes urine production), is safe if used correctly but can be quite dangerous if overused. Many physicians prescribe this drug for extra-special events when the child may worry about being dry, such as a sleepover party or a group camping trip. Another drug that has been used for bedwetting, imiprimine, is actually prescribed for depression. One of its side effects, however, is a decrease in urine production and increased bladder capacity. Again, if taken to excess, the drug can be quite dangerous.

The most negative aspect of these drugs, besides their potential for overdosage, is the fact that they do not cure bedwetting; they simply prevent it from occurring the night the drug is taken. It often returns once the drugs are stopped.

BICYCLE INJURIES

Bicycles are a major form of transportation and source of fun for most school-aged children. Typically we recommend waiting until the child is over the age of six before beginning to teach her how to ride a bike. There are also a number of agreements and understandings you need to negotiate with your child in order to insure her safety while riding.

1. The child (and any other bicyclist) should always wear an approved bicycle safety helmet when riding. The major form of injury related to bicycles is typically a fall after being hit by an automobile or running into something. But it is important to stress that the bicycle rider *must* wear his helmet at all times—whether riding near traffic or on a deserted stretch of playground. There is always a real danger of a rider falling off his bike. Serious head injuries, such as concussions and loss of consciousness, can be easily caused by a child's head striking the ground—especially at high speeds. Insist, as part of the agreement that allows him to ride his bicycle, that *he always wear his helmet when biking!* When purchasing a bike helmet, make sure that it fits properly and check to make sure that the product label includes the following: "Snell Approved" or "This product meets the ANSI Z90.4 Standard."

2. When purchasing a bicycle for your child, make sure that it "fits" properly. This means that both his legs touch the ground when he straddles the bike but has not yet placed his feet on the pedals (that is, when his feet are flat on the ground). The middle bar, if it is a boy's bike, should be just beneath but not touching the crotch area. If you purchase the traditional types of bicycles built for women, you can place a tape measure across the top of the "V" of the midsection of the bike. Both feet should be flat on the ground. This tape measure should be just beneath but not touching the crotch area. Before purchasing the bicycle, make sure that you watch your child try it out. Does he appear comfortable on it? Is he struggling to reach the handle bars or pedals? Although it may be tempting to "re-cycle" an older brother's bike for your daughter, this is really a false economy. Accidents occur when a small child cannot maneuver or master a bicycle physically larger than her abilities allow.

3. Make sure that the bicycle is in good operating conditions, including the brakes.

4. Double riding, handle bar riding, reckless riding, and similar ventures should be avoided. If you are an avid cyclist who wants to take your younger child for a ride, purchase a safety-approved infant or child bicycle seat that has special strap or seat belts. Make sure that his legs do not dangle too far out of the seat and are protected by leg guards in order to prevent his legs from becoming stuck in the moving parts of the bike. If you ride a bicycle on a road, the same rules of traffic apply to the cyclist as to the automobile driver.

5. Young children—and, preferably, most cyclists—should not ride their bikes in

the streets. Sidewalks are preferable simply because there is no fast-moving traffic. Once an older child, say ten or eleven years, graduates to street riding, you need to establish strict rules of conduct including avoiding particularly busy streets, following traffic signs and lights, and avoiding night riding. Sidewalk or bike path bicycling remains the safest bet and should be encouraged over travel on dangerous streets.

 When is a good age to buy my child a mini-bike, motor bike, or all-terrain vehicle?

Never. There is no good age to buy these off-road vehicles. Mini-bikes, all-terrain vehicles, snowmobiles, trail bikes, and similar motorized vehicles are extremely dangerous and a frequent cause of serious head injuries, trauma, and death. Children younger than fourteen should not be riding these at all, and older teens—if they must use them—should always wear helmets, be supervised, and demonstrate that they can safely operate the vehicle. In reality, such motorized vehicles are best left at the department store. Spend the money on something more productive and safe for your child.

BITES

Bites, Animal

Everyone knows that dogs are "man's best friend"—that is, unless you happen to own a cat. Pets can be a very valuable addition to the family and can enrich a child's life with affection, companionship, and a sense of responsibility. But as wonderful as pets are, they are not trouble-free in terms of your child's health. For example, injuries from bites are a definite risk of childhood. Most commonly, children incur bites from household pets and domesticated animals. Since we are discussing bites in general, we will also consider human bites, typically done by a sibling or playmate, and bites from wild animals, insects, snakes, and sea creatures.

Bites, Domestic and Household Pets

The most common animal bites come from dogs and cats. Domesticated rodents such as gerbils, hamsters, white mice, and guinea pigs as well as larger domestic animals, such as horses, have also been known to occasionally bite or nip their owners. In the United States these types of animals are almost always free of rabies, a rare and fatal disease. The greatest risk from this type of injury is subsequent infection at the site of the wound. Some types of animal bites are more dangerous than others. Cat bites are about 500 percent more likely to become infected than their canine counterparts. This is because the size and shape of feline teeth, which are sharp and pointy, lead to puncture wounds. In a way, the cat's teeth act almost like needles, injecting the bacteria it may have in its mouth directly into the wound. Dog teeth, on the other hand, are more broad and flat; while infections can be introduced by dog bites, they are not as common. Minor cuts or claw marks from pets need to be properly cleansed as well, since the claws of most animals are contaminated with saliva and bacteria.

First aid tips for treating pet bites

For mild bites: Mild scrapes, cuts, or abrasions that do not penetrate the skin can be treated at home by gently washing with soap and water and, after drying, covering the injury with a bandage. Wash thoroughly with a gentle liquid soap and cool running water from the faucet to prevent possible infection.

When was the child's last tetanus shot? The child's immunization record for tetanus needs to be determined and his immunization updated, if necessary. Generally referred to as the Td or DPT shot, the tetanus portion of the vaccine needs to be updated for everyone—adults included—every five to ten years. *[See Immunizations]*

Bites that require immediate medical attention

• *Deep cuts, lacerations, and puncture wounds* require medical care and, often, suturing (or "stitches").

• *Animal (and human) bites to the hand* are a medical emergency, regardless of the source, because of their likelihood of becoming seriously infected. The hand consists of many tiny spaces that are walled off from other parts of the hand, making infections there difficult to treat.

• *Bites to the head* should always be looked at by your physician. These wounds are often covered by hair and can be difficult to assess in terms of severity. Because of the very real risk of penetration of the child's skull by an animal's bite, it is imperative to investigate the wound by means of careful examination and, in the case of deep wounds, an X ray or CAT scan of the head. *[See X ray].*

• *Inspect the injury daily to make sure there is no developing infection.* Signs of a skin infection include redness, swelling, or oozing pus at the site of the injury. If these signs of infection are present, you need to call your physician immediately for examination and treatment.

In the event that the animal doing the biting did so without provocation, or if it appears ill, unusual, is a stray, or has no record of a rabies vaccination—whether the bite is serious or not—it is a good idea to consult your physician for advice. Even though rabies is extremely rare in the United States, such animals need to be isolated and observed for a period of ten days after the bite to ensure that they are, indeed, rabies-free. Your local police force can often be of assistance in this pursuit. In a perfect world, all household pets would be vaccinated against rabies, but this is not always the case.

Bites, Wild Animal

All children love to see animals in the wild, but you must teach them to avoid direct contact. When a child is bitten by a wild animal, especially if you notice that a serious or deep wound has resulted, it is best to seek immediate medical attention. One should wash the injury carefully with cool water and a liquid soap for at least fifteen minutes. Be careful not to have any contact with the animal in question, even if it is dead, because of the risk of contracting rabies from saliva-contaminated limbs. It is best to leave the capture of wild animals to professionals.

It is important to note, however, that not all wild animals are susceptible to rabies. Rabies is, in the United States, an extremely rare contagious disease. Spread by animal bites, rabies can result in death. Small animals such as mice, rats, rabbits, chipmunks, and gophers are relatively rabies-free. Animals such as skunks, bats, raccoons, foxes, coyotes, and some types of squirrels, on the other hand, can carry rabies without any outward signs of illness. In addition to the risk of rabies, these types of animals are capable of causing greater harm because of the size of their teeth and the ferocity of their attack. These types of bites, especially bat bites, should always be looked at by a physician and evaluated in terms of the risk of rabies.

 Are there certain types of dogs I should avoid buying as a pet for my children?

Yes. One must always consider the "friendliness" of a particular breed of dog before purchasing it, especially when children live in the household. For example, studies have shown that German shepherds, Doberman pinschers, and St. Bernards are the breeds most commonly involved in childhood bite injuries. Similarly, specially bred "fighting dogs" such as pit bull terriers can often lead to disastrous results in the home.

What is the best age to think about getting a pet for a child?

While there is no absolute age for "pet suitability," one should never leave an infant or toddler alone with a pet. In rare circumstances, infants have been attacked by pets; even less frequently, sleeping newborns have been suffocated by a pet joining them in their cribs. By the age of three or four most children can interact safely with household animals, but they still need to be supervised by a parent. A good way to begin this interaction is to teach the child how to command the dog or cat to sit, stay, and so on. (This type of education may be more difficult with cats than dogs; as one colleague put it, "Cats don't interact with their owners, they control them!") All children should be taught never to tease any animal. Teach your child to respect animals and not to panic when confronted with strange dogs, lest his sudden movement upset the animal and bring about an attack. Instead, your child should be instructed to approach animals with her arms at her sides and the hands open. Children older than the age of five can begin to take some responsibilities in caring for the pet. Begin with manageable tasks such as having your son feed the pet; other tasks, such walking, bathing, and so on, should be added as the child grows. With careful teaching and gentle supervised play, most children beyond the toddler years can succeed at being excellent friends to man's best friend.

Our animal-loving friends remind us that there are other pets that may be easier to take care of than dogs or cats. To be sure, many a child has helped nurture fish, lizards, turtles (always wash your hands after handling turtles!), parakeets, gerbils and other rodents, and, of course, far more exotic creatures. We have patients who are the proud keepers of ferrets, tarantula spiders, and pigs. Before picking out a pet, make sure that the animal can be legally and practically kept in a home. Use common sense, and if in doubt ask your pediatrician or, better yet, a veterinarian about a particular pet's suitability for children.

Bites, Human

First aid and treatment issues

For a variety of reasons ranging from behavioral to accidental, children often experience a human bite at the hands—or should we say mouths—of siblings or playmates. Human bites, ironically, are among the most serious of all types of bite injuries and are especially prone to serious infection—particularly bites on the hand. If your child is bitten by another human, you are best advised to call your physician immediately in order to describe the severity and extent of the injury. This is especially important if the biter's teeth pierced your child's skin or the injury is large enough to require stitches.

For the serious bites that actually pierce the skin, you should carefully wash the injury with cool water and soap before seeing the physician. Again, it is important to know your child's tetanus vaccine status in case she may be behind in her shots. For more superficial bites, such as cuts that barely break the skin or scrapes, good washing with soap and water, followed by bandaging and close follow-up are all that is needed.

Biting as an unacceptable behavior: what to do

As bad as it is to hear that your child was bitten by a schoolmate, many parents of biters report that it is worse to find out your child did the biting. Clearly, this is a socially unacceptable and dangerous practice that needs to be carefully and firmly addressed.

Typically, biting behavior begins during the first year of life after most of the infant's teeth have developed. At first it may be a mild "love bite" in order to get attention, or simply an act of mouthing an object or person. Remember, oral contact and putting things in one's mouth is the principal means by which infants explore their worlds. By the age of two to three, however, toddlers who are prone to bite know that it is an aggressive gesture and typically use it as such.

The most important suggestion is to make clear to your child that biting is un-acceptable. You need to do this in as concrete a manner as possible so that the child understands the rule clearly. Whether the child is biting merely for attention or in the act of aggression, you need to explain to him that there are other ways of getting noticed or showing anger. For example, you might say, "Never bite anyone" or "Biting is never allowed," and you should give the reasons why (it hurts, it can cause serious injuries or infections, and so on).

Some behavioral pediatricians suggest given the biter an alternative object to vent his oral aggression upon. A teething ring or soft, pliable rubber toy might serve nicely. Remember to keep the object clean between uses.

Other helpful tips in the process of stopping biting behavior:

• When you see your child actually biting someone, stop him and emphatically say "No!" This is an issue worth battling over, and you need to be strong, clear, and authoritative. Children who bite frequently may need closer supervision than those who quickly learn the lesson.

• A suitable punishment for biting behavior is necessary. There is no need to hit your child, nor should you bite him in an attempt to show him what it feels like. Instead, a "time out" from playing with his friends or engaging in a particular activity is a good and humane way of enforcing the lesson "Don't bite!" It is important not to get too angry. Remember that children who bite need just as much—if not more—loving attention from their parents as the non-biters.

• As we have noted in so many instances before, children do better with praise than insults. Therefore as the child improves, learns not to bite, and expresses his anger, aggression, or playfulness in a more acceptable manner, you need to congratulate and, perhaps, reward him.

• Since children who bite are far more likely to do so with other children who bite, it might be a good idea to have your children spend less time with other biters, at least until both children improve *[see Discipline]*.

 Do I need to worry about HIV/AIDS if my child is bitten by another child?

To date no case of HIV has been contracted in this manner. If your child was bitten by another infected with HIV, a blood test is suggested [see AIDS].

Bites, Insect

The bane of summer vacation is, undoubtedly, insect bites and stings. While most insect bites are more annoying than serious, it should be mentioned at the onset that some children and adults have severe allergic reactions—particularly to those insects that sting—resulting in difficulty breathing, swallowing, and severe hives or welts within 30 minutes of the injury. This rare but reversible allergic reaction, which is called anaphylaxis, is covered under "Allergies."

Insect bites that cause itching

Insects such as mosquitoes, chiggers, fleas, and bedbugs are all capable of causing an "itchy" child. These insects leave their own body fluid or even body parts at the site of the bite in exchange for a few drops of human blood. The result is a raised, red, itchy bump (rarely, a blister) that serves to drive both child and parent mildly crazy.

Mosquitoes and chiggers—some first aid and prevention tips: Treatments for these bites are temporary and rarely effective. Calamine lotions or newer concoctions containing baking soda, oatmeal, and even topical antihistamines may, however, be of some use. For severe insect bites, such as those caused by chiggers, a trial of hydrocortisone cream (0.5 percent), which can be purchased at any drug store, may bring some relief. Oral antihistamines, on the other hand, are rarely of any use in relieving the itch of insect bites.

Perhaps the wisest course is to prevent the bites from occurring in the first place. When going outdoors (especially in areas that are heavily wooded, contain stagnant waters, or where it has rained a great deal), it is a good idea to apply an insect repellent that contains 15 to 20 percent DEET to the child's clothing and exposed skin. DEET products are not recommended for children under the age of three years. There is no need to drench the child in repellent; the products available on the market today are quite potent. This is an especially important point since the overuse of DEET-containing sprays can cause serious side effects such as seizures or coma. Licking the repellent off and ingesting it can cause similar problems. Used sparingly, however, DEET repellents are safe and effective. With this in mind, be careful to avoid spraying it directly on your child's face, mouth, or hands (which invariably go into the eyes and mouth). You should also avoid spraying the repellent onto open cuts, wounds, and sunburned or injured skin in order to prevent increased absorption of the product. Finally, once your child has come inside, wash the repellent off her.

There are other preventive measures one can take to keep bugs at bay. For example, avoid dressing your child in bright colors, which attract insects. Perspiration odors and perfumes can also attract insects. There are studies to indicate that people who have just eaten foods—such as bananas—that are rich in a substance known as serotonin may give off an odor that attract insects. There appears to be an added benefit to applying sunscreen on your child beyond protection from harmful sun rays: it makes the skin slippery and insects have a difficult time getting a grip necessary to bite. Similarly, the scent that clings to the skin after swimming in a chlorinated swimming pool serves as an excellent repellent *[see Sunshine, Sunscreens, Sunburn, and Sunglasses].*

Remember, chiggers and mosquitoes love exposed human skin. Chigger bites often occur on the skin exposed over a belt, or just above the stocking line in a child wearing shorts. Mosquitoes will bite anywhere they can find a suitable place to land!

Bedbugs: If bedbugs are a problem, they can be easily destroyed with an insecticide called malathion, available at most garden supply stores or from your local exterminator. Children need to be kept away from the sprayed areas, usually the bed and its frame, until *after* it dries, since it is extremely poisonous.

Fleas: Fleas, which are almost exclusively brought into the house by pet cats or dogs, can live for months in your home's carpet. All household animals should be routinely treated with flea powder, and carpets need to be carefully vacuumed. In the case of severe household flea infestations, an exterminator may be needed.

Stinging insects

Bugs that are definitely worth avoiding are hornets, wasps, honeybees, bumblebees, and yellowjackets. The overwhelming majority of stings are caused by the infamous yellowjacket wasp. Typically these stings are painful, inflamed, red, and raised (like a bump). These painful symptoms typically disappear within a period of one or two hours, although the swelling can progress during the first twenty-four hours of the sting.

Since all stinging insects often live and travel together, the child with multiple stings is not nearly as rare as we would all like. For these injuries, particularly when more than ten stings are noted, there is enough venom injected to cause more serious symptoms such as nausea, vomiting, loose stools, generalized achiness, and fever. Unlike the anaphylactic reaction we briefly mentioned above, this response is clearly a reaction to a larger amount of venom. Stings inside the mouth are especially vexing, because they can cause swelling of the involved tissue, such as the lips and tongue, which may interfere with swallowing or breathing.

Some first aid tips

• For the majority of sting injuries (i.e., the child who has less than ten stings, is not experiencing more generalized or serious symptoms, and is not known to be allergic to the insect venom in question), you can treat your child at home.

• Bees often leave their stinger in the victim. If you notice the stinger still present (it will stick out at the center of the bite mark), you can remove it with either tweezers or the edge of a credit card.

• Apply ice or a paste of meat tenderizer and water to the sites of sting injuries (this will counteract the venom), and offer a great deal of hugging and reassurance. If the stinger cannot be removed, the swelling continues to worsen twenty-four hours after the event, or you are simply concerned, it is a wise idea to contact your physician.

Ways exist to prevent these injuries. Insist that your child not walk outdoors barefooted (a wise move for a variety of reasons) and not upset areas where these insects like to nest or feed, such as blooming flowers, clover fields, and fruit orchards. Teach your child what a bee or a wasp or a hornet is, and how to avoid them. One should also beware of leaving open soda-pop cans unattended in the great outdoors. Frequently, wasps fly into them and stings can result. Alas, no repellent currently on the market is of any value in keeping these irritating insects away.

Painful insect bites

Typically, bites caused by red ants, gnats, sand flies, horse flies, deer flies, blister beetles, centipedes, and similar insects, are painful. They may also burn and be quite red in appearance. Fire ants' bites are especially painful and should be looked at by a physician.

The best treatment for this type of insect bite is readily available not in your first aid kit but, instead, in the kitchen. A mixture of meat tenderizer and water applied with a cotton swab to the affected area often brings rapid relief.

Tick bites: a preventive approach

Few parents of the 1990s have neither heard nor worried about tick bites. What has gained these tiny creatures such notoriety is their association with Lyme disease and two less-publicized tick-borne infections, Rocky Mountain spotted fever and Colorado tick fever. While very few tick species actually carry the organisms that cause these diseases, the following advice on tick bite prevention and treatment is offered.

The Deer Tick—A carrier of Lyme Disease. Note that the tick is shown under a magnifying glass; in real life, ticks are about the size of the head of a pin.

1. Ticks live in wooded areas, primarily in bushes, shrubs, or underbrush. Ticks do not fly at their victims. Instead, they commonly attach themselves to humans and animals walking through this underbrush and, literally, suck blood from their host for a period of 3 to 6 days. Most are tiny—no bigger than the head of a pin—making them extremely difficult to see if you do not look closely.

2. The best means of avoiding tick bites, then, includes wearing protective clothing that covers all areas of exposed skin. This means that the hiker walking through a wooded area ought to wear long socks and pants that have been tucked into the top of the stocking, long-sleeved shirts, and solid shoes (as opposed to sandals or walking barefoot). You should also apply a 20 percent DEET-containing insect repellent, as described above, to any exposed skin surface and lightly about the clothed areas as well. When hiking, it is always a wise idea to inspect the exposed

skin of your child every two hours or so for any evidence of a tick bite. Upon return to your home after such a trip, a more complete examination of the child's entire body (as well as your own) is mandatory, followed by a shower.

3. Please note that most tick bites are relatively painless, small in size, and do not produce an "itchy" reaction like other bug bites. Instead, the tick burrows under the skin, in a painless manner to the host, and draws in blood. Consequently, merely asking your child how she feels will not guarantee that she is "tick-free." You must inspect her body with great care and attention. One should also make sure that you include in your inspection some of the tick's favorite hiding spots, the armpits, the groin, the scalp, neck, and hair.

4. Because ticks are typically not firmly attached to a human's skin early on in their "feeding frenzy" and the actual transmission time for Lyme disease requires about 18 to 24 hours, early attention to tick removal is a safe and effective means of preventing this disease.

5. Pets, particularly dogs that roam outdoors, can also spread Lyme disease if they become tick-infested. Make sure that your family pet is thoroughly washed with an antitick soap (at least bimonthly) during the spring and summer. Such soaps are readily available at your local pet supply store. Don't forget to examine your pet periodically for ticks during the warm months, especially if it spends time outside or accompanies you on your hikes.

6. The task of removing ticks is not nearly as difficult or disgusting as it sounds. For the parent who has graduated from changing diapers and feeding an infant, pulling ticks off your child's skin should prove to be a relatively easy task. Here are some tips to aid such a process:

a. Using tweezers, grip the insect as close to your child's skin as possible without pinching. In most cases, the back of the tick is actually sticking out of the skin, and this is the best part of the insect to grab with the tweezers. Once you have a good grip on the tick, you should swiftly but carefully pull the tick out. Do not twist the tweezers or use an unsteady jerking motion: such maneuvers are likely to break the tick in half, leaving its head behind, still firmly embedded in the skin. Don't squeeze too hard with your tweezers or you may crush the tick, causing its body fluids to ooze into the bite area, which can also spread Lyme disease.

b. In the event that the tick does break off, remove the remaining body parts much as you would a wood splinter. One method taught to a number of pediatricians by their mothers involves soaking the affected area in warm water to soften the skin, followed by the careful removal of the tick body with a sterile needle. By now the tick is either dead or soon will be. Do not save or manhandle the removed tick, since it may contain body fluids that carry the causative organism of Lyme disease.

c. Smaller ticks can be literally scraped off with a stiff, flat object such as the blade of a knife or even a credit card.

What is Lyme disease?

Named for the town where it was first discovered (Old Lyme, Connecticut), it is probably the disease most commonly spread by tick bites. Although there are anywhere from five thousand to ten thousand cases of Lyme disease reported each year, it is spread by one specific type of tick—the deer tick—that preferentially feeds on white-footed mice and white-tailed deer. Humans are incidental and accidental feasts for these insects. The most common areas in the United States for Lyme disease are wooded parts of the Northeast, from Massachusetts to Maryland; Minnesota and Wisconsin in the Midwest; and Oregon and California in the West. In other United States locales, Lyme disease can occur, but at present less than 3 percent of the ticks in those areas are know to carry the disease. European cases are also beginning to be reported, especially in wooded areas of Sweden, France, Austria, Germany, and Switzerland.

It is important to note that the overwhelming majority of tick bites do not lead to Lyme disease. Even when Lyme disease occurs, most cases do not go on to the severe complications described below. Usually, within 1 to 3 weeks of the tick bite, most infected people (about 50 percent) develop a specific type of rash called erythema migrans. This rash is a red "bull's-eye" with a pale center that grows in size over time. It is not an itchy or painful rash but is quite prominent in appearance. For those who develop this rash and seek medical attention, commonly prescribed antibiotics such as tetracycline or penicillin can cure the illness with great ease. Those cases that remain untreated, however, either because no heralding rash appears or the rash is ignored, go on to develop severe long-term complications such as arthritis, neurologic problems, and abnormalities of the heart and cardiovascular system. In fact, one of the hallmark neurologic symptoms of Lyme Disease is a condition known as Bell's Palsy. Named for the Scottish neurologist, Sir Charles Bell, it is a sudden one-sided paralysis of the facial muscles that results in a distortion of the face. These frightening and serious complications, it should be reiterated, are entirely preventable by following the tick bite precautions noted above and, if actually bitten by a deer tick, by receiving prompt medical attention.

When should I call my doctor after discovering a tick bite on my child?

You should always call your doctor if you cannot remove the tick yourself or if part of it remains embedded in the skin; if you live in an area of the country where Lyme Disease is a common problem and you are concerned your child may have contracted it; if your child develops an unexplained fever, flulike symptoms or the rash of Lyme one or more weeks after a tick bite; or if you note a tick bite on your child more than 18 hours after the event.

Remember, even if your child is bitten by a tick, most tick-borne diseases, including Lyme disease, may be prevented by prompt removal of the tick.

For more information about Lyme Disease, write or call:

National Lyme Borreliosis Foundation
Box 462
Tolland, CT 06084
(800) 886-LYME

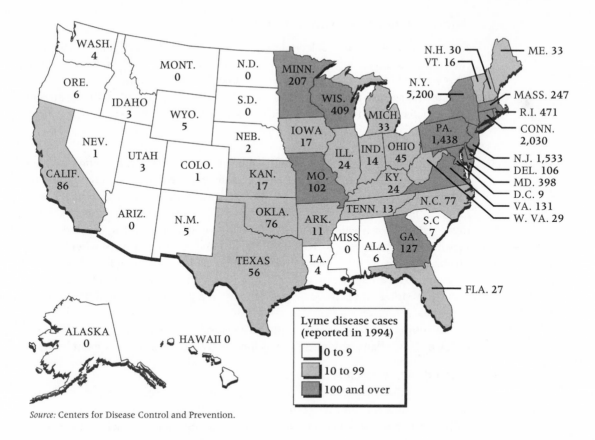

Source: Centers for Disease Control and Prevention.

What is Rocky Mountain Spotted Fever (RMSF)?

This rugged-sounding disease is also tick-spread and infectious. It is caused by an organism called Rickettsia rickettsii. *This rather rare infection occurs most frequently in the Rocky Mountain region of the United States. About a week after a child is bitten by an RMSF-infected tick, he develops achy muscles, headache, a mild to high (100 to 104°F) fever, fatigue, loss of appetite, and sensitivity to light. The child with RMSF also exhibits a characteristic rash during the second week of illness. Light pink splotches break out around the child's hands and feet. Soon the ankles and wrists are involved, and with the passage of twenty-four hours, the pink to purple, bruiselike lesions cover the face, neck, arms, armpits, belly, and buttocks. If your child has been bitten by a tick and subsequently develops the symptoms described above, you need to have him examined by the pediatrician. Blood tests are available to help with the diagnosis. RMSF is easily treated with antibiotics, but it does require medical attention. Some cases are extremely elusive, especially in those 10 percent of all children who do not develop the characteristic rash.*

Bites, Sea and Freshwater Animals

Trips to the seashore are a splendid way for families to relax and enjoy each other's company. But just as you take special precautions to insure your child's safety by always having him swim under the supervision of an adult, you need to follow certain precautions against marine animals that sting or bite such as jellyfish, venomous fish, sea urchins, and the rare electrical shock injury caused by certain types of eels.

Stinging "fish"

The most common type of sea animal injuries are caused by stepping on gelatinous animals (such as jellyfish, man-o'-war, and sea nettles). Frequently the sweeping tide of the ocean washes either the entire animal or parts of its tentacles ashore onto the sandy beach. This is especially a problem after a storm, when more debris is washed ashore, either living or inanimate. The best means of avoiding such injuries is to watch where you and your child walk when you are on the beach. Given the beauty of the ocean and the impossibility of watching every move of a happy boy or girl at the shore, this is not as simple a task as it sounds. Wearing inexpensive "water-sandals" is a good way to avoid foot injuries at the beach.

The stings themselves are painful and cause a burning sensation and redness of the skin. This inflammation can last as long as twenty-four to forty-eight hours.

First aid and treatment:

1. Wipe off the "stingers" with either sand or a thick towel. You need to be careful not to touch the stingers with your own bare hands or you, too, will be stung. Once the tentacle has been removed, wash the affected area with salt water—readily available, considering you are at the beach.

2. The stinging sensation and resultant inflammation is caused by two factors: the sharp tentacle of the animal and its venom or poison. To counteract the venom's toxin, you can apply either rubbing alcohol or a paste of meat tenderizer and water to the injury for at least thirty minutes.

3. A great deal of relief from the burning and itching sensation of these stings can be achieved by applying a 0.5 percent hydrocortisone ointment three to four times a day for a period of three days after the injury. As noted elsewhere, this ointment is readily available at any drugstore and does not require a prescription.

4. Rarely, these injuries can cause more serious reactions, including nausea, headache, dizziness, and muscular weakness. In the event of such symptoms, you should contact your physician immediately.

Venomous fish

The dorsal spines of true fish such as stingrays, catfish, scorpion fish, and stonefish frequently contain a venom that produces intense pain, redness, and swelling at the site of the wound. Sometimes these injuries are serious enough to cause fever, vomiting, weakness, muscle cramps, and, rarely, shock *[see CPR]*. Stingray injuries are especially serious because the fish whips its tail at its victim with a rather muscular snap that can cause a deep cut or laceration, in addition to injecting its venom.

First aid and treatment:

1. Wash the wound immediately with sea water in order to dilute the toxic venom.

2. Remove any remains of the fish's dorsal spine from the wound site. Again, you need to be careful to protect your own hands when removing these sharp spines, since they still contain venom and can cause injury.

3. The venom of these fish is especially sensitive to heat; therefore, if you soak the affected area in a bath of heated water for thirty to ninety minutes, the pain caused by the venom should resolve. The water should be as hot as your child can tolerate, but never hotter than 120° F.

4. It is wise to call your physician for immediate attention if your child develops generalized symptoms such as nausea, vomiting, weakness, or cramping; if the laceration caused by the injury is especially deep and requires stitches; or if you cannot remove the spine itself.

5. Please note that there exist many other kinds of fish that may bite or sting but do not inject venom. These injuries are usually easily treated with an immediate cleansing with sea water or soap and water. One need seek medical attention only if the injury produced is a deep cut or puncture wound, or if the wound is actively bleeding despite the application of direct pressure for a period of ten minutes.

Electric eels

Stepping on or coming in contact with an electric eel results in the child feeling stunned and even partially paralyzed for a brief period. The good news is that the electric "shock" incurred is rarely serious, and your child should start to feel normal within the half hour. The best treatment is to calmly reassure your child that he is all right and have him lie down for an hour with his feet elevated on a pillow or a rolled towel.

Sea urchins

These hard, prickly creatures can be quite painful if inadvertently stepped on. Their barbed spines contain a venom that causes a stinging or burning sensation. It is important to remove the spine, which can become lodged much like a wood splinter, from the skin in order to prevent further inflammation and irritation.

First aid and treatment:

1. After removing the spine from the affected area, apply a paste of meat tenderizer and water or rubbing alcohol for a period of thirty minutes in order to counteract the effects of the venom, followed by careful cleansing of the injury with soap and water.

2. Inspect the injury site carefully for any remains of the spine and remove them much as you would with a splinter, using a sterile needle or tweezers. Sometimes the sea urchin spines leave a purple discoloration at the injury site; this is caused by a dye that exists in the sea urchin itself and will resolve on its own.

Leeches

Leeches are black, wormlike creatures that attach themselves to other animals and suck their blood. Leech bites are a nuisance that can occur when swimming in freshwater lakes or rivers.

First aid and treatment: If you notice the black, wormlike leech attached to your child's skin, it is important first not to panic or scare your child. Nor should you attempt to pull the leech off your child's skin, since the leech's teeth can remain behind and cause prolonged bleeding. These bites are not typically painful and can be easily removed by applying a large amount of salt to the leech until it dries up and falls off. Explain to your child what you are doing and simply dump an entire salt shaker's contents onto the offending creature. Once the leech is off (this should take no more than five or ten minutes), you should clean the site with water and alcohol, followed by a bandage.

Bites, Snake

These creatures have been causing trouble since the time of Adam and Eve. And while they no longer appear to have the ability to convince us to transgress, their bites can be of great concern.

Bites by poisonous snakes such as rattlesnakes, water moccasins (cottonmouths), copperheads, and coral snakes are a true medical emergency. After such an event, call your physician immediately. The most frequently bitten area, for obvious reasons, is the leg. Even with these types of poisonous snakes, the bite can be what has been termed a "dry bite," meaning that no poisonous venom was actually injected. It is easy to distinguish a dry bite from a venomous one in that venom causes a severe burning and painful reaction directly at the site within five minutes of the injury. If your child does not complain of such an injury, he should be considered extremely lucky. If these symptoms do appear, (i.e., burning, swelling, bruising, or other serious symptoms of illness) however, you need to act quickly.

First aid and treatment:

1. Remove the child immediately. It is a good idea to remove any restrictive clothing or jewelry on the affected limb before swelling sets in. Take him to the nearest hospital emergency room available. Antivenin treatments—which are generally only available at a hospital—can prevent serious complications, but they need to be administered within four hours of the bite.

2. If the hospital is simply too far away and the bite was certainly caused by a poisonous snake, you should begin, before making the trek to the hospital,

by removing some of the venom yourself. This can be done by cleaning the area with alcohol and making a small incision with an alcohol-washed pocket knife. The incision should be about a half-inch long and deep enough to go through the skin to the level of the fang mark—about one-eighth to one-quarter of an inch. Follow by squeezing the area very hard to extrude both blood and, hopefully, the venom. With your mouth, suck out as much venom as possible for a period of five minutes. This age-old method, as horrifying as it sounds, can help to save your child's life—but only if it is done within half an hour of the bite. After you have completed suction of the wound, wash it carefully and rush to the hospital.

3. In the event that your are more than two or three hours from a hospital, you should apply a tight tourniquet such as a bandana or a ripped piece of cloth about two inches above the wound—although not on a movable joint—to prevent the venom from moving to the heart. The tourniquet needs to be tight, but not so tight that it prevents blood flow to the affected limb. One way of knowing you have tied it too tight is if you see veins popping out, much as you do when you have your blood drawn at the doctor's office. Too tight a tourniquet will cause further damage. Ice is not recommended, since it can damage the skin further and worsen the effects of the venom. The tourniquet needs to stay in place until after the antivenin is administered.

 Do I need to worry about nonpoisonous snake bites?

No. Bites from snakes such as garter snakes or pet snakes are relatively harmless. Their bites rarely pierce the skin and require little first aid. It is a good idea, however, to make sure your child's tetanus shot is up to date and to wash the injury with cool water and soap.

Bites, Spiders

The "itsy-bitsy" spider is more than just a "teensy-weensy" problem for growing children. Although there exist more than twenty thousand types of spiders in the United States, most are relatively harmless, either because they lack fangs strong enough to break through human skin or do not possess a venom toxic to humans. But some types of spiders exist whose bites are quite dangerous; these eight-legged creatures can cause great pain. We will discuss first those types of spiders that are most dangerous and conclude with a brief discussion of the not-so-dangerous types, which are best left to playground bullies hoping to scare their victims.

The brown recluse spider is perhaps the most common culprit of spider bites in the United States. It likes to live in dark, out-of-the-way places such as woodpiles, the undersurface of basement stairs, garages, and so on. Since these creatures hibernate during the winter, the likeliest time for such a bite is between April and October. It has extremely long legs and a dark, violin-shaped pattern on its head. Because these spiders are rather small, their presence is rarely recognized until it is too late. Their bites yield swelling and blister formation long after the spider had gone on to greener pastures (or darker corners). Typically, four to eight hours after the bite, the area forms a blister and is extremely painful. Shortly after that, the center of the lesion becomes somewhat bruised-looking and sunken or depressed. There are times that the bites may be so severe as to require plastic surgical repair. The good news, however, is that such serious damage is rare. Once you notice this type of lesion on your child, you need to wash the area carefully with soap and water and follow the injury's healing carefully in case some of the skin is damaged.

The black widow spider may well be the most infamous of dangerous and deadly spiders. Reputed to be quite "shy and nonaggressive," the spider will bite when it becomes trapped between, say, a layer of clothing and human skin. Like brown recluse spiders, they tend to hibernate during the winter and, if seen at all, tend to be more common during the warmer months. It is a dark black, eight-legged creature with a reddish-orange hourglass figure on its belly. Unfortunately, because of the location of this tell-tale sign of the black widow, it is not always easy to see—nor should you inspect suspicious spiders by picking them up to verify their species. It is the female spider that is poisonous and a threat to humans; male black widows do not possess fangs strong enough to pierce through human skin. The female black widow is about an inch or so in length. Their bites, like those of the brown recluse, contain an extremely poisonous venom that causes intense swelling, redness, and pain shortly after the event. They can also cause intense muscle cramps—especially in the abdomen—nausea, vomiting, and generalized achiness. Despite popular folklore, black widow bites are rarely deadly, unless one is bitten by several spiders at the same approximate time or if the victim is under the age of two.

First aid and treatment: Spider bites—when caused by brown recluse or black widow spiders—definitely require a physician's immediate attention. Call your doctor for advice. Most likely, your doctor will instruct you to apply ice to the wound for a period of thirty minutes in order to prevent the venom from spreading. If it is necessary, you will be instructed to take your child to the nearest emergency room for close observation and, possibly administration of drugs to provide symptomatic relief from the painful effects of the venom. Antivenin may be indicated, particularly for the extremely young child or the child with multiple bites.

Scorpions are related to spiders. They are extremely poisonous, and their bites are a true medical emergency. They typically live in the desert such as the Southwestern United States. The treatment of scorpion bites is similar to that of black widows. You should call your physician immediately and arrange to meet him or her at the nearest emergency room. As of this writing, only one type of scorpion residing in the continental United States has been reported to be serious enough to cause death: the yellow, stripeless *Scorpionida sculpturatus.*

Are there any other types of spider bites that I should be concerned about?

While relatively few spiders in this country carry a poisonous venom (see above), there are a large number of harmless spiders that do, indeed, bite. For example, common garden spiders cause a bite that is painful and swollen (lasting up to two days). Frequently these creatures do their dirty work at night when their victim is asleep, leaving only a tender bite behind as evidence. The best treatment for these injuries is to wash the area carefully, then apply a paste of meat tenderizer and water. If the pain persists, cold packs or ice packs help to numb the area.

You need call your physician only if the bite does not heal properly, the pain and swelling persists, a blister or a bruise develops at the bite, or your child develops muscle cramping or appears ill.

Remember, spiders like to hang out, so to speak, in underbrush, wooded areas and woodpiles, near garbage, or in dark areas such as outdoor open structures without light. They are easily killed with most household insecticides, so if spiders are a problem in your home, it is wise to do some careful insect removal.

BLOCKED TEAR (LACRIMAL) DUCT

Most newborn babies spend up to two hours a day crying *[see Crying]*. Early in the baby's life, however, the tear ducts (the lacrimal duct system) do not produce much in the way of tears, although this "moisture shortage" resolves within eight weeks of life. By two months of age the baby should be crying regularly with regulation tears!

Tears are important not only for expressing the hallmark symptom of crying; they also help to moisten and lubricate the eyes, keeping them dust- and particle-free. The lacrimal gland, a tiny sac deep between the nose and the eye, produces the salty clear fluid we call tears. It flows from the gland through a tube called the nasolacrimal duct and overflow, much like rain in a gutter, out of the eye.

In about 6 percent of all babies this nasolacrimal duct is blocked, causing a problem in tear flow. Most of these obstructions (61 percent) are the result of a membrane developing where it shouldn't. Some tear duct blockages are caused by infections (24 percent), fewer by trauma (12 percent) and poorly working tear ducts or glands (3 per-

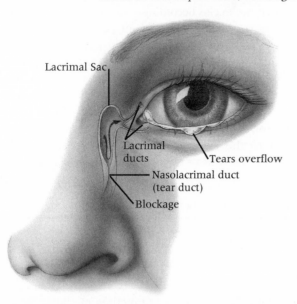

Lacrimal Sac

Lacrimal ducts

Tears overflow

Nasolacrimal duct (tear duct)

Blockage

When the tear duct is blocked, the tears cannot drain properly into the nose. This gives the baby the appearance of crying or looking "weepy-eyed."

cent). Blockage is more commonly found on one side, although a third of all babies with this problem have both tear ducts blocked.

What Does a Baby with a Blocked Tear Duct Look Like?

Given the amount of time the average newborn baby spends crying, you ought to have plenty of opportunities to observe your baby's nasolacrimal duct system in action! Babies with tear duct blockages have a persistent "wet-eyed" or "weepy" appearance; in other words, they appear to be crying or to have just cried even when this is not the case. Such babies will have no discharge coming out of the nostril on the side where the blockage exists. They frequently have persistent or intermittent tearing; occasionally, a whitish or greenish discharge will result when you press on the area where the lacrimal sac is located (medial canthal fold).

Home Care Tips for a Blocked Tear Duct

If you notice these symptoms, your health care provider can show you how to massage the lacrimal sac area with your fingertip. Basically, you rub the tip of your finger along the inner corner of the affected eye (as indicated in the figure) in an upward motion (toward the top of the baby's head), twice a day. Because the baby's eyes are especially prone to infections, make sure you always wash your hands before trying this maneuver. Keep the baby's eye area clean and free of discharge or fluid. If you notice the eyelid becoming swollen or see reddened, green, thick discharge or other signs of infection, call your pediatrician to assess the need for antibiotic-containing eyedrops.

By massaging the tear duct and gland in an upward motion, you will probably force open the plugged up tear duct within two to four weeks. This conservative management tends to work in 90 percent of all babies with blocked tear ducts. For the more stubborn problems, a consultation with an ophthalmologist is warranted. This doctor, who specializes in diseases of the eye, will delicately insert a tiny probe into the lacrimal duct in order to remove the blockage.

BLEEDING INJURIES *[See Cuts, scrapes, and bleeding injuries]*

BOTTLE FEEDING YOUR BABY

Although we strongly recommend breastfeeding as the method of choice for infant nutrition, there are circumstances that make breastfeeding difficult or impractical. If you have begun to breastfeed and are having trouble, do not give up hope. In the majority of cases, a consultation with your pediatrician or a lactation counselor can help solve most problems.

Should you decide not to breastfeed, however, that's okay, too. Infant formulas are safe and nutritious alternatives to breast milk, and your baby will grow healthy and strong on these products. They are also extremely convenient and easy to transport.

There are many different formulas available, most made with cow's milk or soy milk. Some iron-free or low iron baby formulas exist, but most have been taken off of the market because they are not nutritional enough for growing babies. *Do not buy the low iron formulas! Babies need iron in order to develop normally [see Iron Deficiency Anemia].*

How do I Prepare Infant Formula?

These products are available in three formats: ready-to-serve liquid; concentrated liquid that needs dilution; and a powdered form to which you add water. For the latter two forms we suggest the following instructions.

Concentrated liquid formula: Mix equal parts (1:1) concentrated formula with water. Tap water is fine if you are only making one bottle; if you are making a whole day's supply, you should use water that has been boiled. Prepared formula, regardless of its original format, may be kept, refrigerated, for about 48 hours, but not more.

If you are making more than one bottle and you are using boiled water, be sure to cool the finished formula *before* giving it to your baby. If you use well water, make sure it is boiled for ten to fifteen minutes before giving it to your baby in the form of formula. You may also use distilled water, although this is expensive and, like well water, does not contain fluoride.

Powdered formula mix: These products come with a plastic measuring spoon for preparing the formula. Add two ounces of water for every level scoop of the powder. The suggestions regarding water, boiling, and refrigeration are the same as above.

Some Good Rules to Follow

• It is *never* a good idea to make up your own proportions of formula. Read the directions carefully and do not try to make an extra-concentrated or an extra-dilute formula. This may seriously harm your child. If you follow the formula's directions carefully, adding the measured amount of formula to water, your baby will be assured of getting his nutrition in a safe manner.

• Never rewarm formula in a microwave. It heats the milk unevenly, and there have been several reported instances of babies burning their mouths after being fed formula that has just been taken out of the microwave—or off the stove. It is important always to check the formula before giving it to your baby to make sure it is not too hot. The age-old method of squirting a drop or two on your wrist should suffice.

When and How Much to Feed the Baby

Pediatricians in the early twentieth century used to give mothers detailed and complicated schedules of when to feed their babies. In retrospect, these hourly feeding schedules look like a monitor at the airport detailing the day's arriving flights! The simplest way to figure out the minimum amount of infant formula your baby needs is to simply divide his weight (in pounds) by two. The resulting number (one-half the baby's weight) is about the total number of ounces of formula that baby needs each feeding. When the baby is about five to six month of age, he will settle into a routine of, perhaps, four feedings of seven to eight ounces; if your six-month-old baby is taking in more than thirty-two ounces of formula per feeding and is not overweight, it's probably time to consider adding solid foods. More than likely you and your baby will establish a routine of feeding, probably not dissimilar from the one offered below. Remember, these are simply suggestions. Your baby will tell you when she is hungry, and the feeding schedule should be adjusted to her needs and demands.

Tickle the baby's cheek or lips with the nipple of the bottle. This causes a reflex opening of the mouth called the rooting reflex. Then insert the nipple into the baby's mouth.

Newborn to one month: Most newborns will want to be fed every three to four hours; indeed, this is a pretty good rule of thumb, since newborns need the nutrition and energy provided by formulas at least every three hours. Try six to eight feedings per day (three to four ounces per feeding). Separate the feeds to every three to four

Make sure that you support the baby's head with the crook of your arm. Always hold the bottle at an angle so that the infant formula completely fills the bottle's neck and the nipple. This prevents the baby from sucking in air, which will make her uncomfortable.

hours, depending on your baby's level of hunger or satisfaction. Do not feed the baby more than every two-and-a-half hours.

One to three months: Try six feedings per day (four to six ounces) but make sure that they are three to four hours apart.

Three to six months: Four to five feedings a day (six to eight ounces) every four hours or so.

Six to nine months: Try four bottle feedings (eight-ounces) a day. You will also begin adding solid foods to your baby's diet. Try to restrict the bedtime feeding to just formula. Try to keep the feedings at least four hours apart *[see Feeding Your Baby]*.

Nine to twelve months: By this point your baby will be eating more and more solids, such as strained baby foods and even finger foods. Give him three bottle feedings (at least eight ounces) a day, and offer solids with each meal. These meals should be separated by about five hours. You can also offer two snacks between meals.

As with breastfeeding, it is important for both parent and baby to be comfortable and calm. Try supporting your arm with a pillow as you place the baby in a semiseated position. The baby's head should be supported by the inner portion of your elbow.

When feeding a baby with a bottle, make sure that the bottle is tilted or "propped" at an angle that allows the nipple and the bottle's neck to be always filled with formula; otherwise the baby will suck in air, and this will cause abdominal discomfort *[see Burping Your Baby]*.

 Why can't I just give my baby whole cow's milk?

We do not recommend introducing whole cow's milk into a baby's diet until she is older than twelve months. The reason we prescribe infant formulas is that they are modified for a human baby's special nutritional needs and digestive system. Introducing whole cow's milk too early can increase the risk of your baby developing a milk allergy. Perhaps more importantly, whole cow's milk can cause iron deficiency anemia in babies under a year of age, which can seriously affect the baby's physical and mental development. Indeed, one of the

authors of this book (F.A.O.) spent a major portion of his career disproving the older practice of introducing whole cow's milk to six-month-old babies. During the first year of life, the best food for babies is either breast milk or iron-fortified infant formula.

Does my baby need extra vitamins or other essential nutrients?

Most infant formulas currently being sold contain all of the essential vitamins, minerals, and nutrients your baby needs to grow up to be healthy and strong. The one exception is fluoride, which we need for strong teeth and the prevention of cavities. If you live in an area where the water is fluoridated, simply use that water in making the baby's formula and his nutrition wants will be complete. In the event you live in an area where fluoride is not added to the municipal water supply or you are using well or distilled water to prepare the baby's formula, you need to ask your pediatrician to prescribe fluoride supplements [see Tooth Care, Tooth Decay, and Toothaches].

BREASTFEEDING YOUR BABY

In the United States, as in many industrial nations, the development of safe and health cow's milk or soy milk formulas for babies has largely displaced breastfeeding. This is most unfortunate for a variety of reasons, including the fact that breastfeeding is a *learned* experience. It does not just happen! You need to work at it. A century ago, for example, most women did breastfeed for a period of time and most young women and girls grew up in a house where another woman (typically their mother) had experience in breastfeeding. With the advent of the bottle—with which even a father could feed a baby—this process was disrupted. Today, many young mothers have no one in their immediate family who can offer instruction on the art of breastfeeding. Discouragement with the early days of the process too frequently gives way to simply reaching for the bottle.

Why Should I Breastfeed?

Breast milk is nature's perfect food for growing human infants. An enormous amount of information supports breastfeeding as the best means of providing nutrition for your baby, and the benefits to your baby persist long after weaning has occurred. For example, breastfed babies experience fewer infections (including diarrhea, ear infections, and more serious problems) and allergies than those who are fed cow-milk or soy-milk formulas. Breast milk is better digested by human babies. It is inexpensive (free, compared to a cost of $1400 annually for formula) and produced at just the right temperature. There also exists evidence that breastfeeding reduces the mother's risk of developing breast cancer. Finally, the act of breastfeeding promotes infant-mother bonding in the most delightfully productive fashion. Even the baby who is breastfed for only a month appears to receive enormous benefits from this experience.

Consequently, we will try to convince you that breastfeeding is worth the extra planning and effort for both you and your baby. We are also aware that breastfeeding is a dance with two partners—mother and baby. If one chooses to stop, for whatever reason, that's perfectly okay. What we are most interested in is providing advice and information that works in your life. Bottle-fed babies do grow up healthy and normal—one of the authors (H.M.) of this book was a bottle-fed infant!

Tricks of the Trade

Don't be afraid to ask for advice: Study after study on breastfeeding shows that the single most important factor in a mother's successfully breastfeeding her child is good advice from those who are qualified to help. Fortunately, a number of excellent sources regarding breastfeeding, such as La Leche League and other breastfeeding and lactation support groups, are available to you. Many community centers, for example, offer classes on breastfeeding as well as other parenting skills. These classes are extremely valuable not only for the information given but also because they create networks of support with other mothers who are right there in the trenches with you! Many a great friendship, filled with support and warmth, has been generated this way.

Most community and children's hospitals today have lactation consultants available on staff to consult with even before your child is born. Ask your pediatrician or the local community or children's hospital if they know of a lactation consultant practicing in your area. These professionals are glad to make an appointment with you and begin instruction on prenatal concerns, problems that may arise during your hospital stay, and, of course, concerns that emerge after the baby is born. Before we undertook to write this essay, we were fortunate in consulting with our two favorite lactation experts, Susan Nehring, R.N., of the C. S. Mott Children's Hospital at the University of Michigan and Judy Vogelhut, R.N., at the Johns Hopkins Hospital Children's Center.

The importance of support: Successful breastfeeding demands support not only from the baby's doctors but, more importantly, from the family. Again, studies of breastfeeding consistently show that the most successful and longest breastfed infants also had supportive fathers who helped in the process. Early on in the pregnancy, both parents need to participate in the decision of how to feed the baby, based on a clear understanding of the realities of breastfeeding. Talk together about your fears and concerns regarding this decision. You will both be happier for a frank discussion of the topic and a sound grasp of what it entails.

The first days of breastfeeding: Babies enter the world with extra fluid and sugar on board as nature's way of taking care of the two- to five-day delay in mother's milk production. During the first days of life, the fluid that the baby suckles from his mother is called colostrum. Primarily made up of antibodies and other infection-fighting substances, water, and proteins, colostrum is thick and rich in appearance but much smaller in volume than the milk you will produce in a few days. Colostrum also has a gentle laxative effect on the baby. The baby will fill itself on colostrum, but may want more frequent feedings during the day. Don't worry, and keep a-going. The "real thing," human breast milk, will be coming shortly. Frequent small feedings during the first days of life will encourage milk production with minimal engorgement of the breasts. You will know when the baby is actually suckling because the feedings are not painful and you can often hear the baby swallowing. (You can also see the baby's ears wiggle up and down as he swallows!) Early feeding with colostrum also helps to prevent jaundice *[see Jaundice of the Newborn]*.

1. As soon after birth as possible, hold the baby to the breast. During the first few hours of life, most newborns are alert and ready to nurse. The newborn baby may want to breastfeed two or three times shortly after birth. She may then go through a period where she sleeps deeply for a period of two or three hours. (Apparently, the process of being born is exhausting!) While you should attempt to wake the newborn baby every three or four hours for feedings, remember that the baby needs to sleep as does the mother after the birth process.

2. An important sign of what the baby is taking in, is what is coming out! The baby should have a blackish, tarlike stool within the first day of life. Babies who do not have a bowel movement before the end of the second day of life need to be examined by a pediatrician. Frequent wet diapers (six to eight or more a day) are the best way of knowing that the baby is getting enough fluid.

3. After the first day of life, both mother and baby will have rested enough to begin a routine of feeding. The baby should have had at least one more bowel movement and several wet diapers by this point.

4. By day three of life, many babies are hungry and appear to breastfeed almost non-stop. Again, nature has designed a perfect system. The third day or so is when the calorie-rich breast milk begins to appear. Frequent suckling will stimulate the mother's milk glands to produce more. This is an extremely important point—the more the baby nurses, the more milk is produced. Nursing mothers also need to be reminded to drink plenty of fluids and to be aware that breastfeeding during the first few weeks after the birth may cause uterine contractions in the mother; these are normal but can be painful. If this happens to you, feel free to speak with your lactation consultant about them.

5. Some babies are simply slower than others in learning the concept of waking up to nurse. Whether they are deeper sleepers or are less aware of the pangs of hunger is not clear. It may seem sinful to waken a sleeping baby, but these "slower" babies need to learn about nursing on a regular basis and your milk supply needs the stimulation of the suckling infant. These "sleepy babies" should be allowed to sleep for no more than two and a half hours during the first days of life; newborns need to be frequently fed to prevent low blood sugar (hypoglycemia). Gentle stimulation, such as stroking the baby's cheek and un-

wrapping the blanketed baby, is a good way to achieve this. Once the baby learns to wake up to his own hunger cues, you will no longer need to awaken the baby for nursing. He will know, and very quickly will let you know. During the third day, the baby should have another stool and at least three wet diapers.

6. On day three to four, your breasts will begin to feel full. This fullness can be a mild sensation for some women; in others, the breasts can be quite tender. This firmness, called *engorgement* (see below), is caused not only by the milk production but also by the increased blood flow to the mother's breasts, hormones, and extra milk production.

7. By day four, the baby should be wetting his diaper at least four to six times daily and producing yellowish or "mustardy" looking stools. They are yellow because there is beta-carotene in mother's milk, and its presence in the stools is an excellent indicator that the baby is actually getting and digesting the milk. If the baby is not having yellow stools, is rarely wetting his diaper, or is simply having trouble feeding, call the pediatrician and lactation consultant. They will be only too glad to help you troubleshoot the problem. Many breastfeeding problems can actually be handled on the telephone. Most others can often be solved simply by having the lactation consultant examine the baby and observe the way you are nursing him.

Some women do have a delay in their milk production. Examples are women who underwent a Cesarean section, those who lost a large quantity of blood during the delivery, or those who experienced pre-eclampsia, a complication of pregnancy that includes symptoms of fluid retention (edema) and high blood pressure.

8. On day five, the nursing baby should be feeding eight to twelve times in every twenty-four-hour period. If you are *not* experiencing fuller breasts and seeing at least six to eight wet diapers and two to three yellow stools per day from your baby, call the pediatrician or lactation consultant and arrange to be seen at the office.

How to hold the baby
Some things do not come naturally, and for these situations it is wise to look at instructions. Positioning the baby on your breast is an extremely important issue, since lactation counselors find poor positioning a frequent source of sore nipples and poor infant weight gain. Alternating positions is an excellent means of preventing sore nipples by spreading out the pressure onto different parts of the areola. This also yields the stimulation of different milk ducts, preventing any from clogging. You will find a few positions, as you breastfeed, that are more comfortable than others for you and your baby. Use them, alternate them, and enjoy them. For example, some nursing mothers use a pillow on their laps to help the process; others have different styles. Here are a few suggestions on holding the baby during breastfeeding.

1. To begin nursing, make yourself comfortable and hold the baby in your arms with his body entirely on its side. His lower arm should be around your waist, with his head in the bend of your elbow.

You should hold the baby (as shown above) and let her nurse for about ten minutes.

2. Support your breast with your free hand, placing the thumb above the areola and your four fingers below it (like a "C"). Make sure to keep your fingers off the areola so that they do not get in the baby's mouth and interfere with the breastfeeding. Healthy babies will suck, and suck vigorously, on anything that gets into their mouths!

3. Gently tickle the baby's lips with your nipple until the baby's mouth opens as wide as a yawn. When the baby's mouth opens wide, pull the baby toward you with the nipple centered in his mouth. The baby will close his jaws, in a gumming motion, over the area of the breast where the milk sinuses are, just behind the nipple. This is called "latching-on." Make sure that the baby has the areola of

your breast in his mouth. Once the baby learns to "latch on" correctly and is feeding well, you do not have to limit feeding time. Infants have a very specific way of showing they are satisfied—after some minutes of nursing, they stop feeding and frequently fall asleep! As an aside, it is important to distinguish between your baby being satisfied and a more serious form of sleepiness called lethargy. Satisfied and healthy babies are aroused by gentle stimulation such as stroking. Lethargic babies, who may be ill, will fall asleep shortly after beginning to feed and are difficult to awaken.

4. When you are feeding the baby, his body

Take a break and burp the baby.

should be in a straight line, with his abdomen positioned against your chest.

5. It is normal for the baby's nose to be touching your breast while nursing. Since newborn babies routinely breathe through their noses, you need to make sure his nostrils are not blocked. One way of repositioning the baby, to allow simultaneous nose-breathing and mouth-nursing, is to raise the breast with the supporting hand or lift the baby's buttocks higher. As complicated as this may sound, you do get better with time and learn a routine that best fits both you and your baby! Some babies need more instruction than others. Be patient and ask questions if you have concerns.

Let the baby "latch on" to the other breast, and continue the feeding for another ten minutes, or until the baby indicates that she is full.

 What do I do when I develop sore nipples during the nursing process?

Positioning the baby properly can prevent most cases of early nipple soreness. Limiting the time the baby nurses does little to alleviate nipple soreness. Alternating the breasts during feedings is a good idea. Skipping feedings will simply cause the hungry baby to nurse more frantically and less efficiently when he finally does get to latch onto your breast. Some tips include frequent repositioning of the nipple in order to relieve the pressure; avoiding the use of nipple shields, which do little to protect your nipples and may help to decrease the amount of milk your baby is getting; expose the nipples and areolas to the air a few minutes before nursing; use a wet, warm washcloth to clean your nipples (rather than soaps); express milk onto the nipple and let it air dry in order to promote the healing process (see below). Rubbing olive oil on your nipples can also assist healing.

What is engorgement?

Engorgement refers to the sensation of breast fullness that occurs as the milk begins to be produced. Commonly, after the first few days, the breasts can become full and hard as a result of milk production and the increased blood flow to the breasts. When a breast is engorged, the full areola may cause the nipple to flatten; this makes nursing difficult for the baby. If your breasts do become engorged, apply moist heat to them, such as warm compresses or a warm shower, and gently massage the breasts before nursing. Another useful technique is to hand express or pump milk from the breast until the areola

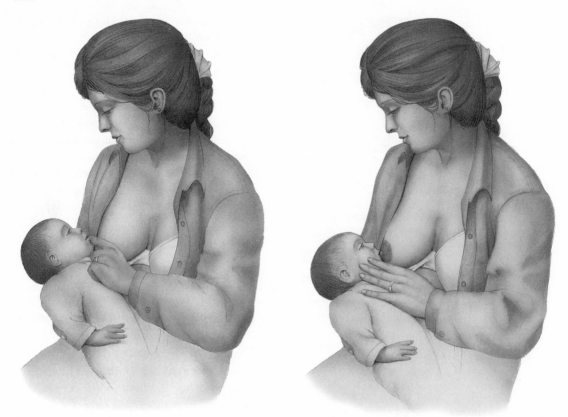

Begin by tickling the baby's cheek with your nipple or finger. This causes a reflex opening of the baby's mouth (the rooting reflex). The stimulated baby will turn to the mother's breast, open her mouth, and latch onto it, followed by intense sucking (left). Some newborn babies may need a little extra help in "latching on"; simply guide your areola into the baby's mouth (right).

softens and then proceed to nurse the baby. Simply place your thumb and index finger opposite each other on the areola, about an inch behind the nipple. Push your fingers inward, toward your chest. Then roll your thumb forward to compress the milk sinuses behind the nipples, and expect milk to come out!

After nursing, apply an ice pack to the breasts, briefly, in order to relieve swelling. It is perfectly all right to take ibuprofen or acetaminophen as a pain reliever for this discomfort. Breastfeeding often helps to prevent serious engorgement.

What is the "let-down" reflex?

This refers to the sensation that develops approximately two to three weeks after beginning to nurse. It is noticeable as a tingling sensation at the nipples or the actual ejection of milk just before feeding—sometimes even just when you think of feeding. It can also occur in the other breast while you are nursing. Once you experience the "let-down" reflex, you know

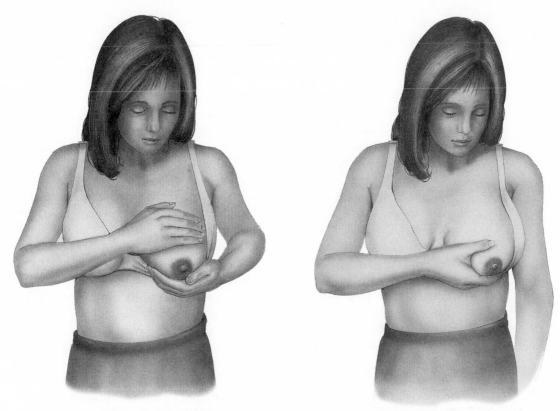

*Begin by stimulating your breast with gentle massage. Cup your breast in your hand
with your fingers placed around the areola. Press the areola inward in a steady motion.*

*that the breastfeeding mode has really kicked in. This process is obviously helped by making
sure the mother has enough rest, adequate fluid and food, a restful environment, and a
minimum of stress (just what every new mother has an easy time finding!). Remember, if
you have any questions or problems, call your pediatrician or lactation consultant for helpful advice and encouragement.*

How do I know if the baby is getting enough nourishment from nursing?

*Concern about the baby "getting enough" milk is one of the major reasons women stop
breastfeeding, although other causes include painful breasts, the baby's refusal to take to
breastfeeding, maternal distaste for breastfeeding, illness or fatigue in the mother or baby,
and the need to get back to work after delivery. Of all these reasons, the baby not getting
enough nourishment should be the least of your worries.*

*The best means to make sure a newborn infant is getting enough to eat—whether from
breast or bottle—is to measure how she is growing (in terms of weight, length, and head
circumference) over the first months of life. As long as the baby is gaining weight, you are
providing enough nutrition! Your pediatrician will measure these parameters carefully dur-*

ing your child's well-baby visits and judge how the baby is growing. Generally, breastfed babies lose about 7 percent of their birth weight during the first seven to ten days of life. (No baby—whether breast- or bottle-fed—should lose more than ten percent of birth weight during this period.) After the mother's milk has come in, the baby will gain about an ounce per day.

Most breastfed babies, but certainly not all, will nurse eight to twelve times per twenty-four-hour period during the first weeks of life—or up to every two to three hours. Breastfed babies typically wet their diapers at least six times a day and have no fewer than two or three loose bowel movements per day. They also appear satisfied after each feeding, as opposed to fretful, crying, or restless. Remember, breastfed babies do not always eat exactly on schedule. Indeed, schedules are better suited for the comings and goings of airplanes than a newborn baby. On some days, your newborn will seem to want to nurse all the time; at others, she may be less hungry and less anxious to nurse. The days of frequent feedings tend to correlate with the infant's growth spurts. Allowing the baby to breastfeed for the length of time she desires serves to increase your milk supply in order to meet your particular baby's increasing growth demands. As the baby grows and takes more milk, your body will produce more.

It is estimated that *less than 5 percent* of all mothers produce inadequate amounts of milk, so the chances are excellent that you will be successful. Moderate exercise that improves cardiovascular fitness but does not cause the breastfeeding mother to expend too much energy (and, thus, lose calories), as well as adequate food intake, will improve rather than harm lactation. Breastfeeding mothers can safely take part in recreational activities without fear of providing inadequate nutrition for their babies. By the way, another advantage to breastfeeding is that the mother expends about 500 calories a day simply by nursing.

Breastfeeding and the Working Mother

Many mothers today work at demanding careers and need to continue that work shortly after the baby's delivery. Fortunately, employers are becoming increasingly aware of the health benefits and importance of breastfeeding. Innovative programs across the country are in place to make breastfeeding a viable choice for working mothers. Ask your employer what is available at your workplace. Another positive point is that not much is needed to implement a "breastfeeding program" in the workplace—simply a quiet, private room, a refrigerator, and a breast pump!

The most important point of all breastfeeding is establishing a good milk supply. The principle is simple: the more milk the baby demands (by suckling), the more milk your breasts will produce. Therefore, it is important to take advantage of your maternity leave and establish a steady breastfeeding regimen in the early weeks of your baby's life before returning to work. Once you have stored the breast milk in a proper manner (see below) you—or someone else—can feed it to your baby using the techniques discussed above in "Bottle Feeding Your Baby."

Even though the baby is not always "nursing" using this method—in the literal sense of breastfeeding—he is getting the nutritional and healthy benefits of continuing on human breast milk.

Breast pumps

A compromise solution to the perennial maternal problem of "how can I be at two places at the same time?" is a device called the breast pump. There are a number of different electric breast pumps that you can purchase or rent. For information on breast pumps and home lactation consultants you can call Sanvita Programs-Medela, Inc. at (800) 435-8316.

It is best to avoid the smaller hand-held or piston-type breast pumps currently available at toy stores or child care stores. These devices have hand suction controls that make it easy to damage swollen breast tissue.

A working mother needs to plan her time to both maintain a steady supply of milk and perform all her other responsibilities. This is no easy task and may, at times, appear frustrating and difficult. A reasonable pumping regimen for the working mother of a nursing baby is to pump her breasts at the times she would have been breastfeeding at home. Keeping a journal of your breastfeeding during the early weeks is a good way to gauge this schedule. The mother should also breastfeed the baby in the morning before work and frequently during the evening (every two hours or so). If the baby awakens during the night, a feeding often helps him to fall back to sleep. During the weekends or on vacations the baby should be breastfed as often as possible.

As the infant grows (age three months or older), you will reduce the breast pumping at work to perhaps once or twice a day. You should continue along this schedule as long as the baby continues to feed frequently during the night. As discussed elsewhere, most babies learn to sleep through the night after the age of two to four months *[see Sleep and Sleep Problems]*.

Weaning

Human breast milk is the *only* food your baby needs to help her grow and develop normally during her first six to twelve months. Ideally, you will be able to nurse her for that period. After six months, most pediatricians would be willing to give the still-nursing mother a gold medal! Although some babies will want to breastfeed until they are two years or older, most infants begin to lose interest in nursing once solid foods are introduced (about age six months), and the breastfeedings will gradually diminish.

There is no ideal or set way to wean your baby, although the more gradual the process the more comfortable it is for both baby and mother. Here are a few tips that may be applied to either the breast- or bottlefed baby:

• Introduce the baby to a bottle or cup. Continue to use breast milk or specially prepared infant formula during the baby's first year of life; whole cow's milk is not suitable for a baby under one year old. (Remember, at the age of six months many, but not all, babies are developmentally able to hold a bottle or cup with two hands. This skill, obviously, improves with age.)

• Replace one nursing session a day, for several days, with a bottle or a cup feeding. Do this until your milk supply has adjusted to fewer feedings.

• With time, continue to decrease the number of daily breastfeedings.

• Weaning mothers should continue to drink fluids when thirsty. Remember, restricting your fluid intake will *not* prevent engorgement. Typically, this late form of engorgement passes one or two days after beginning the weaning process.

• If you do wean your nursing baby before nine months to one year of age, a commercial formula should be used for supplementation. After the age of one year—but not before—when the baby is taking a variety of solid foods (equaling three quarters of a cup per day), you may use whole cow's milk.

Storing breast milk

The best and safest means of handling breast milk is as follows:

• Always wash your hands before touching your breasts or breast milk containers. Avoid touching the inside of the bottles or caps.

• Pump the breast milk into a clean collection cup or use a breast pump where the baby bottles connect directly.

• If necessary, transfer the milk into a clean storage container.

• Label the container with the date, and be sure to use the milk in its order of storage.

• Breast milk will typically be safe for a few hours at room temperature, provided that you carefully washed your hands before expressing or pumping. Immediate refrigeration, however, is best and suggested.

• Breast milk may be kept safely in the refrigerator for up to seventy-two hours.

• If you are going to store breast milk for longer periods of time, you should freeze it. Fill the container to about three-quarters full in order to allow for expansion during freezing. Let the milk cool before freezing by swirling the container in a bowl of ice water. Freeze each container separately. It may be kept in a regular kitchen freezer for up to six months and for twelve months in a −20°F deep freezer. Never refreeze breast milk!

• When you are ready to thaw the frozen breast milk, simply place the container in a bowl of warm water for about thirty minutes, frequently "swirling" during the thawing process. Feed the baby the thawed breast milk immediately, or store it in the refrigerator for less than twenty-four hours. Do not microwave breast milk!

 I am currently taking several medications for various health problems and am concerned that this will prevent me from breastfeeding my baby. What should I do?

Your concerns are valid, since almost any drug that the mother takes will find itself—even if in minute amounts—in the breast milk. Because the actual dose the baby gets through the breast milk is so small, however, drug side effects in nursing babies are not as big a problem as one

may fear. A large number of drugs are safe to take during the nursing period, including aceta-minophen (Tylenol), penicillin, erythromycin, stool softeners, and antihistamines. Sulfa drugs and aspirin should not be ingested during the nursing baby's first two weeks of life, since they can cause jaundice in the newborn. If the baby is older than two weeks and does not suffer from jaundice, these drugs are safe as well.

More potent drugs and medications—cancer chemotherapeutic agents, thyroid medica-tions, chloramphenicol, and radioactive agents—can harm your baby. Such other drugs, as large doses of Vitamin B6, some birth control pills, migraine medications (such as ergota-mines), and antidepressant medications can also cause some problems. If you have any questions about the medications you are taking and their interactions with nursing, ask your physician.

The nursing mother who consumes caffeinated beverages, chocolate, or nicotine some-times notices that the baby becomes more alert and even "jumpy" after breastfeeding. This can be ameliorated by restricting your caffeine-containing beverages to less than twenty-four ounces per twenty-four hour period. You should not smoke or drink caffeine during the hour before each feeding. Alcohol, which can get into the milk, should not be consumed less than an hour before feeding. In general, it is wise not to drink more than two alcoholic drinks (one ounce of alcohol) per day. If you notice the baby having consistent problems after you have consumed a specific food, it is cer-tainly worthwhile to try eliminating it to see what happens.

The Football Hold

I am expecting twins, but am a bit un-sure how I can possibly nurse both of them at the same time. What advice can you give me?

This is not as strange a question as you might think. In nursing twins, you might choose the simplest option of feeding them one at a time; if you decide on a simultaneous approach, the positioning of the babies is all-important. You will need to experiment with the twins, the right chair, the need for pillows, and so on as you progress. Some techniques you may want to try include:

The football hold: *Sit up and place each baby under an arm, with the babies' heads resting on supportive pillows on your lap and feet, near your back. Lactation counselors call this "the football hold."*

The criss-cross hold: *Hold both babies in front of you and let the babies criss-cross over one an-other as they each feed.*

The Criss-Cross Hold

What about night feeding?

Try to make the night feedings brief and quiet. You should position yourself and the baby so that you are both comfortable. Do not turn on all the lights or sing or interact vigorously with the baby. Simply let him nurse and then fall back to sleep.

Should I supplement my newborn baby's diet with bottles of formula or water?

No! Do not offer supplemental bottles to the newborn who is breastfeeding, especially during the first four to eight weeks of life. During this period, the infant is learning specific cues and techniques that allow her to breastfeed. If you interrupt that process by changing the hardware—from soft, pliant breast to rubber-nippled baby bottle—this process will be disrupted and difficult to put back on track. Equally important, during these early weeks of breastfeeding, the mother is going through a number of physical changes that makes breastfeeding easier (see engorgement; letdown*), above and these physiological processes should not be interrupted. If the baby is not gaining weight well, this will be picked up during your newborn's visits to the pediatrician. With encouragement, patience, and the help of a friendly lactation counselor, supplementing with extra milk can be avoided. Later on, after the baby is older than a month, you may want to express or pump human breast milk and bottle feed it to your infant. This is especially popular with working mothers who must return to the workplace but still want their babies to have breast milk. When the mother comes home she can nurse, if she desires, or continue to bottlefeed her breast milk.*

As to supplementing your baby's diet with water, simply forget about it. Remember, the newborn baby's stomach is about the size of a golf ball. Therefore, it is important to fill the baby's belly with fluids that are rich in calories, i.e., breast milk. Milk helps the baby grow; water contains no calories and only makes the baby too full to nurse. Studies of nursing babies living in desert climates of the Middle East, where the temperature routinely rises as high as 120°F, revealed that even these babies get all the water they need from breast milk. As a prominent pediatrician once said, if newborn babies really needed extra water, women would be born with three breasts, two for milk and one for water! In all seriousness, babies—whether they nurse or are bottlefed—get all the water they need by nursing. Incidentally, another way to make sure your baby is getting enough fluid is to look at her urine-soaked diapers. Urine is clear, like water, in a well-nourished baby. Dark or golden urine or pinkish-tinged urine (caused by uric acid crystals in the urine) can be a sign that the baby is not getting enough fluid.

Does my breast-fed baby need any special vitamins or minerals?

Yes. Although breast milk is the ideal food for human infants, it is not rich in Vitamin D or fluoride. Most full-term infants with light skin and adequate exposure to sunlight will produce enough Vitamin D by natural means. For those breast-fed babies who are dark-skinned and receive less than 15 minutes of exposure to the sun twice a week, we recommend a dose of Vitamin D (400 units, which comes in a liquid form, combined with Vitamins A and C, that you can drop into the baby's mouth daily). Premature infants, regardless of their complexion or the climate, should also receive this daily dose of Vitamin D.

Fluoride, the other important substance not found in breast milk, helps strengthen growing teeth. Although some pediatricians will wait until the breastfed infant is six months of age before prescribing fluoride, we typically begin at age two to four weeks. Fluoride is a safe substance and the dose, 0.25 mg per day, helps promote the development of tooth enamel even during this early stage of life. After you discontinue breastfeeding, you should note that most municipal drinking water supplies in the United States contain fluoride: a daily dose is present in an eight-ounce glass of water. If your water supply does not contain fluoride, there is a need to add more to the diet. [see Tooth Care].

Iron, an important nutrient that prevents anemia and other problems, is adequately provided with a diet of breast milk. You do not have to worry about adding iron supplements until the baby is not longer nursing [see Iron Deficiency Anemia].

Nursing mothers themselves should take a daily multivitamin tablet that contains the daily requirements for iron, vitamin D, calcium, and phosphorus. The same nutrients, incidentally, can be found in one quart of milk or its equivalent in dairy products.

For additional information on breastfeeding, consult the following:

The American Academy of Pediatrics, *The Art of Mothering*. Available in both book and video versions by writing to:

American Academy of Pediatrics
P.O. Box 927
Elk Grove Village, IL 60009-0927
(800) 433-9016

Your local chapter of La Leche League: your pediatrician will have their local telephone number and address, or you can contact them at their national headquarters:

La Leche League
9619 Minnesota Avenue
Franklin Park, IL 60131
(708) 455-7730

BREATH HOLDING

This behavior is typically seen in toddlers under the age of four, especially during a temper tantrum. Children can become quite adept at this skill and will, literally, hold their breath until their faces bulge, turn red, and—if the breath is held long enough—show the bluish color that indicates that not enough oxygen is being inhaled. In severe cases of breath holding, the lack of oxygen can cause fainting, involuntary jerking movements, and seizures *[see Seizures].*

For most children, these spells are not severe; they may occur occasionally to daily; and tend to fade away as a means of expressing anger by the age of four or five.

When you first notice your child holding her breath, make sure that she is not in danger of hurting herself if she falls. Discuss this behavior with your pediatrician, since rare conditions exist that might be confused with simple breath holding spells. Once it has been established that the spells are behavioral rather than caused by a medical problem, here are a few techniques to help them resolve a little easier.

• During a spell, make sure your child is comfortable and safe. If you can, time the event. Seconds often seem like hours when your child is not breathing, but damage seldom occurs when breath holding lasts less than one minute.

• In the rare event that the spell lasts longer than one minute; or if the child appears blue-colored at the lips and very pale in the face; or when the child is younger than six months of age—call 911 (Emergency Services).

• Similarly, if during a breath holding episode your child is unconscious for more than a minute or develops a twitching or jerking motion *[see Seizures],* you need to call your pediatrician. Tilt your child in a forward-leaning position and make sure he is breathing normally.

• During the less-extended breath holding spell, try to distract your child by talking calmly to her or pointing out something of interest. Screaming or hitting only makes these spells worse. Similarly, paying a lot of attention to the episode gives the child a motive to do it again. You are walking a fine line, and if you need help or advice, feel free to call your pediatrician. Above all, remember to stay calm and be firm about putting an end to these episodes.

• Children with a history of breath holding often do so when they are tired, cranky, scared, or stressed. Try to minimize these situations before a spell occurs.

• Sometimes when a young child becomes especially frightened, she may hold her breath out of fear. Be calm, loving, and reassuring; this, too, shall pass.

BURPING YOUR BABY

Whether you bottle- or breast-feed, it is important to make sure that your baby is sucking in milk rather than air. Air simply takes up much-needed space in an infant's tiny stomach. The gas and bubbles actually stretch and expand the stomach and may cause bloating, abdominal discomfort, and pain. Burping—as any adult who remembers his last Thanksgiving dinner can tell you—helps rid the stomach

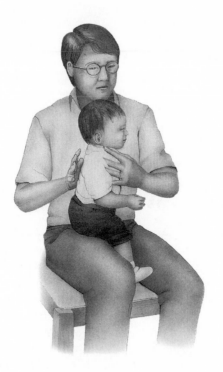

of excess gas and relieves the sense of full-ness one can get after eating.

We recommend three ways to burp your baby.

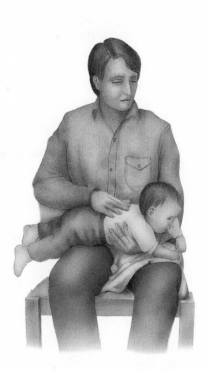

1. Sit the baby up in your lap and support his chest with your free hand, while you gently pat the baby's back.

2. Place the baby over your shoulder and gently pat or rub his back.

3. Drape the baby across your knees (or lap) and gently pat or rub the baby's back.

Finally, as a word of advice to the unsus-pecting parent, it is often useful to protect your clothing with a towel when burping your baby *[see Bottle Feeding; Breastfeeding; Spitting Up]*.

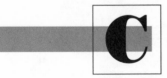

CAR SEATS, SEAT BELTS, AND AVOIDING MOTOR VEHICLE ACCIDENTS

Injuries resulting from motor vehicles—particularly car crashes—are one of the most common sources of accidental injury and death for both children and adults. For Americans between one and thirty-four years of age, car crashes are the leading cause of death; even for older Americans, they remain the leading cause of accidental deaths. Each year more than 50,000 Americans lose their lives in this type of accident. Teens and young adults make up 40 percent of these deaths, with males being most likely to get into a car accident. The next most vulnerable group for car-related injury and death are infants in the first year of life.

There are a variety of ways to avoid being injured in a car crash, including safety measures, defense driving techniques, and the scrupulous use of car seats (for infants and small children) or seat belts (for older children and all adults). It is important to buy a safety-approved car seat and to read the owner's manual and instructions carefully. Car seats should be equipped with a special locking clip to hold the car seat in place.

Some Guidelines for Infant and Child Car Seats for Seat Belts

For infants up to nine months and weighing under twenty pounds

As shown on the facing page, always place your infant in a specially designed infant car-seat carrier that has been approved by rigid federal safety guidelines and the American Academy of Pediatrics. Use the seat belt to fasten the car seat to the car, using the directions included with the car seat. The infant must be securely held in place, without discomfort, by the car seat's restraints and locking-clip system and should be placed in a semireclining position facing the rear of the car. Use the middle of the back seat. Do not place the baby in the front seat because of the risk of a front-end collision. Front seats with airbags are dangerous because their action is forceful enough to smother the baby; also, the powder used to lubricate airbag systems can irritate a baby's lungs.

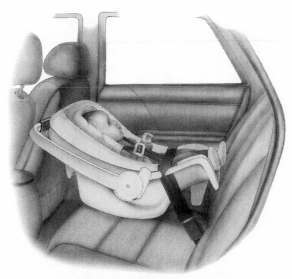

Infant car seats: Make sure to place the car seat facing the rear of the car. Strap the baby securely in the car seat. Make sure that your infant car seat (and any other car seat) is safety-approved and includes "locking clips."

For toddlers nine months of age to three or four years, who weigh between twenty and forty pounds and can sit without support

Always place your child in a specially designed child car seat that has been dynamically tested (i.e., under crash conditions) and approved under federal guidelines. The seat belt should be a "three-point" design, one that has lap and shoulder belts. Make sure that the seat belts fit the child well. Adjust as needed. Fasten the seat to the car, using the seat belts, as specified in the product directions. The toddler needs to be securely held in the car seat and should be placed facing the front of the car.

Children who weigh more than forty pounds, adolescents, and adults

All these passengers and the driver must ride in the car with the car's seat belt fastened snugly—but not uncomfortably—over the thighs (not the abdomen). A shoulder harness should always be worn once the child is tall enough for the strap to pass over the shoulder rather than the neck.

Other Safety Precautions

1. Never drive under the influence of drugs or alcohol, regardless of who is in the car.

2. When purchasing a car, obtain one with airbags on both the driver's and the passenger's side of the vehicle.

3. Always use common sense, courtesy, and intelligence when driving a car.

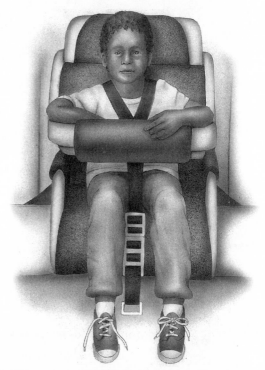

Toddler car seats: All toddlers need to be placed in a three-point safety seat (one that restrains the child at both shoulders and at the lap). The seat should face the front of the automobile.

Children in a car wearing seat belts: An excellent rule is to never start the engine unless everyone in the car is wearing seat belts.

In the wrong hands, it can easily transform itself from a modern-day convenience into an instrument of death.

4. Establish a rule that the car goes nowhere until everyones seat belt is secured.

 Why don't school buses have safety belts?

Based upon United States Department of Transportation regulations, school buses or similar vehicles do not contain safety belts because each passenger is compartmentalized within his seat. In other words, in the event of an accident, the child is theoretically protected by the padded seats in front of him and by his own seat. This causes an inconsistency that is not lost on children; why do they have to wear safety belts in cars but not in buses? As time progresses and older buses are phased out for newer ones, you should expect to see the intro-

duction of safety belts on these vehicles. Since we are on the topic, we should mention that there is another source of danger on school buses: active and boisterous children who fail to keep seated on the moving bus or actively distract the driver. Teach your child the importance of good behavior on a school bus. Perhaps the most serious types of injuries associated with bus rides occur when a child runs to or off the bus and does not acknowledge traffic. Teach your child to be careful both in getting on and off the bus. Teach your child never to run into the street after a bus.

CHICKEN POX

Chicken pox is caused by an extremely contagious virus called varicella-zoster, a member of the herpesvirus family. It is one of the most easily transmitted of contagious diseases: 90 to 95 percent of those who are susceptible to the virus and are exposed to it will develop chicken pox within twenty-one days. But because there is such a long incubation period between exposure to the virus and the appearance of the telltale rash, many children are unknowingly exposed to chicken pox by their seemingly healthy playmates or siblings. Typically, contaminated respiratory droplets enter the air after an infected but not yet symptomatic child sneezes, coughs, drools, spits, or, of course, exhales; the infectious material is then inhaled by a nearby and unsuspecting child (or susceptible adult), and so the contagion spreads.

Recently, a new chicken pox vaccine has been developed and approved for use by the United States Food and Drug Administration. The American Academy of Pediatrics suggests that children receive this vaccine at twelve to fifteen months of age. Until chicken pox vaccine becomes universal, however, it seems likely that we will still see cases of this childhood infection *[see Immunizations]*.

Listed below is a timetable, of sorts, explaining the events of chicken pox.

Day 1: Exposure to the varicela-zoster (chicken pox) virus.

Days 11−20: Incubation period of the virus; during this time there are no symptoms in terms of rash, fever, or discomfort. Ironically, it is precisely now that the child is most contagious to others.

Days 11−21 (variable in each child): The rash of chicken pox appears, along with fever and achiness. The rash, in its earliest appearance, has been described as "dew drops on rose petals": it looks like tiny blisters or water droplets on reddened skin. Generally the rash begins at the head. Soon the rash, which is quite itchy, marches its way down the child's body, leaving him uncomfortable. Because most children scratch this rash constantly, open, weeping sores soon progress to crusted-over lesions.

Please note that although this timeline includes the lengthy incubation period of chicken pox, your child should be actually ill for only seven to ten days.

Days 22−28: Your child really has chicken pox now, and your main job will be the provision of tender loving care, comforting foods and liquids, and a healthy dose of diversionary entertainment. As these days progress, your child will gradually improve and begin to feel normal; most importantly, to prevent the passage of chicken pox to another child, you must keep your child home from school until *all* of the chicken pox blisters have crusted over. At this point the child is no longer contagious to others, however he may look.

Helpful Prescriptions for Chicken Pox

There are a number of things you can do to make your child feel somewhat better during her bout of chicken pox.

Itchy skin is the most prominent feature of chicken pox. Unfortunately, the constant scratching of these blisters can cause spread secondary infections at the site of the open sores. No medicine completely takes away the urge to scratch the pox, but there measures help.

1. It is an excellent idea to bathe your child once daily with an oatmeal-based bath powder (e.g., Aveeno®) or a baking soda bath (add one half cup of baking soda to the bath water). Both these products soothe sore and itchy skin. Remember the adage, "more is not necessarily better." Bathing more than once a day can actually dry your child's skin, which makes it even more itchy!

2. Calamine or calamine-antihistamine lotions are one of the mainstays of symptomatic therapy for chicken pox. The advantage of these pink, gloppy lotions is that children enjoy putting on the lotion themselves. One can become quite creative about such a process. One of our patients was given clean paint brushes to apply his calamine lotion, and he was delighted to have a chance both to get some relief and paint his body as he saw fit!

3. Some children who have severe chicken pox about the body and who cannot sleep because they are so uncomfortable may require oral antihistamines, such as Benadryl. You need to read the directions of these over-the-counter medicines carefully in order to give the proper dose. Remember, antihistamines can make a child quite sleepy or, more rarely, hyperactive. Children under two years of age should not be given oral antihistamines.

4. Clip your child's finger- (and toe-) nails to make his scratching less efficient and less damaging to the skin. Scarring is the most common result of overzealous scratching during chicken pox.

5. Have your child wear loose-fitting clothes or pajamas, preferably made out of cotton, so as not to irritate the skin further.

Some other important treatments include:

1. Plenty of fluids. Children with fevers are at risk of dehydration, so it is important to make sure they are drinking enough. Some children develop chicken pox in their mouths and throats. Because these lesions can hurt, it may be difficult to get them to drink. Popsicles, gelatin, and ice cream are palatable, and numbing, means of getting liquids into your child.

2. Acetaminophen (Tylenol) is useful in holding down the fever that accompanies chicken pox and reducing the aches and pains brought on by the virus. Aspirin should *never* be used for chicken pox because of its association with a rare central nervous system disorder called Reye's Syndrome. In general, it is wise not to use aspirin at all for your child.

When to call your doctor
Call your physician if your child develops any of the following:

• Confused behavior

• Severe cough and complaints about breathing

• Difficulties in urinating, blood in the urine

• Chicken pox that have become infected and are red and oozing pus

 I read in the newspaper that a medication exists to actually reduce the severity of chicken pox. Is it safe, available, and effective?

The antiviral drug Acyclovir® has been used in the United States since 1982 as a medication for genital herpes. In 1992, the FDA approved its use for chicken pox. Studies suggest that if Acyclovir is taken within 24 hours of the appearance of the chicken pox rash, the duration and severity of the disease is lessened. The bad news is that the virus's severity is reduced by only one or two days at most. Because of the drug's rather high cost (about $50 to $75 for a five-day course) and the controversy generated by prescribing a drug to reduce symptoms by twenty-four hours, most pediatricians elect to use Acyclovir for only the most severe cases of chicken pox or to prevent chicken pox in those children who have been exposed and who have a pre-existing medical condition that requires them to take medications called steroids.

Is there a vaccination against chicken pox?

Yes, a vaccine called Varivax® has recently been approved for use by the United States Food and Drug Administration. This vaccine should make chicken pox far less common in the years to come. The vaccine is safe and can be given after the child's first birthday. If you have concerns or questions about this new vaccine and your child, discuss them with your pediatrician [see Immunizations].

I have read that chicken pox can be quite serious and even deadly. Should I simply keep my child home from school every time I hear some other child has contracted it?

No, not if you want him to graduate! In all seriousness, chicken pox is so common that it would be extremely difficult to keep your child from contracting it sometime during his childhood years. Predictions are often fraught with error, but we believe it is safe to predict on these pages that almost every single child whose parents read this book will contract chicken pox at some point before leaving elementary school or have it prevented entirely, thanks to the new chicken pox vaccine.

There are, rarely, some serious cases of chicken pox that result in hospitalization. Symptoms of this more severe form of chicken pox include confusion, difficulty in walking, a stiff neck, bleeding into the chicken pox sores, and many episodes of vomiting (more than three per day).

Your point about the potential severity of chicken pox, however, is a good one. With almost every disease there exists a spectrum of severity that may span from harmless to deadly, depending on such factors as the virulence of the infectious disease and the health of the human host who contracts it. Chicken pox is one such disease. Although the most severe cases are rare events, for some children—especially those with other serious illnesses such as cancer or immunodeficiency syndromes—chicken pox is no trivial matter. If your child does have one of these other illnesses, discuss chicken pox prevention and specific vaccination precautions with your pediatrician, before the event occurs. For the majority of healthy children, however, chicken pox is an annoying, itchy, but manageable experience.

My fifteen-year-old daughter never contracted chicken pox, even though all of her sisters, brothers, and friends have. Does this mean she will never contract it? Are adult cases more serious than childhood ones?

Because chicken pox is so common and contagious, people like your daughter are extremely rare. While we do not recommend that she spend her spare time in a day-care center in order to achieve this dubious milestone, it is likely that at some point she will contract it—particularly if she has children of her own or works with children. Adult cases of chicken pox can be more serious than those of childhood. We recommend that older children who have never contracted chicken pox and are otherwise healthy be vaccinated against it.

CHILD-PROOFING THE HOME *[See the following "fold-out" section; Injury and accident prevention]*

CHOKING: PREVENTION AND TREATMENT

Choking occurs when foods, liquids or other objects become lodged at the level of the vocal cords near the airway. The natural response to such an event—for all humans—is to begin choking, coughing, and, at times, vomiting. This is a good thing, as it often serves to clear the airway without more intensive means.

At the risk of being alarming, it is important to note that every five days a child dies in the United States as the result of choking on food. For children under five years of age, this is the fourth leading cause of accidental death in the United States. Yet the overwhelming majority of these tragedies need not happen. The following simple and important tips will prevent your child from choking. In the event that choking does occur, we offer first aid advice that will prevent serious injury.

How to Prepare Your Child's Food in Order to Avoid Choking

Typically, most toddlers want nothing to do with strained baby foods or formula. Instead, parents adapt to their requests—and their seemingly scanty diets—by preparing "finger foods" that they can help themselves to at mealtime. We suggest the following food preparation tips.

1. Most children begin solid foods at about six months of age. Although every mother has heard of a three- or four-month-old baby who wolfs down solids, most babies this young simply do not have the neuromuscular coordination or digestive abilities to handle solid foods. Since, in addition, an infant's airway is especially narrow and easy to block, it is wise to discuss introducing solid foods with your pediatrician before doing so, and then to do it slowly with careful supervision.

2. Cut the baby's (or toddler's) food into small pieces. For example, grapes should be quartered; meats should be cut lengthwise into small strips.

3. Remove all bones from meat, chicken, or fish before feeding it to your child.

4. Remove all pits or seeds from fruits.

5. Slippery, small, round, or firm foods are often called "choking foods" by pediatricians: they include items such as hot dogs and cocktail frankfurters, sausages, raisins, nuts, popcorn, seeds, chewing gum, hard candies, and, for infants, teething biscuits or cookies. These are best avoided for children under the age of four years and should *not* be part of the toddler's diet. Foods such as hot dogs or hard, raw vegetables (e.g., carrots, celery, hard peas), are notorious for lodging themselves in a small child's airway. You should be extremely careful when introducing these into your child's diet (only after the age of four years).

Other Environmental Causes of Choking

Some cases of choking and asphyxiation (suffocation) are caused by objects other than food. Tiny objects like uninflated balloons, marbles, little balls, soda pop caps, coins, safety pins, makeshift pacifiers, bottle nipples, and jacks may be swallowed by a curious toddler. These objects especially cause problems when they become lodged in a child's small airway and prevent adequate breathing. They must be eliminated from the child's environment before such accidents can occur. Some commercial pacifiers are built in a substandard way that allows them to break into smaller pieces. Always purchase safety-approved pacifiers *[see Pacifiers]*.

Children are at risk for accidental hanging or asphyxiation around draperies (particularly the cords and sashes), ropes, and even pacifiers that have long strings attached to them. Other potentially suffocating items are large toy boxes with lids (which can easily fall on a small child, trapping his head), plastic garbage and laundry bags, the folds of a playpen, and, for older children, old refrigerators and excavation sites.

1. Always purchase age-appropriate toys for your child and inspect them carefully to make sure there are no removable parts—such as the "eyes" of a stuffed

animal—that might be bitten off, ingested, and cause choking. Toys with tiny "button" batteries should also be avoided. They may look harmless at the store, but the older infant or young toddler can easily remove and swallow the batteries. Be especially careful with balloons. Studies have shown balloons to be one of the leading causes of choking in children.

2. If you use a playpen, make sure that it is well constructed and baby-safe. Mesh playpens with the sides down and older models with slats spaced widely enough apart for the baby to stick her head through should be avoided.

3. Avoid long cords, strings, hanging toys, and similar objects in a house with young children. Do not make a medallion out of your baby pacifier. It may seem like a great time-saver, but it is far safer to pick up and wash a pacifier that falls out of the baby's mouth (and it will!) than to have it hand around her neck when not in use. The potential risk of choking on the pacifier string is not worth the assumed convenience.

4. Do not allow your young child to eat the "choking" foods mentioned above or to swallow pills and similar products until at least the age of three or four years.

5. Warn and keep children away from tunnels, caves, wells, excavations, or construction sites into which they may crawl or fall. Fascinating as they are to a young child, they are extremely dangerous.

6. Avoid accordionlike stairway barriers. A young child can easily get his head stuck between the openings. Lightweight, mesh-type barriers are readily available and infinitely safer.

7. Remove the lids from toy boxes and the doors from old refrigerators or freezers that are no longer in use.

8. Teach your older children (and yourselves) the following first aid techniques for choking accidents. A good rule of thumb is, when the choking child is still able to speak or breathe and is coughing, no attempt to perform a choking maneuver should be performed. Listed below are the maneuvers you need to familiarize yourself, based upon the child's age.

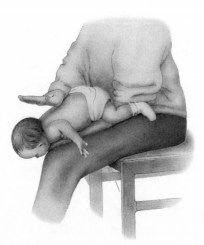

Responding to the Emergency of a Choking Infant or Child

We recommend that all adults take a CPR/Choking Emergency course, with annual refresher sessions. This is especially a good idea for parents. You need to acquaint yourself with these techniques *before* an emergency occurs. The following guidelines are offer to help you maintain these skills.

Call your local Red Cross or the American Heart Association for information on free CPR classes available. Most local hospitals also offer these classes *[see CPR]*.

Infants

1. Place the infant face down on your forearm at a 60° angle. The baby's head should be pointing down toward the floor with his neck and head stabilized. You may brace your forearm against your body for additional support.

2. Use the heel of your hand to give four firm—but not striking—blows between the infant's shoulder blades.

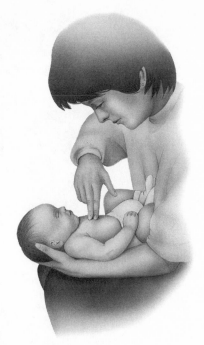

3. If the infant is still choking and you cannot see the "obstruction", turn the baby over and place him in a supine (lying face up) position on a firm surface such as the floor. Deliver four rapid chest thrusts with *two fingers only* to the middle of the chest (at breastbone or sternum) at the level of the nipples.

4. If the baby is still not breathing properly, instruct someone to call 911 (Emergency Services) while you attempt to open the mouth by lifting the jaw open. This maneuver moves the tongue away from the back of the throat and may make it easier for you to see an obstruction. *If you actually see the obstruction*, use your index finger to sweep it out. In the event that you cannot see such an obstruction, do not perform a "blind" finger sweep.

5. If the infant still does not breathe spontaneously, you should attempt infant CPR (cardiopulmonary resuscitation) *[see CPR]*.

6. Repeat steps 1 through 5 if there is still no resolution, while you are awaiting emergency services.

Small children (two to ten years of age)

1. Place the choking child on his back and kneel next to him. At this point, place the heel of your hand on the child's abdomen (belly) in between the child's navel (bellybutton) and his rib cage. Apply six to ten abdominal thrusts (often referred to as the

Heimlich maneuver) until the foreign object he is choking on is expelled from his mouth. Remember, the Heimlich maneuver is most successful when the person administering it delivers rapid *inward* and *upward* thrusts.

If the child is standing up or seated, you should get behind her and encircle her chest. Place the thumb side of your fist against the middle of the child's abdomen between the bellybutton and the breastbone (sternum). The fist should not be touching the ribs or breastbone. Grasp your fist with the other hand and apply six to ten separate abdominal, upward thrusts. Continue to apply the thrusts until the obstruction is expelled out of the child's mouth.

2. If the obstruction is not relieved with the Heimlich maneuver, you should open the child's mouth by tilting the head back and moving the lower jaw (chin) forward. This maneuver lifts the tongue and the epiglottis from the rear of the throat and usually helps to open the airway. Look into the back of the child's throat. *If you can actually see the obstruction*, manually remove it with a finger sweep. Again, blind finger sweeps should not be attempted; they frequently result in further obstruction.

3. If the child still does not begin to breathe spontaneously, you should attempt artificial respiration by blowing air into his mouth or nose five to six times, followed by a repeat of the Heimlich maneuver. At this point, it is wise to have the 911 (Emergency Services) on their way.

4. Repeat steps 1 through 3 and keep attempting to remove the obstruction, until Emergency Services arrives.

[Adapted from the American Academy of Pediatrics Guidelines for Cardiopulmonary Resuscitation, and the American Heart Association CPR Guidelines]

CHOLESTEROL AND FAT: A HEALTHY AND NUTRITIOUS APPROACH

For some time now, we have all been inundated with warnings about the dangers of diets rich in fat and cholesterol. After centuries of fat-laden, deep-fried gastronomic excess, we have finally become aware that a bountiful table isn't all that it was once cracked up to be. Unfortunately, the doomsayers are right: elevated levels of cholesterol and fats such as triglycerides lead to atherosclerosis and coronary artery disease, the major killer of Americans. Indeed, between 30 and 40 percent of today's children will eventually die of a heart-related disease. Risk factors such as cigarette smoking, diabetes mellitus, hypertension, obesity, and sedentary lifestyles increase the chance of cholesterol-related heart disease. Fatty diets also lead to fat children.

Medical studies have shown that atherosclerosis, a deposition of cholesterol on the walls of an artery leading to it's becoming blocked, begins as early as the second decade of life (ten to twenty years) and advances significantly during the third and fourth decades. In light of this work and of the high incidence of cholesterol-related heart disease among the public at large, the expert panel of the National Cholesterol Education Program (NCEP) has suggested a plan of prevention for all children over two years of age.

A Preventive Approach for Children Two Years and Older: Diet and Exercise

• Your pediatrician will advise you about the importance of exercise and a diet that is moderately low in fat content; it is also important to check the child's blood pressure (for evidence of hypertension or high blood pressure) and his height and weight (for evidence of being overweight).

• Your pediatrician will suggest a moderately fat-restricted diet that includes low-fat (skim) milk and similar fat-reduced dairy products, increased amounts of bran and fiber, vegetables, and foods that are baked or broiled rather than fried. Junk foods, such as potato chips and ice cream, taste great but are extremely high in fat and need to be enjoyed sparingly. When grocery shopping, make sure that you read the nutritional labels on products. Choose only those packaged foods where the "percent calories as fat" is equal to or less than 35 percent.

A good way to gauge your child's food intake is to consult the food pyramid pictured below. There are basically five major food groups:

1. Bread, cereal, rice, and pasta group
2. Vegetable group
3. Fruit group
4. Dairy food group
5. Meat, fish, poultry, dry beans, eggs, and nuts group

Always use fats, oils and sweets sparingly!
No one food is more important than another. Indeed, your child needs some of all the five food groups to insure normal growth and development.

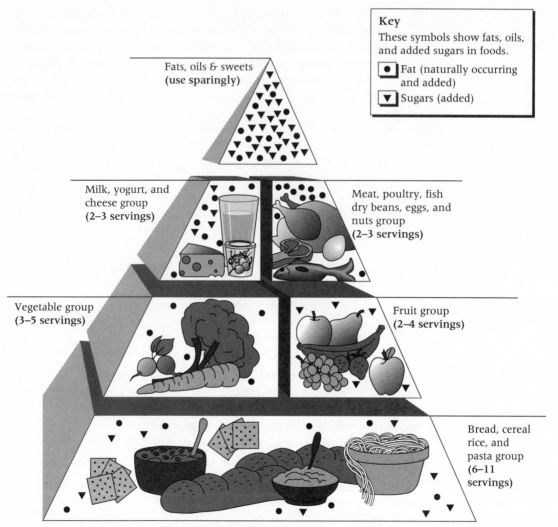

Key

These symbols show fats, oils, and added sugars in foods.

● Fat (naturally occurring and added)

▼ Sugars (added)

Fats, oils & sweets
(use sparingly)

Milk, yogurt, and cheese group
(2–3 servings)

Meat, poultry, fish dry beans, eggs, and nuts group
(2–3 servings)

Vegetable group
(3–5 servings)

Fruit group
(2–4 servings)

Bread, cereal rice, and pasta group
(6–11 servings)

Source: U.S. Department of Agriculture and the U.S. Department of Health and Human Services.
Provided by: the Education Department of the National Live Stock and Meat Board

What counts as a serving?

Bread, cereal, rice, and pasta group:

½ cup of cooked rice, pasta, or cereal
1 slice of bread
1 tortilla
1 sheet of matzoh
1 ounce of breakfast cereal

THE PRACTICAL PEDIATRICIAN

4 plain crackers
½ bagel, roll, or muffin
1 pancake (4" in diameter)

Vegetable group:

½ cup of chopped or raw vegetables
1 cup of raw, leafy vegetables
¾ to 1 cup of vegetable juice
½ medium potato

Fruit group:

1 piece of fruit
1 cup of fruit juice
1 slice of melon
½ cup of chopped, canned, or cooked fruit
¼ cup of dried fruit

Milk, cheese, and yogurt (dairy) group:

1 cup of milk (skim milk is preferable for children over the age of two years)
1 to 2 ounces of natural or processed cheese
1 cup of frozen yogurt or ice milk (both are preferable to ice cream in that they contain less fat)

Meat, fish, poultry, dried beans, eggs, and nuts group:

3 ounces of cooked lean beef (round tip, top round, eye of round, top loin, tenderloin, or sirloin); lean pork (tenderloin, boneless top loin chop, boneless cured ham, center loin chop); lean lamb (loin chop, leg); lean veal (cutlet, loin chop), poultry, or fish

Note that every ½ cup of cooked beans, 1 egg, two tablespoons of peanut butter, or ½ cup of nuts are counted as 1 ounce of meat. Eggs and nuts tend to be high in fat and cholesterol, while most dried beans are relatively low in fat.

You and your child should regularly engage in physical activities such as walking, athletics, swimming, and so forth for at least twenty minutes, three times a week. As soon as your toddler can walk, encourage her to engage in active games rather than passive ones. Frequent (at least three times a week) aerobic exercise is essential for keeping one's weight and cholesterol down as well as for feeling healthier. As one athletic shoe company implores us, "Just do it!"

How safe is a low-fat diet for children?

For the overwhelming majority of children over the age of two, *it is safe and effective in helping to lower serum cholesterol. For babies under the age of two years, however, fat re-*

stricted diets are not recommended. Babies require a fat-rich diet in order for the brain and nervous system to develop appropriately. In fact, restriction of fat and cholesterol during this important period of development can lead to serious problems.

For older children and adults, the only required or essential fatty acid, a building block of fat, is linoleic acid. Linoleic acid is a polyunsaturated fatty acid and readily available in sufficient quantities using the diet proposed above.

Although this diet is safe, however, there can be too much of a good thing. Some of the adolescent patients that we see with anorexia nervosa (refusal to eat based on the desire to remain thin) differ markedly from the frequently described obsessive teens who only want to look slimmer. Instead, some of our patients are merely devout followers of severe fat-restricted diets. Indeed, the most common concern we hear from those teens (both girls and boys) who have restricted their fat intake so greatly that it has become a health issue is: "But doctor, if I drink the whole milk and other fatty foods you are suggesting, won't I corrode my arteries?" The answer, obviously, is no. Moderation does not mean starvation. During rapid growth, such as the toddler years and puberty, it is clearly important to keep in mind that some fat and cholesterol in the diet are needed to "keep the engine going." If such a child is restricting his fat content to less than 35 percent of daily intake, one way of increasing that fat intake to a more healthy level is to use 2% or whole milk (not to mention other dairy products). This doesn't mean you should serve your child greasy cheeseburgers from afternoon until night, but it also means you needn't restrict your child's diet only to grains and legumes. A growing child needs some fat in his diet.

What is an abnormal cholesterol level?

This is a good question that is still being heatedly debated among medical experts. Generally, those children found to have serum cholesterol levels over 200 mg/dL (or two successive levels above 170 mg/dL) need to be further evaluated by their pediatrician. Options for treatment range from dietary and exercise regimes to drugs that lower cholesterol in adults but have not yet been established as effective for children.

High cholesterol and heart disease run in my family. How should I help prevent these problems in my own children?

There are a number of rare diseases (affecting 0.2 percent of the entire population) called the hypercholesteremias. They are inherited disorders where the affected child has a markedly elevated serum cholesterol level. The severity of disease depends on the cholesterol levels, but affected people have a 75 percent chance of dying of cardiovascular disease before the age of 60 years. Men are generally affected earlier than women. Pediatricians, pathologists, and epidemiologists are not in entire agreement of how to manage children with these elevated LDL cholesterol profiles, although any child with a cholesterol over 220 mg/dL is at risk for the future development of cholesterol-related heart disease.

But most children are not routinely screened for cholesterol, given that the overwhelming majority of them do not have elevated serum cholesterols and the test is an expensive one. Consequently, many physicians rely on the family medical history for guidance. In our practices, when we encounter a family with a history of parents or siblings with cholesterol levels greater than 240 mg/dL or family members who died before the age of 55 from choles-

terol-related heart disease, we screen the child annually for cholesterol levels. Similarly, the child with diabetes mellitus, hypertension, kidney disease, or a lipid metabolic disorder needs close medical attention to this matter. For most normal children, annual screens are probably not necessary as long as the child is active, there is no family history of early cholesterol problems, and the diet is not rich in fat. Other pediatricians disagree, however, and may suggest annual screenings beginning when the child enters school.

Further reading

Kwiterovich, P. *Beyond Cholesterol: The Johns Hopkins Complete Guide for Avoiding Heart Disease.* (Baltimore: Johns Hopkins University Press, 1989).

Schoenberg, J., and JoAnn Stichman, *The Heart Family Handbook.* (Philadelphia: Hanley and Belfus, 1990).

Hotline and information services

The American Heart Association
7272 Greenville Ave.
Dallas, TX 75321-4596
(800) 1-242-8721

CHOOSING A HEALTH-CARE PROFESSIONAL FOR YOUR CHILD

There are a variety of ways parents go about selecting a health-care professional for their child. Advice from friends, firsthand experience with a particular physician, or even advertisements in the newspaper are some of the more common routes.

Perhaps the best time to start thinking about the issue is during the pregnancy. All women need sound medical advice throughout their pregnancies for prenatal care. During these visits with the obstetrician, you will discuss issues of how to have a healthy pregnancy, signs and symptoms that need to be investigated, and advice on diet, exercise, and the avoidance of drugs, alcohol, and cigarettes. A perfectly reasonable topic to discuss with your obstetrician is his or her knowledge of excellent child health-care professionals in the area.

Parents you especially admire or respect are a good resource to use in selecting a pediatrician. Ask them why they like or dislike their pediatrician. Ask if there are any specific features of the practice they like or dislike. Most people have strong opinions about their doctors, one way or another, and are usually only too glad to discuss this topic. Also call the county medical society, the local board of health, or the office of the chair of pediatrics at a nearby medical school or large hospital for references.

In terms of credentials, your prospective physician should have graduated from an accredited medical school and, if a pediatrician, completed at least three years' postgraduate training (after the M.D.) in an accredited pediatrics residency program. You should also inquire if your pediatrician is board-certified by the American Board of Pediatrics. If your physician is a family practitioner, he or she needs similar post-graduate residency training in Family Practice that has been approved by the American Board of Family Practice.

Pediatric nurse-practitioners (PNPs) are steadily becoming an important part of our child health-care system in this country. These are registered nurses who have spent additional time training in the health maintenance and common diseases of childhood, with a special emphasis on parent education. To learn more about this option, you can obtain information from the National Association of Nurse Associates and Practitioners. You need to check the individual situation with your region and decide if this is an option for you.

Once you have generated a list of potential candidates, arrange a "prenatal conference" with each. This is becoming an increasingly popular means of meeting and "interviewing" a pediatrician. During the conference parents should ask questions about the physician's style and philosophy of medical practice. Some frequently asked questions in our experience include:

• Specifics on the physician's education, training, and qualifications and his or her philosophy on specific issues of concern to you, such as toilet-training, behavior, immunizations, and so on

• Arrangements for emergency calls if the physician is not available

• Does the physician have specific "telephone hours" for questions that do not require a specific visit? Are there charges for this service?

• What are the insurance plans, managed care programs, or health maintenance organization plans with which the physician is affiliated?

• What are the fees and medical insurance schedules?

• Does the clinic have evening or weekend hours?

• What hospitals and medical centers is the pediatrician affiliated with? Does the pediatrician admit patients to a children's or a general hospital?

• When would the doctor like to be called about a problem with your child? (The answer to this one should be whenever the parent is specifically worried) *[see Well-Child Pediatric Examination Schedule]*.

CIRCUMCISION

Circumcision is an ancient Jewish ritual signifying the covenant that Abraham and his son Isaac made with God. Specifically, the tissue (foreskin) that surrounds the head (glans) of the penis is surgically removed. All Jewish males are commanded by religious tenet to undergo a circumcision on the eighth day of life unless the child is ill. Moslem males often undergo circumcision at the age of thirteen years. For these parents, the decision about circumcision is easy; for others, there is little to help them decide.

Circumcision became an especially popular procedure for male infants during this century in most English-speaking countries. At one point during the early 1960s more than 80 percent of all male infants born in the United States, Canada, and England were circumcised; less popular a procedure today, circumcision is currently practiced on about 60 percent of these boys. Other nations, however, diverge, and more than 85 percent of all males around the world are *not* circumcised. Is circumcision necessary? Frankly put, the research on the value of having a circumcision can be interpreted as supportive evidence by both those for and opposed to the procedure.

What Do We Know about the Benefits of Circumcision?

1. There is a lower incidence of penile cancer, an extremely rare form of cancer, among circumcised males compared to uncircumcised males.

2. There is a slightly higher incidence of urinary tract infections among uncircumcised infants than their circumcised peers. The incidence of this problem, however, among both uncircumcised and circumcised males is so low that it remains difficult for physicians to recommend the procedure only on this account.

3. There is a distinct psychological advantage, especially during puberty, to being "just like everyone else." This is especially true with respect to the boy's father and brothers. The boy who is the rare uncircumcised fellow in a group of circumcised males—or vice versa—may feel self-conscious about himself.

4. There is evidence to suggest that circumcised males are less likely to contract or transmit sexually acquired diseases (such as HIV/AIDS, syphilis, and gonorrhea) than uncircumcised males.

What do We Recommend?

As noted, for those of the Jewish or Moslem faiths, the question is made moot by religious doctrine. For all others, we agree with the conclusions of the American Academy of Pediatrics on the question: it really depends on how comfortable the parents feel with the decision, one way or the other. One good rule, however, is that if you are going to circumcise your son, do it during his newborn stay in the hospital. All studies of circumcision show that delayed circumcisions (done after infancy) are the procedures most frequently associated with complications. Many insurance companies only reimburse for those circumcisions performed during the initial newborn hospital stay.

Make sure you pick a competent and experienced physician or mohel (a rabbi who has received special training to perform circumcisions) to perform the procedure, and take note of the necessary aftercare for the surgical site listed below. The procedure is not without pain, but this does resolve within a few days. If a physician is performing the procedure, ask if he or she uses local anesthesia. A number of studies have shown that much of the discomfort and stress during circumcision can be avoided with this technique.

Special care for the newly circumcised boy

1. The circumcision site will be red and sore in the first few days after the procedure. While the tenderness at the site should resolve within three days of the circumcision, a scab will form at the incision line where the foreskin was removed from the glans (head) of the penis. This scab—which is often yellowish and thick—will fall off about ten to fourteen days after the procedure.

2. Some physicians prefer a device called plastibel ring to perform a circumcision. Do nothing to help this process along, lest you cause slight tearing or bleeding at the incision site. The plastibel device will work itself off in due time (seven to fourteen days).

3. You should clean the area gently every time you change the baby's diaper (or at least three times a day) with water only. Soap may irritate the sensitive skin. You may apply an antibiotic ointment (such as Bactroban® or Bacitracin®) or petroleum jelly to the incision line. This will keep the sensitive skin and wound from sticking to the inner lining of the diaper.

4. It is a good idea to call your physician after a recent circumcision if any of the following are noted:

- The head of the penis become black or blue
- The circumcision site appears abnormal
- Excessive bleeding (more than a few drops) occurs
- The shaft of the penis appears red or inflamed
- The baby develops a fever (greater than 100°F) shortly after the procedure, or your baby appears ill

 My husband and I decided not to have our son circumcised. Are there any special precautions we need to take?

No precautions, but there are a few points of hygiene that need to be reviewed. During infancy, the foreskin is connected to the glans (head) of the penis, but as the boy grows— usually by age six to ten—the foreskin is less firmly attached and is easily retractable from the head of the penis. It is important not to force this process of retraction along. If you retract the foreskin too abruptly while there are still skin cells attaching it to the glans, bleeding and inflammation can occur that may lead to scarring and abnormal retraction of the foreskin; specifically, such scarring can cause the foreskin to remain retracted below the head of the penis (paraphimosis). Consequently, most physicians suggest simply keeping the exterior of the foreskin clean during the first two years of your son's life.

Beginning at the age of two, you can clean the area with a washcloth during bath time by partially retracting the foreskin. This is best done by grasping the shaft of the penis and drawing the skin downward to the child's abdomen. The key word, again, is gently. The point is to clean the area but not to retract the foreskin too vigorously, so as to avoid scarring and future retraction problems.

You should only use water when you wash the area because of the harsh effects of soap on sensitive skin. As you retract the foreskin you will find a whitish, cheesy substance called smegma, which is a collection of dead skin cells and debris. The area is easily cleaned with a washcloth. After finishing this task you should draw down the foreskin to its natural position. As your child gets older (by the age of five), he should be taught—and, knowing the hygienic habits of most five-year-old boys, frequently reminded—to wash himself.

How will I know if I retract my son's foreskin too vigorously during washing?

If you pull back too hard, the baby will experience pain and probably cry.

COLDS *[See Upper respiratory tract infections]*

COLIC

Colic is the term applied to an usually long crying spell in an infant. These spells typically begin at the age of two weeks and resolve by three months of age. They last more than three hours straight and occur every day (or almost every day), usually at the same time (generally between six P.M. and 1 A.M.). Between spells, "colicky" babies are well fed, healthy, and often reasonably happy. During the spells, the infant replaces the "reasonably happy" part of his personality with angry, loud crying. It is a self-limiting, albeit trying, condition. Most colicky babies stop by age three months. Colic probably has nothing to do with the intestinal tract or excessive gas. Instead, behavioral pediatricians are finding that it is more a result of the baby's temperament, requirements for sleep, and, perhaps, the anxiety level of the baby's parents.

The baby with colic often cries in the late afternoon or evening, tensing his abdomen and drawing his knees to his chest for as long as three hours. The spells can occur three or more times a week. Parents who survive these marathons, rather than the colicky baby (who won't remember this hurdle of infancy), deserve a special merit award.

Not all lengthy crying spells can be dismissed as colic. When concerned by your infant's crying, you need to recall the last time of feeding, check his diaper and other aspects of his environment that might affect him, and make sure nothing is hurting him. One also needs to be certain that the crying baby does not appear sick and can be consoled when comforted in the arms of a parent—a sign most pediatricians feel is the most predictable measure of health in a crying infant. Settling babies with colic can be an exasperating experience, but eventually they calm down.

Colic and Diet

Some recommend that mothers who breastfeed restrict their intake of caffeine-containing drinks, such as colas, sodas, coffee, tea, and so on. The breastfeeding mother may also note that certain new foods she consumes disagree with the nursing baby a few hours later. The baby's diet, however, rarely has an impact on the colic spells. Although "milk allergies" may present as colic, these allergies are quite rare; changing formulas, therefore, is a popular but probably futile effort *[see Food Allergies].* Another important reminder is that colic is not cured by feeding the baby every time he or she cries. Most breastfed babies require feeding every two hours; bottle-fed babies can last three to four hours. Remember that infants have very small stomachs, so overfeeding a baby can potentially worsen his discomfort.

Can colic be caused by the way you hold a baby?

This theory has some value if you are clutching the baby like a basketball, but most people can be taught how to hold a baby properly and gently. Rocking or gently cradling the baby is a time-honored technique of quieting an infant. A variety of devices can help the tired parent in the rocking effort: front-pouches [Snuglis], mechanical swings, rockers, and special baby chairs are widely available. One such product, called "Sleep-Tight," is available by calling (800) NO-COLIC. The key to all methods of rocking, whether its power source is electric or human, is gentleness: remember that rocking the baby is done in preparation for sleep, not as training for a trip to Disney World. The best method is also the oldest and, not surprisingly, the easiest: holding the baby next to you and reassuring him.

Are there any medications to alleviate colic?

No, other than the old physician's prescription, Tincture of Time. Medicines that slow down the movement of baby's gastrointestinal tract (e.g., anticholinergics, opiates, and barbiturates) cause a good many serious side effects and should not be used for colic. Similarly, the more invasive "therapy" of inserting suppositories or a thermometer into the baby's anus in an effort to correct the baby's "gas" problem can only serve to annoy a colicky baby even further.

Will keeping my baby awake all day alleviate her colic?

Perhaps. Babies with colic may have a lower requirement for sleep than other babies. But it is important to realize that newborn infants spend the majority of their time sleeping, up to fourteen to twenty hours a day during the first three months. The baby, regardless of colic, should be gently awakened for feeding, play, and loving every three hours. This may reduce nighttime awakenings.

My husband and I are at our wit's end. For four weeks now our two-month-old son has had colic. He looks normal but then cries in high-pitched wails for what seems like hours. Nothing we do works. If we try to feed him, he rejects it; if we play with him, he becomes angry and

fussy; if we lay him down, he again squeals. Finally, he tires himself out. Should I feel like a bad parent?

No. You both need to realize that you are doing everything possible for your infant and hope this phase soon passes. Colic can be so frustrating and maddening that it has driven some parents to child abuse. There are ways to avoid the natural feelings of anger, fear, and stress that this situation engenders. First, talk freely about it with your spouse and work together as a team in the arduous work of dealing with a colicky baby. Second, seek help from family members and professionals if you require physical care of the home and baby, or if you need to discuss how you are feeling. Third, there will be a time during this episode where you will both, after making sure nothing is physically wrong with the baby, lay him down, shut off the lights, and leave the nursery. Special tapes of heartbeats, ocean waves, rainstorms, or other "white noise" devices may soothe the baby. Earplugs may be necessary aids for the parents. And try to spell each other for occasional breaks. The colic will eventually stop on its own, and new parents deserve some sleep.

COMPUTERS AND THE INTERNET

Computers are becoming increasingly more common in American homes. While parents are often limited in both computer skills and curiosity, most school-aged children (especially teens) are not. Just as with television, video games, and other forms of popular entertainment, you need to keep aware of your child's computing habits. What computer games is he playing? Are they violent or sexual in content? Have you reviewed them? Do you find them appropriate for your child?

A wide variety of information and materials are available to your child on the Internet, including terrific new tools for learning and potential pen pals. Your child may be communicating with children (and adults) around the world. But feel free to discuss the content of those communications with your child to make sure they are appropriate interactions. Do not allow your child to enter cyberspace unescorted. Remember, this is the equivalent of letting "strangers" into your house. You need to be aware of everyone who plays a significant role in your child's life.

This is *not* a plea for censorship. Just be aware that there are some bulletin boards on the Internet that are not appropriate for children because of their explicitly violent or sexual content. Specific computer programs can help you block certain bulletin boards on the Internet if you feel they are inappropriate. If necessary, discuss these products with your local computer software dealer.

Finally, too much of anything can cause problems. As with movies, television, and other forms of popular entertainment, we suggest that you should limit the recreational use of the computer to under two hours a day, *after* the completion of homework. This does not apply, of course, to homework-related computer use *[see Television; Videos Games and VCRs]*.

CONJUNCTIVITIS (Pinkeye)

These infections, often called "pinkeye," irritate the white portion of the eye and the tissue that surrounds them. Pinkeye is frequently associated with ear infections. This is probably due to mutual drainage systems and other anatomical connections between the middle ear and the eyes.

When you notice that your child's eyes appear a bit more bloodshot than usual and there is no evidence of trauma or recent crying, chances are good that she has pinkeye. Before rushing to the doctor, however, make sure that other events that can make one's eyes red with irritation have not occurred (getting soap or shampoo in the eyes, exposure to smoke fumes, a recent swim in a chlorinated pool, rubbing one's hands in the eyes after eating spicy foods, and so on).

Conjunctivitis that is not caused by irritation, on the other hand, is most commonly caused by a virus such as adenovirus and can be linked to colds and ear infections. Viral conjunctivitis can last up to a week and is extremely contagious to others. More often than not the child rubs his eyes and spreads infection to both; similarly, other members of the household are at risk for pinkeye, especially if they do not wash their hands well after contact with the child with pinkeye. The same risk exists when sharing towels or washcloths among family members. Viral conjunctivitis does not require any specific medication and is usually self-limiting. Currently, no antiviral medication "cures" this condition any faster than nature.

Occasionally, a bacterial infection will cause a case of pinkeye. These infections are notable for sticky pus or a yellow discharge in the eye. You might also note dried pus on your child's face, or see her eyelids stuck together upon awakening because of dried secretions. These secretions distinctly differ from the minimal crusting that our mothers used to call "sleep in the eyes," which appears in the inner corner and is not nearly as copious as that seen with true infections.

Currently there is a great deal of controversy over whether to treat this problem with antibiotic-containing gels or eye drops. Given that most cases of conjunctivitis are viral in origin, antibiotics will do little for their relief *[see Medicines, Antibiotics]*. For those cases that appear superinfected with bacteria, it may be necessary to prescribe an antibiotic. We prefer the gel or ointment products because they can be easily rubbed onto the external surface of the eye and absorbed into the infected area. Eye drops, on the other hand, frequently burn and require a great deal of coordination on the part of the parent and even more cooperation on the part of the child. These products require a prescription from your physician, who will be able to assess whether or not your child needs the medication and who will discuss any questions you may have. These medicines need to be applied, as directed, three to four times a day until the child has two morning awakenings without evidence of pus or dried secretions in the eye. All cases of pinkeye—bacterial or viral—are extremely contagious and require good handwashing by everyone who comes in contact with the child and avoiding the sharing of towels or washcloths.

Finally, a word or two about pus. Pus refers to fluid that develops when an infection is present. Whenever you notice a yellow-green discharge in the eye, or when the eyelids are swollen shut or stuck because of pus, or you note sacs of yellowish fluid behind the eyelids, infection is present and needs to be looked at by a physician for definitive treatment. A good rule in general is that whenever cases of pinkeye do not resolve in three to seven days, consult your physician.

 My child was sent home from school today with pinkeye. The teacher says it's contagious and that he cannot return to school without a doctor's clearance. What should I do?

Pinkeye—whether it is caused by a virus or by bacteria—can be extremely contagious. If the pinkeye is caused by a virus, it may take three to seven days to clear up. Quarantines or restriction from school are not necessary, as long as the child is careful to wash his hands (this may be difficult to insure for the toddler or child under the age of five or six). If the pinkeye is caused by bacteria, the child is no longer considered contagious after twenty-four hours of treatment with an antibiotic.

Do eye drops that "get the red out" help in the treatment of pinkeye?

Probably not. Most of these products contain drugs called "vasoconstrictors," which temporarily shrink the blood vessels in the eye that make them appear blood shot. While these products can provide some comfort for irritated, tired eyes or for allergic conditions involving the eye, they do nothing to treat viral or bacterial conjunctivitis [see Eyes, Emergency Eye Problems].

CONSTIPATION

There is a delightful book entitled *Everyone Poops* by Taro Gomi (Kane/Miller Publishers, 1989) that you should read and read to your children as they approach toilet training *[see Toilet Training].* While it is certainly true that "everyone poops," this title needs to be expanded to include the reminder "but not every day!" Many people believe that a day without a bowel movement is like a day without sunshine. In reality, different people have different bowel movement patterns, and this includes babies and children. Before talking about what to do *for* constipation and how to prevent it, it is useful to talk about what constipation is and what it is not.

What is Constipation?

Specifically, we define constipation as:

1. The painful passage of stools. Typically, the constipated child will tell you when he has difficulty having a bowel movement or when he experiences pain in the anal area and cannot pass a stool.

2. Infrequent bowel movements. While not going to the bathroom every day is

not necessarily a sign of constipation, not having a bowel movement for more than three days, accompanied by straining when trying to go to the bathroom, may be considered constipation. Having written this, we know that there are many children who may have bowel movements only once every three days and are doing fine.

What Constipation is Not?

Constipation is *not* the passage of infrequent stools (e.g., once every two days or so), nor is it the passage of large, hard stools. Many people normally have large bowel movements without any pain.

As you get to know your baby, you will invariably notice how she has a bowel movement. Babies less than six months of age typically grunt, push, draw up their legs, and become flushed in the face while having a bowel movement. It is important to note that these babies having normal bowel movements are not crying. This makes sense, since it is a normal event and should not hurt the baby. As the baby grows, she will learn how to coordinate the bowels and the rectum to better facilitate this process. Remember, it is not easy to have a bowel movement while lying on your back; consequently, the baby having a bowel movement appears somewhat strange and scary to new parents. Don't worry, you'll get used to it soon enough. One way you can help your baby with her bowel movements is as follows: when you notice her trying to pass a stool, try holding her knees against the chest to stimulate a squatting position—the natural position for pushing out a bowel movement.

Some Causes of Constipation

• Constipation is typically due to a diet deficient in fiber. Fiber is commonly found in fruits, vegetables, and whole-grain foods. Because the human body cannot digest fiber, it remains in the stool and causes the stool to be larger, softer, and easier to pass.

• A rare cause of constipation in the newborn baby is a disease called Hirschspring's Disease. With this illness, the nervous tissue in the gut that coordinates a bowel movement is simply missing. More than 95 percent of all normal newborn babies have their first bowel movement by forty-eight hours of age. If your baby has not had her first bowel movement by this point, she needs to be examined by the pediatrician.

• One of the more common forms of constipation occurs during toilet training. This suggests that the parent may be putting a bit too much pressure on the child to succeed. Back off a bit and try to remain encouraging *[see Toilet Training]*.

• For older children, a common cause of constipation is repeated postponement of the urge to go because of embarrassment about school toilets or public toilets, or as a result of long waits for use of the bathroom at home. Feel free to talk with your child about this problem, if you detect it, and try to encourage her that it is really okay to go, when you've got to go! Otherwise, a vicious cycle is set up: when the child avoids going to the bathroom to have a bowel movement, the stool stays in the colon, becoming bigger, harder, dryer and more difficult to pass. When the child does pass this bowel movement, she experiences pain and may develop a rectal fissure (a tiny tear in the anal area), which causes more pain and more reason to postpone a bowel movement *[see Encopresis]*.

Some Home Treatments for Constipation

Common foods that help alleviate constipation:

Prunes
Peaches
Plums
Cherries
Bran
Whole-grain cereals such as oats and barley
Kale
Broccoli
Cabbage
Popcorn (only for children over the age of five) *[see Choking]*

Common foods that may worsen constipation:

Dairy products (milk, cheese, ice cream, butter, and so on; for those children with lactose intolerance, dairy products may actually cause diarrhea)
Rice products
Applesauce
Bananas
Pears
Cooked carrots

Babies younger than one year

Constipation can be cured by placing your child on a soy-based infant formula (rather than one based on cow's milk), or by adding fiber to the diet in the form of fruit juices (prune juice is a perennial favorite for this problem). Adding more fluids to the diet (again, fruit juices) may also help relieve constipation. You may also try some of the strained vegetables (peas, beans, spinach), the whole-grained cereals (such as barley, oatmeal, but not rice), and strained fruits (apricots, peaches, prunes, plums). Avoid the potentially constipating foods listed above.

Children over one year

The initial "therapy" is similar to that above, only now you can offer a greater variety of fiber-rich foods, since the child is more experienced with issues of feeding. Again, the key is to bring on the fiber! In addition to offering those foods mentioned above, you may try concealing fiber in the diet. This is not as difficult as it seems. There are various ways to make bran or oatmeal palatable to a toddler—they are called bran muffins and oatmeal cookies! Popcorn (unbuttered) is another fun food that happens to be rich in fiber. (Remember, because of the risk of choking, reserve popcorn for the child over five years *[see Choking].)* Make sure your child drinks plenty of fluids. Sometimes drinking soda pop can help a constipated child insofar as the gas bubbles fill up the stomach and colon, giving a sense of fullness and helping to pass a bowel movement.

The "Okay, Doctor, None of These Worked" Department

For those cases of constipation that do not resolve with dietary changes, your pediatrician will likely prescribe a natural laxative for babies and children such as Maltsupex.® This is made from the malt extract of barley and is much safer than some of the more industrial-strength laxatives marketed to adults. It comes in a liquid and a pill form and can be mixed with any type of drink. Recommended dosage is as follows:

Infants: ½ tablespoon daily
Children: 1 tablespoon daily
Teens: 2 tablespoons (or two tablets) daily

Older methods of "curing" constipation, such as adding corn syrup and similar products to the infant's formula, are no longer suggested because they carry a risk of botulism (food poisoning).

The constipated child who is toilet-trained should be encouraged to practice sitting on the toilet every day in order to help set up a regular bowel movement pattern. Try doing this for ten minutes after breakfast. Many people have a bowel movement after eating the first meal of the day, and this is a good way to go about introducing a pattern. If mornings are too rushed by the American family ritual of hurriedly getting out to school and work, try initiating these daily exercises after dinner, when things are calmer. Remember, simply practicing this maneuver—a regularly scheduled trip to the bathroom—helps to train a constipated person to be regular.

When to Call the Doctor

You should always feel free to call your physician with questions regarding this problem. The overwhelming majority of these situations can be handled during his or her office hours. Call the physician immediately, however, if your child appears to be in pain that lasts longer than two hours. You should also call your physician for an appointment if your child is, after adjusting his diet as suggested, having stools less frequently than every three days, if the bowel movements are causing pain, or if the anal fissures bleed more than three times.

My constipated child has now developed a painful rectal fissure. How can I attend to this so it doesn't make matters worse?

This is, indeed, a common and painful complication of constipation. If you notice streaks of fresh blood on the toilet paper, diaper, or mixed with the stool, your child probably has a rectal fissure. It is important to have this checked out by your physician, however, because there are rarer, more serious causes of blood in the stool. Remember to change the diet as discussed above. Treat the fissure by putting your child in a warm bath for twenty minutes three times a day. You may apply a 0.5 percent hydrocortisone ointment to the sensitive area to relieve some of the inflammation. This ointment is available at your drug store without a prescription.

What do you think of suppositories, laxatives, and enemas to help things along?

Generally, we like to avoid these medications. Suppositories are especially problematic since they need to be inserted into the rectum and can themselves cause painful rectal fissures or irritation. Laxatives, other than the barley agent recommended above, should also be avoided, since they can cause cramps and may be habit-forming. Enemas are devices that spray water into the colon in an attempt to clean the bowels of retained stool. Some children with a particularly severe form of constipation retain hard, dried-out stools to such a large extent that they, literally, need to be "cleaned out." We reserve enemas for these severe cases [see Encopresis].

CONTAGIOUS AND INFECTIOUS DISEASES: A FEW WORDS ON PREVENTION

There are hundreds of contagious or infectious diseases that your child could potentially contract; fortunately, we live in an age where many of the most serious contagious diseases are entirely preventable. You can avoid such illnesses as diphtheria, polio, mumps, hepatitis B, German measles, measles, tetanus, hemophilus influenza, and whooping cough, to name but a few, by immunization and a variety of public health measures *[see Immunizations]*. Nevertheless, there are still contagious diseases that parents need to try to prevent. Listed below are some of the major culprits and the precautions you need to take.

Respiratory Infections (Such as Influenza, Common Colds, and Upper Respiratory Tract Viruses)

These infections are, perhaps, the most common ones your child will experience. It is extremely difficult—if not impossible—to avoid all contact with them. They are usually spread from mouth, eye, and nose secretions of the infected person to noninfected persons. There are a number of ways this can occur; for example, if a child has a cold and begins sneezing or coughing, he will expel respiratory droplets into the air, which can then be inhaled by another child (or adult, for that matter). Remember when your mother told you not to let sick kids breathe on you? She may have been right—although this is impossible to prevent in reality. Colds and similar infections are also spread when the child in question sneezes or coughs into his hands or onto an object. If someone else touches the ill child (or the contaminated object), then touches her own face, the disease will spread. To help prevent these infections:

1. Encourage hand washing, especially after blowing the nose, sneezing, or coughing.

2. Do not smoke around your child *[see Smoking]*. Study after study shows that a child who lives with a smoker is more likely to contract upper respiratory tract infections.

3. Remind your child not to rub her nose or eyes and not to put her fingers in her mouth. This is a common way to spread upper respiratory tract infections as well as eye infections *[see Conjunctivitis]*. Unfortunately, toddlers tend to explore the world through their mouths, so such reminders may not help younger children.

4. Remember to use good hand washing techniques yourself (lots of soap and water, and scrub away). Use disinfectants for cleaning up the kitchen, bathrooms, nursery, and other places where your child spends a lot of time.

Gastrointestinal Infections

These infections, involving the digestive system, are spread by eating under-cooked food or by touching another person who is experiencing diarrhea and has not adequately washed his hands. These can be potentially serious, and you need to take great care to prevent them. Such measures include:

1. *Always* cook meat, fish, and poultry products thoroughly. The gastrointestinal bacterium called *E. coli* can live in uncooked beef and poultry. Fortunately, the high temperatures of thorough cooking will kill these deadly bacteria.

2. Make sure that you thaw frozen meat in the refrigerator rather than at room temperature. Never refreeze meat or poultry products. Always wash all utensils such as knives, forks, and other kitchenware after cutting or manipulating raw meat, fish, and poultry products.

3. Use a plastic cutting board rather than a wooden one, to prevent the spread of germs.

4. Never eat raw eggs. Make sure all foods that contain eggs are well cooked. Avoid using raw eggs for drinks like egg nog or in foods such as Caesar salad.

5. Always wash your hands before and after handling food.

Other Helpful Hints to Prevent Infections in Your Child

1. Keep your child's immunizations up to date. The immunization checklist included in this book will help you in your record-keeping process *[see Immunizations; Well-child Pediatric Exam Schedule]*.

2. Don't let your child kiss animals on the mouth (this can spread worms and some forms of diarrhea).

3. If your child is exposed to someone with tuberculosis, meningitis or hepatitis, call your doctor for an office visit as soon as possible.

4. If you rely on day care, make sure that your day care attendants practice all of these safety measures.

5. Encourage your child to wash her hands after every visit to the bathroom.

[For more specific information, see AIDS; Chicken Pox; Croup; Day-Care and Child Care Issues; Diarrhea; Hand, Foot, and Mouth Disease; Immunizations; Impetigo; Lice; Mouth Sores; Scarlet Fever; Sore Throats; Upper Respiratory Tract Infections; Worms]

COXSACKIE A VIRUS *[See Hand, foot and mouth disease]*

CPR (Cardiopulmonary resuscitation)

We strongly urge that all parents learn CPR techniques before their first child is born. Because these techniques require some practice, we also advise that you take an annual refresher course. Your local medical center or hospital offers these courses, which are most likely free. Ask your pediatrician about these resources. *The instructions that appear below are in no way a substitute for an American Heart Association CPR or CPR-refresher course.* They serve only as a reminder of the CPR instructions.

What to do in an Emergency

If you notice that your child is not breathing or that his heartbeat has stopped, it is important to act quickly to prevent heart and brain damage or death from lack of oxygen. Speak loudly to your child—"Are you all right?"—to see if he will respond. If the child is unresponsive, begin by calling the local Emergency Service (911). You must next quickly assess the "ABC's" of CPR—Airway, Breathing, and Circulation.

A = Airway. Is the child's airway free of any obvious obstruction? Is his tongue blocking the airway? *[see Choking.]*

B = Breathing. Make sure that the child is moving air in and out of his lungs. Can you feel air moving out of the mouth and nostrils? Is the child blue around the lips or nails? Is he wheezing or gasping for air? Is he conscious and responsive?

C = Circulation (heartbeat). Check your child's pulse at the neck, wrist, or right over the heart. Make sure that there is a heartbeat.

If you detect an absence of heartbeat or breathing, do not panic. You need to begin CPR.

CPR for the infant (newborn to one year old)

1. Place the baby on his back on a firm surface, such as the floor.

2. Tilt the head back and elevate the chin (unless you suspect a head or neck injury). Make sure that the mouth is clear of any obstruction, including the child's tongue. Check the pulse by placing your fingers on the sides of the child's throat (over the carotid artery).

3. Listen with your ear over the baby's mouth to make sure that he is breathing. Look at his chest to see if it is moving air.

4. If the infant is not breathing, begin CPR breathing techniques. Pinch the baby's nose and blow two light puffs of air into the infant's mouth. Be gentle; too forceful a burst of air can cause vomiting.

5. Make sure the baby's chest rises and falls with your two puffs of air; if it does not, you need to suspect an airway obstruction.

6. If you suspect an airway obstruction, turn the baby over and place him across your knee, supported by your forearm. With the heel of your hand, deliver four firm blows to the baby's back at the level of the shoulder blades. If this does not work, try a modified Heimlich maneuver where you place the baby's back on your lap (the infant is now chest up) and place three fingers in the middle of the chest at the level of the nipples. Give the baby four quick thrusts. Be firm but gentle! Keep the baby's mouth open when doing the thrusts *[see Choking]*.

7. After these maneuvers, if the baby is not breathing on his own, try the two puffs of air again as described in step 4. Make sure the baby's chest wall moves with the puffs of air. Give a few more air puffs, three seconds apart.

8. Check the baby's pulse. Pulse points include the wrist, the sides of the neck, and the inner arm. Place your fingers over these pulse points and measure the heartrate (or pulse) over a ten-second period. If there is a pulse but still no breathing, continue to give the baby air puffs by mouth every three seconds (about twenty per minute). Recheck the pulse every twenty breaths.

9. If there is no pulse, you need to give the baby chest compression. Put two or three fingers on the breastbone, which is in the middle of the chest between the nipples. Press down gently on the chest (compress the chest by one-half inch to one inch) five times over a three-second period.

10. After applying the five chest compressions, give the baby a puff of air, as described above.

11. Continue giving the chest compressions and the puffs of air, alternatively, for ten cycles. Follow this by checking for a pulse. Continue CPR on the infant until the heartbeat and breathing return or until the medical emergency team comes to relieve you.

12. Continue these alternate rounds of compressions and rescue breaths until emergency help arrives.

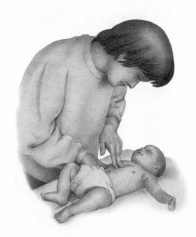

CPR for the toddler and child (one to ten years)

1. Place the child flat on his back on a firm surface, such as the floor.

2. Tilt the head back and elevate the chin (unless you suspect a head or neck injury). Make sure that the mouth is clear of any obstruction, including the child's tongue. Check the pulse by placing your fingers on the side of the child's throat (over the carotid artery).

3. Listen with your ear over the child's mouth to make sure he is breathing. Look at his chest to see if it is moving air. If necessary, repeat the finger-sweep to remove anything obstructing the airway.

4. If the child is not breathing, begin CPR breathing techniques. Support the chin with your fingers, open the mouth, pinch the nostrils shut, take a deep breath and blow two gentle, shallow breaths into his mouth.

5. Make sure that your child's chest moves up and down with the two puffs of air.

6. If there is no movement of the chest with the air puffs, you need to perform the Heimlich maneuver to remove any obstruction to the child's airway. With the child on his back, place the heel of your hand below the lower tip of the breastbone, at the middle of the chest and above the bellybutton. Point your fingers toward the child's head. With

a firm but gentle upward thrust, push. Repeat five to ten times until the obstruction is removed. Check to see if the child is breathing on his own *[see Choking]*.

7. If the child is not breathing, try two more puffs of air as described in step 4. Check the mouth to see if there is still some obstruction. Watch the child's chest for movement.

8. Check the child's pulse at the neck or wrist. Check for at least ten seconds. If the pulse is present but breathing is still not restored, continue to administer the rescue breaths at the rate of one puff of air every four seconds or fifteen breaths per minute. Continue to check for signs of breathing and movement of the chest wall. Check the pulse every fifteen puffs of air.

9. If there is no pulse, you need to begin chest compressions. Place either four fingers or the heel of your hand, depending on the size of the child, on the chest just below the sternum (breastbone).

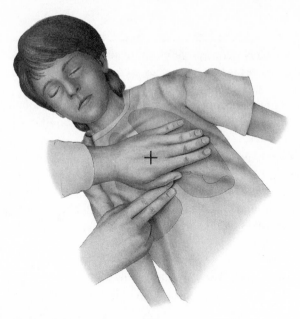

10. Compress the chest by pressing down firmly about one inch to one and one-half inches, five times every three to four seconds.

11. After each round of chest compressions, tilt the head back, lift the chin, pinch the nostrils, and give a puff of air. Repeat this cycle ten times and then check for a pulse and breathing.

12. Continue these alternate rounds of compressions and rescue breaths until emergency help arrives.

[Adapted from the American Heart Association *Heart Saver Guide: A Student Handbook for Cardiopulmonary Resuscitation and First Aid for Choking*, 1995.]

 What is shock?

To the health-care professional, shock is a condition unrelated to electricity or strong emotion. Rather, shock is the medical term for the human body's response to extreme injuries and infections. Its earliest symptoms may include a weak but fast heartbeat, cold or "clammy" skin, difficulties in breathing, thirst, and slowness or "cloudiness" of thought and speech. More serious forms of shock can lead to a complete dysfunction of many organ systems in the body including the brain, heart, kidneys, lungs, and liver. Shock is a true medical emergency, since it typically causes a cardiac or respiratory arrest (stopping of the heart or breathing). Call 911 (Emergency Services) immediately and begin the CPR techniques described above.

For information on CPR courses and materials:

The American Heart Association
National Center
7272 Greenville Avenue
Dallas, TX 75231-4596
(800) 242-8721

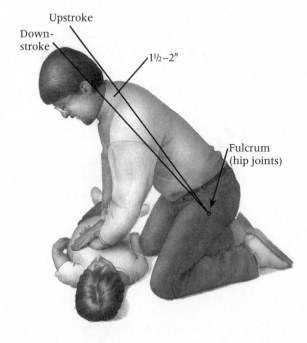

Upstroke
Down-stroke
1½–2"
Fulcrum (hip joints)

CRIBS

- You need to make sure that the baby's crib is safety-approved and was built after 1974—when special regulations regarding baby cribs were first implemented in the United States. This means that the slats of the crib can be no further apart than 2⅜" to prevent a small head poking through them and becoming stuck; more commonly, slats that are too wide allow an active baby to stick her legs and body through the spaces, again getting stuck.

- Make certain that the mattress, blanket, or pillows are not easily lifted, shifted, or removed by the baby, allowing him to get caught under them and suffocate. The mattress should be the same size as the crib, without gaps at the edges that can trap the baby. If you can fit the breadth of two fingers between the mattress and the edge of the crib, your mattress is too small and a more appropriate one needs to be purchased.

- Avoid cribs that are not smooth, rounded, and knobless at all edges and borders. Although the older, ornately carved wooden cribs are beautiful, their sharp edges and carvings can be a place where clothing can catch and put the baby at risk for choking *[see Choking]*.

- The corner posts of the crib should be flush with the "headboard" and "footboard" of the crib. When clothes or toys are strung across lower endposts, there is a risk of the older baby strangling himself. All parts of the crib should fit snugly and well. Hanging toys need to be placed well out of a baby's reach. Repair sharp or rough crib edges.

- Even when lowered, the crib sides should be at least 9" above the mattress level to prevent the baby from rolling out. Raised, the crib sides should be at least 26" above the mattress level. Make sure that the crib-side mechanism is stable and safe. Do not use cribs where the crib sides can accidentally fall down on their own.

CROUP

Croup is a quaint name of Scottish origin for the harsh, barking or honking cough that is a symptom of infections of the throat and larynx (voice box). One apt description of the "croupy" cough is the sound of a barking seal. Typically, it is accompanied by vocal hoarseness, harsh or raspy breathing noises when the child inhales, and difficulty with breathing.

Most cases of croup are caused by a viral infection of the vocal cords and voice box called parainfluenza. The virus causes coldlike symptoms in addition to the "croup" *[see Upper Respiratory Tract Infections]* and occurs in epidemics, frequently during the fall and spring months. The parainfluenza virus inflames the upper airway and the vocal cords, which leads to the characteristic cough. It generally lasts about five to seven days, although the child will often display a variety of symptoms, from mild to severe, at different times during that week. Children under the age of three have an especially difficult time getting over the croup; they display the most prominent breathing symptoms of all children who develop the illness.

For some reason, warm, moist air helps to relieve some of the upper airway swelling and tight breathing that children with croup can develop. Instead of playing around with humidifier devices or complicated tents, we suggest you simply turn on a hot shower in your bathroom for about ten minutes; when the room is sufficiently "steamy," turn off the shower and bring the baby with you to sit on your lap in the steamy bathroom. Creative parenting and artful distractions are an important part of this therapy. If you can actually read a story book to your child in the steamy bathroom, do so; otherwise, cuddle him, talk with him, and try to get his mind off the discomfort. Remember, crying children breathe harder, and this can make a croupy cough sound worse. We do not recommend warm air humidifiers because if they spill, they can accidentally cause a burn.

As an aside, there are some children who appear to get great relief when breathing cold air for a short period. The classic story is a croupy infant who is coughing and having difficulty breathing. Upon taking the baby outside, into the cold winter air, for a visit to the pediatrician, the symptoms suddenly diminish. No one is quite sure why cold air sometimes relieves the croup, but you might want to give it a try.

Another croup remedy is the warm drink. Hot chocolate, soup, and other warm beverages can help loosen secretions and reduce the upper airway swelling. Cough medicines that contain dextromephorphan may be of some help in alleviating the cough in older children (two years or older), but we do not recommend stronger cough remedies such as codeine because it can suppress breathing and worsen matters. Fever reducers should be used as needed. Anyone in the house who smokes needs to be away from the baby with croup, since passive smoking can make a case of croup far worse *[see Smoking].* If there are other children in the house, remember that the virus that causes croup is quite contagious until the infected child no longer has a fever or three days into the illness.

Most children with croup get better without too much difficulty, although the condition needs to be watched closely, particularly for children under three years of age. You need to call your pediatrician immediately, however, if you begin to notice that your child is having difficulties in breathing. For croup, these difficulties may appear as:

- Noisy breathing upon inhaling (stridor)

- Blue-colored skin, mouth, lips, or nails

- Drooling and great difficulty swallowing

- Breathing with great exertion so that you can see the muscles of the child's neck, abdomen, or chest working (retractions)

CRYING

As every parent knows, normal babies cry. In one famous study by Dr. T. Berry Brazelton it was noted that the normal baby cries about two hours a day during the first two weeks of life. Between two and six weeks, crying increases to about three hours a day. The amount of wailing generally decreases to one hour a day by the age of three months. Ironically, the most common time for infants to cry during the first three months of life is the evening, a time when both parents are typically at home and tired from the day's activities.

Before merely ascribing your baby's crying to "nature," however, you should make sure that nothing is bothering her. For example, overfeeding or inadequate burping or sucking can be a cause of crying, as can hunger. Physical complaints such as illness, fever, infections, corneal abrasions, hair tourniquets (a hair wrapped so tightly around a finger or toe that it results in pain), and intestinal hernias can result in crying. These are usually easily ascertained upon physical examination or with the help of your doctor.

If the baby appears to be simply crying for no clear reason, but it is not a night-time sleeping issue, try picking him up and consoling him with gentle and soft re-assurances. Songs, cooing, or whatever best fits your parenting style and your baby's pleasure should be attempted. Walking with the baby in your arms, gentle rocking, and a lot of patience generally save the day. The best advice is to remember to observe your baby as she grows. No one will know your child better than you. Recall what has worked before (and what hasn't) in these situations. Experiment, and remember that babies do cry—some more than others. Don't become frustrated or angry. Neither you or baby is being "bad" *[see Colic]*.

CUTS, SCRAPES, AND MINOR BLEEDING INJURIES

All children fall, and all children occasionally cut, scratch, and hurt themselves. Some children do this far more often than others. For mild scrapes, scratches, and cuts that do not appear too deep and are small in size, the minimalist approach to first aid will suffice.

• Try to stop the bleeding by applying firm pressure to the injury with a clean and sterile piece of gauze or cloth *[see Medicines]*.

• If the bleeding persists after a few minutes of pressure, try placing an ice pack on the wound, followed by more pressure with the gauze.

• Once the bleeding is under control, take a look at the wound to better assess its severity. Sometimes small cuts bleed a great deal, such as those on the tip of a finger, but do not require any further treatment once the bleeding has stopped. If the wound looks particularly deep, it may require sutures ("stitches"), and you need to call your physician to make the appropriate arrangements.

• Clean the minor cut or scratch with liquid soap and water. Scrub gently to remove any dirt. Pat dry with gauze or clean cloth. Dress with a clean bandage, if necessary. Healing ointments should be left on the shelf.

• For those wounds that become infected and are weeping pus or become red and extremely tender, your physician may prescribe an antibiotic *[see Impetigo]*.

• If the child experienced the cut by stepping on a rusty nail or somehow punctured his skin with a dirty object lying outdoors, he may need to have a tetanus booster shot to prevent the possibility of an infection called lockjaw. Make sure your child always has an updated tetanus shot *[see Immunizations]*.

• You should call the doctor if these minor wounds do not appear to heal within a few days, or are showing signs of a skin infection (such as redness, severe pain, pus, poor healing, red streaks emanating from the wound, and fever).

What should I do if my child's bleeding injury will not stop?

In the event of more serious bleeding emergencies that do not stop with the simple techniques described above, you need to maintain pressure at the bleeding site and make sure the child is resting flat on the ground. If possible, elevate the affected limb or wounded area so it is above the level of the child's heart. Continue to apply pressure with compresses. Arrange to call the Emergency Medical Service (911) for more definitive bandaging, tourniquets, stabilization, and treatment of the wound. Make sure that your child is not in shock, is breathing well, and has a normal heartbeat [see CPR].

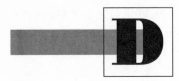

Day care and child-care issues

In 1991, the United States Department of Labor estimated that about 58 percent of all mothers with children under the age of six were working. Most of these mothers were working full time. Among those employed mothers with children under the age of five, about 30 percent were using some type of child-care center during the workday. Currently more than eleven million American children spend some or all of their day in a day-care center. Some experts predict that by the year 2000, 80 percent of all American mothers will be part of the workforce. Consequently, day-care issues have become of great concern both to parents and those who care for children. Whether you choose care in a private home, employer-based day care, parent cooperative day care, or individual in-home infant and toddler care (e.g., a baby-sitter), here are some tips to help you pick the best situation for your child.

How to Begin Finding Out about Day-care Alternatives

It is extremely important that parents thinking about day care do their own leg-work and investigate the child care options in their community. Ask your friends who have children in day care what they like or dislike about the programs they have selected. Other sources of information include your local state office of human and social services, which keeps on file a list of all the day-care homes it licenses; social groups where parents may be members, such as school Parent Teacher Associations and church and synagogue groups; local colleges or universities that have departments of child development; local hospital departments of pediatrics; your pediatrician or other health care provider; your employer (some firms actually provide day care); local children's welfare societies, newspapers, bulletin boards, and the telephone book. You also need to ask yourself where your child might be most comfortable—at home with a baby-sitter or with a group of other children? Generally this is decided by the age of the child, since many center-based day-care operations only accept children over the age of two years who are toilet trained. Smaller children and babies are frequently cared for by "baby-sitters."

Once you have generated a list of potential day-care options, based on location, cost, and reputation, you need to start contacting them in order to inspect the child care arrangements and facilities. We suggest you begin by telephoning all of the candidates, as there may be some that appear unacceptable to you even over the telephone. Questions that you should ask include:

1. Are there any openings? What are the requirements for admission?

2. Can you arrange a meeting with the director and the staff to discuss your concerns and your child's needs?

3. Are references from other parents who use that facility available for your review?

4. What is the ratio of children to caregivers at the day care center? Current standards set by the National Association for the Education of Young Children suggest staffing ratios of one adult for every 3 to 4 infants; one adult for four or five two-year-olds; and one adult for eight to ten four-year-olds.

5. Is it licensed by the state or local municipality?

6. Does it have caregivers with child development certificates? (This typically means that the caregiver spent nine or more months training for the job.) Child care providers should have this as a minimum qualification. You might also want to inquire of staff members have degrees in early childhood education.

7. What does the staff do to ensure cleanliness at the day-care facility? Are sinks available to wash one's hands between handling different children or changing diapers? Have any serious infectious diseases been reported at the day-care facility?

8. What are the financial arrangements, hours of operation, vacations, and related matters?

9. How are ill children taken care of in the facility? Are they kept separate from the healthy children?

10. What practices are followed to ensure safety, such as not having the children exposed to strangers or unsafe situations?

11. Can parents drop in and visit the day-care center without an appointment?

After narrowing down the numerous possibilities to fewer selections, you need to arrange to visit these day-care facilities (preferably both parents make this trip!) in order to interview the staff, inspect the premises, watch other children in the facility, assess the daily activities, and, if possible, arrange to speak with some of the parents of the children who use that center. You might also try bringing your child for a trial visit. Let her play in the area where she will be cared for and meet those who will be assigned to take care of her. Remember, a thorough interview and inspection is essential to this process. A similar process of scrutiny and interviewing is also essential if you plan on hiring an at-home baby-sitter.

Interviewing a Prospective Caregiver or Baby-sitter

The interview process is an important one. It gives you a chance to discuss the caregiver's perceived responsibilities and your expectations. Some questions to ask include:

1. What is your background and experience in child care?

2. Do you have children of your own?

3. Do you smoke or have any health problems?

4. What type of training have you had in infant and child first aid?

5. What is your philosophy on issues of discipline, television, meals, and so on?

6. In the event of a medical emergency, what would you do with my child?

7. Do you have references from other parents who have used your services?

8. How many other children do you presently care for? How many people in the home?

9. What safety precautions have been taken in the home or site of day care?

You also need to inquire about the specific program of activities your prospective child-care provider will plan for your child.

1. What activities will the provider employ to promote your child's physical development and milestones? Are rest periods (naps) used to balance the physical activities with restful ones? Are the suggested games or activities child safe and developmentally appropriate?

2. What activities are employed that will help your child develop socially and emotionally? Does the caregiver encourage the child to try to speak and express himself? How patient is the caregiver in helping the toddler or young child to solve problems on her own? Are elements of positive reinforcement (i.e., praising the child for a job well done) used, or more punitive methods of discipline? Is there a safe, predictable, and defined set of activities planned each day?

3. How do the planned activities help your child to develop intellectually? Are structured activities that involve learning and gradual goals employed? Is the television or videocassette recorder a peripheral part of the child's activities? How does the provider encourage and facilitate language development in the younger child?

4. What are the health and safety precautions, such as posting emergency numbers near the telephone, that should be taken by the provider and the day care center? Are there established guidelines for handling medical emergencies? Are the caregivers trained in first aid and infant or child CPR? *[see Choking, CPR]*. Has the day care facility been "childproofed"? *[see Injury and Accident Prevention]*.

EMERGENCY PHONE NUMBERS

Pediatrician: _____

Hospital: _____

Emergency Medical Service (EMS) 911 or: _____

Poison Control Center: _____

Police: _____

Fire: _____

Work Phone Number #1: _____

Work Phone Number #2: _____

Car Phone Number #1: _____

Car Phone Number #2: _____

Pager Number #1: _____

Pager Number #2: _____

Neighbors: _____

_____

_____

Your Home Address: _____

Your Home Telephone Number: _____

5. Are there kitchen facilities at the day-care center? How clean are they? Is food served in a fun and pleasant manner? Are the snacks and meals provided well balanced, healthy, and enjoyable?

6. Finally, you need to ask yourself how you feel about the arrangement. Are you impressed by the facilities and the staff? Do you have any concerns about their abilities? How does this potential caregiver interact with your child? Most importantly, what does your "gut instinct" tell you about this person? Remember, always trust your parental instincts. Few tests in clinical medicine are more accurate!

[See Working Parents]

DEATH AND GRIEVING

Perhaps the greatest tragedy in life is the loss of a loved one. Young children have a particularly difficult time with the loss of a parent or sibling. The death of other close relatives and friends can also be difficult for a child.

Children's responses to these events are closely related to their developmental age. Some children may at first disbelieve the event and fantasize about the loved one's return. As with adults, an element of sadness develops when the child begins to realize that the person who died is, indeed, not coming back. Grieving signs for infants include poor feeding, crying, and fussiness; for toddlers, crying, uncooperative behavior, and tantrums. Older children typically withdraw from others, including close relatives and friends. Sleep problems and increased fears may also occur among grieving infants, toddlers, and young children.

Many questions will come up when a child loses a sibling, parent, close relative, or friend. And, of course, each situation is different. Try to make sure that your child's daily routine remains as normal as possible. Discuss the death as freely as your child wishes to explore the issue, and make sure that he can understand what you are saying. This may seem trying, as some children have endless questions about what happens after someone dies. Tell the truth as you understand it within your own belief and value system, as opposed to making something up. In general, it is unwise to hint that the person who died may come back to life someday.

Guilt over a death can become a big issue for a young child. Recall that children still rely on magical thinking and tend to be quite egocentric. The child, for example, who becomes angry at an adult and yells "I hate you" or "I wish you were dead" may experience intense feelings of guilt if that person actually dies. Magical thinking leads her to believe that she somehow caused the death. Some children blame themselves for the death of a parent or a sibling—understandably, a most difficult issue to work through. Reassure your child, if she asks, that she had nothing to do with the other person's death.

Above all, rely on your friends, loved ones, and family to help out as much as you need them. And be prepared to discuss the death openly with your child in the days, weeks, and even months and years to come.

Should a child attend the funeral of a close family member?

Children who are school-aged (over five years) may want to attend the funeral of a sibling, parent, or close relative. Sometimes younger children attend funerals, but this depends largely on the child's emotional and intellectual development. You should discuss this option with your child. Children who appear nervous or extremely anxious about the prospect of attending a funeral should probably not attend; other children will express a desire to say "good-bye" to their loved one, and that is perfectly appropriate. As a "fail-safe" mechanism, it is wise to arrange a backup system of child care, in case the child wishes to leave early and you need to remain at the funeral. As the child grows, she may wish a more informal visit to the gravesite.

Should a child who experiences the death of a loved one obtain professional psychological help?

We generally suggest that, in such an event, you discuss the situation with your pediatrician. With time and observation, both of you will be better able to assess the type and level of grieving your child is experiencing. Most children think about the death of a loved one for a long period, but they return to their normal daily lives soon after the funeral. The child who continues to withdraw, stay at home from school, and allows the death to occupy most of his thoughts and time, however, probably needs to be referred to a mental health professional.

The death of a sibling can be difficult because the sister or brother was close in age to the surviving child and children are "not supposed to die." Surviving children may worry about their own health and experience problems with parents who are themselves mourning.

Many children who appear to be "all right" also benefit from articulating and discussing the pain that they are experiencing after the death of a loved one. Your child may be one of those who needs to talk about his feelings with a qualified and skilled grief therapist.

Fortunately, there are a large number of well-trained psychiatrists, psychologists, and social workers or grief counselors in all areas of the United States. Your pediatrician will be able to help you find one to consult, if necessary.

Parents also have difficulties with deaths. For example, the death of a parent also means the death of a spouse, and this can make the healing process especially difficult for both the surviving parent and the child. Make sure that, in these tragedies, you take care of your own mental health needs, and, when appropriate, seek out professional counseling, too.

Most hospitals and many disease-centered organizations (such as the American Cancer Association) have support groups directed at children who have lost siblings, parents, or significant loved ones, as well as for adults. Your pediatrician will know about the resources in your area. There are also a number of books available to help children cope with issues of death and loss, including:

Lamerton, R. *Care of the Dying* (New York: Penguin Books, 1980).

LeShan, E. *Learning to Say Goodbye: When a Parent Dies.* (Boston: Atlantic Monthly Press, 1986).

Your pediatrician can help direct you to other learning resources and books on death and grieving issues.

DIAPER RASH

Diaper rash is an annoying and painful irritation of the skin that a diaper covers. Most of these skin irritations are caused by bacteria, enzymes, chemicals, and the acidic quality of the baby's urine and bowel movements. The rash is usually red and irritated and always in the area covered by a diaper. With proper care, it should get better in three days, unless it is worsened by a fungal infection called candida *[see Thrush].* Given that most infants wear diapers for pretty good reasons, it is the most common rash of infancy. Typically, babies with fair skin tend to suffer from diaper rash more frequently than their darker-skinned counterparts. The chemicals and bacteria in bowel movements are especially hard on a baby's sensitive diaper area, so babies who are experiencing diarrhea are more prone to develop diaper rash.

Home Care Tips for Handling Diaper Rash

When your baby has diaper rash you need to pay attention to her bowel and urinary patterns in order to *change diapers frequently* (every hour or so—during the day—is a good rule of thumb). Remember, the best treatment for diaper rash is to *keep the irritated skin dry and clean.* Frequent diaper changes and cleansing the diaper area help to heal the skin. Warm tap water and a gentle soap are all that is needed. Wash the baby's diaper area gently after changing the diaper, and make sure to pat the area dry with a towel (see the following comments on "air-drying"). With extremely angry-appearing diaper rashes, you might want to bathe the baby two or three times a day in a warm tap-water bath for ten to twenty minutes. Adding a tablespoon or two of baking soda to the bath water will promote the healing process. Incidentally, the new disposable baby-wipe products are best avoided in the treatment of diaper rash. Some contain alcohol or other chemicals that can further dry and damage the sensitive skin. Save them for travel or similar occasions. At night, make sure the baby has a dry diaper before putting her down. You may want to check the baby once before you go to bed and once during the night to see if she requires changing until the diaper rash has resolved.

Allow the diaper area to air-dry between changes to encourage healing. Diaper rash irritations heal best when the baby's bottom area is as dry as possible. Between diaper changes and bathing, you need to make sure that the baby's sensitive and raw skin remains dry. Simply put, wet skin makes diaper rash worse. A time-honored means of achieving this goal is air-drying. Many old-time pediatricians used to recommend that the baby be allowed to play and amble about sans diapers. If this is impractical, simply make sure the area stays dry by increasing the amount of air-drying between changes (you might even try a hair blow-dryer—set at low—for a few minutes). Diapers that incorporate heavy rubber or plastic pants are to be avoided, since they render the diaper area air-tight and the rash process continues to worsen.

Okay, Doctor, None of these Tips Really Worked

There are some diaper rashes, of course, that require more treatment than just the suggestions discussed above. These are some symptoms of more severe cases of diaper rash and skin infections that necessitate a consultation with your pediatrician:

• The rash is not responding significantly after three days of applying the cleaning and drying suggestions.

• The diaper rash appears especially angry-red or infected, has a honey-colored sticky discharge from open sores, or is spreading to other parts of the body.

• The baby has a fever greater than 102°F, or appears especially cranky.

• Evidence of a yeast or candidal diaper rash: Because of the baby's immature immune system and the breakdown of skin caused by the diaper rash, a secondary, yeast (candidal) infection frequently follows in its path. This causes a severe red rash with "satellite lesions" around the diaper area, especially in the folds or creases of the skin. This type of skin infection is painful to the baby but can be easily cleared up with an antifungal ointment prescribed by your pediatrician *[see Thrush]*.

 Does diaper rash occur more frequently in babies who wear disposable diapers rather than cloth?

As much as we would like to advocate cloth diapers in terms of environmental wisdom, there is no evidence to suggest that there is any difference in the incidence of diaper rash between those babies who wear cloth or disposable diapers. All babies get diaper rash at some point, unless they don't wear diapers. In the event of a severe diaper rash, it is not necessary to change from a disposable to a cloth diaper, although this is commonly suggested for more severe diaper rashes. Note, however, that the worst diaper rashes are seen in those babies who wear the newer air-tight, "super-dry" diaper products. These diapers prevent leakage but do not allow in air, and combined with urine, sweat, and stools can lead to a more severe rash.

Do creams or soothing lotions help reduce diaper rash?

Sometimes, especially if the baby's skin is especially dry and cracked, both parent and baby find some relief in the hands-on experience of a protective barrier such as ointments containing zinc oxide (e.g., Desitin®) or petroleum jelly with vitamins A and D—not baby lotions, which can dry out sensitive skin. There is no need to slather it on. It's diaper rash, not a greased watermelon contest. After the diaper rash begins to heal, some parents find that applying cornstarch to the sensitive skin helps. Cornstarch does not, incidentally, increase the incidence of yeast infections. Talcum powder, on the other hand, is best avoided with all babies and children, since it is easily inhaled and can cause an irritation of the lungs.

Does the detergent used to wash cloth diapers make a difference in the incidence of diaper rash?

Not really. It is rare that a detergent, soap, or cleaning product is implicated as the culprit in a diaper rash case. But there are some precautions you may want to take. Wash the cloth diapers with a detergent and *bleach, in order to sterilize the diapers. We consulted our own mothers for some more explicit washing instructions and here they are:*

1. *During the first wash cycle, add one cup of detergent and use the hot temperature setting.*

2. *During the second wash cycle, add a cup of bleach in order to assure sterile diapers.*

My husband and I are undecided about using disposable diapers or cloth ones. We like to think we are pro-environment, but we are also working parents who would like to avoid one extra hassle of parenthood. Do you have any suggestions.

It is important to note at the outset that many studies have been done to compare the two. With the exception of the air-tight, plastic-enclosed diapers, there is little difference in the incidence of diaper rash between wearers of cloth and disposable diapers. Perhaps, then, the two issues most pertinent to the debate are the convenience factor and the role disposable diapers play in our rapidly expanding landfills. We would never presume to suggest that the choice of diapers is a significant reflection on one's parenting skills. Nine out of ten American parents use disposable rather than cotton. Instead, we urge you to consider this: a responsible parent is concerned not only about her child's immediate welfare but also for his future. This concern for the future, of course, takes many different aspects. For example, we plan for our children's college education at earlier and earlier ages. Indeed, some of our financial expert friends suggest putting aside money for college before the child is even born! And so, too, should we plan, as parents, to act as stewards of the earth's environment for our children's future sake.

At present, disposable diapers make up less than five percent of the nation's burgeoning landfill problem. Environmental groups who track the landfill problem estimate that every infant soils between seven thousand and ten thousand diapers before mastering toilet training. If you further estimate the average dirty diaper to weigh about eight ounces, we accumulate some thirty-one hundred tons of soiled disposable diapers every six hours—that's about four and one half million tons *of dirty diapers a year! The problem becomes more serious when we recall not only the energy and resources that go into making these products but also the fact that many take upward of five hundred years to biodegrade. Newer products that are more environmentally correct than earlier models are being developed, but they still remain untouched by natural degradation processes far longer than other "disposable" products.*

In most major cities in the United States, cloth-diaper services both launder and deliver steady supplies of this more environmentally safe product. They can be used between 150 to 200 times and are easily biodegradable. It also winds up far cheaper to use cloth diapers, especially if you do the laundering yourself. For example, parents who use disposable probably spend about fifty cents per diaper or about $26.00 per week. Many cotton-diaper services deliver and launder their product for fifteen to twenty cents a diaper or nine dollars to fifteen dollars per week. If you launder them yourself, the cost drops to about a nickel a diaper—two bucks a week!

DIARRHEA AND DEHYDRATION

Although etiquette sometimes prevents us from admitting it, we are a nation obsessed with our own bowels and bowel movements. The briefest reading of a daily newspaper or a minimum of time in front of a television set confirms this theory, as you will be inundated with advertisements for laxatives, cathartics, stool softeners, and diarrheal aids. The national fascination with the size, frequency, and consistency of our stools extends, of course, to our child-rearing practices. Not surprisingly, questions about the subject are among the most frequently heard by pediatricians and other child health-care providers.

In reference to the term diarrhea, we are *not* terribly concerned with the occasional loose or runny or watery bowel movement that often accompanies eating a particularly disagreeable food, too much candy, too much fruit, or other dietary indiscretions. Instead, pediatricians and parents need to become concerned with the child (especially those under the age of two years and particularly infants under six months) who is having several of these episodes a day (more than five to six watery bowel movements), as typically seen in infectious causes of diarrhea. Quantity rather than quality is the issue here; not all watery stools portend diarrhea. A lot of loose watery stools, especially in a small infant or child, is how you need to define diarrhea.

Severe diarrhea is very serious as it can cause dehydration, a potentially life-threatening condition for the infant or small child. Babies are more easily dehydrated than larger children and adults. Because our bodies are mostly made up of water, serious reductions in the amount of total body water can seriously impair normal function. Normally, the internal gauges of our bodies maintain regular organ function and metabolism even when there is a reduction in body water. In serious cases of rapid fluid loss, however, the body simply cannot keep up with the demand, and serious illness results. This process is accelerated in small infants, who store less water in their bodies. Indeed, not that long ago one of the major sources of infant mortality in the United States was epidemics of diarrhea and resultant dehydration. With the advent of better means of refrigeration of food products, the development of intravenous and oral rehydration techniques, and earlier methods of recognition and intervention, relatively few American infants die of diarrhea today, although it remains a significant cause of death for babies around the world, especially in underdeveloped nations where medical resources are scarce.

Important Questions to ask When Assessing Your Child's Diarrhea

When confronted with an infant or toddler with diarrhea, you need to ask yourself several key questions (in addition to the important concern of where the toilet paper and cleaning supplies are):

1. How often is your child rushing to the bathroom with a diarrheal stool (or in the case of the infant still in diapers, how often is she soiling the diaper)?

2. What is the consistency and quality of the stool? Is it well formed? Is it completely liquid or watery? (The greater the water content of the stool, the more serious should be your concern about dehydration.)

3. How does your child look? Does she appear dehydrated? Is she still urinating? (Golden or dark-colored urine signifies evidence of mild dehydration, while clear-colored urine suggests that the child has retained most of her body fluids.) Does your child cry with tears? (dehydrated children produce fewer tears than well-hydrated ones.) Does the child have saliva in her mouth or does her mouth feel dry and parched? (older children will tell you that they are thirsty.) Does her skin feel dry and lax?

If the answer to any of these questions suggests dehydration, call your pediatrician for advice. Sometimes the level of dehydration is minimal enough for you to merely rehydrate the child orally with sips of cold, but flat soda pop, popsicles, gelatins, ice cream, and similar liquids. If the child appears, on the other hand, listless, irritable, and quite "dry," more serious measures, including the administration of intravenous fluids at the doctor's office or a hospital, may be necessary.

Preventing Dehydration: What do I Feed My Child When he has Diarrhea?

This is a question that has been plaguing pediatricians for years. If you ask ten pediatricians this question, you are likely to get ten slightly different answers. In the past, we were hesitant to continue feeding milk-based formula to an infant with diarrhea because of the concern that it would be difficult to digest and might even worsen the diarrhea. In actuality, it probably doesn't matter too much what you feed your child during this crisis, as long as she can 1) hold it down and 2) the food or liquid is palatable to the child.

For infants who are still on the bottle or who nurse, formula or breast milk is best. Continue feeding as the baby tolerates it. Oral rehydration solutions (such as Pedialyte®) may also be tried.

For children older than one year, with copious diarrhea, we often recommend a bland and binding diet that includes foods such as bananas (rich in potassium, an essential electrolyte in normal body function that may be in short supply during bouts of serious diarrhea), plain boiled rice, applesauce (but not apple juice, which can actually worsen diarrhea), and plain toast. Pediatricians often call this a B.R.A.T. diet, from the first letters of each of the prescribed foods, and they are a good place to start during the first day of a serious bout of diarrhea. Other improvisations, depending on your individual child's likes and dislikes, are welcome; for example, adding fiber to the diet may actually help the child retain fluids. Given that, in the majority of cases of diarrhea, your child will *not* lose significant weight during his illness, it is best to concentrate on getting fluids down rather than focusing on calories. It is essential to make sure the child is drinking, urinating more frequently, and complaining less of being thirsty.

Is There a Best Fluid to Rehydrate My Child?

Not exactly, but some rehydration fluids are better than others. Although water seems the obvious answers, it is *not* a good liquid to rehydrate someone who has lost a lot of fluid. The reason for this is that the vital electrolytes, minerals, and other substances that make up normal blood volume are already in short supply and become more scarce when the body fluids are diluted with plain water. Attempting to give a severely dehydrated infant or child pure water may worsen problems because of this dilutional effect.

Instead, we recommend special fluids that have been concocted to be more or less similar to the chemical composition of body fluids: Pedialyte®, ORS (Oral Rehydration Solution), and similar products. These liquids are specially formulated to maintain the delicate balance of fluid and important electrolytes and other substances in infants and children.

Larger children, on the other hand, call be well hydrated with less exotic liquids such as flat sodas, soups, and teas. They are less sensitive to the metabolic derangement of diarrhea and fluid loss. Nevertheless, they still need to be watched carefully for signs of improvement or worsening. Even a big, strapping teenager is capable of getting into fluid problems if the diarrhea is severe and copious enough. We generally avoid high-solute drinks like Gatorade® and similar products for rehydration.

Diarrhea, bloody

More serious forms of diarrhea accompanied by bloody stools may be caused by specific bacteria (e.g., salmonella, shigella, *E. coli,* and so on) that are extremely pathogenic (disease-producing). These bacterial agents frequently secret a toxin or poison that not only causes blood in the stool but can seriously interfere with the function of the gastrointestinal and other organ systems. For this reason, it is wise to always wash your meat, fish, poultry, and food products before preparation with cold running water, then cook them completely. If you are marinating meat, fish, or poultry, remember not to place the cooked food back into the raw marinade, since the juices may still contain bacteria. Similarly, if you are using kitchen utensils to manipulate raw foods, make sure you wash them thoroughly before using the same utensils on cooked foods. Most of these serious causes of bloody diarrhea are easily rendered harmless by proper cooking, but for those who prefer their meat rare, the health risk is definitely there.

If you note blood in your child's stool or are concerned about some food product your child may have recently consumed (such as undercooked meat or poultry), call the pediatrician immediately *[see Contagious and Infectious Diseases]*.

It is also important to note that there are some rather harmless causes of so-called "bloody" diarrhea in children—for example, ingesting foods containing red dyes, beets, tomatoes, colored soft drinks, and other products can cause a red-colored diarrhea. With specific lab tests, it is relatively easy to distinguish this problem from the real thing.

Diarrhea: Local Skin Care for Your Child

Sometimes with repeated diarrheal stools—whether bloody or non-bloody—the child's sensitive perirectal area becomes red and inflamed. Skin often breaks down in this area and occasionally it can bleed mildly. Careful washing after each stool and application of petroleum jelly or A and D ointment ought to help somewhat. This tender situation is, fortunately, self-limiting.

[See Diaper Rash]

DISAGREEMENTS BETWEEN PARENTS

All married couples disagree from time to time. The added stresses of a new child or the complex activities of the average American family may lead to the occasional disagreement or "fight" in front of the children. Excessive fighting in front of your children may have an adverse effect on their behavior and even their health. Children rarely thrive in combat zones. Consequently, you need to be extra careful in your disagreement techniques. Indeed, the best way to understand how a child fights or disagrees with others is to observe his parents in a disagreement. Quite simply, children imitate the fighting (and loving) skills they learn at home.

Some children observing a fight between their parents may become unsettled about the stability of the marriage. Fear of divorce is quite common among American children *[see Divorce; Long-distance Parenting]*. It is wise not to fight in the presence of those children who appear especially sensitive to family discord. In the event that a fight does occur in front of the children (typically in a car, on a family outing, or during a family crisis), here are a few tips that should help.

• Avoid using a harsh tone of voice. Children tend to react more to the tone of an adult's voice than to his or her words. Try to calm yourself down and refrain from speaking with anger, hatred, or malice.

- Avoid name-calling of any kind.

- Avoid "gunny-sacking." Don't hit your spouse with a list of complaints or errors dating back to your wedding day. It will not help your marriage or resolve the fight; it will, however, upset your children and may inspire them to use similar tactics in their own fights or arguments.

- Fight fairly rather than fighting to win. Defeating your partner in an argument rarely strengthens a marriage and often causes conflict in the child's mind. Whom should he side with? How does he feel about the victorious partner? The defeated partner?

- End the fight promptly! You, your spouse, and your children will all benefit from prompt closure of a fight. Lengthy disagreements that last for days will only have negative ramifications in your child's life as well as your own.

- After concluding a disagreement with your spouse, make sure to hug, kiss, and make up *in front of* the children. This lets them know that things are back to normal and that the marriage is doing well.

For additional reading on this topic we suggest: Taffel, R. *Why Parents Disagree.* (New York: William Morrow, 1994).

DISCIPLINE

Parenting is an ongoing and difficult task. There will be many times during your child's life where you will need to discipline him or, at least, set some limits. Most parents often look for guidance in this task. There are, of course, no easy solutions to the age-old question, "How should I raise my child?" We asked Dr. Eileen Mollen, a child psychologist at the University of Michigan Medical Center and the mother of three, to share her views on better parenting through effective communication between parent and child. This chapter should not be interpreted as a cookbook or "how-to" approach, but rather as a guide to thinking about how you interact with your children.

Respect and Listening

Children who cry, whine, or otherwise misbehave often do not have insight into their own behavior—they need their parents to interpret and understand the reasons for their behavior. In fact, the misbehavior in question may be the only way your child can communicate his feelings. A first approach to understanding and, we hope, ameliorating these negative behaviors is to respect and carefully listen to your child.

Perhaps the most effective tool for promoting positive child behavior is a strong, loving, and nurturing relationship between parent and child. Such a relationship begins with respect. Children are individuals, with temperaments, styles, strengths, and weaknesses different from their parents'. Consequently, they must be respected as individuals with their own needs, desires, and goals. A child's self-esteem soars when he is complimented; conversely, his self-esteem is negatively affected by criticism. When children are treated with respect, they usually respond in kind.

How do You Interact and Speak with Your Child?

Many adults make the mistake of speaking harshly or condescendingly to their children, especially under stress. To measure your own verbal interactions with your child, try this exercise. Take a moment to think about the last five verbal interactions you had with your child. Think about your tone of voice, your facial expression, and the words you used. Was your facial expression angry or mean? Was your voice louder or sharper than the tones in which you would like to be spoken to? If you think such a problem may be interfering in your relationship with your child, some good ways to correct it are to consciously modulate the volume and tone of your voice; relax your facial muscles; and, above all, make eye contact to indicate that he is important and that you require his attention.

We often think that we hear what our children are saying, but we don't always listen to what is behind their words. In fact, we often don't give them a chance to talk. On the whole, parents don't like to see their children in pain or struggling with a problem, so often they are often tempted to "answer" for their children. Instead, it might be better to hold your tongue and *be quiet* for a bit longer than usual. Give your child time to think and share his thoughts.

Our efforts as parents to guide our children in positive ways depend largely upon our abilities to understand the reasons or motivations behind their actions. Fortunately, they frequently give us clues, if we listen carefully without comment, judgment, or advice. Many times your child may not even want your input. He may just need to vent his feelings verbally or share his own experiences that day. When we "jump the gun" and respond before knowing why a child is openly communicating about some aspect of his day—troubling or not—we may reduce the chance that he'll want to communicate openly on subsequent occasions.

It is important to convey to your child that you value his ideas and opinions. For example, the next time you are reading the evening paper and your child approaches you with conversation, try responding with: "Wait, let me put this newspaper down so I can really listen to what you have to say." Even if you have just planted yourself in front of the television for a night's hibernation, remember how important it is to interact with your children and pay attention to them. This display of respect will not only make your child beam that evening, it also helps to build a lifelong sense of self-worth.

Always avoid insulting your child. Instead, try to listen with your heart and put yourself in the place of your child. Ask yourself what he might be feeling. It is possible to state your feelings—even the angry ones—without insult. For example, if your child is explaining why he got into trouble in school, avoid yelling or getting upset and, instead, try something like: "It sounds like you had a problem in school. We should talk about it." Similarly, when your child erupts with anger, instead of responding in kind, try: "I don't like being spoken to that way. I would like you to talk to me in a respectful way."

We hear a lot about "quality time" these days, and certainly spending significant time doing special things with your child is important. But don't underestimate the importance of *quantity time* for communication. This is the casual time around the home when children can approach you at odd moments and give you a quick clue as to what's going on in their lives. It is usually unplanned and achieved simply by spending time with your child. Children don't save up their conversation; they like to communicate when they feel the urge to do so. More frequently, children pick ordinary occasions to share their thoughts and ideas. As children get older, you may find that they communicate better not face to face but in the context of doing something else—riding side-by-side in a car, doing dishes, cooking together, and so on. If those times are not available, you may miss some important opportunities to share in your child's life.

Problem Solving

If our children are to become independent, thinking adults who make good choices in life, then we must teach them early how to become effective problem solvers. Children who become adept at solving their own problems tend to make better decisions and also behave in a more parent-friendly manner.

It is very important that parents allow their children to solve their own problems as long as those problems are developmentally appropriate. Learning this skill involves an active process of communication between parent and child that leads to a sense of responsibility and follow-through in children. Many parents make the mistake of trying to solve their children's problems for them or offer too much advice. Instead of providing a solution for your child, it is more productive to help him think through the solution himself.

How do I help my child learn to solve problems?

You can begin by giving your child lots of opportunities to make choices for himself. For the young child, such choices may include "Do you want milk or juice?" or "It's time for dinner; do you want to run into the house or hop into the house?" Older children, of course, need larger problems to solve and this requires some creativity on a parent's part. Make sure that the school-aged child, for example, is actively involved in decision-making regarding his extracurricular activities (either organized or with the family).

As with any other new skill, children must learn *how* to make decisions. They are not born with those skills. Some children are better than others at decision-making. This is a process they learn by observing the decision-making processes of the adults in their lives and of other children around them.

When your child is attempting to solve problems on her own, don't immediately give advice, even if you feel you know the best solution. Instead, hold back and think of questions you could ask to guide her to the solution herself. Similarly, for homework problems, don't immediately give the answers. Rather, ask some questions about the particular assignments at hand. For example, if your child is having trouble reading an assigned book, try asking questions about some of the characters. If you have read the book in question, explain why you think it is worth reading.

With good role models, time, and the chance to make age-appropriate decisions on his own, your child can become adept at social problem solving from a very early age. The problems, of course, become more complex as children grow older, but the thinking through of choices, consequences, and compromise continues to be part of the process. Finally, it is often helpful to review with a child both good and ineffective decisions to help her learn new skills for future choices.

Control

Struggles for control are commonly a major issue for both children and their parents. Too often, however, control issues degenerate into a power struggle. Keep in mind that for a parent to "win," the child must "lose," and vice versa. For parents, force usually wins ("You'll do it because I said so"); this is a resolution that typically leaves both parent and child angry and frustrated.

Every parent and child fall into this control rut every so often. Problems occur when the parent-child relationship turns into a repetitive cycle of power games and rebellion. In this case, parents too often resort to the same techniques they may have been raised on—such as screaming, spanking, or inducing guilt—to communicate with their children.

Many families experience conflicts because the parents fail to recognize developmental shifts in their children. Just when you think you know "what makes your child tick" and you are feeling effective as a parent, he moves on to the next developmental stage and you have to regroup and adapt to the next exciting phase of parenthood. Keep in mind how stressful this can be for your child. If you are confused, your child may be far more confused by his emotional growth. Many child psychologists believe that the behaviors of the "terrible twos" (such as egocentricity, tantrums, and the struggle between dependence and autonomy) are revisited at every major developmental shift.

If your child continually displays a certain type of negative behavior in these conflicts, it might be helpful to begin a log or journal to determine a pattern in the conflicts; this record can also help you interpret your child's and your own behaviors. The log needs to include a description of the behavior, what led up to it, and how it was (or was not) resolved. A pattern may emerge that clarifies the problem—perhaps a link to hunger, anxiety, or fatigue. Are the behaviors to get your attention? Do they occur at certain times of the day? Are they associated with separation (such as before school in the morning)? Are there any new stresses your child may be experiencing?

Once you have figured out the pattern (and especially if you haven't), *ask* your child about these behaviors. Try to elicit *his* observations during a time when things are calm and you are not in the throes of conflict. This gives your child the message that you respect his thoughts, needs, and feelings. The encounter, more neutral than at the time of conflict, is more likely to be productive. Equally important, this type of communication allows your child to take part in the problem-solving process.

Anger

It is normal for all parents to become angry at their children at some times. Such feelings are natural and to be expected. What we would like to discuss is *how* those feelings of anger are best expressed. In fact, parental anger can play a positive role in child-rearing: it sends a message to the children that parents care enough to be affected by their behavior. It also provides an opportunity for parents to show their children effective ways to deal with anger as it periodically emerges.

The difficult trick is to express anger in such a way that you do not attack the character or self-esteem of the child. Consequently, destructive statements, insults, and other negative, unproductive means of expressing your anger need to be replaced with more positive methods. Instead of shouting or acting physically, parents should use statements that inform rather than destroy. For example, "I feel angry when I call you to dinner and no one comes. I say to myself—I cooked a great meal and I want some appreciation, not frustration!" This illustrates how to give vent to anger in an appropriate way.

[Sometimes parents become angry at one another. For information on how to handle disagreements with your spouse in front of the children, see Disagreements Between Parents]

Children are quite uninhibited when expressing anger. The very young child, for example, is primitive in his expression and typically responds with hitting, biting, screaming, tantrums, and other negative behaviors. As children get older, they become more complex in their methods of expressing anger, adding defiance, mouthiness, aggression, and sometimes destructiveness to their repertoire. Children need to express anger, just as adults do. Therefore, we must teach our children more acceptable ways to be angry. The earlier this process starts, the better. Begin by exposing your toddler to the words that will help him to identify his emotions—for example, "You seem very angry when you scream like that" or "Your face has a very angry look." This technique helps a child to read his own body cues and to place a label on those feelings.

You need to set limits as to how anger can be expressed within your family. For example, you might explain to your child: "It's okay to be angry, but you cannot hurt anyone." Instead, suggest that your child uses words to express his anger rather than fists. You also need to remind the older child that, while being angry is okay, using destructive or hurtful words is not. This is a quiet but remarkably powerful tool in helping your child deal more effectively with anger.

When children are angry all the time, you must explore the source of the anger. Constant anger usually indicates that something is bothering the child. Strategies for exploration include asking the child at a calm moment to help you understand what is bothering him; talking about your concerns with a day-care provider or teacher to gain insight into his behavior or stressors in other settings; or, if necessary, discussing your concerns with your pediatrician. A referral for professional intervention may be indicated.

Positive Parenting Techniques

1. **"Catch them being good"**: Our favorite parenting approach is a technique widely referred to as "Catch Them Being Good." What parents often want is un-interrupted time to complete a task like reading the paper or cooking dinner. What children want is frequent parental attention. As a result, when parents are unavailable to give attention, children will find ways to gain access to mom or dad, often with negative behaviors. For example, if you are sitting in the living room reading and your children are playing nearby, one of the children is likely to try to gain your attention with a negative behavior such as hitting her little sister. In the short run, this usually works—the parent stops reading to reprimand the offender. Instead, we suggest that you try giving attention when the child is compliant. For example, after five or ten minutes of reading the paper, get up, go over to the children and say "I like the way you are playing so nicely" or "What an interesting block house you two have built." Adding a smile, a quick hug, or touch on the shoulder cements this positive behavior further.

2. **Positive feedback:** Children need positive feedback specifically directed at their behavior. Reinforcing the behaviors you approve of with praise will increase the likelihood that they will be repeated. If you tell a child he is "being good," he will be pleased. But depending on the child's age and developmental level, he may ask himself "Am I good because I am coloring within the lines or because I am not swinging from the chandelier?" Specific (and genuine) praise is much more effective. If your child succeeds at a particular task, tell him directly and positively: "Thank you for putting your dish on the counter"; "You got those shoes on without any argument. Thank you so much!"; or "I am so proud of how you tried to figure out that math problem on your own."

Once you are involved with such positive approaches, you are in a position to ignore many of the behaviors that you want to disappear. If a child is no longer getting attention for a certain behavior, he will commonly conclude "what's the point?" Often the negative behavior disappears.

3. **Setting limits:** Children need to know what is expected of them. Children—including older children and even teenagers—feel safer when they know the

boundaries of their behavior and what the adults in their lives will tolerate; these boundaries create a framework from which they can explore and test their independence. So, in fact, you do your child a favor by setting limits. Those children for whom there are not limits, inconsistent limits, or chaotic living situations are much less secure and may not function as well.

When setting limits, be clear and specific. Again, "Be good" doesn't tell a child much. "When we are in the store, we keep our hands to ourselves and we walk, not run" is more specific. These "instructional" statements need to be easy to follow *[see Surviving Shopping Trips with Your Child]*.

Temper Tantrums Throughout Childhood

There is a common misperception that toddlers have a corner on the market for temper tantrums. In fact, temper tantrums may occur at any time when children are struggling between autonomy and dependence. This is a big issue during the toddler years because the child is learning "new tricks" almost every day involving motor development, language development, and individuation from mom and dad. But similar struggles occur throughout childhood and adolescence.

What can I do about my child's temper tantrums?

Perhaps the most effective technique is to prevent the tantrums in the first place! Observe your child throughout his entire tantrum scenario. What happened just before the tantrum occurred? What body cues, words, or actions precipitated the outburst? You will begin to see a pattern with your child. They key is to identify those behaviors that occur *before* the tantrum and intervene at that point.

Unfortunately, even the most astute and responsive parent cannot head off all tantrums. What can be done when a child is in the middle of a tantrum? The short answer is, "nothing." Once a child is out of control in the throes of a tantrum, techniques such as reasoning, threatening or cajoling are often ineffective and may even escalate the tantrum. Instead, remain calm and reassuring. First, make sure the child is safe, which may entail moving objects out of the way or moving him to a safer spot. Then, ignore the child and go about your business in the same area. The child who gets no attention for a tantrum will realize that his behavior doesn't "buy" him anything and the tantrums will become less frequent and less intense over time. As you begin this new approach to temper tantrums, keep in mind, that as you ignore him, he will "up the ante" to see if you will respond. Expect that things will seem worse before they become better. However, if you remain consistent in your lack of response, the temper tantrums will diminish.

Following a tantrum, it is helpful to praise the child's ability to regain control over himself. Then it is important for both sides to agree that the incident is over. Parents do not need to punish, lecture, or demand an apology; instead, think about what precipitated the tantrum and move to repair things (e.g., feed the child if he is hungry, remove the child from an overstimulating environment, and so forth). Calmly resume the activity at hand. Take care that you do not yield to the demands of a child in a tantrum. If you give in, you are demonstrating that tantrums pay off, and it becomes that much more difficult the next time.

For the older child, try discussing the matter *after* everyone has regained their composure. This allows the event to serve as a problem-solving session. A positive approach like this tells the child that "in control" behavior gets responded to, and you will be able to reinforce good listening and problem-solving skills with your child.

Whining

Whining is certainly one of the most annoying behaviors among children (and many adults). They learn quite early how quickly it garners our attention, so it is very effective from the child's point of view. While some parents can easily ignore whining, for others it is like fingernails on a blackboard. To eliminate whining, two things need to occur. First, children need to hear the message that whining will no longer get them what they want; and second, they need to learn an alternative behavior that *will* get them what they want.

For example, the next time your child begins to whine for a glass of juice or some other want, be sure to inform him that you cannot understand him when he uses a whining tone. Continue with what you are doing. Stand your ground even if the whining escalates. After a while, most children get the message and try more appropriate methods for requesting an item. Remember to praise your child when he does ask in a more appropriate manner! And remember, whining is rarely "cured" in one day or one week. The need for periodic reminders throughout childhood are essential.

Finally, keep in mind that children whine the most when they are tired, hungry, or bored. So it pays to resolve those needs in order to reduce whining. When those situations cannot be avoided, a little extra understanding and tolerance for whining is in order.

Time out

"Time out" has been a popular disciplinary technique in recent years. There is a lot of variation regarding how the time out is implemented. The purpose of a time out is not as a punishment for bad behavior but rather to provide an opportunity for the child to remove himself from an out-of-control situation and use that isolation as a means of regaining control. The expectation should be that time out results in a more in-control child who is ready to reenter the social situation.

Parents often begin using time out with toddlers; however, this may be too early in a child's development, for a couple of reasons. First, toddlers often act (and react) impulsively and cannot reflect sensibly about their behaviors. Time out may be perceived by the toddler as a power struggle and a punishment because he doesn't have the necessary verbal understanding of the parent's expectations. Second, by the time the child is older and could learn from this technique, he may be "burned out" by its overuse and failure in earlier years. Other techniques for toddlers, such as redirecting his attention to another activity or presenting him with some choices ("Do you want to continue playing or should we bring you inside the house for a nap?") are often more effective.

Time out is, however, a particularly effective tool for older children, generally over the age of three or three-and-a-half years, who have learned to express themselves and have gained some insight into their behaviors. Sometimes it is helpful to explain to your child about time out at a quiet moment before you actually implement the technique. Playing "time out" with a teddy bear who is misbehaving is a good way to illustrate to the child how to use time out to calm down.

When you child's behavior is becoming out of control, a time out should be instituted. Begin with words to mediate the problem—for example, "Megan, you look very angry and out of control. You need to take a time out until you can calm down." Then escort her to a quiet, safe place (such as the bottom step of the stairs, a chair in the living room away from the family, or the rug in her bedroom) and tell her that when she is back in control, she can rejoin the group. With these directives, you are giving the child the message that it is her responsibility to remain in control and that she can judge her own readiness to return. Initially, this will take some teaching ("Megan, you are not ready to return to play. Your face is really angry; you are still shouting. When you can talk in a quiet voice and are calmer, you may return.") If your child tries to rejoin the group activities too early, then redirect her back to the time-out spot.

During the time out, except for the brief sentences noted above, no attention should be paid to the child. If you do give her your attention, she is likely to maintain the power struggle in an attempt to continue getting it, and the purpose of the time out will be lost. Instead, tell the child what you expect and then walk away, ignoring any tantrum behavior. It is her responsibility to calm down.

There are times when your child may need more assistance to regain control. For example, sometimes a child needs to be rocked or held in that quiet place in order to calm down. Again, keep in mind that time out, as described here, is a teaching tool to help children manage their own behavior, not a punishment.

When the child returns, say something like "I like the way you have calmed down. Come join us." Then continue with the activity at hand. Don't rehash the incident or make the child apologize or you will be setting yourself up for another battle. It is more important to comment on the child's accomplishment of pulling herself together and thus reinforcing her skills (even if it took her a long time). If the incident needs to be discussed, find a time when you can both calmly go over what happened.

Spanking and physical forms of punishment

There is a simple response to the question "When is it okay to spank?" *Never!* Spanking is generally administered when parents are angry and out of control. It is an aggressive and counterproductive response that gets used when parents are at the end of their rope *or* if they do not have more effective techniques at their disposal. When parents who are out of control spank their children, they are sending the message that aggression and physical force are permissible responses to angry feelings. Parents then serve as a model for violent behavior and, as a result, hitting begets hitting. Because adults are so much bigger than children, these "spankings" can be quite painful and dangerous. Any activity that involves hitting has the potential for getting out of control.

If you feel that you are about to lose control, try giving yourself a break. Children are often told they need a time out. Parents sometimes need one, too. Take a time out for yourself. Close yourself in the bathroom or bedroom and take a few deep breaths. When you have composed yourself, you will be able to respond to your children more rationally. It doesn't hurt to tell your child "I am very angry right now, and I don't want to lose control. I am going to take a time out in the other room. I will come back when I am calm." You have given your child the message that you are angry, but you are taking control and thereby serving as an excellent model for your child.

If need be, call a neighbor, friend, or relative, just to talk with another adult. Sometimes that brief contact will help you feel supported enough to function more effectively.

If you are still in danger of hurting or abusing your child, call a professional immediately. You can phone your pediatrician or a Parent's Anonymous hotline (listed in your local telephone directory) for immediate support from someone trained to help you through this type of situation.

DIVORCE

One of the harshest statistics of American society is the current divorce rate. And while no one wants to contemplate the problems encountered when a marriage breaks up, when children are involved, careful and sensitive planning is absolutely necessary. The most important factor in announcing such a decision to one's children is establishing a plan that both minimizes the obvious pain of the situation and reassures the child that both her mother and her father will continue to love and support her. No matter what the situation, divorce is always hard on the parents and, of course, the children. Careful planning, maturity, honesty in answering your child's questions, and maintaining a loving and caring with the children can, however, go a long way in their healthy adjustment to such an event.

A child's response to divorce depends greatly on his or her age and level of maturity. Here are a few common responses to divorce that are divided by a child's age and developmental level.

Infants to two years:
- Lack of energy
- Withdrawal
- Changes in eating patterns
- Increase in spitting up or vomiting
- Easily angered or upset

- Increased crying
- More difficult to console when crying
- Changes in sleep patterns or restlessness
- Clingy behavior (child always wants to be held and is upset when he is not)
- Increased or exaggerated fear of strangers or new situations.

Toddlers:
- The child hopes and believes that the separation is only temporary
- Denial (Mommy and Daddy will get back together)
- Regression into more immature behaviors
- Fear
- Guilt
- Confusion
- Separation anxiety
- Child fears he may be replaced or cast aside
- Changes in child's playtime behaviors

Early middle childhood (six to eight years):
- Child can understand, after awhile, that the divorce is final
- Child wonders if he is somehow the cause of the divorce
- Displays of anger directed at the parent who lives with the child after the separation
- Increased displays of affection for the departed parent
- Fear
- Grief reactions (such as tearfulness, sadness, anger, and so on)
- Conflicted feelings over which parent to be loyal to

Here are a few tips to make the transition a bit easier.

1. Before announcing the decision to divorce to your children, discuss the situation thoroughly with your spouse. Even though you may be angry and hurt by the actions of your spouse, you must reach an accord over how to make the announcement in a calm and nonaccusatory manner. Blaming mom or dad for the decision, citing the actual problems that may have led to the break-up, or displaying anger are best confined to your attorney's office. Such behavior only inspires children to feel that they must choose sides—a choice that inevitably leads to anger, resentment, or guilt.

2. When you tell the children, do so together in a relaxed and calm atmosphere. You should not pick a time when your child is distracted or unreceptive. You might be surprised to know that even children as young as age three or four sense that their parents are not getting along, so the announcement may even be

expected by older children. Another point to remember is that every child responds differently to bad news. Some children may respond quite matter-of-factly, others may cry, others may become angry. Recall that you are the bearer of bad tidings and the response to bad news is not always immediate. Instead, responses typically develop over the weeks and months to come.

3. Explain to your children that the reason you are divorcing is because you two are not getting along. It is important to assure children that the divorce is not because of their behavior or actions. Commonly, children become convinced that they are the cause of their parents' divorce and try to change their behavior in an attempt to bring their parents back together. These changes can include playing the model child or the angry, bad child who garners a lot of attention from both parents.

4. Reassure the children that both his mother and father love him and always will, regardless of their living arrangement or marital status. It is all too common for a young child to misconstrue her mother or father leaving a marriage with leaving her.

5. The decision to divorce is a final and firm one—except in the minds of the children, who will attempt almost anything to get the parents back together. Your announcement, then, needs to be both firm and gentle to avoid future disappointment when the child realizes his attempts to reunite his parents must fail *[see Long-distance Parenting]*.

DROWN-PROOFING THE HOME: CHILDREN AND WATER SAFETY

After automobile-related injuries, drowning (or submersion injuries) are the second leading cause of accidental death for Americans between the ages of five and forty-five. Fifty per cent of all drowning deaths in the United States occur among those under the age of twenty. Children between the ages of one and two years are especially vulnerable to this risk because few know how to swim and fewer still can accurately judge for themselves the true danger of jumping into a pool of water significantly deeper than one's height.

Typically, these accidents occur as an unattended toddler discovers a swimming pool, home whirlpool, hot tub, or spa device and simply jumps in. Toddlers and infants, however, can easily drown in any amount of water that is deep enough to cover the mouth and nose—a toilet bowl, a bathtub, or a pail of water. Always supervise your baby or child when she is in or near water. Stay alert! *[see Bathing Your Baby]*.

Older children, on the other hand, typically are pushed or accidentally fall into a body of water and drown. These areas are frequently unapproved swimming sites such as unsupervised rivers, creeks, or quarries. Other occasions of drowning injuries among this age group include boating accidents, body surfing, and more rarely, scuba diving.

There are a number of ways to prevent drowning accidents *before* they even occur.

1. Maintain constant adult supervision of young children while they are bathing. This means that you are in the bathroom, watching them at all times. An amazing number of bad things can happen when a toddler is left to his own devices in a bathtub or larger body of water.

2. If you have a swimming pool in your backyard, fence it in completely, on all four sides, and keep it locked so that young toddlers or children cannot come in to explore. If you live near a lake or ocean, fencing the water in may be impossible. You need to set strict rules forbidding your child to swim without the supervision of an adult. *Never let your child swim in an unsupervised environment.*

3. If you live near a quarry, creek, or river, do not allow your child to swim there. Under the surface there can be large and virtually invisible obstacles, such as rocks or branches, against which she can hit her head, become unconscious, and drown.

4. If you have a boat, make sure it meets all of the United States Coast Guard Safety regulations, including a suitable flotation device (life jacket) for *each* passenger. Avoid high-speed or unsafe boating practices. *Never* drink alcohol and boat at the same time.

5. Children should always swim *only* in guarded and supervised areas.

6. All teens and adults in a family should learn CPR techniques to be used in the event of an emergency *[see CPR].*

7. Although many debate the proper age to begin swimming lessons for your child, most four- or five-year-olds can be safely taught to swim with excellent results. Whenever swimming, all children need to be supervised by adults.

[See Injury and Accident Prevention]

DRUGS AND ALCOHOL

Saying "No" to Drugs and Alcohol

Unfortunately, we live in an age where children are inundated with the temptations of drug and alcohol. Although we have no means at present to predict which person will actually become addicted to a particular substance, it is clear that initiating drug or alcohol use at an early age can lead to future addiction problems. The dangerous combination of youthful energy with lifted inhibitions or unclear thinking can often lead to a variety of risky behaviors, ranging from sexual promiscuity to reckless driving.

Physicians who treat drug and alcohol abuse problems remind us that it is probably never too early to begin teaching your child about its dangers. While the phrase "Just Say No" is a catchy one, remember that education and example are the keys to raising drug-free children. Just as you might sit down with your child to explain to him the importance of looking both ways before crossing the street, you need to warn him about the problems encountered when using or abusing these substances. You might also think back to your own experiences as a means of personalizing the lesson including the difficulties of avoiding peer pressure which children so often experience when "saying no to drugs" or episodes where such substances may have caused problems for you or your close family members.

Perhaps the earliest lesson on drugs and alcohol a child receives has less to do with a "lecture" on prevention or exposure through movies and television than it does with the example set by one's parents. Clearly, the best defense against this problem—and many other unhealthy habits—is personal example. Indeed, experts have shown that it is the parent's pattern of drug and alcohol use that serves as the child's most potent teacher. The parent who abuses drugs or alcohol—even those who casually use these substances as an artificial means of relaxation or stress reduction—frequently raise children who grow up with the belief that such behavior is acceptable.

 What are some reasonable ways to prevent my child from using drugs and alcohol?

Aside from the advice offered above, you need to take an active role in your child's life outside of the home. Well before adolescence, children are frequently exposed to those who abuse alcohol and drugs. This is as true for children raised in small towns as it is for those raised in large cities. Besides careful guidance and education on these issues, you should keep aware of where your child spends his free time and with whom he spends it. If your child is invited to a party, make sure there is adult supervision and do not be afraid to ask if there will be drugs or alcohol present. Finally, do not hesitate to set reasonable limits on your child's social life. There are excellent reasons why you are the parent and your child is the child; therefore you should not hesitate to state a given time when you expect him to return home or to state definitively that using drugs or alcohol is not "okay."

How can I tell if my child is experimenting with drugs?

Although every child is different, there do exist specific patterns to early drug abuse. The first message you should understand is that experimentation is a normal part of childhood and adolescence. What makes this type of experimentation so objectionable are the inherent dangers of the substances themselves rather than the curiosity displayed by the child. Many signs of early drug abuse are ignored or not recognized by parent, either out of fear of discovery or a lack of knowledge of the specific warning signs. It is vital, however, to become acquainted with them. If prevention by means of education does not work, early intervention to break the pattern is the next best solution.

Early warning signs include:

• *Unexplainable shifts in behavior such as drowsiness, hyperactivity, mood swings, appetite changes, weight loss, or changes in physical appearance*

• *Secretive behavior, such as hiding out in one's room, keeping locks on drawers, late-night phone calls from strangers, and so on*

• *New friends whom you suspect of drug or alcohol abuse*

• *Lack of interest in formerly enjoyed activities; sudden change in school performance; lack of energy or desire to be with others*

• *Frequent requests for money; stealing, lying*

• *Smells of drugs such as alcohol, tobacco, or marijuana in your child's room or on his person*

• *Drug paraphernalia such as pipes, cigarette papers, eyedroppers, and so forth left in the child's room*

Many children will experiment on a limited basis with drugs and alcohol. Nevertheless, those who do are at risk for problems with addictions, accidents, and related injuries or death. This is a battle definitely worth fighting. No parent wants to see his child potentially injured or destroyed by drugs or alcohol. If you see or suspect drug and alcohol use, it is always best to discuss it openly with your child. Rather than mere confrontation ("I caught you red-handed"), you need to explore how deeply your child is into using these substances and whether or not more serious interventions are needed. Feel free to talk with your pediatrician for advice about these issues.

Useful Information and Resources:

National Council on Alcoholism
1511 K Street, N.W., Room #320
Washington D.C. 20005
(202)737-8122

Al-Anon Family Group Headquarters
P.O. Box 862, Midtown Station
New York, NY 10018
(800)254-4656

Ears

Ear Infections: Otitis Media, Earaches, and Middle Ear Infections

Ear infections are the bane of early years of childhood and parenthood, and one of the most common reasons a child is taken to see a pediatrician in the United States. Otitis media or middle ear infections occur when a bacteria or a virus infects the middle ear, right behind the baby's ear drum. Fluid containing inflammatory cells begins to collect in the middle ear space with the result being a bulging, red, inflamed eardrum and raging middle ear infection.

To make matters worse, the tube that connects the ear space to the mouth (the Eustachian tube) is quite floppy in a young child. The best analogy are the old paper straws we used to drink milk with when we were in kindergarten; remember how floppy and collapsed the paper straw would get when it became wet? A child's Eustachian tube is much like that (the technical term is patulence) and this makes the drainage of fluid from ear space to mouth difficult, leading to a build up of fluid behind the ear drum and a risk of ear infection.

Middle ear infections typically occur in children between six months and two years of age, but for those children who have a particularly difficult time with frequent ear infections, the age range can be much wider. The overwhelming majority of children (greater than 70 percent!) will experience at least one middle ear infection. Many children experience more than one ear infection. The overwhelming majority do quite well with either simple observation and pain relief, or—for those more serious ear infections—about ten days of antibiotic therapy. Some newer studies recommend only three days of antibiotic therapy to reduce the risk of penicillin resistance. Other recent studies suggest that up to 80 percent of all ear infections will clear up on their own without antibiotics. You should discuss these issues with your pediatrician in order to develop the best and safest treatment for your child. Remember, the infection should clear up in about two weeks but the fluid behind the ear drum can remain for up to twelve weeks. This puts the child at risk for repeated ear infections.

Some children with an ear infection, (less than 10 percent) may still have an ear infection after one course of antibiotics and may need a different medication.

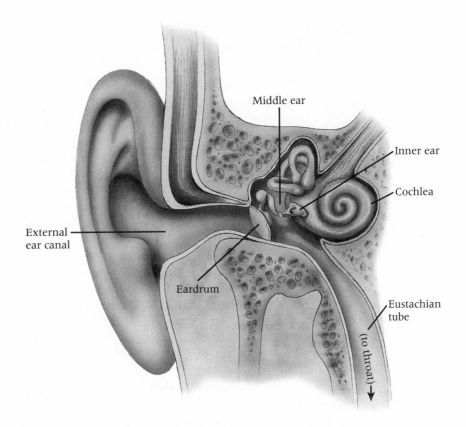

About 10 percent of all children with otitis media will experience a ruptured eardrum, with fluid dripping out of the ear. These cases also do quite well with antibiotics, and the eardrum does indeed, close back up with resolution of the infection. A smaller minority of children with frequent ear infections, scarring of the ear drums, and possible hearing loss may require placement of tubes in the eardrum to provide a semi-permanent drain for the build up of fluid behind the drum.

Ear infections can be a complication of colds and upper respiratory infections, but they are not contagious. It is especially difficult to diagnose ear infections in younger infants under the age of three months, because there is still some amniotic fluid behind the baby's eardrum.

Ear infections can be quite painful. While not a true emergency in the sense of life-threatening illnesses, they do warrant a call to your pediatrician, particularly if your child has ear pain in association with fever. Acetaminophen as a pain reliever should be of some help. Sleeping on several extra pillows in a more upright position may also help alleviate pain. The antibiotics do not really begin to resolve the infection for at least forty-eight to seventy-two hours. Your child should feel some resolution of the pain by this point. Call your doctor if pain, ear pulling, repeated irritable episodes or worsening symptoms develop.

Ear Piercing

Ear piercing is a relatively safe procedure. Many of our adolescent patients are expanding this concept with nose and body piercing. The decision for pierced ears may be based on cultural, social, or aesthetic reasons, and we prefer to leave this decision-making process to you and your child. There is no minimum age for ear piercing; in many cultures, baby girls have pierced ears. Instead it is important to remember that earrings are tiny and could be ingested by a small baby. You can prevent this risk of choking by thinking ahead and by *never* leaving earrings (or other small objects) near a baby's curious grasp *[see Choking]*.

We suggest that if you *do* decide to have your child's ears pierced, have it done by an experienced health-care professional who pays scrupulous attention to both the procedure itself and the cleanliness required. Pierced ear infections come in two major varieties: those caused by an unclean piercing itself, where bacteria got into the pierce hole and caused a skin infection; or those that occur after wearing an earring that irritates the pierced hole, breaks down skin, and then allows disease-causing bacteria into the area.

Preventing pierced ear infections
• Choose a health care professional to perform the piercing, someone who will employ the procedures of cleanliness required of all "surgical procedures"

• Purchase only stainless steel or 14 K gold posts. These metals are the most reliably safe. Avoid nickel and copper posts

• The first posts should be left in for six weeks after their placement. Once six weeks have passed, the skin lining the pierce hole has healed and the child may change earrings as often as she likes

• Apply posts loosely, especially in the early weeks when there may be some swelling

• Always keep the ears clean

• Always keep the earrings and posts clean. Wash with rubbing alcohol between uses and air dry

• Remove earrings and posts at night

Signs of an infected pierced ear
• Redness and pain at the pierce hole

• Rubbery lymph nodes in the neck region or behind the ear *[see Lymph Nodes]*

• Fever of 100° to 101°F

• Pus at the pierce hole

For mild infections (those without fever or pus)

1. Make sure your child removes the earring and cleans the post and earring with rubbing alcohol; soak them for about ten minutes and then rinse well with tap water. Do this three times per day.

2. Clean the ear lobes with rubbing alcohol.

3. Rub a triple antibiotic ointment (available at the pharmacy without a prescription) on the post of the earring and reinsert it. Remove the posts for washing (see #1) and reapply the ointment three times a day. Do this for two to three days.

For more serious infections

1. Consult your physician by phone if there is pus, fever, or both; or if there is no improvement after a few days of following the directions above.

2. If there is high fever (102°F or greater), complaints of a stiff neck, sensitivity to light, or unresponsiveness, you should contact your physician immediately.

Earwax

Every human being develops wax in their ears. It is a natural, albeit not terribly appealing, substance that helps protect the eardrum and the lining of the external ear canal. Its color and odor can be offensive, but it is quite normal. Interestingly, earwax works itself out of the ear on its own, aided by chewing movements, which is why we often notice ear wax at the opening of our own ears when cleaning them in the morning. Rarely, if ever, does ear wax build up enough to actually cause an obstruction in the ear canal. Earwax does not impair hearing! If you do notice a waxy build-up in your child's ears, it is best not to push small objects such as cotton swabs into the ear canal to "pick it out." This will only cause potential damage to the eardrum. We routinely advise never putting anything smaller than your elbow into an ear. In other words, a warm washcloth at the ear's opening, but not inside the ear canal, is usually sufficient. For those really waxy ears, consult your physician, especially before experimenting with water syringes and similar devices.

Foreign Body in the Ear

Children frequently stick things in their ears, ranging from tiny toys to pieces of candy. One of the most common "foreign objects" we find in children's ears are insects. Once the offending insect has made its way into a child's (or anyone's) ears, the sensation of the insect moving is felt as a tickling sensation in the ear and, potentially, dizziness. Neither you nor your child should panic. Once ascertaining that the object in the ear is a living one rather than inanimate, you can try placing the child in a dark room and shining a flashlight into the "bugged" ear. This may make the insect climb out. Placing several ear-droppersful of alcohol (rubbing alcohol, or even clear spirits such as gin or vodka) into the ear canal may paralyze the insect. Vigorous shaking of the head, for the energetic child, or careful suction of the involved ear with a plastic bulb syringe frequently helps. In the event that these techniques do not work or if the object is lodged in the ear canal (as is commonly the case with foreign objects that are not insects, such as pieces of candy, popcorn, toy parts, and many, many other things), you need to call your physician to have it removed. Do *not* attempt to insert tweezers or similar devices into the ear canal on your own. It is far more likely to cause harm than good and will probably push the object even deeper into the ear canal.

Swimmer's Ear (Otitis Externa)

A different type of ear infection from middle ear infection is the outer ear infection commonly called swimmer's ear because it is often associated with swimming. It is an infection of the sensitive lining of the external ear canal and results in an itchy and painful sensation in the canal. Other features of this annoying problem are a sense of the ear being "plugged up," pain when the child pushes on his ear, and a clear, watery discharge coming from the ear canal.

Swimmers who frequent swimming pools are more prone to swimmer's ear than those who favor fresh water or the ocean, primarily because of the effects of chlorine on the sensitive linings of the ear canal. But all swimmers are liable to this problem, largely because of the irritative effects of submerging one's ears in water for long periods of time.

There are a variety of treatments for swimmer's ear. The simplest one, recommended for uncomplicated cases, is white vinegar. Please note, this does not include balsamic, flavored, or other fancy vinegars, which are better suited for a salad. Using a small eye-dropper (one that measures 5 cc is fine), instill the white vinegar into your child's ear while he lies down on his side. The best way is to explain first what you are doing. Explain that the fluid will "tickle" his ear as it goes in, but it will not hurt. Emphasize that if he lies still, the process will be quite easy and painless. After the vinegar has been "dropped" in, plug the ear with a piece of cotton and let your child remain in his recumbent position for five minutes. After this period, have your child "jiggle" his head around in order to help the vinegar run out. Making a game of this can both make the job easier and enhance the speed with which the vinegar runs out of his ear! Repeat the process for the other ear. This should be done twice a day, and the problem should resolve within three days.

More complicated cases of swimmer's ear include those associated with a fever higher than 101°F, extreme pain, swelling, inflammation or redness of the outer ear, and swollen lymph nodes behind the ear. If your child is suffering from any combination of these symptoms associated with swimmer's ear, he needs to be examined by a physician.

Prevention tips

A child who swims needs to take care of her ears! This means that once she gets out of the water, she reaches directly for a towel and dries out her ears with it. Younger children who swim need the assistance of their parents. Jiggling one's head around from side to side also helps to get water out of a child's ear safely. As noted above, this can be made into a game with smaller children; ten-year-olds may regard you as an alien from Neptune if you try to engage them in this maneuver. Another useful method is to use a hair dryer set at low and cool. With some simple blow drying, the water will be removed from the ear canal.

Incidentally, swimmer's ear is entirely different from another condition called swimmer's itch. This red, bumpy skin rash is caused by parasites called schistosomes. These parasites live in freshwater lakes and accidentally penetrate the skin of human swimmers. The rash lasts for one to two weeks. The best medicine is prevention. Avoid dirty bodies of fresh water or areas where schistosomes are known to dwell. Always thoroughly dry your child off with a towel after swimming in a lake.

EATING: RULES OF BEHAVIOR AT MEALTIME [see also Choking]

Mealtimes should, of course, be fun for the family and a chance for everyone to catch up on the day's events. It is important, however, to set some specific rules during meals to make them safe as well. Here are a few of our favorite tips:

1. You need to teach your child to chew slowly and well before swallowing. Typically, an infant or toddler "bites off more than he can chew"—no doubt where that expression came from!

2. Do not rush meals. This will not only protect your child from choking, it will also make your family's life more pleasant.

3. Limit distractions or game playing, such as running about the table, throwing food into one's mouth, and television watching, during meals.

4. Teach your child to sit up at the table, rather than eat in a reclining position, and to sit still while eating.

5. It is never a good idea to let your child run about, talk, walk, or play with food, gum, or candy in her mouth.

6. Young children, especially, need to be supervised while they eat to protect them from choking. Do not let your infant or toddler eat unsupervised.

7. Children should not eat while you are driving the car. Although the idea is a tempting one because it insures some amount of quiet during the ride, you cannot pay attention to both the road and your child's eating. In the event of a choking episode, you may not have enough time to stop the car and help the child.

EATING UTENSILS

Cups, Spoons, and Forks: Things You can do to Help Your Child Learn How to Use Them

As the infant graduates from formula to solid foods (six to twelve months), parents begin to think hard about her learning how to manipulate a cup, spoon, or fork. Most one-year-olds begin to develop the fine-motor (or hand) control that allows them to take on such a task, but remember, it is a slow process with many a spill on the way. As the baby progresses to her second birthday, she will improve her finger-feeding skills gradually. Typically, most toddlers master the cup before the spoon, followed by the fork. The fine line between hovering as a parent and giving your child independence is probably never more clear than with the child learning how to feed herself. Here are some age-appropriate techniques you can use to help.

Preparing Your Infant to Grasp Eating Utensils

Encourage your year-old baby's grasping skills by offering her toys and baby-safe objects of varying size, shape, color, texture, and weight. Offer these objects to your baby from all positions: the front of the baby, the left, the right, far away from the baby, near the baby, above and below. These activities not only help the baby learn to grasp and hold onto objects, they also improve her visual sense of depth perception.

Learning How to Use a Cup

Make sure that the cup you give your child is heavy enough to be stable on a flat surface such as a table or the baby's high-chair tray. You also need to make sure that the cup is small enough for the baby to hold easily. Remember, if there is a possibility that the baby will spill a cup of milk, chances are good that she will! Spilling is always a problem when learning how to use a cup. As the baby's arm, hand, and lip control improves, you will be able to back off a bit and offer less help. Gauge your baby's progress before relaxing assistance with cup drinking. Special training cups with spill-proof tops are readily available from any department store and help avoid excessive spills. Another helpful product is the baby floor mat, a plastic sheet that fits under the baby's high-chair, making the floor far easier to clean after a feeding session. This mat is also helpful when instructing your infant how to use a spoon or fork! Inexpensive plastic shower curtains are a good alternative.

Learning How to Use a Spoon

As the baby's finger and hand control improves during the second year of life, she will be able to grasp a spoon and learn to manipulate it properly. Begin with a *broad*-handled spoon, which is easy for a one- to two-year-old to grip. As she grows, you may vary the size of the spoon handle gradually until she masters "regulation" tableware.

Early in the baby's "spooning" career, she is likely to scoop randomly or dip the spoon from side to side. This can cause quite a mess if you do not stabilize the baby's bowl or plate for her. A "skidless" place mat is also helpful at this phase of your infant's eating development, since it, too, helps keep the dish or bowl stable while she spoons her food.

As the baby grows, she will gradually learn to steady her dish with her other hand. Make sure that you choose bowls or plates with deep, vertical sides; this allows the baby to trap the food against the side of the bowl with the spoon.

Spilling is bound to occur as the baby learns how to use a spoon, especially in the first few months. A common "spoon-spill" frequently occurs when the spoon is being lifted by the baby to her mouth. This happens because the baby has not yet mastered moving the spoon from the bowl through space, directly into the mouth. We adults don't think much of this action since we do it so well, but it actually takes quite a bit of hand, arm, mouth, and eye coordination as well as practical experience. To help avoid spills, make sure that the size of the spoon's bowl (the rounded part) is appropriate for the baby's mouth. The spoon's bowl must be deep enough to hold food and still shallow enough for her to manipulate her lips around it and swallow the food. By eighteen to twenty-four months of age, the baby will be better able to keep the spoon level and hit the right target—her mouth rather than the floor.

One excellent way to help your baby learn how to use a spoon is to serve foods that have a thick texture and adhere to the spoon (e.g., oatmeal, applesauce, and so on). As the baby improves in spooning skills with the thicker foods, you can experiment (slowly) with foods of thinner textures.

Learning How to Use a Fork

After the baby begins to get the hang of a spoon, you will want to begin introducing a fork to the ensemble. You will still need to cut up the solid foods she will eat with the fork, just as you would for the "finger-feeding" child. Make sure that the pieces are small enough to prevent choking *[see Choking]* but large enough to allow the baby to pick them up with a fork.

Early on, the baby will use the fork in much the same fashion as she uses a spoon—with a scooping movement. Patiently, demonstrate to the baby how a fork works (i.e., spearing the food). Use soft but solid foods such as cut-up boiled potatoes, cooked vegetables, and so on. Add a variety of textured foods as the baby's skills improve with the fork as well as the spoon.

ECZEMA (Atopic Dermatitis)

Eczema or atopic dermatitis is a common skin condition seen in about 5 percent of all children. It is frequently associated with allergies. Indeed, 50 to 80 percent of all children with eczema go on to develop allergic rhinitis or asthma *[see Asthma, Allergies]*. Eczema tends to run in families. The skin gradually improves as the child grows up, but such children often seem to have sensitive skin throughout life, especially after the use of a drying soap and during the winter months when artificial heat makes the skin especially dry *[see Xerosis (Dry-skin).]*

Atopic dermatitis begins with patches of dry skin that are extremely itchy. The child begins to rub and scratch at these areas until they become quite angry-looking and may even weep clear fluid. As the exzema continues, the affected skin may become thickened and dark in appearance. It is most commonly seen in the folds of the arm (especially at the inner aspect of the elbow) and behind the knees, although all areas may be affected.

The Keys to Treating Eczema

For children with eczema, it is essential to keep the skin as moist as possible. By preventing the skin from becoming dry, you prevent the skin from becoming itchy; and by preventing itches and scratches, the incidence of extensive rash, skin thickening, and other problems of long-term eczema are reduced. The prevention of dry, itchy skin also helps lower the occurrence of secondary skin infections that come in the wake of overzealous scratching.

Here are a few tips to help that process:

• Use alcohol-free skin lotions that keep the skin moist and prevent it from drying. Avoid lotions with added perfumes.

• For younger children who have difficulty in reducing their scratching, you may want to clip the finger- and toenails to prevent damage to the dry skin *[for further suggestions, see Chicken Pox]*.

• Wash clothes with a mild detergent, and instead of "dryer sheets" use one fourth cup of vinegar in the rinse cycle as a fabric softener.

• Make sure your child bathes daily with non-drying soaps and, if it helps, oatmeal-based bath products. Bathe less frequently (every other day) during the winter or when the skin is especially dry.

• Avoid itchy or coarse clothing such as rough woolens and polyesters.

• For inflamed and itchy skin, your pediatrician may suggest a steroid-containing ointment such as hydrocortisone. These lotions are fairly safe but need to be used under the guidance of a physician in order to prevent side effects from overuse.

ELECTRICAL INJURIES AND HOW TO PREVENT THEM

Although electrical injuries are not nearly as common as some of the other childhood injuries discussed in this book, they are potentially quite serious, even deadly, and best prevented before they have a chance to occur. Despite the common fear of being struck by lightning and incurring electrical shock, this is not the major source of this type of injury among children or adults. Usually there are about one hundred lightning-related deaths in the United States each year, with a third of the victims being children and adolescents.

Instead, the more common causes of electrical injuries include:

1. Touching an electric appliance while wet. Wet children (or adults) should never touch anything that may carry electric current.

2. Loose cords lying about the house that are bitten by a young toddler or infant. Severe mouth burns can occur when a child chomps down on an electric cord. You need to be especially careful about keeping these well out of reach of the curious baby.

3. Putting metal objects into an electric socket. An all-too-frequent accident occurs when a toddler or child inserts a seemingly harmless metal object into a socket. One of the authors (H.M.) of this book well remembers a personal shocking experience with a paper clip and an outlet in his first grade classroom. At the time—during a particularly boring story—it seemed like a perfectly good idea to see what might happen! Although the child usually escapes injury in this activity, serious electric shocks, cardiac arrest, and electrocution can occur. Ground all of the sockets in your house with special safety plugs that cannot be easily manipulated by children.

4. Older children, especially teenage boys, tend to be fascinated with electrical wires and poles. They appear fun to climb and play near, yet they can truly be deadly considering how much electric power is surging through these wires. Instruct your child never to play near electric utility apparatus, poles, or loose wires. They are potentially disastrous.

Some Safety Tips to Prevent Electrical Injuries

1. Make sure your local electric company has buried all transmission lines (or, at least, placed them well out of reach) to the house so that they are not a temptation to children playing outdoors.

2. Do not allow your children to play near or with high-tension electric wires, ever! Warn your child to never try to retrieve a toy, such as a kite, that has become tangled or caught in high tension electric wires. (This is a job for the local electric company—not a child *or* a parent!)

3. Place an outlet "blank" into all outlets that are not in use. This device prevents the transmission of electricity to a curious child placing a piece of metal into the outlet, just to see what happens.

4. Do not use long extension cords in a house with young children who might bite them and be injured.

5. Keep all electric cords in excellent repair. Frayed cords can potentially injure anyone who touches the noninsulated portion. They are also a fire hazard. Replace such cords immediately.

6. Keep all electric appliances out of the reach of toddlers and young children.

7. Keep all bathroom electric appliances unplugged when not in use, far away from the sink or bathtub, and out of the reach of children. All outlets in the bathroom, kitchen, and near sinks should be grounded with a special safety device available from your hardware store. Water and electricity *never* mix!

8. Do not let your child swim or go boating during rainstorms—especially if you see lightning.

9. Teach your child to take cover in a thunderstorm to avoid lightning injuries. A common scenario for a lightning accident involves a Little League team that continues to play during a summer electrical storm. Teach your child to come in out of the rain! The best place to be during an electrical storm is a car, because the rubber tires ground any lightning that hits it. Most houses are safe as well. Do not hide under a tree; lightning can strike a tree and cause it to topple over.

What to do if Your Child Experiences an Electrical Injury

If the electric shock in question is minor and no obvious damage has occurred, simple reassurance will suffice.

More serious electrical injuries can cause burns to the skin. Electrical shock can also cause twitching muscles, brain damage, heart problems, and affect other body organs.

Immediate concerns

1. Make sure you have removed your child from the area of electrical contact. If an active current is going or the child is in a body of water that is being accidentally electrified, you need to make sure *you* do not get electrocuted. Use a neutral, non-charge conducting instrument to help, such as a wooden hockey stick or a plastic sled.

2. Check to see if he is conscious and breathing normally.

3. Check the heart beat and pulse *[see CPR]*.

4. Is your child's skin cold and clammy? Is the heartbeat or pulse slow or weak? Has he fainted? Is he breathing abnormally? All of these problems are signs of shock. If one or more is present, make sure your child is warm and covered by a blanket and that his legs are elevated (place two or three pillows under his legs).

5. If the child is having trouble breathing or appears in shock, you need to call 911 (Emergency Services) immediately *[see CPR].*

ENCOPRESIS (Soiling)

Encopresis is defined as the regular soiling of a child's underwear with liquid or formed bowel movements. The child has encopresis only if he is at least four years old (past the age most children are successfully toilet-trained) and if there is no associated organic or physical disease present that might be causing the symptoms. This problem occurs in about 1 to 2 percent of all school-aged children, with boys affected more often than girls.

What Causes Encopresis?

A number of factors can lead to encopresis. A major cause is called chronic stool retention. For reasons of constipation, embarrassment, or difficulty in getting to the bathroom, these children hold back from evacuating their bowel movements. This creates a vicious cycle where the rectal wall becomes overstretched and the nerve fibers in the rectum become less sensitive to the sensation of being full and, hence, less sensitive to the need to have a bowel movement. The retained stools then become dry, hard, and painful to pass. The child experiencing this cycle of retention, constipation, and pain becomes quite anxious to avoid having a bowel movement. Liquid stool that has not yet formed then leaks around the harder, formed stool, and the result is soiling. In about 25 percent of these cases, there is an associated problem with bedwetting or enuresis *[see Bedwetting].*

If this problem is occurring with your child, a consultation with the pediatrician is indicated. At this visit, a full medical history will be taken and a complete physical examination will be performed in order to make sure that there are no other reasons for this problem.

Perhaps the most important part of this meeting will be to demystify the problem of encopresis—for both the parents and the child—by explaining what is occurring and how to correct it. This is not an issue of blame or the child behaving badly. It is a medical problem that needs to be addressed by both the parents and the child, working together over at least a six- to twelve-month period. Your doctor will discuss with you methods of cleaning out the retained (and hard) stools with prescribed (and supervised) use of laxatives. If enemas are indicated, the physician and the parent need to rehearse this plan with the child before instituting it. The pediatrician will also work out a maintenance plan that includes daily sitting on the toilet (generally after each meal is best), attention to the diet in terms of constipating or non-constipating foods *[see Constipation],* continued use of gentle laxatives (such as bran or barley-based products), if indicated, and, frequent follow-up with the pediatrician. Above all, be patient, be calm, and be reassuring. Do not force your child to have a bowel movement. It will do little good and may, in fact, cause more problems.

It is also vital to be as understanding as possible. This problem is extremely embarrassing to your child, and he risks being taunted in school and by play-mates. Work at improving his self-esteem and praise him for the success he does achieve while being treated *[see Constipation; Toilet Training]*.

ERYTHEMA INFECTIOUSUM *[See Fifth disease]*

ERYTHEMA TOXICUM *[See Newborn appearance]*

EYES

Emergency Eye Problems

Trauma

Damage to the eye can occur in a variety of ways. For children, traumatic injuries are the most common culprit. Indeed, over 160,000 school-aged children suffer from traumatic eye injuries of varying severity each year. Although "trauma" is the descriptive word used by physicians to describe these injuries, the variety of offending causes includes balls, sticks, fists, fingers, falls, glass, animal bites, and metallic foreign bodies.

The overriding concern with these types of injuries is, what damage did it do to the child's vision? One way of addressing this vital question is to find out ex-actly what type of object actually hit the eye. Scraping objects, such as a stick or a piece of glass—even if they are tiny—can be more dangerous to one's vision than, say, a football thrown at the eye. Consequently, it is important to ask your child immediately if he or she has noticed any problems in vision. Ask her to close one eye and then the other to ascertain any type of visual damage. This problem is especially vexing when it occurs in a child under the age of three, who may not be able to tell you in understandable terms that some damage to vision has occurred.

Eye trauma that requires a physician's attention

We suggest that, in the event of eye trauma, you consult your physician immedi-ately if your child complains about the following:

- Severe eye pain
- Visible lacerations or cuts either very close to the eye (such as the eyelid) or on the eyeball itself
- Bleeding either from the eye or around it
- Tearing from the injured eye that does not appear to stop within thirty minutes of the traumatic event
- Constant blinking

- An eyelid that is swollen shut or swelling shut
- Complaints of blurred vision, double vision, or blindness
- When the child covers her eyes and will not let anyone look at them
- Trauma caused by a sharp object or one that was propelled at high speeds, such as an object thrown by a lawnmower
- Unequal pupils (the black part of the eye)
- When the child is under three years of age and cannot communicate to you adequate information about the extent and the severity of the injury.

Minor eye trauma that can be treated at home

Many types of eye trauma can easily be treated at home, in the event that the more serious symptoms described above are not present. For example, one of the most common foreign bodies that get stuck in eyes are eyelashes. This can be quite painful, not to mention a source of great irritability in an infant or toddler. If you see such a lash in the eye, it can easily be removed using the sticky side of a sterile bandage (Band-Aid). This is most appropriate for the older child (over five years of age), since it is extremely difficult explaining to a toddler the need to hold perfectly still while his mother or father shoves a Band-Aid—or anything else—at his eye. If your child is uncomfortable with this, or if you are, try washing the eye out with cool water and reassessing the situation.

When foreign bodies, such as particles of dust, cinders, insects, and other annoying tiny objects, find their way into the eye, they too can be removed using the "bandage" technique or steady washing out the eye with cool water, plus a lot of reassurance. If the foreign body in question is a piece of glass or other sharp object, we do not recommend taking care of the problem at home to avoid serious damage and scratching of the eye's cornea.

Eye injuries, regardless of their severity, are often quite frightening for a young child. Perhaps one of the reasons for this is that the child is not allowed to use one of the primary coping mechanisms for pain or fear of pain: closing the eyes. Try to be as gentle as possible and avoid forceful gestures or yelling at the uncooperative child.

For superficial cuts to the skin around the eye, such as the bony orbit or eye socket that serves as a protective layer around the more fragile eyeball, you should wash the injury with soap and cool water followed by ten minutes or so of applied pressure in order to stop the bleeding and clean it up. For cuts that do not stop bleeding or appear rather deep, stitches or sutures may be necessary.

Finally, if you are unsuccessful at such removal attempts, the child still complains about vision problems, pain, constant tearing or blinking, you should contact your physician within two to three hours of the injury, as opposed to the next day. It is possible that the "dust" particle is still in the eye; at worst, a scratch to the cornea—the clear covering of the eyeball—may have occurred. By the way, foreign bodies (like contact lenses) cannot get caught *behind* the eyeball; a layer of tissue behind the eye prevents such an occurrence.

The proverbial "black eye"

This well-known and frequent injury of childhood comes from a direct blow to the skin and underlying tissue surrounding the eye. It is essentially a bruise and may frequently be accompanied by a small area of bleeding on the white part of the eyeball (subconjunctival hemorrhage), far more frightening in appearance than dangerous to your child's vision. The black eye typically appears slowly over the first day or so after the injury, and the resultant "shiner" lasts upward of two weeks. Acetaminophen and ice packs are reasonable ways of reducing the pain of such injuries. Save your prime aged beefsteaks, on the other hand, for the dinner table.

The chemical eye injury

Almost as frequent as the traumatic eye injury caused by a foreign body is the event where a chemical may splash into one's eyes. If the chemical in question is an acid (household cleansers often contain acid) or an alkali (such as the products used to unclog drains), you need to act quickly to avoid a serious burn and scarring of the cornea of the eye. The best way to do this is to wash the eyes with cool, continuously running water for at least ten to twenty minutes. The least cumbersome way to do this is to place the child under the shower and have him look up at the water source, making sure water is actually getting into the eye. Other methods include dripping water into the eye with an eyedropper or straw or squeezing a water-soaked wash cloth over the eye. You should then take your child to the nearest emergency room for a more complete evaluation.

Chemical products that contain alcohol or hydrocarbons are not as dangerous in terms of chemical burns and can be easily treated with water, but to be safe you should call the local Poison Control Center or your physician with information about the specific chemical to ensure that it does not contain more dangerous substances. Remember, a great many household products that you purchase can be quite damaging if they enter the eye, or worse still, are ingested by your child. These include floor wax, wax remover, makeup, nail polish, nail polish remover, furniture polishes, dishwashing detergents, laundry and soap products, and drain cleaners—to name but a few. All of these products need to be kept safely out of the reach of the curious hands of a toddler or child *[see Poisoning: Prevention and Treatment]*.

Prevention of eye injuries

Prevention should be the hallmark lesson of this discussion. Specifically, do not allow your child to play with projectile-like toys such as BB guns, bows and arrows (regardless if the tips are real or made of foam rubber), and similar "toys." They are dangerous and all but guaranteed to cause damage. Be careful when mowing your lawn—not only to avoid hurting any bystander with the lawnmower itself but, more commonly, because of the danger that the mower will pick up an object inadvertently left on the lawn, only to shoot it out at high velocity. Wear goggles or protective eyewear when engaging any type of power tool or machinery, and keep *all* dangerous chemicals out of the reach of children.

Allergic Reactions of the Eye

Allergies to specific substances or irritants can make your child's eye red, watery, and itchy. The important distinction between an allergic reaction and an infection of the eye, however, is that in an allergic reaction, the eyes should not be painful nor should there be any pus in the eye area *[see Conjunctivitis (Pinkeye)]*. Your child may experience crusting over the eyes when he awakens in the morning. Some allergic conditions irritate both the eyes and the nasal passages. Other allergies, such as those to pollen, pet dander, feathers, and eye makeup can cause these symptoms as well. The best way to distinguish those allergies due to pollen from other allergies is the seasonality of the symptoms. If your child develops allergic symptoms of the eye during the same season, year in and year out, pollen is the most likely culprit. These "pollen seasons" can last up to six weeks, and the symptoms typically disappear as the season changes. If, on the other hand, the symptoms only occur after playing with a cat or exposure to some of the above-mentioned allergens, their removal from your child's environment should work wonders *[see Allergies]*.

How should I treat my child's eye allergies?

Other than removing allergens from the house and avoiding areas with pollen-rich air, there are a few treatments that, while they do not cure the allergy, can provide some relief. For example, after he has been playing outside during a pollen season, you should carefully wash your child's eyes with cool water and a washcloth. You need to pay special attention to the eyelids, where pollen likes to hide. A long shower with vigorous shampooing—hair is another favorite haven for pollen—is also a good idea after outdoor play.

Some medications may provide temporary relief. Eye drops that contain vasoconstrictors can diminish symptoms of itchiness, dryness, and redness.

Eyeglasses and Contact Lenses

It is difficult to assess the vision of an infant or toddler, although obvious deficits, such as an inward or outward turning of the eye (esotropia or exotropia) need to be corrected as soon as possible to avoid further damage to the child's vision *[see below, Cross-eyes]*. Similarly, if the infant does not appear to respond to visual cues (such as a parent's face), following brightly colored objects, and so on, this needs to be reported to the physician in order to assess the situation and, if necessary, treat it.

The need for eyeglasses depends largely on the actual shape of the child's eyeballs and his ability to see things either from afar or up close. Detecting visual problems and the need for glasses becomes easier as the child becomes older and either tells you she can't see well or performs poorly on visual screening exams given either at school or your doctor's office. Most frequently these issues present themselves as complaints ("I can't see the blackboard in school very well") or the child who sits extremely close to the television set in order to see more clearly. All children over the age of three should have a vision test every year.

Contact lenses are a popular alternative to glasses, especially for those who are self-conscious about their appearance. Because these require a great deal of responsibility and care, they are best prescribed for the child ten years or older who has demonstrated both the desire and the ability to handle them.

It is important to remember that contact lenses cover the eye and prevent the entry of oxygen to the eyes (although gas-permeable lenses do exist). Consequently, they are not to be worn twenty-four hours a day, and the child needs a backup pair of glasses to wear at night or when giving her eyes a rest.

Contact lenses can also be a problem for the child with conjunctivitis or who develops a problem because of a foreign-body or chemical injury to the eye. In these cases, the contacts should be placed in their protective case and glasses worn until the problem resolves itself fully, to prevent further injury.

When should I first begin having my child examined by an eye doctor?

By the time the child enters school, he or she should have had several vision screens at the pediatrician's. A formal vision examination by an optometrist (a health-care professional who specializes in assessing and correcting vision problems) or ophthalmologist (a physician and surgeon who specializes in eye diseases) should be instituted on an every-other-year basis beginning at the age of five years, unless your child complains of a vision problem or you or the child's teacher notices problems [see Sunshine, Sunscreen, Sunburn, and Sunglasses].

Eyelid, Swelling

Mild swelling of the eyelids can be expected in all of the eye problems described in this section. Another common cause of eyelid swelling is an insect bite, such as a mosquito bite. The hallmark of eyelid swelling related to an insect bite, as opposed to more serious cause, is that the lid is flesh or pink-colored but not an angry red.

Other problems that can cause severe eyelid swelling include:

1. Infections of the sinuses *[see Sinusitis].*
2. Serious infections of the eye itself or the surrounding skin and soft tissues.

These severe infections, called periorbital cellulitis and orbital cellulitis, include the following symptoms:

- Severe eye pain
- High fever (greater than 104°F)
- An inability to move the eye(s) from side to side or up and down
- Extreme sensitivity to light

• Severe swelling of the lid, eye, and areas around the eye; may be associated with a bluish or reddish bruise. These situations require medical attention, particularly if your child appears to be generally ill.

"Bags" or Dark Circles under the Eyes

Although many people commonly associate bags under the eyes with a lack of sleep, in children they are more often associated with nasal congestion and allergies involving the nose. For this reason, pediatricians often refer to these as "allergic shiners." Other conditions that cause "bags" include chronic sinus infections, frequent upper respiratory tract infections, and swelling of the tonsils and adenoids *[see Nasal Congestion]*.

Cross-eyes and "Lazy Eyes" (Strabismus and Amblyopia)

The appearance of cross-eyes, or eyes that appear misaligned, in an infant or child needs to be carefully examined and, if necessary, treated. Sometimes the shape of a baby's face can give the impression of misaligned eyes, but after a careful examination, this is found not to be the case. For example, babies who have broad folds of skin on either side of the nose, or a broad bridge of the nose, often give the appearance of being cross-eyed; this "optical illusion" has no effect on the child's vision or, as he grows out of a more infantile facial pattern, his looks! Newborn babies are especially difficult to examine for this problem; many infants have poor neuromuscular control, and frequently their eyes appear misaligned. By the ages of three to nine months, these examinations become easier to interpret.

In those families where there is a history of *strabismus*—the actual turning in of the eyes—a more detailed eye examination by an ophthalmologist is mandatory. In many cases, these conditions are not recognizable until six months of age. Some forms of strabismus involve the shortening or lengthening of the muscles that control and coordinate the eyes and may require surgical intervention.

Each time you bring your baby to the pediatrician, however, the doctor will be looking carefully at the baby's eyes to detect or rule out a number of birth defects and problems that can be associated with the turning in or out of the eyes. The earlier the diagnosis of these problems the better.

For the long-term problem of *amblyopia*, a loss of vision caused by disuse of one eye and the dominant use of the other, patching of the good eye typically arrests the process and restores good eye alignment. Amblyopia may not be detected until the child begins school and undergoes his first eye examination. The child who squints all the time may have amblyopia.

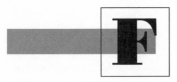

Falls: PREVENTION AND TREATMENT

First things first: all children (and many adults) fall down. It seems to be a prerequisite for learning how to walk and more complicated maneuvers. This is not surprising, given the toddler's and young child's unrealistic understanding of danger, distance, and their own physical capabilities. Add to this the child's motivation to always want to be somewhere she is not, and one can understand the importance of careful planning and prevention. Falling is always a risk better prevented than treated.

Falls perennially lead the list among nonfatal childhood injuries. Although they can occur at almost any age, falling injuries among children tend to hit their peak at the age of one year. Given that this is the age most toddlers are beginning to learn to walk, such a peak makes sense. The next highest group of falling children, unsurprisingly, are those aged one to three years. Falls down stairs make up a significant portion of these injuries, as do falls related to the use of walker-type products *[see Walkers]*.

Clearly, the injuries related to falling are a matter of the force of the child falling down on a hard object. The higher the distance, the greater the velocity and force with which the falling body crashes to earth. For example, a child falling from a second-story window onto the pavement hits the ground with a resounding force capable of causing serious damage, including broken bones or worse. On the other hand, the toddler falling from a standing position onto a carpeted surface is likely to be scared or upset, but not as likely to injure herself. Carpeted or padded surfaces, often referred to by injury prevention specialists as "forgiving" surfaces, are the preferred places for children to fall!

Preventing Falling Injuries among Toddlers
(Child-proofing the home)

One of the most difficult accident-related issue for new parents (and new pediatricians, for that matter) is that all children fall—a lot! Most of these falls are relatively harmless, so you do not want to further scare your child by overreacting. Young children sense this quite easily, and when their parents display fear or a sense of upset, are likely to follow suit. Relax, check out the situation, make sure no serious damage was done, and (provided all these "checks" clear), reassure your child with a hug and loving words.

Perhaps more importantly, you must "child-proof" the house in order to keep potentially dangerous situations from occurring at all. Here are a few tips:

Windows: Do not leave open windows (especially on second floors or higher) that are not protected with screens or storm windows. Children, once they can climb out of a crib or playpen, can put these same skills to more dangerous use, such as climbing out of a window, often to disastrous results. Window latches, locks, and guards are readily available from your local hardware store and easy to install. These are well worth the money and should be installed in every home where a child spends time.

Staircases: If you live in a home that has a staircase, you need to supervise your child (especially younger children) as they negotiate these stairs. Young toddlers who have only recently learned to walk are probably not coordinated enough to master stairs and may still have to be carried or helped down. Another useful aid are specially made barricades for staircases that cannot be overcome by a two- or three-year-old. One must be careful in purchasing a "child-safe" stair barricade (one without large gaps in the device through which a toddler can stick his head and become stuck). Do not allow these barricades to replace good old-fashioned supervision of your child's play. Small children often learn how to push through or overcome these barricades. You need to keep an eye on mobile babies and toddlers when it comes to staircases.

Playgrounds or the backyard: Ladders, monkey bars, jungle gyms, and similar objects are fascinating and fun for children of all ages. Children under the age of four or five should always be supervised during play to prevent falls and other types of accidental injuries. As the child grows and displays evidence of understanding playground rules, you can begin to back off a bit. As a parent, you will need to find a happy medium between careful supervision and too strict or imposing a safety program. This is not such an easy task for most parents, but rest assured that with experience you will become the most reliable judge of your child's skills and almost every other aspect of his health and well-being. Remember that as the parent you are the one with the years of maturity and experience. Therefore, you must be willing to supervise your child's play—don't leave this task to a slightly older sibling.

Climbing is fun, but it carries some risks. Watch your toddler carefully as she negotiates these playground toys and make sure she is truly able to handle them. Give assistance where needed (and accepted). As the child progresses, allow her more and more independence while still being available for potential accidents. Do not let your child play at obviously unsafe climbing activities, such as a scaffolding, a ladder, or other items not intended for a child's play. It is also a good idea to use those playground toys—whether they are in your own backyard or at a nearby park or school, that have a cushioned and "forgiving" surface at the bottom, such as wood chips or, better still, grass as opposed to concrete.

The bedroom: Despite the fond memories of old Hollywood movies or television situation comedies, leave those charming bunk beds in the furniture store. Young children, who often argue who gets to sleep in the exciting top bunk, frequently fall from these perches. Children under six are especially prone to this type of accident. Children under the age of two or three should sleep in a crib *[see Cribs].* Make sure that all of the nursery furniture is baby-safe. Babies should not sleep in bed with adults *[see SIDS; Sleeping].* You should *never* leave your baby unattended at a changing table or other perch. They can and will roll over, wiggle off, and (potentially) serious hurt themselves if they fall. Cribs, especially, need to be checked over each night to make sure that the side railing is firmly fastened and cannot come down. Once the child has learned to master getting in and out of the crib himself, little can be done to unlearn such a potentially dangerous lesson. It's time to think of purchasing a safe bed, preferably with a removable side rail that stays in place as he gets adjusted to the bed *[see Sleep].*

Cellars and outbuildings: Doors to the basement, sheds, outbuildings, or other underground and outdoor locations should be locked (or latched) in order to prevent the young, exploring child from reaching out, opening the door, and accidentally tumbling down.

If your child does fall

1. Make sure he is safe, breathing normally, and conscious.

2. Assess the wounds, if any. Is there any bleeding? Any signs of serious damage?

3. Is the child complaining of difficulty moving a limb? Are the limbs in any way deformed or severely bruised?

In the event of serious falls, you need to call to your physician or the emergency services (911) or treatment.

In the event of minor falls with minimal cuts and bruises, simple first aid should suffice.

FEEDING YOUR BABY: A DEVELOPMENTAL APPROACH

Infants and babies, of course, need help feeding. This is most obvious when they are newborns. As you watch your baby grow, he will develop all sorts of new skills and abilities. It really is quite exciting to watch how the baby develops. One important thing to remember, however, is that babies can only progress to the next stage of development when they are physically, mentally, and socially ready. Be patient; not all children learn skills such as self-feeding as quickly as others. See the table on pages 158–161 that charts what the baby, from birth to eighteen months or older, can do in terms of physical, cognitive, communications, and social abilities. Listed alongside these milestones are tips you can use to help your infant and child with feeding issues.

Fever: measuring the temperature and fever-reducing medicines

A child's temperature normally fluctuates between 98.6 and 99.5°F during the course of the day. It is usually lowest in the early morning, rises to its peak in late afternoon, and increases predictably in response to exercise, excitement, eating, and environmental conditions. This is entirely normal. In some children the body temperature may fluctuate by as much as 2.0° in the course of a typical day. The average normal body temperature is 98.6°F or 37°C.

The body's temperature control center, much like a thermostat, is located in an area of the brain known as the hypothalamus and is regulated by a variety of substances carried to it by the blood. In response to infection, the white cells of the body produce a substance termed interleukin-1, which can reset the body's thermostat to a higher level, resulting in fever.

Fever is just one sign of illness and not a very important sign. Fever is one way by which the body fights infection; in animals it has been shown that blocking the fever response increases the mortality rate from infections. Fever is a friend. Fever should only be treated when it is extreme and produces discomfort, such as chills, headache, or muscle aches, in your child.

Remember, fever is a symptom, not a disease. It is the body's normal response to infection. The usual fevers, often up to 104° are not harmful. Most are caused by viral infections, others by bacterial infections. Rarer causes of infection include fungal and parasitic agents. The height of the fever is *not* related to the seriousness of illness. Just because a child has a fever of 104°, this does not mean that it is going to climb higher to, say, 106°. Brain injury from fever does not occur until the temperature exceeds 106.5°—an extremely rare event.

Approximately 4 to 6 percent of children may experience a "febrile convulsion" during a fever. These seizures, which usually last for two to ten minutes, are frightening to observe but rarely result in permanent injury to the child. Although most parents believe that fever-related seizures occur with temperatures above 104° F, this is not typically the case. Febrile seizures commonly occur during the first twenty-four hours of an illness, often before the parents know that their child has a fever or is even ill. It is generally believed that febrile seizures

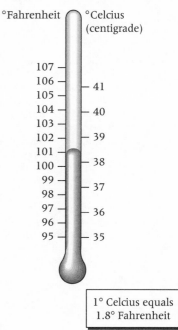

°Fahrenheit / °Celcius (centigrade)

107
106 — 41
105
104 — 40
103
102 — 39
101
100 — 38
99 — 37
98
97 — 36
96
95 — 35

1° Celcius equals
1.8° Fahrenheit

(continued on page 162)

157

FEEDING YOUR BABY: A Developmental Approach

Age of the Infant	Physical Abilities	Cognitive and Social Abilities
Newborn– nursing baby (0–3 months)	Poor control of the head, neck, and trunk. Most of the baby's movements are random and reflexive. For example, the baby randomly moves arms and legs; the child reflexively "mouths" small objects and hands. These features reflect the newborn's poor neuromuscular coordination.	Baby responds to internal (such as hunger) and external (e.g., noise) stimuli. The baby communicates emotions, needs, and thoughts by means of cooing sounds and crying. The baby begins to learn about textures, flavors, and shapes of food (and other objects) by reflexively "mouthing" them.
Older infant (3–6 months)	At this point the baby should have "doubled" the birth weight. Explores world through the mouth. The baby begins to develop better stability in terms of head, trunk, and extremity control; when placed on the stomach, the baby lifts head and supports weight with straight elbows. Newborn reflexes diminish. Baby learns to "bat" objects with fisted hands.	The baby begins to settle into a "schedule" in regard to sleeping habits. Baby responds to social interactions with spontaneous smiles and body movements. The baby believes that objects he/she cannot see do not exist; hence, the fascination with "peek-a-boo."
6–9 months	Baby is now able to sit up, without support. This postural control, as well as improved muscle control and swallowing ability, is the reason why 6-month old babies do far better with the introduction of solid foods than their younger counterparts. Improved independent movement, such as rolling from back to front and "creeping" (pulling oneself, while on the floor, using the arms). Improved fine-motor or "hand" skills, such as raking a small object towards oneself into a fisted hand and transferring objects from one hand to the other. Teeth begin to develop at 6 months of age, at a rate of 1 per month.	The baby begins to learn about the concept of "object permanence," i.e., the realization that an object still exists even if you don't look at it or close your eyes. This allows an easier time of feeding with a spoon because the infant realizes that a "loaded spoon" is out there even when not looking directly at it. The baby begins to use specific sounds and gestures to communicate desires or needs.

Feeding Skills	Communication	What the Parent can do to Help with Feeding	Food Choice
The newborn roots in search of a nipple (a reflexive reaction). The newborn can only suck and swallow liquids. They simply don't have the coordination of their nervous, muscle and digestive systems to eat solids. The newborn can hold liquids in the mouth with the help of "fat pad" in the cheeks.	The newborn cries and sucks intensely when hungry. The satisfied baby will release the nipple or fall asleep while feeding. Newborn infants are able to regulate their food intake to meet their caloric needs by the age of 6 weeks.	Learn to read (and respond) to the baby's hunger cues as well as their satiety (fullness) cues to prevent under or over feeding.	Breast milk is the best nutrient source for all newborn babies. Alternative formulas include: cow's milk formulas, soy milk formulas.
The baby uses the tongue, in a coordinated manner, to push food to the back of the mouth in order to effectively swallow without gagging. Although some like to "push" solids onto infants at this age, all the necessary nutrients to grow and develop normally can be found in breast milk (or infant formula). Stay the course!	The baby becomes more sophisticated in expressing wants such as hunger, wet diapers, happiness, etc.	Pay close attention to the baby's "eating-readiness" cues. Make your feeding approach flexible enough to correspond to the baby's eating style and rhythms.	Breast milk is the best food source for a growing infant. Alternative formulas include: cow's milk formulas, soy milk formulas. Try to hold off introduction of solid foods until 6 months.
Begin your feeding of solids, one at a time, introducing a new food once a week. This makes it easier to resolve a potential food allergy. Begin with cereal solids (e.g., rice, barley, etc.) mixed with formula. Introduce "sweet" or dessert foods last. This prevents early favoritism of sweets over vegetables, etc. The baby will begin to be able to drink from a lidded cup, if assisted. The baby will "experiment" with the different textures and thicknesses of the introduced foods and learn to swallow without gagging.	Baby grabs spoons and similar utensils; infants frequently bang these utensils against the table almost as if to say "I want to eat!" If still hungry, the baby looks for more food when parents remove the feeding dish.	Remember: learning about new foods and how to eat them takes time. Have a patient, relaxed attitude and have fun! A spare towel to cleanup potential messes is also a good idea. If the baby doesn't seem to like a particular food offer it at other meal times—this frequently improves acceptance. Try to build on the prior "food experience" your infant has gained; it is often easier to introduce a new food when it is served with a helping of another "favorite" food.	Breast milk (or infant formula) remains the best source of infant nutrition. Begin with thickened cereals and purees.

FEEDING YOUR BABY: A Developmental Approach *(continued)*

Age of the Infant	Physical Abilities	Cognitive and Social Abilities
9–12 months	Infant has stable posture and body control. Infant can reach out for a toy without losing balance. Infant's mobility improves; infant can crawl well and pull self to a stand. Infant shows improvement in hand (fine motor) control; uses thumb and finger to pick up small objects.	Infant begins to learn the cause and effect of specific events e.g., how things "work." Infants begins "problem solving." The baby shows assertiveness by reaching for objects that were taken away. The baby participates in basic interactive communication; begins to connect words with gestures.
13–24 months	The baby should weigh 3 times the birth weight. Good mobility; the baby begins to walk with assistance; baby can stand alone. Baby exhibits efficient hand skills; uses finger-tips to pick up small objects; reaches out with palms to receive an object from someone else.	Infant begins to learn self-control. Responds to simple commands and limits imposed by a parent's voice or gesture. Infant uses a variety of gestures and some words in order to express wants or to label things. Infant imitates behaviors of others.
Toddler (18 months or older)	The toddler has learned to master physical milestones; walks and plays with confidence. The toddler masters fine-motor or hand-control skills, including a number of different hand grasp patterns; manipulation of objects within one hand; toddler shows clear preference for right or left hand.	Toddler exhibits intentional planning and exploration. Toddler begins to balance the desire for independence with need for reasonable parental limits. Toddler communicates with words, phrases, and gestures to express wants. Shows assertiveness by saying "No" to a request and then doing something else.

Adapted from L.A. Barness (ed.) Pediatric Nutrition Handbook-American Academy of Pediatrics Handbook. Committee on Nutrition. (3rd ed), Amer. Acad. of Ped.: Elk Grove Village, IL, 1993; Dietary Guidelines for Infants, Fremont, MI: Gerber Products Co. Medical Services Dept., 1994.

Feeding Skills	Communication	What the Parent can do to Help with Feeding	Food Choice
The infant learns to use the tongue in order to move food to the side of the mouth for mashing. Infant holds lidded cup while drinking without help. Infant begins to show interest in self-feeding by reaching out for utensils to either "mouth" or play with.	The infant vocalizes, points, and touches parent's hand during meals in order to control what and how much is being fed.	When introducing a new food or a different textured food, remember to introduce it with an already established favorite food. Parents should continue spoon-feeding as the baby's finger-feeding skills develop and improve; this helps make sure that the baby is still getting adequate nutrition while developing self-feeding skills.	Breast milk and formula remain the key-stone to infant nutrition during the first year of life. Add textured foods that encourage chewing.
Infant keeps lips closed and most of the food in mouth when chewing. The infant can use the upper and lower teeth to bite through many different textured foods. Can easily feed self with fingers. Learns to spear foods with a fork and scoop with a spoon. Infant drinks from a cup and desires to stop using bottle.	Will mimic parents' mealtime behaviors. Uses words or sounds to articulate the desire for specific foods.	The parent needs to balance the child's need for independence and the need for a varied, healthy diet; offer a wide variety of foods at regularly scheduled meals. The child at this age is in a critical period for acceptance of new foods and the development of healthy eating habits. Take advantage of this developmental phase!	Whole cow's milk (in the form of skim or 2% milk) may be introduced as the child begins to consume a variety of solid foods.
Toddler effectively uses lips, tongue, and teeth to draw food and liquid into the mouth for efficient feeding. Uses one hand to adjust spoon into more efficient position when scooping a variety of textures and consistencies. Can bring spoon to the mouth with minimal spilling.	Toddler expresses mealtime desires with simple phrases such as "Want that!" "All done," "More milk," etc. Toddler will lead parent to the refrigerator or pantry and point out a desired food or drink. Toddler develops definite food preferences.	Many toddlers develop erratic eating behaviors. As long as the child is growing normally, he or she is consuming enough calories. One approach to sporadic eaters is leaving a plate of non-perishable finger-foods (e.g., raw vegetables, fruits, etc.) available for the toddler-on-the-go to grab as desired. Some toddlers develop finicky eating patters. Be patient and creative. Provide healthy foods at regularly scheduled meals and allow the child to make independent eating choices, both in terms of how much and which foods will be eaten. Remember, that children lay down life-long eating patterns early during their lives. Offer a healthy and nutritious diet!	The widest variety of foods with interesting textures and flavors within the confines of a nutritious diet that includes the four major food groups and essential minerals and vitamins.

are more closely related to the rate of rise in temperature than to the height of the temperature. Early in an illness the temperature is most likely to increase abruptly, making it difficult to prevent the febrile seizure *[see Seizures with Fever]*.

When to be Concerned; When to Call the Doctor

If the height of the temperature should not be a reason for concern, then what should you look for? Dr. Barton Schmitt provides the following guidelines in an article that appeared in *Contemporary Pediatrics*. We have made slight modifications.

Call your pediatrician when you note fever in your child if:

- Your child is less than two months old
- The fever is over 105°F
- Your child is crying and can't be consoled, or if your child is whimpering
- Your child is difficult to awaken
- Your child cries if you touch or move him
- Your child's neck is stiff
- Breathing is difficult and rapid (more than sixty respirations per minute in a child under one year of age; more than forty respirations per minute in a child over one year of age)
- Breathing is noisy, crowing, or barky
- Your child is unable to swallow anything and is drooling saliva
- Any purple spots are present on the skin
- Your child looks or acts very sick (child appears pale or dusky blue)
- Your child's pulse is weak and rapid (pulse rate greater than 160 beats per minute in a child less than one year of age; greater than 120 beats per minute in a child more than one year of age)
- Burning or pain accompanies urination
- Your child is having diarrhea with blood in the stool

This list may not be complete, but it covers about ninety percent of the situations where the presence of fever may signify the presence of an illness that may require medical attention for your child.

Measuring the Temperature

Body temperature can be accurately and inexpensively measured in a variety of ways. Precision to a tenth of a degree is not important. You shouldn't fret about getting the exact number—this is not the stock market.

Glass thermometers containing mercury are perfectly satisfactory but are slow and may be difficult to read. To improve your reading, find the probable spot where the mercury ends by rotating the thermometer slightly until the line appears.

Glass thermometers come in two forms: oral and rectal. The oral thermometer has a thin tip and is designed for taking temperatures in the mouth, while the rectal temperature has a broader, rounder tip and is designed to take temperatures in the rectum. The rectal thermometer can be used for taking oral temperatures, but naturally it should be cleaned carefully before use in the mouth. Both oral and rectal thermometers can be used to measure temperatures under the arm (axillary temperature). The majority of thermometers record in both degrees Fahrenheit (F) and degrees Celsius (C).

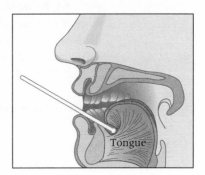

Rectal temperature

For children less than four to five years of age, rectal thermometers are probably the most accurate means of obtaining the temperature. Moreover, many young children will not hold an oral thermometer in their mouths for the required two or three minutes. In children over five years of age, oral temperatures are usually taken. Axillary temperatures can be used in patients of any age.

Tongue

Oral temperature

Before using a glass thermometer, make certain that the mercury line is below 98.6°F. Shaking the thermometer will bring the mercury column to the desired location. Always clean the thermometer with rubbing alcohol after every use.

When taking a rectal temperature, always lubricate the end of the thermometer with some form of petroleum jelly such as Vaseline. Lubricate the opening of the anus as well. Have your child lie on his stomach or place in infant in your lap and then carefully insert the tip of the thermometer into the

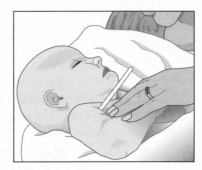

Axillary temperature

lubricated anus, with the mercury bulb about one inch beyond the opening of the anus. Never force it and never insert it more than two inches beyond the opening of the anus; it may break or get lost. Hold your child still, and press his buttocks together to hold the thermometer in place. Keep the thermometer in the rectum for just about two minutes in order to get a reasonably accurate reading.

To take an oral temperature, place the tip of the thermometer under the tongue and toward the back of the mouth. If possible, have your child hold the thermometer in place with his lips and fingers. Instruct your child to keep his mouth closed and breath through his nose for the three minutes or so it takes to record the temperature. Remember that if the child has had a cold or hot drink within a couple of minutes of taking the temperature, this will distort the accuracy of the measurement.

If you wish to take an axillary temperature, place the tip of the thermometer in your child's dry armpit. Hold your child's elbow against the chest to keep the thermometer in place for four to five minutes.

Ear (tympanic membrane) thermometers are becoming popular. They record temperatures within two to three seconds and are painless. They are still expensive and the information they provide is no better than that provided by the traditional and inexpensive mercury thermometer. Don't run out and buy one until the price comes way down.

Temperature strips and temperature-sensitive pacifiers have not proven to be sufficiently accurate. They are good ideas that require further development.

Treating the Fever

Temperatures below 101° Fahrenheit rarely require medicine to lower the fever. When your child has a mild fever, provide her with extra fluids and dress her in light clothing. When the temperature goes beyond 102° Fahrenheit and is associated with discomfort and irritability, treatment can be justified.

Treatment should be with acetaminophen *[see Acetaminophen Dosage Chart]*. Children two months of age or older can be given an acetaminophen-containing product to reduce fever. Tylenol®, Anacin-3®, Liquiprin®, Panadol®, Tempra® and similar acetaminophen products can be used as described in the acetaminophen dosage chart. They are the same product with different brand names. When used in the appropriate dose, they can bring the temperature down by two to three degrees in two to three hours. Their effects generally last for four to six hours; giving the drug more often than every four hours is unnecessary and can even be dangerous.

The response to acetaminophen provides no clue to the nature of the fever. Fever from either bacterial or viral infections may or may not respond to acetaminophen. Serious or trivial, an illness may or may not respond to acetaminophen.

Age	Weight	Total Amount	Infant Drops (1 dropperful = 0.8 ml = 80 mg)	Elixer or Syrup (1 tsp (5cc) = 160 mg)	Adult Tablets (1 tablet = 325 mg)
FEVER AND PAIN RELIEVERS: Acetaminophen Dosage Chart					
3 months	9–11 lbs	40 mg	1/2 dropperful (0.4 ml.)		
4–11 months	12–17 lbs	80 mg	1 dropperful (0.8 ml.)		
12–23 months	18–23 lbs	120 mg	1.25 droppersful (1.2 cc)	11/2 tablets	
2–3 years		160 mg	2 droppersful	2 tablets	
4–5 years		240 mg	3 droppersful	3 tablets	1 tablet
6–8 years		325 mg		4 tablets	1–11/2 tablets
8–10 years		485 mg		5–6 tablets	2 tablets

Administer acetaminphen every 4–6 hours.

Another medicine that is soon to be available over the counter for fever reduction is ibuprofen (e.g., Advil®, Motrin®, and similar ibuprofen-containing products). This medicine is generally used as a second choice for fever reduction (in the event that acetaminophen is not working), for fevers greater than 102.6°, and only for children over the age of six months. It is given every six to eight hours. In the overwhelming majority of cases, however, acetaminophen works just fine *[see Ibuprofen Dosage Chart]*.

If your infant smiles, plays, and drinks adequate fluids, don't worry about her fever. Never wake a child to give her fever medication. Sleep is more important and more effective in treating an illness than any benefit that can be derived from fever reduction.

Do not treat a fever for more than three days without checking in with your doctor. If you wish to use other medications for temperature reduction, consult your physician first.

Remember, never bathe your child to bring down her temperature until you have given acetaminophen a chance to work for at least an hour. Bathing without first lowering the child's thermostat can make the child uncomfortable, producing shivering as the child generates heat in an attempt to get her temperature back to the setting on the internal thermostat. If you bathe the child, use luke-

FEVER AND PAIN RELIEVERS: Ibuprofen Dosage Chart

Age	Weight	For Fever over 102.6°F
6–11 months	13–17 lbs	1/2 tsp (50 mg)
12–23 months	18–23 lbs	1 tsp (100 mg)
2–3 years	24–35 lbs	1 1/2 tsp (150 mg)
4–5 years	36–47 lbs	2 tsp (200 mg)
6–8 years	48–59 lbs	2 1/2 tsp (250 mg)
9–10 years	60–71 lbs	3 tsp (300 mg)

Ibuprofen is suggested as a second choice for fever reduction in the event acetaminophen is not working. We recommend it only for children with fevers greater than 102.6°F who received little or no relief with the acetaminophen. It should be given every 6–8 hours. Ibuprofen is not recommened for children younger than 6 months.

warm water—avoid alcohol baths. Alcohol can be absorbed through the skin and produce alcohol intoxication.

Finally, never forget that fever is designed to help fight infection. It does not require treatment until it gets to be about 104°F unless the child is very unhappy. (Even doctors sometimes forget this fact).

FIFTH DISEASE (Slapped cheek syndrome; erythema infectiosum)

In the late nineteenth and early twentieth centuries, pediatricians used to number the contagious diseases associated with specific rashes. Measles was the first disease, scarlet fever was the second, rubella was the third, and a scarlet-feverlike illness named Fikatow-Duke disease became Fourth disease. Erythema infectiosum is—you guessed it—the fifth rash-related infectious disease of childhood. It is caused by an infectious microbe called parvovirus B19. It tends to be most common in the late winter and early spring months.

Fifth disease, or erythema infectiosum, is an extremely mild infection of childhood. Sometimes parents don't even know that their child is "sick." Its classic features are:

• Bright red splotches on the child's cheeks (it appears as if his cheeks were slapped and have become red). Generally, the rash develops seven to fourteen days after exposure to the virus.

• A lacy, pink rash on the chest, belly, and legs or arms.

Does Fifth Disease Require Medical Attention?

• In most cases, no. Generally, children with Fifth disease have no more symptoms than the slapped-cheek appearance. If they feel well and have no fever or other complaints, they can return to school and the rash should resolve in about a week.

• If the child also complains of a sore throat, headache, itchy skin, watery eyes or nose, muscle aches, or has a mild fever (100° to 102°F), treat the symptoms with warm drinks and other fluids, rest, and, if needed, pain relievers *[see Fever]*. Feel free to call your pediatrician if your child appears especially uncomfortable or you are concerned.

• Children with Fifth disease should not come in contact with pregnant women. Most adults have had parvovirus B19, but for those pregnant women in the first trimester who have not yet been infected, the virus may harm the developing fetus.

Fires, smoke inhalation, and burns: Prevention and treatment

Fires in the home cause about two thirds of all fire- and burn-related deaths each year in the United States. Typically, it is the inhalation of smoke—rather than actual burning—that causes these deaths. Fires are especially dangerous for infants and young children; they may not yet be able to run out of a burning house, or they may become panicky and not know what to do.

Common Causes

Matches
Despite the common belief that playing with matches is a common cause of these tragedies, national statistics show that only 2 percent of house fires are caused by children playing with matches.

Cigarettes, cigars, and pipes
Perhaps the most common cause of house fires is the burning cigar, pipe, or cigarette. The most common scenario is that the burning ash of a cigarette or a lit butt accidentally falls onto carpet, furniture, and similarly combustible objects. The burning ash then smolders away—unknown to anyone—leading to a potentially large fire several hours later. If you must smoke, do it safely and preferably out of the breathing space of children. Never smoke in bed, and pay careful attention to your ashes *[see Smoking]*.

Wood-burning stoves, electric space heaters, and fireplaces
Many fire-related injuries are caused by portable space heaters or wood-burning stoves. This is an especially important problem among poorer families living

without adequate heat during the winter months. They are dangerous, can easily explode, set fire to nearby objects, or (in the event of the burning stove devices) yield high levels of carbon monoxide in a closed room, resulting in inhalation injuries and death. If you use gasoline, kerosene, or other flammable fluids in the home, you need to keep them far out of a child's reach—both to avoid burns and to prevent carbon monoxide poisoning. Wood-burning stoves can irritate the air passages of children with asthma or allergies *[see Asthma].* These heat sources are also dangerous in their risk of causing contact burns if a child accidentally brushes against them. It is a good idea to purchase children's sleepwear that carries a flame-retardant label, to minimize potential burn injuries.

Hot water

Finally, a word about scalding—an important source of burn injuries in children. You need to be especially careful about your home's source of hot water. Hot water heaters can be adjusted to produce water no hotter than 120 to 130°F, which will not cause a scalding burn if a child accidentally comes in contact with it. Similarly, be careful about spilling hot things when young children are underfoot in the kitchen. Have you ever tried to sit down to a nice, hot cup of coffee while watching an active toddler? Hot beverages falling from counters onto a small child are a leading cause of scald burn; so are food spills, especially when the stove or oven is in use and hot liquids are simmering. Contact with these hot objects and foods can cause significant and serious burns.

Be careful near the summer "barbecue" grills; make sure that the hot coals are doused with water after use and that the grill is kept in a safe place away from children and free of fire hazards.

Prevention Techniques

1. Smoke cigarettes, cigars, and pipes away from your child. Be careful when disposing of the ashes. To insure non-impaired judgment, do not drink alcohol or use other recreational drugs while smoking.

2. Improve your home's heating system to avoid space heaters or portable stove devices. If you live in a rented apartment or home, push your landlord to make these improvements.

3. Teach your children to respect, and even to fear, fire or burning objects. You need to teach them the importance of using these objects carefully and safely. Do not play around with fires or fireworks in front of your child, unless you want him to imitate this reckless and dangerous behavior.

4. Place both a smoke detector and a carbon monoxide (CO) detector on each level of your home. Check them regularly to make sure each battery is working. Change the batteries every six months!

5. If you are building a new home, insist that the contractor place "sprinkler" systems that automatically turn on in the event of smoke or fire.

6. Make an emergency plan to follow in the event of a fire. Discuss it with your children, and practice it at regular intervals. Emphasize safety tips such as the best means of exiting the house, keeping one's head and body at floor-level while exiting (to prevent inhaling poisonous smoke fumes), and the importance of not panicking. Repetition, in the form of fire drills, will aid this process immeasurably.

7. If you live in a two (or more)-story home, make sure that you install escape ladders. These can be attached to the outer walls of the home, or portable ladders can be purchased that are kept inside and are placed out the window in the event of a fire.

8. Teach your child the "drop and roll" technique of walking through the fire. Drop to the ground, preferably with a towel around your head, and roll out to a place of safety.

What do You do in the Event of a Burn Injury?

First-degree (mild) burns: These are minor burns that only involve the outer-most layer of skin (the *epidermis*). They are red and slightly painful, but do not cause blisters to form.

• Run the burned area under cool tap water.

• The injury should be air dried and may be left unbandaged. If the burn is especially large or looks more involved, you may want to bandage it.

• Pain relievers such as acetaminophen may help.

• Check the burn injury in a few days to make sure that it is healing rather than becoming worse.

• If the injury is not healing or involves the eyes or face, seek the advice of your physician.

Second-degree burns: These are more serious burns that involve two layers of skin, the epidermis and the dermis. They cause more extensive damage, such as redness and blister formation, and typically hurt a great deal.

• Run cold cap water over the burn injury for several minutes; follow by applying an ice pack to the injury for twenty to thirty minutes.

• Pat dry the injured area and place a clean bandage over it; you may wish to give your child a pain reliever such acetaminophen or ibuprofen *[see Fever]*.

• If the arms or legs are involved, make sure to keep them elevated.

• Call 911 (Emergency Services) immediately if there are large burns across the body (more than 10 percent of the body), the burns involve the eyes or face, the burns involve a moving joint, or the child is having trouble breathing. For less serious second-degree burns, you should call your pediatrician for advice on treatment.

Third-degree burns: These are the most serious types of burns, involving all the layers of skin and the underlying nerves. Because the nerves are destroyed, third-degree burns may not be perceived as painful; they appear ash-white in color and are severe in nature.

• Call 911 immediately for medical help.

• Make sure your child is breathing well and the pulse is normal; check to see if CPR is necessary *[see CPR].* Continue to monitor your child's pulse and breathing until the Emergency Medical Team comes to relieve you.

• If legs or arms are involved, make sure they are elevated.

• Place cool compresses on the burn injuries.

• Keep your child as calm and comfortable as possible.

FONTANELLE *[See Newborn appearance]*

FOOD ALLERGIES *[See Allergies]*

FOOD POISONING *[See Poisoning]*

FRACTURES, DISLOCATIONS, AND ORTHOPEDIC EMERGENCIES

Fractures or broken bones tend to be different in children when compared to adults (especially small children) because their bones are still growing and are more flexible. Fractures should always be considered emergency situations that require a visit to the hospital emergency room.

Fractures that do not Involve the Head or Neck

If your child falls or is involved in an accident where you suspect a broken bone, begin by checking the "A,B,C's" of CPR *[see CPR].* Serious bone fractures can cause shock. Ask your child about the level of pain and examine the injury for evidence of swelling, redness, bleeding and bruising, if she can move the injured limb, and in more serious situations, a bone actually sticking out of the skin.

If the fracture involves a body part other than the head or neck, such as an arm or leg, make sure the child is lying down on a flat surface and try to keep him as calm as possible. If the area is bleeding, you may place a cool compress on the injury. In general, it is not wise to move this child, test out how "bad" the fracture is by putting weight on it, or other maneuvers. Do not feed the child food or water in the event that the fracture requires surgery. Make sure that the child is comfortable and call either your pediatrician or the 911 service to transport the child to a hospital where the fracture can be assessed, stabilized and casted. Never try to "re-set" a bone fracture yourself.

Once the initial crisis of the fracture and the visit to the Emergency Room is over, purchase a laundry-marking pen so when your child returns to school his friends may "sign the cast"!

Fractures of the Head or Neck

If you suspect a fracture to the skull or neck, you should call 911 immediately, make sure that the child is breathing normally, that his heart is beating, and that he is comfortable. Do not attempt to move the child with a head or neck injury *[see Falls; Head and Neck Injuries; Injury and Accident Prevention]*. If CPR is necessary, do not attempt to manipulate the head and neck as you would for a normal "jaw-lift maneuver" when assessing the child's airway *[see CPR]*.

Dislocations

This is an injury where the ligaments—or stretchy bands of connective tissue that holds muscles, bones, and joints together—stretch or tear following some type of trauma. Sometimes, this injury causes the bone to be pulled out of its alignment and prevents the joint in question from working properly (a dislocation). As a rule, we suggest that in the event of a dislocation, you begin by calling your physician. Different dislocations, of course, can be more serious than others, but most heal well.

The most common dislocation of early childhood is *nursemaid's elbow*. This condition, also known as dislocation of the radial heads of the arm, is accidentally caused by a parent picking up or swinging an infant or toddler by the arm. The child will hold her arm in a protected fashion and will cry in pain. Fortunately, nursemaid's elbow is easily fixed in minutes by a physician who realigns the bones with some physical maneuvers.

Other dislocations may involve the hands, thumbs, elbows, shoulders, and knees. In general, it is wise never to attempt to realign a dislocated joint yourself. Place an ice pack on the injury, elevate it if possible, and bring your child to the physician or an emergency room for safe and definitive treatment.

FROSTBITE, HYPOTHERMIA, AND THE GREAT OUTDOORS

After being exposed to extremely cold weather, the skin becomes painfully cold, numb, or feels tingly (like "pins and needles") and appears white in color. Those severe cases of skin exposure that do not resolve quickly after warming up inside are called frostbite. This painful condition results from the actual freezing of the skin and occurs at temperatures of −2° to −10°C or 14° to 28°F. The risk of frostbite is increased by the duration of the exposure to cold weather, the wind-chill factor, previous injury, and general health. We most commonly see frostbite in those areas of the body that are difficult to wrap up during the cold weather, such as the cheeks, ears, nose, and, if gloves or boots are forgotten, the fingers and toes.

A less common form of frostbite is called *popsicle panniculitis*. This refers to the skin damage that occurs to the cheeks of a child sucking on a popsicle or ice cube who leaves the frozen object against the skin for too long. The cheeks often appear reddened and bluish and can be somewhat painful.

Treating Mild Frostbite

• Most cases of simple frostbite can be treated at home by warming up the affected area with a warm and wet compress. You should apply warm, wet compresses to the frostbitten area until the white skin becomes pink again; this signifies that blood is flowing freely in the affected area. Rubbing or massaging the frostbitten skin will not cause additional damage, but it is not necessary as long as you use the warm compress technique described above.

• A bath that is nice and warm but not burning to the skin is also a good way to warm someone up quickly.

• Frostbite injuries can be quite painful, especially after the numbness wears off. You may want to give your child a pain reliever *[see Fever]*. Make sure that he has plenty of warm fluids to drink. Despite rumors to the contrary, it is unwise to place a frostbite injury in a pile of snow. This will only worsen the injury.

Hypothermia

Hypothermia is a lowering of the core body temperature caused by overexposure to the cold or by wearing damp clothes during cold weather. It can be dangerous and even life-threatening. You need to call your pediatrician immediately if your child has been exposed to extreme cold for an extended period of time and appears sluggish, unresponsive, or complains of feeling very cold.

When to Call the Doctor

• The frostbitten area is large and does not respond to the warm compress treatment, and it develops blisters.

• The child is shivering, even inside the house, and does not seem able to stop.

• The child was exposed to cold weather for a long period of time or fell into cold water during a period of cold weather.

• The child is so cold that her core temperature, when taken with a regular thermometer, is lower than normal (below 98.6°F).

• The child appears confused, or speaks with slurred speech.

What can I do to prevent frostbite and hypothermia?

• *Always make sure you check the weather report before sending your child outside to play in cold weather. Days that are especially bitter and below the 0°F mark are not good outdoor days. Remember always to take the windchill factor into account along with the air temperature. The winds of winter can make the actual temperature significantly colder than the thermometer tells you. Again, most weather news services provide both the air temperature and the temperature adjusted for wind chill factor.*

• *Make sure that your child wears protective gear including a warm coat, gloves, and boots. Hats are especially important in the cold weather, since most people lose about 50 percent of their body heat from the head.*

• *Talk with your child to ensure that she understands when to come in from the cold. The first sign of tingling or numbness of the skin is a good time to grab a cup of hot chocolate, indoors! Call your child inside the house after a romp in the snow, even if only for a break. Chances are good that the child absorbed in play will forget to come inside on his or her own.*

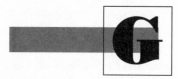

GENITALIA

Swelling of the Scrotum and Groin

Hydroceles (fluid in the scrotum sac)

There are a number of reasons for swelling in the groin or scrotal area of a little boy. The most common (and an essentially harmless) cause is a collection of fluid near the testicle, present at birth. Physicians call this fluid collection a *hydrocele;* it is usually present above both testicles and is painless. This condition generally resolves with time and requires no special treatment.

Lymph nodes, hernias, and orchitis

A swollen lymph node in the groin area may be another cause of swelling. These can be quite sensitive and painful. They frequently accompany an infection or severe rash in the area of the groin *[see Lymph Nodes].*

Inguinal hernias are a condition where a loop of bowel protrudes through a small opening in the baby's abdominal wall. It usually presents itself as a mere swelling in the groin. If the area is bulging, blue in color, painful to the child and cannot be pushed back into the abdomen, you need to get your child to an emergency room for medical attention. If it is not causing immediate pain, you can arrange for the pediatrician to look at it in the next day or so. It is important that inguinal hernias are surgically corrected.

Orchitis is an infection or inflammation of the testicles; the testicle becomes swollen and painful, and this condition requires rapid medical attention. One of the most common causes of orchitis is an infection of mumps. Fortunately, this can be avoided with the mumps vaccine, which is given along with the measles and rubella vaccines at the age of 15 months *[see Immunizations].*

Cryptorchidism

This is a condition where one of the boy's testicles has not descended into the scrotal sac and remains in the abdomen. Your pediatrician will check your son's scrotal sac during the first few years of life to ensure that both testicles are where they belong. In the event of cryptorchidism, a surgical procedure is required to bring the testicle down into the scrotal sac before the child reaches the age of two years in order to prevent the risk of testicular cancer.

Torsion of the testicle

The most serious cause of swelling in the scrotum is a torsion of the testicle. This occurs when the testicle twists upon itself, cutting off its own blood supply. The area is painful, sensitive to the slightest touch, swollen, and may be bluish in color. For different anatomical reasons, boys during infancy or early adolescence can experience this problem. In general, painful, swollen, tender, or red testicles is a medical emergency and it needs medical attention as soon as possible.

Vagina, Foreign Bodies

Sometimes, as little girls explore their genitals, they stick something in the vagina and forget about it. The foreign bodies pediatricians are asked to remove from this area most commonly are wads of toilet paper, although anything small can be inserted. (Later on, when the girl is older, the most common foreign body found is a forgotten tampon.)

The hallmark symptom of a foreign body in the vagina is a foul smell coming from that area. Greenish discharge, occasional bleeding, itching, discomfort, and signs of irritation can also be present. Consequently, children with this problem are typically brought to the attention of a pediatrician over concerns of a vaginal or urinary tract infection.

It is important to remove these objects when discovered, and your physician can help with such a process. It is important to make sure that no sexual abuse has taken place.

Labial Adhesions

Sometimes the *labia minora* (Latin for tiny lips) of an infant girl's vagina become fused, or stuck together, by a thin membrane. We are not exactly clear what causes this vexing but easily treated problem, although some have identified poor hygiene as a cause. Because it is usually not a serious problem, it is often missed until the baby is a little girl.

The proper way to wash a baby's genitals (girls *and* boys) is from the front to the back. This prevents the chemicals and bacteria from the rectal area getting into the baby's urinary tract. Careful washing with a washcloth and warm tap water (soap is not necessary) is all that is necessary. Soaps can cause a chemical urethritis or irritation of the opening of the urinary tract *[see Urinary Tract Problems]*.

Upon noting that your baby girl has labial adhesions, make sure that her stream and flow of urine are not blocked. Sometimes, the fusion of the lips can extend all the way to the urethra—the tiny opening where urine comes out—

and obstruct the flow of urine. A physician needs to know about this situation as quickly as possible.

In terms of treatment, there are two options. The first is simply to wait. If there is no obstruction to the urine flow and the child is not bothered by the labial fusion, nontreatment is a good option. As she grows up and reaches puberty, the estrogen secreted by her ovaries will separate the fused lips on its own.

For those who desire more immediate results, a physician prescribes an ointment that contains estrogen (the female hormone). Holding your little girl's vaginal lips so there is *gentle* (but not tearing) pressure on the thin membrane, you apply this ointment with a cotton swab to the membrane fusing the two labia minora, two to three times a day. Gradually, after about four weeks of therapy, the estrogen cream thins the membrane, and with gentle pressure the labia come apart. Many times your doctor will ask you to continue applying the ointment for another week or so to prevent the lips from refusing, which they often do.

We realize as we write this advice how difficult in reality it is to get your infant or little girl to sit still through this process. It's somewhat uncomfortable and definitely not fun. In the case of an older child, try to explain what you are doing and why you are doing it. If you have trouble applying the ointment or simply have questions, call your health care professional. This is not an easy task and help is usually available. *Remember, never attempt to split the fused lips with pressure alone.* This maneuver temporarily separates the fused lips, but the raw edges created by such a ripping motion will almost certainly yield a refusion of the labia and pain for the child.

GROWTH AND DEVELOPMENT: MEASURING THE HEIGHT, WEIGHT, AND HEAD CIRCUMFERENCE *[See Well-child pediatric examination schedule]*

GUNS AND FIREARMS: PREVENTING INJURIES

Although this is a controversial topic, for political rather than safety reasons, we will emphatically state that firearms and children are a deadly combination. Guns are readily available in American society and are increasingly portrayed on television and the media as a means of resolving conflicts. Children are especially vulnerable to gun injuries and deaths, not only because of their lack of judgment or understanding of the deadly nature of these weapons, but also because most children today have a cavalier attitude toward guns. Watch any school-aged (or younger) group of children at play and you will invariably see either a fairly accurate replica of a gun used as a toy or even sticks or fingers as pointed fantasy weapons. Indeed, variants of "Bang! Bang! You're dead" are probably more commonly heard on American playgrounds than almost any other expression of play.

The ways children can be hurt by guns include unintentional injuries (being in the wrong place while gunfire occurs, or accidentally finding a real gun and mistakenly playing with it as if it were a toy); homicides; and, for older children, suicides. Each year, the number of injuries and deaths of children and teens from these events increases.

Simply put, children need to be kept as far apart from firearms as is humanly possible. Together, they are almost always a disaster waiting to happen.

If you do decide to let your child learn to handle a firearm, it should only be when he is of the age to handle such a dangerous responsibility (older than 14 years) and always under the strictest of parental supervision.

Those families who insist on keeping firearms in the home (whether for professional or personal reasons) must always:

1. Keep them hidden and locked away from children.

2. Never leave them loaded. Ammunition needs to be locked up and stored away separately.

3. Avoid hunting under the influence of drugs or alcohol with your child. It is not a safe outing for either of you.

4. Remember that many so-called toy guns, such as the non-gunpowder firearms called BB guns, are *not* toys. They, too, are quite dangerous and need to be handled as such.

5. Educate your children about the dangers of guns. Instruct them to run away and immediately tell you whenever they are confronted with one.

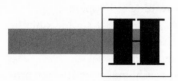

Hand, Foot, and Mouth Disease (Coxsackie A virus)

This conveniently named rash is caused by a family of viruses called Coxsackie A. Despite its quaint name, this infection has nothing to do with the similarly named disease of livestock, "hoof and mouth disease." Usually appearing during summer months (and more specifically, usually during your family summer vacation), the infection causes tiny fluid-filled blisters or ulcers on the tongue, mouth, lips, palms of the hands, soles of the feet and, at times, between the fingers or toes and even on the child's buttocks.

The infection is common among children aged six months to four years. It is commonly associated with a low-grade fever (about 100°F) and complaints of a sore mouth. Indeed, the mouth sores, which make drinking and eating quite painful, are the biggest hurdles of this minor infection. You will need to be creative in getting fluids into a younger child with several mouth ulcers. Some recommend acetaminophen for the pain and small dabs of an antacid such as Maalox® painted on the mouth sores with a cotton swab *[see Mouth Sores]*.

Typically the child improves within three to four days, and the rash resolves by seven to ten days, with the mouth sores disappearing before the skin lesions. There are no curative medicines that will shorten the course of this illness.

Although this infection is usually harmless, there are occasions when it can become more serious. If you notice any of the following symptoms in your child, discuss them with your pediatrician:

• Fever greater than 102°F

• Signs of dehydration such as dry cracked lips, dry tongue, or mouth; or if the child is rarely urinating or has not urinated in more than eight hours; or complaints of being thirsty from a child who will not drink

• Your child complains of a stiff neck or appears confused, difficult to awaken, or simply appears more ill than your comfort zone allows

 Is Coxsackie A virus a contagious disease?

Yes. Coxsackie A virus is easily transmitted, and it is likely that if your child has it, so do some of his playmates or siblings. Generally, it takes about three to five days

after *close contact with someone with the infection for it to develop in another child. In the overwhelming majority of cases, however, this is a harmless part of growing up and attempts at isolation or removal from school seem cruel and unnecessary. Once the child no longer has a temperature and is drinking enough fluids, he is well enough to return to his normal activities.*

Some Tips for Home Treatments

As with other mouth sores in infancy and early childhood, the immediate concern is whether or not the child is taking in fluids. Remember, the smaller you are, the more likely you are to develop dehydration—lack of body water—if you stop drinking. You need to avoid giving your child drinks or foods that are salty, spicy, hot, or otherwise painful to the tender and sensitive mouth lesions. A good rule of thumb is that if it hurts your mouth, it will definitely irritate a mouth that contains open sores. Cold fluids, popsicles, ice cubes, ice cream, and other "numbing" foods are excellent ways of getting your child to eat or drink something with a minimum of arguing. Be patient—your child is experiencing some pain—but also be persistent!

HEAD AND NECK INJURIES

Children frequently fall down and hit their heads. Fortunately, the human head is quite "hard," and most blows to the head are not as serious as they are frightening. Begin by looking at your child and making sure he is alert, responsive, and in no immediate danger. Examine the spot where the head was hit.

Signs of a Mild Head Injury

- Red lump, cut or scrape where the head was hit
- Headache
- Double vision
- Vomiting (fewer than two or three episodes in a twenty-four hour period)
- Drowsiness for one to two hours after the head blow
- Confused behavior for a short period of time after the head blow

What You can do for Mild Head Injuries

If your child suffers from a mild head injury *without* significant bleeding or loss of consciousness, and if the child appears to be recuperating after one to two hours, you can give supportive care.

- Apply cold compresses to the injury site
- Give acetaminophen as a pain reliever
- Wake the child up every thirty to sixty minutes during the night and observe his behavior over the next day or so for evidence of sleepiness, falling, paralysis,

uncoordinated movements, slurred speech, or loss of consciousness. If anything concerns you, a telephone call to your pediatrician is in order.

Signs of More Serious Head Injuries

- Loss of consciousness for any period longer than a few seconds
- Bleeding from the head injury that will not stop with pressure
- Clear, watery-to-bloody discharge coming from the ears or nose
- Extreme sleepiness or unresponsiveness
- Vomiting several times after the head blow without nausea
- What appears to be a misshapen head
- Altered pulse or breathing rate

If you notice these signs, call your physician *immediately.* Make sure the child is not in shock and check for the need to give CPR *[see CPR].*

Neck or Spinal Cord Injuries

If you suspect any type of injury to the neck or spinal cord, do not attempt to move the injured child. Make sure that the child is comfortable, is breathing normally, and has a normal heartbeat. Begin CPR if needed *[see CPR].* Be careful not to move or manipulate the head and neck. Call 911 (Emergency Services).

HEAD CIRCUMFERENCE *[See Newborn appearance]*

HEAT RASH

Although this annoying rash is most common during the warm summer months, it can appear anytime the child perspires heavily. Situations leading to heat rash include exposure to high temperatures, either indoors or outdoors, and wearing too much clothing. Remember, if you are warm, chances are your child over the age of two months is also feeling the heat.

With too much heat and excessive sweating, the pores and the sweat glands of the skin become clogged and the tiny pink "heat bumps" appear. Some have described the rash as irritated and angry-looking "goose bumps."

How can I make my child more comfortable?

There are no specific medicines that will instantly make heat rash go away. The rash typically clears up on its own within two to three days. The most important thing you can do is to keep your baby or child as cool and comfortable as possible. This may be difficult to do during the shank of summer, especially if you do not have access to an air conditioner. Frequent baths (every few hours or so) with cool tap water but no soap often help. After bathing, let the child's skin air dry, rather than rubbing it with an irritating towel. Electric fans are best avoided if your child is old enough to get up and stick his hands in them, but not yet old enough to realize the consequences of such an action (six months to four years). Lotions, oils, and similar products are best left untouched since they only worsen the rash by clogging more sweat glands.

Tender loving care, patience, and keeping your child comfortable, dry, and sweat-free should clear up the heat rash within three days. For more extended cases, you should consult your pediatrician.

Hives (Urticaria)

About 10 percent of all children experience urticaria, or hives, at one time or another. This hypersensitivity reaction is an allergic response to a newly introduced food, medication, infection, or other substances. In more than 85 percent of all cases of hives, the specific culprit is not found; however, you can take heart in the fact that most children who do experience hives only get them once in a lifetime.

What do hives look like?

This unforgettable skin rash is extremely itchy and consists of irregular, splotchy, slightly raised red patches. They can appear anywhere on the skin, although the face and lips are common sites. They can be the size of dimes to quarters. In more severe cases, they can be bigger and even blend in with other, nearby hives. They typically last three to four days and then disappear.

What can I do to make my child more comfortable?

Unfortunately, the treatment is largely supportive rather than curative. No medicines available will actually cure hives or make the rash resolve any faster. Frequent cool baths with an oatmeal-containing bath soap such as AVEENO® can help. Slippery, cooling lotions such as calamine make a mess but temporarily soothe itchy skin. You might clip your child's nails if she is too young to understand the importance of not scratching excessively [for more tips on treating the child with itchy skin, see Chicken Pox].

Antihistamines, readily available with or without a prescription, may be of some help in relieving the itchy condition, provided that they are given when the rash first begins and regularly throughout its course. The side effect of this medication is usually excessive sleepiness or, more rarely, hyperactivity. You should discuss this medication option with your pediatrician, depending on the severity of your child's rash.

Once in a while, hives can be a harbinger of the more serious allergic reaction called anaphylaxis [see Allergies, Anaphylactic Reactions]. If you do notice that in association with hives, your child complains of thickened lips or tongue, difficulty with swallowing or breathing, abdominal pain ,or any other serious problem, you should call your pediatrician immediately.

Hyperbilirubinemia *[See Jaundice of the newborn]*

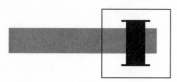

Immunizations

Immunizations—or as their recipients refer to them, "shots"—are both a bane of normal childhood and one of the major contributions to reducing childhood mortality. They have also become a great concern to parents worried about their minor and major side effects or adverse reactions. In actuality, the immunizations for the major infectious diseases of childhood are quite safe and effective.

In some parts of the United States, as few as 43 percent of children have completed their primary immunization series by the age of 2 years. Indeed, some of the recent epidemics of measles, German measles, whooping cough, and mumps in this country have been largely the result of failure to vaccinate children at the recommended age. Therefore, you should always keep an up-to-date record of your child's immunizations. If, for whatever reason, you note that he or she is behind in these important vaccines, you should call your physician to correct the situation.

There are actually only a few reasons for a normal child *not* to receive an immunization. They are:

1. A concurrent severe illness

2. Previous severe allergic reaction (what doctors refer to as a severe anaphylactic or a hypersensitivity reaction) to a specific vaccine or a vaccine component

3. Vaccines consisting of live viruses should not be given to those who are pregnant or have compromised immune systems

The following situations are *not* reasons to delay vaccination: a mild reaction of soreness, redness, or swelling at the injection site or a temperature less than 105°F with the diphtheria-pertussis-tetanus (DPT) shot; current antibiotic therapy; mild illness with low-grade fever or mild diarrhea; prematurity; the mother is pregnant again or the child is still breastfeeding; a history of nonspecific allergies; recent exposure to an infectious disease; a family history of sudden infant death syndrome; or a family history of convulsions.

Listed below is the schedule for the routine immunization of healthy infants and children as recommended by the American Academy of Pediatrics and the Centers for Disease Control. We have also included a more elaborate Immuniza-

Age	Immunization
Birth	HBV #1
1–2 months	HBV #2
2 months	DTP #1; OPV #1; H. flu #1
4 months	DTP #2; OPV #2; H. flu #2
6 months	DTP #3; OPV #3; H. flu #3
6–18 months	HBV #3; DTP #4; OPV #4
12 months	Tb test; H. flu #4, Chicken pox vaccine
15 months	MMR; H. flu [if not given at 12 months]
4–6 years	DTP #5; OPV #5; MMR
14–16 years	Td

Key to abbreviations:

HBV: Hepatitis B Vaccine
DTP: Diptheria-Tetanus (Lockjaw)-Pertussis (Whooping cough)
H. flu: Haemophilus influenzae type b [H. flu is a severe bacterial infection of infancy that can cause meningitis and a number of other serious infections; there are several H. flu vaccines on the market, and the exact schedule of administration may vary with the type your physician offers]
OPV: Oral polio vaccine, administered in syrup form. An OPV at six months is optional.
Tb test: This is merely a test to see if your child has been exposed to the germ that causes tuberculosis. There is a TB vaccine, but it is not used in the United States. A positive Tb test is one where hard bumps (*not* red marks) appear after forty-eight to seventy-two hours at the site of the test. A positive test requires a physician's attention.
MMR: Measles-Mumps-Rubella
Td: Tetanus-diptheria [Update tetanus shots every five to ten years]

tion Checklist to record your child's immunization series in the "fold-out" section of this book. Please note that these ages are recommended, not absolute.

Side Effects Associated with Immunizations

One of the primary reasons why children enjoy such excellent health today is that many major killers of children—diphtheria, whooping cough, polio, and so on—are now completely avoidable with the administration of the vaccines described above. To be sure, with any medicine, vaccine, or medical treatment your child receives, there are some risks. It should be noted, however, that the risks are infinitesimal when compared to the chances of an unimmunized child contracting one of these contagious diseases and suffering serious consequences. For example, the child who contracts poliomyelitis has a 50 percent chance of being paralyzed, while only one in about three million children who receive the polio vaccine contract polio from the vaccine itself. Similarly, the chances of an unimmunized baby contracting whooping cough and succumbing to the illness are far greater than the risks of a serious side effect from the vaccine itself.

When your child is immunized by your pediatrician, you will receive an informed-consent leaflet that explains these rare side effects and the benefits of the vaccine. As with any medical therapy, you should read such forms with great care and make sure that any question you have is answered. But to put it succinctly, all children should be immunized according to the schedule above.

The more common, minor reactions to the vaccines your child receives are listed below:

Diphtheria-Tetanus-Pertussis (DTP) vaccine: This vaccine can produce mild fever (101° to 102°F), mild tenderness, swelling, or redness at the injection site, and mild fussiness in the baby in the first day or two after vaccination. Most or all of these symptoms are well treated with a dose of acetaminophen and, if necessary, a warm washcloth applied to the area of swelling. Some children develop a bump at the injection site; this bump does not hurt and usually resolves within two weeks of the vaccination. You should call your physician if the bump suddenly becomes bigger or is causing the baby pain. Other reasons to call the doctor include symptoms that last longer than two days, a fever greater than 105°, or if the baby is not consolable in a parent's arms, cries for spells lasting more than three straight hours, or is unresponsive.

The pertussis or whooping cough component of this vaccine has received a great deal of attention recently as a potential cause of brain damage, sudden infant death syndrome (SIDS), and death. In reality, the risks of such events occurring as a result of the whooping cough vaccine are all but nonexistent. This is especially important to note if you are considering not immunizing your child against whooping cough. Whooping cough is an extremely serious disease that carries risks of respiratory problems, brain damage, and death that are far greater than serious side effects from the vaccine itself.

A slightly different pertussis vaccine, called the acellular pertussis vaccine, contains none of the cellular elements of the whole cell pertussis vaccine and, hence, has fewer side effects such as sore arm, low-grade fevers, and achiness. It is currently licensed in the United States only for the fourth and fifth doses in the pertussis immunization schedule for children aged fifteen months to seven years. Infants are still recommended to undergo the whole cell pertussis vaccine.

Measles vaccine: In some cases, recipients of a measles vaccine can develop a mild fever and rash a week or so after the vaccination. You should call your physician about these symptoms, but they are usually mild and require no special treatment. Children who are allergic to eggs need to have special precautions taken when considering whether or not to immunize against measles, since the vaccine contains egg products. If your child has only a mild allergy, the vaccine should be given. If her allergy is severe (meaning that within two hours after ingesting eggs the child has problems in breathing or swallowing), consult an allergist for special skin testing to determine if a measles vaccine is safe.

Mumps-German Measles vaccine: At present, there are no known side effects or complications to these vaccines other than a mild swelling at the injection site and occasional joint pain two weeks after the German measles vaccine. These vaccines are usually combined with the measles vaccine.

Polio vaccine: In extremely rare circumstances, a child may develop polio from the vaccine itself. The odds of this happening, however, are about 1:3,000,000. Polio vaccines are made of "live-attenuated virus," meaning they consist of polio virus that has been cultured so that it does not produce the disease but does provide immunity against the virus. Consequently, if someone in the family has a compromised immune function (e.g., AIDS, cancer, or is receiving chemotherapy), you may want to discuss other options, such as the recently reapproved inactivated (Salk or IPV) polio vaccine or a combination (OPV/IPV) immunization schedule with your pediatrician.

Hemophilus Influenzae vaccine: In a few children receiving this vaccine, side effects such as soreness at the injection site and low-grade fever may develop.

Chicken pox vaccine: Side effects are generally mild and include redness, stiffness, soreness, and swelling at the injection site; tiredness, fussiness, nausea, and a low-grade fever (less than 101° F); and, in a few children, a mild rash at the site of the injection or on other parts of the body. These reactions can occur up to one month after the chicken pox immunization and can last several days.

 I remember having to get a smallpox vaccination before starting kindergarten. How come my child is not given this vaccine?

Fortunately, mass vaccinations have succeeded in wiping out smallpox altogether. Vaccination is no longer necessary.

Impetigo

This rash begins as a series of red, raised bumps that rapidly progress to form blisters, pimples, and open sores. The sores themselves can grow in size and spread to other parts of the body. Frequently, the sores will drain a honey-colored, sticky pus that is the hallmark of an impetigo infection.

What causes the rash?

Impetigo is a skin infection caused by bacteria called streptococcus or staphylococcus. These bacteria normally live harmlessly on intact skin but, like other agents of skin infection, will attack skin that is broken down by cuts, scrapes, and other minor injuries. Impetigo is especially common during the summertime, when a lot of skin is exposed and likely to be injured or broken for other reasons [see Bites]. Sometimes it begins with a small sore in the mouth or nose area. Given the propensity for children to pick at their noses or open sores in that area—followed by touching almost any other body part—you can begin to see how impetigo may spread.

Is it contagious?

Yes, it is extremely contagious! Remember that if your child picks at an impetiginous sore, followed by scratching another area of his body, he is likely to spread the infection to that body part. You need to explain the importance of not scratching the sores—no matter how itchy—and to keep the child's nails as trim as possible. Impetigo is also contagious to others, so it is important for the affected child not to share his clothing, towels, linens, and other personal items that may be contaminated with the infectious impetigo drainage (pus). Wash these items with a bleach-containing detergent to sterilize them.

How is it treated?

Antibiotics that kill the organisms streptococcus and staphylococcus are prescribed by your physician for about a week. There are two options. The older option is a syrup or pill that needs to be taken three to four times a day, such as erythromycin. If your child has no problem taking oral medications, this is not a bad way to go, although some children complain of upset stomachs or diarrhea as side effects.

A newer form of this antibiotic, called Bactroban, comes in an ointment form and can be applied directly to the sores.

Both methods are equally effective but depend greatly on the likes and dislikes of your individual child. Feel free to discuss these options with your pediatrician.

When can my child return to school?

The child may safely return to school twenty-four to forty-eight hours after *initiating antibiotic therapy.*

Complications of Impetigo

Some cases of impetigo are more severe than others. Because this is an infectious disease with the possibility of spreading, you need to keep a close eye on the rash's progress and your child's health during the treatment period.

If you notice the following, these may be signs of a worsening infection and you need to consult your pediatrician.

• Red streaks or lines emerging from the impetigo site

• The face, or much of the skin, is bright red in color and extremely sensitive to touch

• The child has red- or tea-colored urine

• Any of the above symptoms plus a fever or sore throat

• The lesions continue growing in size and location despite treatment with an antibiotic for more than two days (forty-eight hours)

INFLUENZA ("The flu")

Although we all confuse a common cold or upper respiratory infection with "the flu," true influenza is a specific type of viral infection with specific symptoms. Moreover, the person with influenza may be far more ill than those with a "common cold" or other upper respiratory tract viruses *[see Upper Respiratory Infections; Pneumonia; Croup].* The influenza virus tends to attack the lining of the nose, mouth, throat, and airway (trachea and pulmonary bronchi) of humans. Those unlucky enough to contract the disease usually complain of serious aches and pains, runny or stuffy nose, annoying cough and raw, painful throat in far greater proportions than those with less serious respiratory tract infections. It is also associated with headache, muscle aches, and a much higher fever than that accompanying the common cold.

Serious complications, such as pneumonia and other secondary infections, are more commonly associated with the true influenza virus than ordinary colds, probably because the influenza virus takes a far greater toll on one's immune and respiratory systems and general state of health.

Because the actual structure of the virus is constantly changing, humans do not build up a long-lasting immunity against influenza and can be reinfected with each year's new strain of virus. Indeed, Italians named the virus "influenza" during the Renaissance because they could not explain these annual visitations of influenza other than as due to the influence *("influenza")* of the stars. The disease is rapidly spread, with an incubation time between infection and actually becoming ill of about twenty-four to thirty-six hours.

How do I care for my child with the flu?

For most children and adults, influenza is nothing more than a bad cold with the complaints described above. Tender loving care, fever reducers such as acetaminophen, fluids, throat lozenges for the child over five years, and plenty of tissues should help to make your child more comfortable.

I understand that an influenza vaccine exists. should I have my children immunized each year for flu?

The vaccination is not a guarantee against contracting influenza, unlike more successful vaccines, and because of the potential side effects of the flu shot (e.g., a flu-like syndrome after vaccination, sore muscles, soreness at the site of injection, and so on), we do not recommend annual flu shots for healthy *children. Currently, however, the American Academy of Pediatrics recommends annual vaccination with the influenza vaccine for children with pre-existing medical conditions listed below. Such children are at greater risk serious complications from influenza, including pneumonia and even death. It is, therefore, wise for the parents and siblings of children with the medical problems listed below to be vaccinated as well, so as not to contract the flu and potentially infect the child in question. Please note that the influenza vaccine is made with proteins from eggs; if your child is known to have an allergy to eggs, he should* not *receive an influenza vaccine.*

Pre-existing Medical Conditions that Warrant Annual Influenza Vaccines for Children

- Immunodeficiency syndromes (such as HIV/AIDS)

- Cancer

- Congenital or rheumatic heart disease

- Long-term lung disease (for example, cystic fibrosis, severe asthma, chronic lung problems of prematurity)

- Endocrinologic or metabolic diseases (for example, diabetes mellitus)

- Neuromuscular disorders (such as muscular dystrophy)

- Illnesses that require long-term administration of aspirin, such as juvenile rheumatoid arthritis

INJURY AND ACCIDENT PREVENTION: CHILD-PROOFING THE HOME

Although the majority of the problems described in this book have to do with illness or behavioral issues, the sad fact of the matter is that *more children die or experience serious medical problems because of injuries and accidents than as a result of almost all of the other medical conditions described in this book combined.* Typically, both pediatricians and parents focus on the fragile state of the newborn or infant, worrying about their contracting an infectious disease, exhibiting signs of metabolic or inherited problems, and issues of feeding, growth, development and the like. Only recently, however, have child-care specialists focused on the *far more pressing problem of injury control and prevention* as an avenue of protecting the health of children in industrialized countries.

This section will discuss means to prevent or control injuries before they occur. Nowhere in pediatric medicine does the old adage "an ounce of prevention is worth a pound of cure" apply more than in this aspect of your child's health. A good thought to begin with is to recall how your baby is changing and developing with each passing month. This means that the infant (and child) is learning new skills, abilities, and thought processes. Some of these new developments can actually get a child into trouble. Since your infant and toddler changes each month, your "child-proofing" plan needs to change, too. For example, a newborn infant that cannot yet roll over or sit up is at far different risks for injuries and accidents from a mobile, walking toddler. We have provided you with a fold-out "Child-proofing the Home" checklist. Each month, say on the day of the child's birthday, do a child-proofing inspection (in other words, if the child was born on April 23, do this inspection on the 23rd of each month).

The Hard Facts of Accidents and Injuries During Childhood

Injuries make up over half of all childhood deaths and three-quarters of adolescent deaths each year in the United States. Boys tend to have a higher rate of injuries and accidents, throughout their lives, than girls. For example, infant boys have injury rates that are about 1.2 times greater than girls; by the teen years, boys experience 3.2 times as many deaths from injuries as their female counterparts. Similarly, children of impoverished backgrounds experience higher rates of injuries. African-Americans experience the highest homicide rates, while native American (North American Indian) children and teens have the highest suicide and unintentional injury rates. Rural children tend to suffer more unintentional injuries than their urban peers, and the summer months tend to be the peak season for injuries of all types. Not surprisingly, school vacation periods and weekends come as a close second. Infants and children of differing ages naturally suffer from different injuries and subsequent problems.

Many of these age-specific injuries have to do with the developmental stage of the child and the dangerous stimuli confronting him. For example, the small infant who is being bathed can easily drown in the bathtub without careful parental supervision. An older child, on the other hand, who is just beginning to ride his bicycle near traffic is at risk for automobile and bicycle injuries. Similarly, the teenager who is a new driver may be at risk for automobile accidents. Therefore, parents need to think especially hard about potential dangers that befall children and work toward age-appropriate preventive or protective efforts.

Because so many different types of injuries and accidents can occur, we will begin by discussing how specific injuries tend to be associated with specific ages or developmental stages. Specific prevention techniques for problems linked to poisoning, falls, walker devices, car seats, burns, choking, and other topics are offered elsewhere in this book.

Infants (Newborn to one year)

Infants are at especially high risk for injuries because they are small, poorly coordinated compared to older children, typically fearless, and without understanding of the concept of danger.

Common injuries

- Automobile crashes or accidents
- Falls
- Choking
- Suffocation
- Fires and burns
- Drowning
- Poisoning

Keys to prevention

1. Purchase and learn to use an infant car seat correctly whenever traveling by car with your baby *[see Car Seats]*.

2. Never leave babies unattended on high places from which they may fall. *[see Falls]*.

3. Avoid baby walkers at all costs! *[see Walkers]*.

4. Tiny objects, especially balloons and foods such as nuts or small candies, can easily become lodged in an infant's airway, causing choking or suffocation. These should not be given to babies *[see Choking]*.

5. Babies and children should not be left near hot water, hot stoves, hot liquids, or any other source of heat *[see Fire]*.

6. Every home should have a working smoke detector installed.

7. In the event of an accidental poisoning, it is important to have syrup of ipecac in the house. This liquid induces vomiting quickly and helps get the offending poison out of the child. Not all poisons require ipecac, however, so it is always important to have at the ready the telephone number of your regional poison control center. These helpful people can give you exact instructions on managing any poison in question within a few minutes *[see Poisoning]*.

8. Learn how to save a choking infant *[see Choking]*.

9. Lower your water heater thermostat to no greater than 120 to 130° F.

Toddlers (One to two years)

At this point, children are beginning to explore their world, typically the home, on their own. The toddler may crawl, cruise, and eventually walk on his own two feet. Other explorations include putting objects in his mouth, pulling open cupboards, emptying things, climbing, and falling. Such activities are not seen only in "bad" or wild children; they are a normal part of early childhood. Nevertheless, this mobility and curiosity add a significant amount of injury risk, especially when one considers that children this age have no control of their impulses (they see, they want, they do!) and do not understand the concept of cause and effect (e.g., if I touch this hot stove, I will be burned).

Common injuries

- Poisonings
- Falls
- Choking
- Fires
- Burns
- Drowning
- Automobile crashes

Keys to prevention

1. Child-proofing your home in terms of keeping medicines, poisons, and household cleaning agents far out of reach of children. As an extra safety precaution, if childproof caps are available for these products, they should be used *[see Medicines; Poisoning]*.

2. Place special locking or child-guard devices on cupboards and cabinets that contain such items.

3. Prevent infants and toddlers from potential falls down stairs or against sharp objects such as furniture *[see Falls]*.

4. If you have a room or a garage that contains dangerous objects, tools, chemicals, or the like, keep it locked at all times.

5. Windows, especially above the second floor of a building, should never be left entirely open. Instead, place screens and barricades in order to prevent the toddler from accidently falling out.

6. You need to supervise your toddlers as much as humanly possible. Left to their own devices, they typically find trouble.

7. Keep all electrical cords out of reach of toddlers. A frequent type of injury is the electrical burn that comes from biting down on a household cord *[see Electrical Injuries]*.

8. Continue to be careful about hot objects (pots, pans, and so on), the stove, hot liquids, and similar sources of heat. These are common causes of childhood burn injuries *[see Fire]*.

9. Toddlers should never be left unattended near any body of water *[see Bathing Your Baby; Drownproofing the Home]*.

10. Once the baby outgrows the infant seat, advance to a toddler's car seat *[see Car Seats]*.

Older Toddlers (Two to four years)

Older toddlers tend to get into many of the same types of accidents as their slightly younger counterparts. Unfortunately they are even more mobile, curious, and interested in exploration, so your level of supervision and prevention must be kept up. Developmentally, preschool children are not adept at judgment and continue to act on impulse. They still do not recognize danger as well as an older child and tend to think in an almost magical manner. For example, the preschool toddler watching a television show about a superhero flying in the air will frequently assume that he has similar powers and abilities. It is necessary, therefore, that you spend time with your child explaining the potential dangers of household living in a careful and complete manner. You also need to continue your supervision of the child, in the event he "forgets" or his magical thinking overpowers your preventive tactics.

Common injuries
- Falls
- Fires
- Burns
- Poisoning
- Drowning
- Automobile crashes
- Pedestrian injuries

Keys to prevention

1. Continue locking doors to rooms or closets containing dangerous tools, chemicals, and the like. Special locks, guard devices, and screens can be easily purchased at your local hardware store.

2. If you have weapons such as guns or knives, they need to be kept locked up and completely *out* of the reach of a child. This cannot be emphasized too strongly. Children, particularly toddlers and young school-aged children, are absolutely fascinated with these objects. A brief review of the types of television shows geared to children this age—with their glorification of weaponry and violence—serves as a partial explanation for this fascination. If you must keep weapons in the house, *keep them far away from the kids! [see Guns and Firearms].*

3. You need to teach your toddler about the dangers of automobiles, the importance of avoiding going into the street—even if a toy accidentally makes its way there—and to be careful of driveways where cars are parked. Continue to supervise your child's outdoor play to reinforce these important lessons.

4. Medicines, poisons, household cleaning products, and similar toxic substances must continue to be locked up out of reach. Remember, toddlers love to explore their world using all of their senses—including taste. The more colorful

or interesting-looking the product, the greater the risk it may find its way into a toddler's mouth *[see Poisoning]*.

5. Matches, blowtorches, and similar combustible products should always be kept out of reach and sight *[see Poisoning]*.

6. Once the child reaches the age of four or five years, arrange for her to begin swimming lessons. Drowning, as you may recall, is a major cause of death and injury among infants and young children. Although some have advocated swimming lessons even earlier in a child's life, including during infancy; this is probably not a good idea. Children under the age of three rarely have the coordination, strength, or cognitive ability to learn how to swim *[see Drown-proofing the Home]*.

7. Always supervise your child when she is in the bathtub or a swimming pool.

8. Continue to use the toddler's car seat when traveling in the automobile. When the child grows out of the seat, change to a regular seat belt. If this seems cumbersome, transitional booster seats can be restrained with regular safety belts *[see Car Seats]*.

9. Continue to have syrup of ipecac in the house and an up-to-date phone number for your regional poison control center nearby. Most poison centers will give you, free of charge, bright stickers to place near the phone with their hotline telephone numbers *[see Poisoning]*.

10. Teach your child to avoid strange animals and to treat even well-known or familiar ones with respect and care *[see Bites, Animal]*.

Early to Middle Childhood (Five to nine years)

The good news is that children this age have the lowest incidence of accidental injuries and deaths of any period in the lifespan. Nevertheless, such injuries still cause the most serious medical problems of children this age. Children may be walking to school, crossing streets, and bicycling around the neighborhood. Elementary school-age children, while certainly better at judging danger than their younger brothers and sisters, still have difficulty accurately estimating the speed, distance, or danger of a moving vehicle; car accidents or related injuries—whether the child is walking or biking—are therefore most common and serious at this age. Fascination with guns, knives, and heavy household machinery (such as lawn mowers) continues among this group, along with a tendency to misjudge how dangerous these objects can be.

Common injuries
• Automobile accidents
• Pedestrian injury
• Bicycle accidents
• Drowning

- Firearm (gun) injuries
- Burns

Keys to prevention

1. Spend a lot of time, on repeated occasions, discussing issues of pedestrian, automobile, and bicycle safety with your child. Positively reinforce key lessons such as holding hands with an adult when crossing the street, looking both ways, and similar safety issues.

2. Children this age should *not* be bicycling on busy streets. The sidewalk should be the site of their activities.

3. The child should *always* wear a bicycle helmet when biking. If he becomes involved in other types of exercise and fun such as rollerblading, ice skating, skiing, or similar activities, you need to make sure he wears appropriate protective gear (helmets, elbow, wrist, and knee pads, and similar guards). These are readily available from your local sporting goods, toy, or department store, and the staff there will be only too glad to sell them to you! *[see Bicycle, Injuries]*.

4. Your child should continue swimming lessons as she improves her skills; but you still need to supervise her when she is in the water.

5. Continue to keep any type of weapon you have in the house locked up and out of sight.

6. Avoid off-road motor vehicles such as minibikes, motorcycles, mopeds, all-terrain vehicles, and the like. They are dangerous and inappropriate for young children, no matter how badly the kids want them.

7. Continue to be vigilant about matches, burning objects, and sources of heat. Elementary school children should *not* be playing with matches.

INSECT BITES *[See Bites]*

INTUSSUSSEPTION

Intussusseption is the most common cause of intestinal obstruction or blockage during the first two years of life. It is caused when one part of the intestines folds into another part, much as a telescope collapses on itself. This obstruction can cause belly pain, vomiting, bloating, and constipation. Children who are too young to articulate their belly pain may draw their legs up to their bellies and cry or frown. Fever may accompany this picture and, in extreme cases, the obstruction can cause damage to the gut and an infection of the abdomen.

The baby or child with these symptoms need to be examined by a physician immediately. Intussusseption can be potentially life-threatening if the blockage is not resolved. The procedure used to diagnose intussusseption consists of an enema containing a contrast medium or dye. The enema is inserted into the child's rectum and the fluid is allowed to flow into the rectum and large intestines. An X ray of the intestinal tract is then taken in order to visualize the area of telescoping. The majority of these cases are actually cured by this diagnostic procedure, in that the fluid of the enema pushes out the "telescoped" portion of the gut. In some cases, a surgical procedure may be necessary *[see Abdominal Pain]*.

IRON DEFICIENCY ANEMIA

We all need iron in our diets in order to maintain good health. One of the most common symptoms of a diet poor in iron is a form of anemia called iron deficiency anemia. Children with iron deficiency anemia may have pale or white skin, poor growth, irritability, or decreased appetites. They also may exhibit lower levels of energy and become tired more easily than other children with a healthier diet. Iron deficiency (with or without the resulting anemia) also may adversely affect your child's attention span, behavior, and intellectual performance. Your pediatrician will check your child for evidence of iron deficiency as part of the annual examination *[see Well-Child Pediatric Examination Schedule]*. This involves a simple test that requires a few drops of blood.

Unfortunately, iron is not commonly found in the foods that we give to infants. Consequently, all infants need either iron-fortified infant formula or iron supplements, if breastfed. As they progress to solid foods at the age of six months, make sure you select iron-supplemented baby foods. Listed below are some iron-rich foods that your older child may enjoy and benefit from:

Excellent Sources of Iron

- Lean cuts of pork
- Lean cuts of beef (hamburgers are an especially kid-friendly format)
- Sardines
- Chicken (dark meat contains more iron than white meat)
- Lamb
- Tuna
- Ham
- Salmon and other fish

Good Sources of Extra Iron

- Dried apricots
- Baked beans
- Baked potatoes (with the skin)

- Almonds
- Lima beans
- Raisins
- Enriched macaroni and pastas
- Enriched bread (make sure that you check the label)
- Peas
- Peanut butter
- Eggs
- Enriched or fortified breakfast cereals

JAUNDICE OF THE NEWBORN (Hyperbilirubinemia)

Jaundice (hyperbilirubinemia) of the newborn appears as a yellowish discoloration of the skin that progresses from head to toe. It is caused by the overproduction of a yellow pigment in the blood called bilirubin, which the baby's immature digestive system and liver are incapable of processing appropriately. Most cases appear by the third day of life. As the infant develops over her first weeks of life, her ability to process properly bilirubin improves.

For the majority of babies, an elevation of bilirubin is a common and relatively harmless problem during the first days of life. Breastfed babies, premature babies, and Asian babies are more likely to experience hyperbilirubinemia than other newborns. If you or your doctor notice that the baby is "yellow" in appearance during her first days of life, your pediatrician will ask for a serum (blood) bilirubin level to be measured. The majority of babies with normal or "physiologic" jaundice will have the harmless form of jaundice physicians call unconjugated hyperbilirubinemia. Depending on the baby's level of unconjugated bilirubin and the rate at which it is rising, these babies may be treated with phototherapy: fluorescent bilirubin light packs help break down the bilirubin in the blood into forms that can be excreted in the urine and stool. Rarely, babies with severe metabolic, genetic, and other diseases may display a more serious form of jaundice called conjugated hyperbilirubinemia. These babies require a detailed medical examination at a children's hospital.

 I heard that sunlight is good for my baby's skin and helps to reduce jaundice. Is this true?

While babies do need some sunlight—particularly for the metabolism of vitamin D—exposing your newborn to long periods of sunlight is probably not a good idea for the treatment of jaundice. If you do take your older baby out in the sun, incidentally, you need to protect her against sunburn by using a suitable hat, sunglasses, and sunscreen lotion (with an SPF rating of 15 or higher) [see Sunshine, Sunburn, Sunscreens, and Sunglasses].

My three-day-old baby was diagnosed with jaundice today. Should I stop breastfeeding?

Do not stop breastfeeding your jaundiced baby. The fluid will help to lower the blood levels of bilirubin, and many lactation consultants believe that the first days of breastfeeding are the most critical; unfortunately, this period happens to coincide with the same time newborns develop hyperbilirubinemia. Many breastfed babies do develop some level of normal jaundice, which should resolve with continued feeding and, if necessary, phototherapy.

Should I feed my newborn with jaundice extra water to help "dilute" the bilirubin?

No. Breastfed or bottlefed babies get all the water they need in breast milk or formula. Some studies suggest that feeding the baby water will make the jaundice worse.

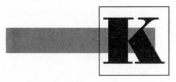

KAWASAKI'S DISEASE (Mucocutaneous Lymph Node Syndrome)

The exact cause of this childhood disease is unknown. Many physicians and epidemiologists believe that Kawasaki's disease is infectious in nature. Currently, the annual incidence of Kawasaki's disease in the United States is low, about 4.5 to 8.5 cases per 100,000 children below the age of five years. In a community outbreak, however, the incidence can rise to 150 per 100,000 children.

Kawasaki's disease is marked by the collection of symptoms listed below. You need to call your pediatrician immediately if you notice these features.

- Fever greater than 101° F for five days

- Red or "bloodshot" eyes

- Swelling and redness in the mouth area: red or swollen and cracked lips; the tongue looks like a strawberry; the throat is beefy-red in color; or other signs of inflammation of the mouth and lips

- Swollen lymph nodes ("glands") around the neck and throat

- Swollen feet, toes, hands, or fingers. A later symptom is the peeling of skin in these areas

- No other explanation for these symptoms or the child's overall illness

The disease can attack other organs in the body, and the heart is at particular risk. About 20 percent of children with Kawasaki's disease develop heart problems as a result of the inflammation associated with the illness. Early recognition of these symptoms and treatment with intravenous gamma globulin and aspirin can be very helpful in preventing damage to the child's coronary blood vessels. These medications are prescribed in the hospital under the careful supervision and observation of doctors. Incidentally, Kawasaki's disease, as well as juvenile forms of arthritis, are among the very few childhood illnesses for which we still prescribe aspirin.

Latchkey Children

More than ten million school-aged children take care of themselves each day at home alone after school. Latchkey children earned their name because they typically have the key to their own homes and are responsible for letting themselves in after school. Leaving your school-aged child home alone for short periods may be the only realistic child-care arrangements you can afford; however, it is wise to explore more supervised options first, such as community-based programs and after-hours programs at church, synagogue, or school.

Not all young school-aged children are ready for such responsibility. You need to discuss with your child whether or not she feels comfortable being home alone, how to take care of herself, whom to call in the case of an emergency, and other important issues. Typically, the child under age six should not be left home alone; as your child becomes older, you will be able to assess better her individual level of responsibility and confidence with such a venture. Some communities have laws that prohibit leaving children under the age of thirteen home alone; check with your local and state law enforcement agency to make sure that leaving your child home alone is not against the law.

It is a good idea to make the daily self-supervision experience LESS than two hours a day. Call your child during her time home alone each day to reassure her that you are thinking about her and keeping a figurative eye on her. Set up clear rules and realistic goals regarding the child's responsibilities, such as letting herself in, preparing a snack, doing her homework, and so on. Homework and a snack are manageable; more complex tasks, such as painting the house, are not! Make sure that your house is child-safe, and have a clear list of emergency numbers, neighbors, and other support in case it is necessary *[see Day Care and Child-Care Issues]*.

For an excellent and nonjudgmental book on the topic, see: Robinson, B.E., B.H. Rowland, and M. Coleman, *Home-Alone Kids: The Working Parent's Complete Guide to Providing the Best Care for Your Child.* (Lexington, KY: Lexington Books, 1988).

Lead poisoning

Lead poisoning is too often a cause of brain damage, mental retardation, and other problems in North America. Lead is a toxic heavy metal found in lead paint and other lead-based products. The ingestion of lead, even at low levels, can cause serious brain damage. Lead paint chips and similar contaminated products taste somewhat sweet, so children, especially young ones who explore the world through their mouths, are likely to eat them. The most frightening aspect of lead is that it is difficult to remove safely and is common in many homes. About 75 percent of all lead ingested by American children comes from lead paint dust in the home; another 20 percent of cases occurs from lead-contaminated drinking water.

Even though federal guidelines in the United States and other countries have been established to prevent new products from containing lead, there is enough lead contamination in homes, soil, and drinking water in various parts of North America to warrant a careful watch by parents. Quite simply, *any* home, particularly those built before the 1960s, can potentially contain large sources of lead, usually in the form of lead paint. Indeed, the federal government suggests that all homes built before 1980 be checked for lead by a licensed lead-abatement contractor who has been certified by the Environmental Protection Agency. These contractors usually advertise in the yellow pages of your local telephone book; their names, addresses, and phone numbers are also typically on file at your city hall or board of health office. Home kits to check for lead exist, but these have not been standardized on a national basis.

Prevention of Lead Poisoning

Inspecting the home

The only way to avoid the damaging effects of lead is not to ingest it. As noted above, this is an especially difficult problem with toddlers, who like to put anything and everything into their mouths. Consequently, parents buying a home need to have it, and the dirt surrounding the home, checked for lead. If lead is found, a professional lead removal, including a thorough cleaning with a high-efficiency particle accumulator (HEPA) device and proper disposal, is mandatory. Older methods such as stripping, sanding off, or burning off the lead paint only serve to make the lead particles airborne and even more easily ingested or inhaled by those living in the home.

 ### Where are the most common places to find lead products lurking in my home?

Lead removal requires good detective work on your part. Here is a checklist for some of the most common household sites for lead contamination.

Inside the home

- *All walls that are painted, from floor to ceiling*
- *Baseboards and molding*
- *Doors*
- *Door casings and jambs*
- *Windows, including the casing, sill, header, sash, well, and exterior*
- *Exposed pipes, particularly those in a vertical position*
- *Floors*
- *Staircases, including stair risers and handrails*
- *Painted or repainted furniture, including drawers, cabinets, shelves*
- *Exposed radiators*
- *Toys (such as painted dolls or soldiers), crystal products, and china*

Outside the home

- *All painted surfaces of the home including siding, trim, and similar structural surfaces*
- *The exterior of the doors, including casings and jambs*
- *Fences*
- *Windows, including those in the basement*
- *Porches*
- *Garages, including doors, windows, and the garage floor*
- *Outdoor decks*
- *Toys and furniture constructed for outdoor use*

Testing Your Home's Drinking Water Supply

The home's drinking water and its pipes also need to be scrupulously checked for evidence of lead. This can be done by obtaining two samples of your home's water supply. Sample #1 should be obtained from the cold water faucet *after* it has not been used for six or more hours. Sample #2 is obtained after running the cold water faucet for about two minutes. Make sure they are properly labeled and analyzed by a licensed lead-abatement contractor. If the first sample contains more than 15 parts per billion of lead or the second sample contains more than 5 parts per billion of lead, you need to obtain a special filter called a reverse osmosis filter for that faucet. Distilling devices can also be used to remove lead from the drinking water. Hot water tends to leech lead from the pipes far more effectively than cold water (thereby increasing the lead content of drinking water). If you live in a lead-contaminated area, be sure to use only cold water that has run several minutes for drinking or food preparation.

Dietary Prevention

A healthy diet that is rich in calcium (found in green vegetables and dairy products), iron, and protein is suggested for all normal children. Children exposed to lead often have dietary deficiencies in these important minerals and nutrients, which may increase their absorption of lead [*see Iron Deficiency Anemia*].

Thorough Handwashing if You Handle Lead

Handwashing is always a good idea before preparing food or playing with your child. This is especially the case if someone in the family works in a lead-related job (such as in metal foundries, chemical plants, shooting galleries, and so on) or has a lead-related hobby (such as making stained glass windows or jewelry).

Use of Lead-free Plates, Cups, and Cutlery

Food and drink should *never* be served in containers or dishes that contain lead paint or crockery treated with lead-based glaze. This is generally not a problem for products manufactured in the United States, where numerous regulations prevent the use of lead paint or lead products. Matters become more risky when you buy products made in countries with less strict rules about the use of lead paint. Similarly, canned goods from other countries may contain lead solder, which can also be ingested. Sometimes, toys produced in other countries may be painted with lead-based products.

When should I have my child checked for lead poisoning?

The American Academy of Pediatrics strongly urges that all children be screened routinely for evidence of lead ingestion. The earlier the intervention, the lower the likelihood that lead will cause damage, since most of the toxic effects of lead on the developing brain occur before the age of three years. We generally obtain a drop of blood from babies during their six-month visit and then repeat the test every twelve to twenty-four months if they are at high risk for lead poisoning. Your pediatrician will go over the results with you. Generally, we do nothing for levels under ten micrograms; if the level is higher, your pediatrician will discuss how to abate lead in the home and any other interventions that may be necessary.

Additional reading for ridding the home of lead

McVay-Hughes, C., and C. Meyer. *Getting the Lead Out.* (New York: NYPIRG Publications, 1995 (Available by writing to the New York Public Interest Research Group, 9 Murray Street, 3rd Floor, N.Y., N.Y., 10007-2272).

Stapleton, R.M. *Lead is a Silent Hazard.* (New York: Walker and Co., 1995).

LICE (Pediculosis)

Head lice are tiny insects that can live only on human beings. They particularly enjoy the scalps of children. If your child is sent home from day care or school with this problem, don't waste a moment of time feeling guilty for not being a "good parent." Even healthy, well-fed, clean children contract head lice.

The lice lay eggs in one's hair and cause an intense itching sensation in one's scalp. After a casual brushing of the hair, you will see dozens of tiny, white eggs (nits) in the brush. Nits are quite adherent to the shafts of the hair, unlike dandruff or dirt. They are especially common in the hair at the back of the neck.

Fortunately, head lice are as easily treated as they are recognized. Your physician can prescribe an anti-lice shampoo or you can purchase (over-the-counter, without a prescription) those called NIX® and RID® 1 percent anti-lice medicated shampoos. Before you put your lice-ridden child in the shower, wash his dry hair with about two ounces of the shampoo. Massage the scalp deeply with the shampoo, adding some warm water to create a lather. Leave this on for about fifteen minutes and then rinse the hair thoroughly in the shower. You and your child can rest assured that the lice and nits have all been killed.

Now comes the disgusting part: the white, now dead, nits are likely to still be sticking to your child's hair. Try to remove them the best you can by picking them out with your fingers or using the small, fine-toothed, disposable comb that comes in the medicated shampoo package. With careful combing and a massage of the scalp and hair, you should be able to master this difficult chore of parenting. There is *no* need to shave your child's hair.

Are lice contagious?

Yes. In fact, if your child gets a recurrence of lice after the treatment, consider whether someone else in the house or a close friend of your child has lice. When one child in a home is diagnosed as being infected with head lice, it is a good idea to check the scalps of everyone else in the household. All new suspects should be rounded up and shampooed as discussed above. The child who has been treated is perfectly healthy and can return to school without worry of infecting others. Make sure you tell your children not to share combs, towels, brushes, or hats to help avoid contracting head lice.

If you discover the lice at home, you should call your child's teacher so she or he can inform the other parents of the class to look at their children's scalps.

My five-year-old son was just sent home from school with head lice. I shampooed him according to directions but was also told to clean my house. Are there any special precautions I need to take?

You can begin by vacuuming the house thoroughly. Soak his combs or brushes in a mixture of water and some of the anti-lice shampoo or bleach for at least an hour. Change the bed linens, pillowcases, and pajamas. Wash the all of the used bedding, plus any clothing he has worn in the past three days, in hot water to kill all the lice and nits that may have stuck to those objects. Some things, of course, are more difficult to wash—hats or winter coats. These objects can be placed inside a large plastic garbage bag. Tie up one end so the bag is airtight and leave the enclosed contents alone for three to four weeks. By the end of the month, there is little chance that any of the nits or lice are still alive. If this is not feasible, try to find a kindly dry cleaner. We do not recommend fumigating the house with special sprays or insecticides. These substances are not only toxic to lice, they can also cause harm to children (and adults). Finally, check your child's head in about ten days to make sure that the lice are not back.

LONG-DISTANCE PARENTING

One out of every two marriages ends in divorce: this is a sad fact of American life. Clearly, one of the greatest problems to emerge from such a process is what happens to the children of these marriages, who need the nurturing, loving, and support of *both* parents. Unfortunately, this is often further complicated by the mobility of most Americans today and what may happen when one parent moves far away from the other—and the children—to "begin again" or for reasons of work. These "long-distance" parents have an especially difficult time maintaining an active presence in their children's lives.

One way to avoid these problems, if you find yourself in a long-distance parenting situation, is to make sure you schedule regular contact with your children. Children over the age of two like to talk on the telephone, and this is not a bad way to establish contact when you cannot actually be present. Another easy way to keep in contact is by keeping a stack of stamped postcards on your desk; whenever you think of your faraway child, jot down a brief note and tell him! Children love surprises, and a seemingly small gesture like a postcard can mean so much to a child. Think of it as an unexpected visit from Dad or Mom. Frequent letters—if the child is old enough to read and write—are helpful. Remember important dates or events in the child's life (such as a holiday, big game, or birthday) with a gift, card, or phone call. Perhaps most importantly, visits are essential. Keeping in touch as a long-distance parent is not an easy task, but it is a crucial one. Remember, no matter where your children live, you need to be interested in their interests and activities in order to maintain an active presence. Ask questions about school and about after-school activities, about what they like to do and what they do not like to do. It's not just on special occasions, like a birthday, that your faraway son or daughter wants to hear from you. Stay involved!

For additional advice on the importance of infant and child bonding, what children experience when confronted with divorce and long-distance separations, and the highs and lows or reunions and good-byes, see Marla Gelper Cohen, *Long Distance Parenting: A Guide for Divorced Parents* (New York: New American Library, 1990) *[see Divorce].*

LYMPH NODES (Swollen glands)

Throughout our bodies, we have a series of channels and nodes called the lymphatic system. These nodes—or, as they are commonly referred to, "glands"—serve as filters against possible infections. Relatively tiny (each about the size of a pea), the more than five hundred lymph nodes in the body are all connected by lymphatic channels. The most common places to feel enlarged lymph nodes are around the neck and in the groin area. Indeed, most children tend to have enlarged lymph nodes in the neck region at some point during any given year, since they develop upper respiratory infections so frequently [*see Upper Respiratory Infections*].

In the event of an infection, the lymph node will enlarge or swell because it is filtering fluid (lymph) and cells that contain elements of the infection in question. You should expect to feel soft, rubbery nodes wherever the infection is most prominent, as a sign that the body is fighting back. They can appear with almost any form of infection or inflammation, ranging from localized cuts or infections of the skin [*see Impetigo*] to more generalized infections like chicken pox or pneumonia. With these more generalized conditions, you may see and feel enlarged nodes at other locations across the body. Enlarged lymph nodes can be quite tender and are generally about an inch or so in diameter.

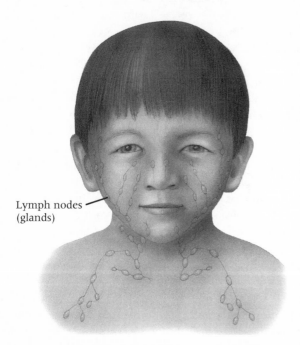

Lymph nodes
(glands)

Swollen Lymph Nodes that Require Medical Attention

Sometimes the child's body cannot adequately fight off a severe infection or inflammation without help. One sign may be persistent large lymph nodes. You should call your pediatrician if you notice any of the following problems.

• Enlarged nodes (two inches across or greater), with the skin surrounding them appearing warm and red

• Red streaks emanating from the enlarged node

• Any node extremely sensitive to your light touch and quite painful

• Swollen neck nodes that are large enough to cause difficulties with swallowing, breathing, opening the mouth, or bending the neck

• Swollen nodes associated with an elevated fever (greater than 102°F) without a clear cause

- Swollen nodes in a child under the age of two months
- An enlarged lymph node that feels "rock-hard" and is difficult to move with gentle pressure from your fingers
- Red-to-blue bruises of varying size associated with the lymph nodes
- Swollen nodes in a child who appears quite ill
- Lymph node swelling that has been present for more than a month without resolution

Treatment

The treatment for the overwhelming majority of swollen lymph nodes is simply to wait. With time—anywhere from a few days to several weeks—the lymph nodes will return to their normal size. Swollen lymph nodes should not be squeezed, poked, prodded, or removed. Indeed, too much manipulation of a swollen lymph node may make it worse.

MASTURBATION

Discussing this topic has led to the dismissal of a United States Surgeon General, but let's face it—almost every human being has masturbated at one time or another. The self-stimulation of one's genitals, regardless of age, is frequently associated with comfort and pleasure. Little boys and girls quickly learn this technique as early as infancy and may practice it when they are especially tired, bored, or—as many parents tell us—whenever you have company! Sometimes, however, frequent masturbation may be a red flag for particularly stressful events in the child's life.

It is important from the outset to note that masturbation is harmless. No one has ever become blind or deformed or a sex offender from this practice! Quite serious, however, can be the psychological damage to a child who is told he or she is evil or who is physically punished for the practice. The main point, then—given that masturbation is a normal part of childhood (and adulthood, for that matter)—is how do you deal with it?

• Remember our principle rule of child care: Pick your battles wisely. There is no point in going ballistic over a harmless activity, especially when it occurs in the privacy of the child's bedroom. If, for example, you notice your child masturbating in his or her sleep, during a nap or at bedtime, ignore it. No harm will come to your child.

• For many years pediatricians and child psychologists urged parents always to ignore the child's masturbation, even if it occurs in public or in the presence of others. This probably is not a great idea, since it sends a wrong message to the child (that it is acceptable to masturbate in public). Instead we recommend, for the child who masturbates openly during the daylight hours, that you gently—and frequently—suggest to your son or daughter that it is not reasonable to do it in public. Instead, you might explain that masturbation is only "okay" in private, such as in the bedroom. You also might explain that it makes others uncomfortable when someone masturbates in public.

• Most toddlers, by the age of three to four, learn not to masturbate in public; the child of five or older certainly can do so. If your concern persists, ask your child's schoolteachers or day care attendants if they are noticing public masturbation in your absence. They, too, need to remind your toddler that such activities are private ones.

I have been trying to get my three-year-old daughter to stop masturbating in public, to no avail. I have explained to her that it is best left to the bedroom or bathroom, but this doesn't seem to work. What should I do?

Certainly some children need more reminders about behavioral change than others. One good method, beyond explaining carefully to the child that it is normal and okay to masturbate as long as it is done in private, is to quickly distract the child from the activity when you first notice it. For example, the child sitting on the floor watching television with the family who begins masturbating should not be allowed to continue. Instead, try to come up with another activity or game to get the child's mind off it. Frequent hugs and other physical contact of a nonsexual nature between parent and child have also been shown to diminish the frequency of masturbation.

When should I worry about my little boy's habit of masturbating?

Unfortunately, in our present day and age, parents need to be concerned about sexual abuse of their children. You need to make sure that the masturbation habit was not taught to your child by either an older child or adult and that your child does not masturbate other children or adults.

Sometimes especially unhappy or depressed children may exhibit excessive masturbation; this, too, needs to be investigated. You might begin by asking the child if anything is troubling him or her. Think back: have you observed a change in the child's behavior of late? Family discord, recent deaths, divorce, and other emotionally traumatic events may also contribute to this behavior.

By the age of five most children, after a month or more of gentle reminders and a good deal of understanding, learn to be more discreet in their habits. If not, a consultation with your pediatrician can frequently be helpful.

MEDICINES

"Over-the-Counter" or "Patent" Medicines

For the overwhelming majority of problems of normal childhood, "over-the-counter" medicines ("patent" medicines) are NOT necessary. Think back to the last time you had a cold: did the patent medicine advertised to cure all of your aches, pains, and symptoms really do that? Or did they simply make you sleepy and, upon wakening, grouchy because the same problems that initially led you to the drugstore were still present? One well-known professor of pediatrics once said that the only children patent medicines help are the children of the people who own the patent medicine companies.

With that in mind, choose your battles carefully with your child. One of your challenges as a parent will be to get your child to take medications he or she does not want to take. If the medication in question will provide temporary symptomatic relief at best, you may want to avoid "medicine-taking struggles" except to get him to accept those medicines really necessary for his recovery. On the other hand, if the child has severe cold symptoms, such as a jagging cough that prevents her from sleeping or a fever higher than 102°, and you find that her cold is helped somewhat by a cough medicine, pain reliever, fever reducer, or decongestant, by all means go for it. Please note, however, that even over-the-counter medicines have side effects (as do all medications). If your child is doing well without them, these products are best left in drugstores.

Antibiotics

These are probably the most frequently prescribed drugs your child will receive. They fight off infections caused by bacteria—ear infections, pneumonia, and more serious illnesses including meningitis (a severe infection of the brain and central nervous system). But antibiotics are only effective against bacterial infections, *not* against viral infections—the type that make up the majority of complaints such as colds and runny noses during the winter. There is absolutely no point in prescribing or taking an antibiotic when the infectious agent in question is a virus, since the antibiotic will do absolutely nothing to shorten the course of a viral illness. In fact, the overuse of antibiotics can cause problems such as diarrhea, allergies, and the development of antibiotic-resistant bacteria. This is a significant problem. A number of studies have discovered new strains of disease-causing bacteria that are completely resistant to almost all of our currently available antibiotics. Overuse of these medications has contributed to this dangerous situation. If your child doesn't need an antibiotic, don't insist on its use anyway; it may cause more harm than good.

Once the course of an antibiotic is completed, throw away any remaining medicine rather than saving it or using it for another family member. Your doctor will prescribe another antibiotic for the next episode, since antibiotic medication that is "saved" can become inactive, rendering it useless for the next application. Similarly, there are hundreds of antibiotics available today, each one with a specific use against a particular bacterial infection; therefore, the antibiotic prescribed for one episode of illness may well *not* be the one of choice for a different illness. We strongly recommend that you discuss all medications with your pediatrician *before* giving them to your child.

Taking Your Medicine ("Just a spoonful of sugar helps the medicine go down")

It is the rare child who eagerly awaits a dose of medicine. Some object strongly, and this can become a major struggle between parent and young child. Fortunately, drug manufacturers have worked wonders in creating medicine-containing suspensions and syrups that actually taste good! For example, most of the commonly prescribed antibiotics are available in flavors ranging from garden-variety grape or cherry to "piña colada." On the other hand, some medicines simply do not taste good. These may require ingenuity. Here are a few tips.

1. You may have to camouflage the medicine by mixing it with a palatable food such as applesauce, ice cream, or fruit juice before giving it to your child. Use a portion of food small enough to make sure you are actually giving all of the medicine prescribed. This approach can be used either for syrups or for pills, provided you grind the pill in question to a fine powder and mix well. Grinding down pills is actually quite simple: merely place the pill on a plate (or in the bowl of a spoon) and crush it with the back of another spoon. If the pill is a capsule, all you need to do is open it into the food product you are using as a disguise. You should also have a nice, tall glass of your child's favorite beverage at the ready to wash down the medicine.

2. Try your best to make the experience a pleasant one rather than a battle. If you grimace when pouring out the medicine, your child is going to realize quickly that the substance in question is a disgusting one and will respond in kind.

3. Refrigerating the medicine or giving the child some ice chips before administering the medicine helps minimize the taste by numbing the child's taste buds.

4. Once the child takes her medicine, praise her for a job well done.

5. Some children like to "control" the situation by holding the spoon containing the medicine as opposed to being fed. Try asking your child what method he prefers.

6. Rather than using regular tableware, purchase a special medicine spoon or syringe from your drugstore that measures an exact amount, usually five cc or one teaspoon, and is designed to be "spill-proof."

7. We admit that some toddlers will refuse to take their medicine even under these conditions. The first thing to do in these circumstances is to call your physician to determine whether the medicine in question is truly necessary for the child's recovery. What we said about choosing your battles carefully should always be taken into account, from the toddler years all the way through adolescence. Let us suppose, however, that the medicine *is* necessary. What then? You can begin by reasoning with the child. Explain to him that you know it tastes bad but that it is necessary so that he can feel better. Being firm and carefully explaining the situation is always preferable to threatening, yelling, or bribes, which in the end will come back to haunt you.

8. After giving all of this advice, we acknowledge that there will be situations where even these approaches do not work and it is imperative for your child's health that she take a specific medication. *As a last resort*, you may have to force-

feed the medicine. Remember, when using this method, that you need to be absolutely certain that the child is not flat on his back, to prevent choking. You should not yell at, hit, or insult your child; and you should always apologize to the child once the ordeal is over, offering reassurance in the form of hugs and kind words. More times than not, during the heat of the moment, the medicine dribbles out of the child's mouth rather than into the child's stomach. If this occurs, try not to get angry. Figure out how much medicine was taken and replace the dose needed. With firmness, and alternative approaches, the child will learn (we hope!) to appreciate that you are serious, and the force-feeding will not need to be repeated.

How can I get my eight-year-old to learn to take pills?

Swallowing pills or capsules is an acquired ability that, while unsuitable for younger children, should be mastered by school age (e.g., six years or older). Gentleness and reassurance are the keys to learning this task. Sometimes it is helpful to have your child practice swallowing, say, a raisin or pill-sized candy before graduating to the actual medicine. If these are too big for the novice pill-swallower, try cutting them into smaller pieces. By making a game out of the exercise, the task can usually be mastered. Given the wide variety of syrups and suspensions and the pill-crushing technique described above, developing such a skill may not be as urgent as it once was.

The Medicine Chest

Medicine chests, like garages, and basements, should be cleaned out completely each year. Such a "spring-cleaning" affords you the opportunity to throw away health-care products whose potency may have expired or which are simply unused and taking up space. Medicine chests need to be either locked or appropriately "child-proofed" to prevent curious children from potential danger. Prescription medicines should *never* be saved beyond either the expiration date or the time when they are no longer needed (whichever comes first). Most medications have a limited shelf life and may not be effective by the time you consider using the remaining amount. Prescription medicines should never be used for other family members, for those who seem to have "exactly the same thing" as whoever required the medication in the first place. Mixing medicines or exchanging prescriptions without your physician's involvement may seem to be a convenient way of avoiding a trip to the doctor's, but it is really a false economy. It can be a game of Russian roulette!

The home medicine chest checklist

1. Thermometers (oral and rectal)

2. Rubber syringe-suction bulb (when used with sterile warm-water nose drops, this device can help alleviate the blocked nose of an infant)

3. Nose drops for severely congested noses; we recommend saline (saltwater) nose drops for infants and small children (under the age of eight)

4. Cough syrups

5. Throat lozenges for the child older than five years

6. Pain and fever relievers: acetaminophen

7. Rubbing alcohol (70 percent isopropyl alcohol), for sterilizing

8. Bandages, gauze, adhesive tape, sterile cotton

9. Antiseptic- and antibiotic-containing ointments (e.g., Bacitracin®, povidone-iodine gel, and so on)

10. Syrup of ipecac (30 cc dose), to induce vomiting for certain kinds of poisoning (This is an over-the-counter medication and does not require a prescription)

11. Ice packs, for sore body parts

12. 0.5 percent hydrocortisone-containing ointment for itchy conditions brought on by poison ivy or mosquito bites. If the child has a history of anaphylactic reactions, keep an epinephrine pen-syringe available in both your home and travel medicine chests. (Epi-pens do require a prescription from your doctor)

13. An antihistamine, such as Benadryl®, for allergic reactions such as hives or hay fever

14. An Ace® wrap bandage for sprain injuries

The portable "first aid" kit on the other hand, which may be used on a variety of occasions ranging from camping trips to car rides and beach vacations, should include: sunscreen, alcohol wipes, bandages, gauze, adhesive tape, tourniquet, insect repellent, adrenaline and syringes (if someone in the family has a severe allergy to bee-stings), meat tenderizer powder (with contains the enzyme papain and is excellent for relief from bee stings), plus scissors, tweezers, and a needle (for splinter removal). Adapt this list to your own travel needs.

Milia *[See Newborn appearance]*

Mongolian spots *[See Newborn appearance]*

Mouth injuries

The best thing about injuries to the mouth, lips, and gums is that they heal quickly with very little scarring. In fact, a cut inside the mouth usually heals within three days, twice as fast as the rate of healing for a cut to the skin. Frequently, the tongue, lips, or the inside lining of the cheeks meet in a "head-on collision" with the teeth. These types of injuries are most frequently seen after falling, being tackled, fighting, and even after eating or chewing. As with most forms of traumatic injuries, the best medicine is prevention. Specifically, you need to instruct your child not to walk with sharp or pointy objects in his mouth, since they can cause a great deal of damage to the back of the mouth or soft palate (at the rear portion of the roof of the mouth). Violent activities from fighting to tackle football should also be strongly discouraged. Incidentally, a common mouth injury (matched by an accompanying hand injury) occurs when one child hits another in the mouth. Frequently, the victim will suffer from cuts to the lips or inner aspects of the mouth, while the aggressor—particularly if the victim wears orthodontic braces—may experience cuts to the hand *[see Bites, Human]*.

Because there are so many blood vessels in the lip and mouth region, these injuries involve a great deal of bleeding, bruising, and swelling. The bleeding can usually be stopped by applying firm pressure to the injury for ten to fifteen minutes with a clean washcloth soaked in cool water. An ice pack wrapped in a washcloth is also helpful and numbing. An important caveat is not to stretch or inspect the wound after the bleeding has actually stopped: this will disrupt the clot (an early form of scab) that has developed, causing further bleeding at the site. Some of the most bloody injuries to the mouth are the deeply cut tongue or tears in the tissues of the mouth. These should not require sutures as long as they stop bleeding during the ten to fifteen minutes of pressure.

It is also important to note that the lips are one of the most sensitive human body parts. The same abundance of nerve endings that makes activities such as kissing or eating so pleasurable can yield a great deal of pain when injured. For the first two to three days after such an injury, the swelling and pain are best treated with understanding, loving care, and plenty of popsicles or ice chips to suck on, numbing the painful area. Acetaminophen or ibuprofen can be used as pain relievers for these problems. (Ibuprofen should be used only after acetaminophen has been tried without success and only in children older than six months.) It is not a good idea to give aspirin to children, for a variety of reasons; it may alleviate some pain, but it can also cause increased bleeding and is associated with a form of encephalitis called Reye's Syndrome.

Anyone who has ever experienced a cut on the mouth or lips knows to avoid acidic foods (such as citrus fruits or tomatoes) or salty foods. These will only irritate the sensitive areas. Instruct your child to rinse out his mouth with cool water after each meal. Mouth injuries should start healing within two days or so, and a whitish scar tissue should begin to appear. If the wound appears worse, looks infected, or the child develops a fever (greater than 102.5°F), call your physician.

When to Call the Doctor

- Extremely deep wounds
- Injuries to the back of the mouth
- Injuries as a result of the child falling with a sharp, pointy object in her mouth.

MOUTH SORES (Canker sores and oral herpes infections)

Canker Sores

We all get canker sores at one time or another. For children, especially young ones, they can be quite painful and a great source of misery for their parents. The exact cause of these annoying sores is not clear. Unlike fever blisters (see below), which appear on the outer portions of the lip, canker sores always appear on the inside of the mouth or lips. They are probably caused by a particle of food that has remained lodged between teeth, lips, and gums, or even a particular type of food. They are not contagious but in some people can be a recurrent problem.

The best treatment for this problem, like so many others, is time and love. Again, as discussed with traumatic mouth injuries, popsicles certainly don't hurt matters any! Sometimes, if your child will cooperate, swishing a teaspoon of antacid liquid in the mouth will help coat the ulcer. Acetaminophen may decrease the pain, but we prefer the popsicle prescription (and so do most of our patients). Avoiding salty or acidic foods, hot liquids, and crunchy or difficult-to-chew foods is also a good idea. Such treatments as numbing or anesthetic medicines and salt-water rinses often create more burning and painful sensations than the sore itself and are best dismissed.

Remember, as with all injuries inside the mouth, the healing sore takes about a week or so and will appear white in color as opposed to pink. This is entirely normal.

There are, of course, situations that necessitate a call to your physician. For example, the child who has several canker sores and will not eat or drink (especially young infants and toddlers, who can become dehydrated rather easily); the child with these symptoms and a fever; the child in whom similar lesions appear on the eyelids, genitals, gums or tongue; and the child with sores that develop after ingesting a particular medicine, may each be suffering from conditions far more serious than a mere canker sore, requiring medical attention.

Cold Sores (Oral Herpes Infections)

This is one of the most common infections of the mouth and is caused by the herpes simplex virus. Unlike genital herpes, which is acquired through sexual activity, herpes simplex of the lips or mouth (herpes labalis) is not sexually transmitted. Oral herpes simplex is typically spread by having close physical contact with someone who has herpes. More than 95 percent of all Americans have suffered from this problem at one time or another.

Herpes infections can be preceded by a burning or tingling sensation of the mouth, followed by the appearance of several small (about one to two-mm in size) "blisters" on the lips or, occasionally, in the corner of the mouth. In a minority of children who develop this problem (less than 5 percent), the infection subsides but quietly lives inside a sensory nerve in the face and may reappear later on, without significant warning. Many times there is some stressful episode associated with an oral herpes recurrence—a severe illness, fever, exposure to the sun, fatigue, or even a young woman's menstrual period.

The lesions of herpes will heal within seven to ten days. Typically, the blisters burst, dry up, and form scabs. The lesions then go on to heal without any serious scarring of the area.

You need to call your physician if the lesions appear to be spreading and worsening over a two-week course, as opposed to healing as described above; or if the blisters appear near the eye.

Extremely small children may have a difficult time with oral herpes (or other mouth infections) and may refuse to eat or drink. These children may need special coaxing and popsicles or ice chips to ensure against dehydration. Some cases of oral herpes in the extremely young child cause enough pain and refusal of liquids that hospitalization is required to correct such dehydration. The child who is dehydrated will produce only small amounts of urine, saliva, and tears. If your child fits these criteria, call your physician for advice and potential therapy *[see Diarrhea and Dehydration].*

 I have always suffered from fever blisters and am worried my child will contract them, too. What should I do to prevent this problem?

Herpes can be contagious, so it is imperative for the parent with an outbreak of oral herpes or fever blisters not to kiss her child (or spouse, for that matter) until the lesions heal completely. Since we each touch our face, mouth, and eyes many times a day without realizing it, good handwashing is a necessary preventive measure. Similarly, if your child is playing with another child who has fever blisters, a little common sense in the prevention department serves nicely. Specifically, do not allow them to share toys that might find themselves in a child's mouth, and discourage kissing or spitting. It is best to have an affected child under the age of five avoid this type of close contact with others for a week until the lesions heal. It is also wise to apply lip balm that contains sunscreen, when the child is going outdoors into bright sunlight; sun exposure is one of the more common triggers of this problem.

Nasal Congestion (Stuffy nose)

A bulb syringe can help suck the mucus out of a baby's plugged-up nose. Since small babies are "obligate nose breathers" and must breathe through their noses, they have a tough time with nasal congestion. The bulb syringe is available from any drugstore. You press the bulb inward to get some suction, insert the pointy end into the nostril, and release the bulb. Empty the syringe before repeating its use. The resulting vacuum will suck the mucus out of the nose and into the bulb.

For older children, we suggest you use nasal sprays (e.g., oxymetazoline, neosenephrine) sparingly, if at all. They can yield some relief for a few days but have the side effect of "rebounding," eventually causing an even worse nasal congestion. Salt-water nose drops, which contain no chemicals or drugs, are far safer. Simply instill a few drops in each nostril, after which a healthy blow into a tissue should provide some relief.

Negotiating with Your Child

Given that one of the major tenets of child rearing is "Pick your battles wisely!", a word or two on negotiations with a small child should be of use. Negotiating with a child, of course, depends heavily upon his or her developmental level. Toddlers apply their unique style of thinking at the bargaining table just as firmly as seasoned labor union officials. You need to appreciate their concrete style of thinking, their lack of interest in delaying gratification, and their impulsivity if you are going to achieve any type of useful agreement.

No matter what your child's age, you will generally do better to sit down calmly and listen to what she is saying before delivering an ultimatum. There will be times when you have a definitive edict to offer (outlawing aggressive or harmful behaviors and activities). But many more issues that divide parents and their children, on the other hand, are really trivial (e.g., cleaning up the toys, television issues, tantrums, and so on). Negotiations are better than orders in these situations. Agreements, contracts, and a system of rewards or positive reinforcement tend to work as well with children as they do with adults.

Consequently, many of the discussions of behavioral issues covered in this book include the suggestion of making a "poster" chart with stickers and similar decorations to document the child's success in modifying a particular behavior. The result is a visual and concrete image of his achievements. *[see Discipline; Sleep and Sleep Problems; Surviving Shopping with Your Child; Thumb Sucking; Toilet Training].*

This system is often most successful with a special prize as a final goal—whatever the child selects, within budgetary reason, for successfully modifying the specific behavior for an agreed-on period of time. This technique can, of course, be adapted for use with older children. A six-year-old boy, for example, may not desire a physical chart of his progress in overcoming bedwetting, but he may want to work toward a goal—perhaps an afternoon of ice skating or a favorite movie—for staying dry. Teenagers frequently do well with "contracts" as well, exchanging behavioral modifications for particular awards. In the case of teens, however, these "rewards" generally cost a good deal more than those for your toddler.

We were recently asked if we considered this technique a form of bribe. Having thought about this issue, we must answer no. If you expect your child to change his behavior based upon the single, transient offer of a cookie, you are right: that *is* a bribe, and it won't do much more than remediate the moment (and, in the case of lots of cookies, create an obese child). Instead, we suggest that you deliberately explain to your child the importance of working, day by day, toward a goal. For toddlers, use actual, visual charting of their progress in a fun, non-judgmental way (including the days they fail). Encourage your child as she works toward her goal. And really reward her for a job well done. Seems to us like a nice way of learning responsibility, the rewards of good behavior, and a sense of self-esteem.

NEWBORN APPEARANCE

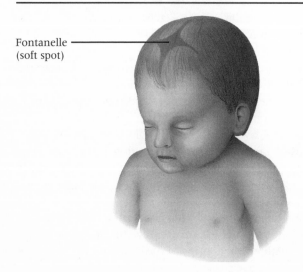

Fontanelle
(soft spot)

Fontanelles (The soft spots on a baby's head)

Although only two fontanelles can be felt or seen by anxious parents and thorough pediatricians, there are actually six "soft spots" where the baby's skull has not fully closed. The anterior fontanelle is the largest and most prominent. This area of the infant's developing brain is covered only with membrane and layers of fibrous tissue and skin, making it an obviously sensitive area to trauma or heavy handling. Gentle care of the baby's head, on the other hand, such as washing her hair or stroking his head, is always welcome.

Doctors use the fontanelles to gain information about the baby's brain and neurological development. For example, the crying infant will have a pulsating and slightly bulging soft spot that resolves once the baby is quiet. Bulging soft spots in the absence of healthy infantile wailing can, however, be a sign your pediatrician needs to know about and act upon immediately. A variety of serious conditions can be heralded by this sign, ranging from meningitis to tumors. Conversely, if a baby's soft spot becomes sunken or depressed, it can be a sign of dehydration (loss of water).

 When will the soft spot in my baby's head close up?

Generally, the anterior fontanelle closes anywhere from four months of age to as late as twenty-six months, with the average infant reaching this physical milestone in seven to twelve months. Delayed closure or a continued large anterior fontanelle may alert the observer to subtle or brewing cases of a variety of infectious, metabolic, and genetic problems. Closure of the soft spot at too early an age (under four months) can also be a harbinger of poor neurologic development.

My newborn son has an extremely funny-shaped head. Should I worry about his appearance?

In most cases, no. Make sure you ask your pediatrician to examine the baby's head [see **Well-Child Pediatric Examination Schedule].** *Molding, the temporary misshaping of the head subsequent to the pressures of labor and delivery, occurs in many babies. It is in no way a birth defect or cosmetic scar. The baby's head will slowly pop into a more desirable shape as his first weeks of life progress. Other mild traumas involving the newborn's head are associated with the birth process, including* caput *and* cephalohematoma. *Caput is a slight swelling on the top of the head or throughout the scalp caused by the pressure of a large head going through the birth canal; it is typically resolved in the first days of life. Cephalohematoma, on the other hand, is a collection of blood caused by pressure between the baby's skull and the mother's pelvic bones during childbirth. Like a bruise, its appearance is slightly delayed. Coming up on the second day of life, it can increase in size for the next five days. Resolution begins shortly after that point but can take as long as two or three months before the blood is completely absorbed by the body. Incidentally, babies who are born prematurely often have more prominent molding than full-term babies. Their heads may take longer to regain a "normal" shape.*

Head Circumference

Your baby's head circumference is an important parameter of his growth, especially in relation to his brain's development. Not that a baby's especially large head destines him to follow in Albert Einstein's footsteps, but it is a measurement pediatricians routinely use to check *normal* growth and progress. A simple tape measure will do to conduct this important test.

During the first three months of life, a baby's head circumference typically increases 2 cm [or 0.8 inches] a month or 6 centimeters [2.4 inches] during the first three months of life. Between four to six months, head circumference only progresses at a rate of 1 cm per month [0.2 inches per month] and during months six to twelve, the baby's head grows at a rate of 0.5 cm per month [0.2 inches per month]. Consequently, the normal baby's head circumference should be 12 cm [4.8 inches] larger at one year than it was at birth *[see Well-Child Pediatric Examination Schedule].*

Skin Conditions Associated with Newborns

Acne of the newborn

Over a third of all newborn babies develop small, red bumps ("pimples") on their face at three to four weeks of age. This condition, newborn acne, can last until four to six months of age. It is probably caused by maternal sex hormones (specifically, androgens) transferred across the placenta and into the baby just before birth. While unsightly, this is a self-limiting problem that goes away on its own and requires no medication or treatment. Try to avoid the temptation to apply lotions or oils to the baby's face; these products only clog the sweat glands and make the acne worse.

Erythema toxicum

By the third day of life more than half of all newborn babies develop a red, splotchy rash called erythema toxicum. It is a collection of red splotches, each red splotch (about $\frac{1}{2}$ to 1″ in diameter) has a tiny central white bump. They can appear anywhere on the baby's skin (with the exception of the palms and soles). No one quite knows the cause of erythema toxicum, but long experience has shown it to be quite harmless. It should disappear by two to four weeks of age.

Mongolian spots

Mongolian spots, black and bluish, flat birthmarks, commonly occur on the back and buttocks, although they can appear anywhere on the skin surface. Children of African-American, Asian, Latino, and native American descent are especially likely to have them. The shape and size of these harmless birthmarks vary from baby to baby. The majority of them fade away by the third year of life, although some may be faintly visible into the adult years.

Milia

Milia are tiny white bumps that appear on the baby's nose and cheeks. Sometimes they also appear on the baby's forehead and chin. They look somewhat similar to pimples and are the result of clogged pores in the skin. They are entirely harmless and will resolve on their own by two to three months of age. No medication or ointments are needed.

Seborrheic dermatitis

This is a common skin condition of infants between the ages of two and ten weeks (although it may reappear during adolescence). It begins at the scalp and is notable for a greasy, yellowish, scaly appearance. As the dermatitis worsens, greasy skin and scales, as well as a pimply rash, may develop on the forehead, cheeks, and even the chest. It is typically not itchy but does look rather unsightly. Fortunately, this is a relatively easy condition to treat: simply wash the baby's hair once a day with a mild baby-dandruff shampoo such as Sebulex®. The scales—and even the pimples on the face and chest—will promptly resolve over the next few weeks.

"Stork bites"

These birthmarks, pink and flat, generally appear on the baby's nose, over the eyelids, or at the back of the neck. The medical name for these birthmarks is capillary hemangioma or salmon patch. They generally resolve on their own during the first year or two of life, although those stork bites on the back of the neck may persist a bit longer. Most are entirely harmless. Physicians will usually measure the size of the birthmark and follow it closely during the baby's life to make sure it is not growing or proving to be a rarer condition of the skin.

NIGHTMARES

Most people begin to dream as early as six months of age. Studies of dream activity in adults, children, and infants suggest that most of us experience four to six dreams a night. Some dreams, of course, are quite unpleasant and downright frightening. Called nightmares, these dreams are often tied to developmental or experiential issues in children. For example, the eight-month-old infant experiencing separation anxiety may have a nightmare about being separated from her parent. The toddler who may enjoy hearing or reading about "monsters" and "bogeymen" may have a nightmare based on this topic. By the age of middle childhood, however, (ages six to twelve), nightmares may be triggered or inspired by real-life fears.

Infants

Obviously, different children react differently to nightmares. It is often most difficult to evaluate the infant who has had a nightmare. She typically awakes and begins crying. But this is also a cue, as you already know, for just about everything else that disturbs an infant in the middle of the night. When attending to the needs of such an infant, always remember the immortal words of Louis, the chief of police in the film *Casablanca*: "Round up the usual suspects!" Check in an orderly fashion to see what is bothering the infant: is she ill? does she have a fever? is there a rash? is her diaper wet or soiled? is she in pain? is she hungry? is she simply frightened? and so on. If all the checks point to a bad dream or minor disturbance, gentle reassurances, hugs, soft words, and placing the infant back in bed should work beautifully.

Toddlers

Toddlers have a fascination, it seems, with scary stories and fantastic figures such as monsters, superheroes, and the like. Not surprisingly, this is closely associated with their developmental states of mind. When dealing with toddlers, it is important to remember that they process and organize information in a far different manner from older children and adults. The line between fantasy and reality is often less clear to a toddler; consequently, frightening dreams, television shows, and such can produce a rather fearful response.

Toddlers and preschoolers frequently awake from a nightmare and run to the people they most associate with reassurance: their parents. A gentle questioning of the child's experience and the reassurance that it was only a dream go a long way toward not only resolving the matter quickly but also to building the child's sense of security and self-esteem. This should be followed by physical reassurances—hugs and tucking the child into bed once again. Typically, the reassured toddler will fall fast asleep. Incidentally, nightlights are helpful for those children "afraid of the dark," especially after a bad dream.

During the next day, it is perfectly reasonable to discuss what happened with your child and try to come up with solutions to making the problems go away. If the child identifies a particularly threatening "monster" or superhuman figure, you need to reassure her that the figure is not real and cannot hurt her.

A good beginning is to comfort the child by saying "Mommy and Daddy would never let a real monster into the house to hurt you." Empowering the child by telling her to say a magic word or phrase (such as "Monster Go Away!") to make the "monster" leave the room often appeals to a toddler's particular way of thinking about the world. Some parents experiment with an empty "squirt" bottle, which they explain to the child as filled with "anti-monster dust"; upon squirting the bottle at the imagined monster, the child is involved in actively ridding her room of the scary figure and learns to trust her abilities to take care of herself. Another approach can be to repeat that "Mommy and Daddy would never let the monster hurt you" and advise the child to seek them immediately if the monster comes back so they can "drive it away."

If, on the other hand, the child spent the night before watching a horror movie on television, your solution is fairly clear: choose a different video next time! In all seriousness, this point cannot be overstressed. We live in a society that is fascinated with macabre and, too often, disturbing imagery. Horror movies are best avoided with young children and can be delayed well into the adolescent years (and certainly beyond!) without any untoward effects. Parents have to be on special guard against children's viewing such movies in their friends' homes, where different tolerances toward these films may exist. Halloween parties that focus on scaring others and campfire ghost story rituals are also sure-fire ways of eliciting a nightmare in a young child *[see Television; Video Games and VCRs]*.

NIGHT TERRORS

Night terrors, on the other hand, are distinctly different from nightmares. They typically occur among children aged one to eight. Their hallmark is the child who is crying, screaming, appears frightened or agitated, but is not awake. His eyes are wide open, yet the child experiencing a night terror does not recognize you. The child may thrash about, run wildly, speak in nonsensical but frightened cadences, and exhibit other irrational behavior. For anywhere from ten to thirty minutes, the child seems inconsolable and may mistake objects or people in his room for threatening figures.

Night terrors may be harmless, but they are especially frightening for those who watch them: parents. The child appears scared and the parent often feels helpless, since no intervention really stops the episode. Instead, it usually ends with the child falling soundly asleep. Even more strange is that children rarely recall these episodes of night terrors upon wakening the following morning.

Night terrors tend to run in families and are found in 2 to 5 percent of all American children. They are benign events in which the child experiences dreams during the deepest phases of the sleep cycle and has difficulty awakening from the dream to the conscious state. It is important to stress that those events are *not* the result of psychological problems and are likely to be triggered by being overtired. Night terrors tend to resolve in the vast majority of children by the age of twelve.

If your child experiences repeated night terrors, it is important to learn how to recognize them and to prevent the child from hurting himself during the event. Child-proofing the room (look for sharp edges, fragile or breakable objects, and nearby staircases) is essential *[see Injury Prevention]*. Speaking clearly, calmly, and reassuringly to the child during the event is helpful. Some children experiencing night terrors calm down with hugging or holding. Some, unfortunately, do not; you will need to experiment with this technique. Although certain authorities suggest frequent awakening of the child to avoid night terrors, we suggest holding this method in reserve for the rare child who experiences them nightly. Discussions with the child the next day rarely help, since the child often does not remember the event.

One final suggestion: if your child does have night terrors, inform your babysitter or day-care worker about the situation, in case it occurs during her watch.

 ### How do I distinguish a night terror from a seizure?

Seizures, a symptom of a neurological condition called epilepsy, are marked by uncontrollable jerks, twitches, drooling, loss of continence, and stiffening. This is quite different from the frightening night terror described above, which is more notable for screaming, crying, and fear. Seizures may sometimes be associated with fever, but not always [see Seizures with Fever; Seizures Without Fever]. Unlike night terrors, they can occur anytime dur-

ing the day or night, although stressful events and being overtired can precipitate them. They typically last longer than night terrors, and the child who suffers one appears "wiped out" or extremely tired, even the next day. Seizures require special examinations by your doctor and the prescription of medication to prevent their appearance. If you are concerned about this in your child, it is important to discuss the event with your physician for accurate evaluation.

NOSEBLEED (Epistaxis)

This common problem of childhood is caused by a number of factors including dry nasal passages, noserubbing, and nosepicking. Sometimes after a cold with a lot of nasal symptoms, sneezing, and noseblowing, a child may suffer a nosebleed. So may the child with nasal allergies such as hay fever. One other cause of nosebleeds is trauma, such as being punched in the nose.

What You Need to do Immediately

1. Assess the injury—if one occurred—and the amount of bleeding.

2. The child should be encouraged to lean forward, so as to not swallow too much blood. A nearby bowl into which the child can spit out blood that enters the mouth from the nose is a good idea. Swallowed blood is quite irritating to the stomach and can cause vomiting; vomited blood typically looks like used coffee grounds.

3. Have your child put his head slightly back while you pinch the soft part of the nose (not the bony part) just above the nostrils with a warm washcloth for about ten minutes. The pinching motion should squeeze the nose so as to stop the bleeding.

Don't forget to remind your child to breathe through his mouth during the nose pressure. You should also try to divert his attention as best you can by talking with and reassuring him.

4. Sometimes the nose pressure needs to be repeated. If, after two ten-minute squeezing sessions, there is still a continuation of the bleeding, call your physician. Some of the questions the physician will ask will have to do with your child's bleeding history (has he had any bleeding from the gums or mouth? any easy bruising? and so on) and similar questions about the child's immediate family. You also need to call the physician immediately if there appears to be a large amount of blood lost or the child complains of feeling dizzy or faints.

 My six-year-old boy has frequent nosebleeds, especially during the winter. What can we do to decrease the number of nosebleeds?

There are a number of nosebleed prevention tips we can offer. Nosebleeds tend to occur more frequently in the winter because we live mostly indoors and breathe heated (and often dry) air. This especially irritates the nasal passages and makes them tender and sensitive to bleeding. A cool-mist humidifier placed in the child's room as well as a humidifying device

connected to your home's heating source should help to moisturize the air. Remember, cool-mist humidifiers need to be cleaned out scrupulously each day to prevent the buildup of mold, fungus, and bacteria in the device. Good daily cleaning with a water-and-bleach solution (one half cup of bleach to one quart of water), followed by rinsing with water, prevents this problem. You can also apply a small dab of petroleum jelly to the inside of the child's nostrils, especially before bed, to help moisturize his dry nasal membranes.

Some children pick their noses more than others; this, of course, can easily lead to nosebleeds. If this is a problem, explain to your child that while we all pick our noses, he is going at it a bit too much. Try to reward him for not picking his nose and gently remind him not to do it when you find him in the middle of a hunting expedition. Make sure that your child's fingernails are trimmed weekly! Physical reminders such as brightly colored stickers on the fingers are sometimes helpful.

For the child with frequent nasal allergies or colds, try to keep her nose moist with petroleum jelly, salt-water nose drops, and plenty of fluids to drink.

NUTRITION *[See Bottle feeding your baby; Breastfeeding your baby; Cholesterol and fat; Eating; Eating utensils; Feeding your baby; Iron deficiency anemia; Obesity]*

OBESITY

In general, we do not worry about chubby babies and rarely prescribe restrictive diets for normal, healthy infants or toddlers under two years of age. Children experiencing the growth spurts of toddlerhood and, later, adolescence and puberty need some amount of fat and cholesterol in their diets to ensure normal growth and development. As the child grows into the middle childhood years (ages five to eight), it may become clearer whether or not he is becoming overweight. About one of every four American children is obese. We define obesity by weighing the child and comparing him to other children the same age, gender, and height. If the child is 20 percent or more heavier than the average child in his age, gender, and height class, then he is probably overweight *[see Well-Child Pediatric Examination Schedule, Growth Charts].*

Many problems, both physical and emotional, are associated with obesity. For example, excellent medical evidence shows that obesity contributes to the development of heart disease, high blood pressure, and diabetes. On the emotional side, many children tend to ridicule overweight children. Such cruel treatment is difficult for any child and can contribute to low self-esteem.

The overwhelming majority of overweight children (and adults) are obese for two reasons: too much eating and too little physical exercise. Obesity tends to run in families. It is difficult to pinpoint the exact cause of obesity. Some physicians believe that there may be a genetic predisposition to being overweight; others warn that the child's environment plays a large role in a child's becoming overweight, since heavy parents who overeat and live a sedentary life style tend to raise children who do the same. Often it is best, in an overweight family, if the whole family participates in learning how to eat a healthier, low-fat diet, exercise regularly, and make a concerted effort to lose excess weight.

Some children may respond to family stress by overeating. The comfort and gratification of food has consoled many a child who is being picked on by a sibling or is responding to family discord such as parental fighting or a divorce. If this is likely to be the case, speak with your child to see what is troubling him. More rarely, organic or physical causes of obesity require a physician's examination.

What can I do to help my obese child?

• *Make sure that you take a positive approach to your child's problem. Maintain his self-esteem and avoid ridicule. Losing weight is hard! If you have experience with this issue, try to use it to understand your child's problems.*

• *Begin with regular physical exercise. Make it fun! Pick a vigorous activity that both you and your child enjoy and set a regular schedule (at least three twenty-minute sessions a week) of exercise. Avoid couch potato activities such as watching television or sitting at the computer. Encourage walking to school rather than riding in a bus, if this is feasible.*

• *Get rid of the junk foods in your house—candy, cakes, doughnuts, cookies, potato chips, and similar "empty calorie" items. Replace them with healthier foods like fresh fruits and vegetables, cereals, skim rather than whole milk, and juices instead of soda pop.*

• *Provide a healthy diet that includes pastas, grains, vegetables and fruits, smaller servings of meat, fish, poultry, and fat-reduced dairy products, and avoid high-fat foods* **[see Cholesterol and Fat].**

• *Make mealtimes fun and nutritious. Do not use food as a punishment or as a reward. Eliminate between-meal snacking.*

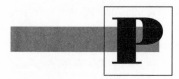

Pacifiers [See Thumb sucking and pacifiers]

Pinkeye [See Conjunctivitis]

Pneumonia

Pneumonia is an infection of the lungs that can be caused by bacteria or by a virus. In cases of bacterial pneumonia, the germs are carried in the air and may be inhaled by a susceptible baby or child. Typically, pneumonia is heralded by a high fever (usually greater than 102°F), cough, and possibly breathing difficulties such as rapid breathing. Pneumonia is a serious disease that needs to be treated with antibiotics. It is easily diagnosed in older infants and children by listening to the chest with a stethoscope and obtaining an X ray of the chest *[see X rays]*. Viral pneumonia, which is transmitted in much the same manner as bacterial pneumonia, must, unfortunately, resolve on its own.

Poison ivy, poison sumac, and poison oak

Certain plants, bushes, and trees that grow across the United States contain oils that, when touched by humans, causes an angry, swollen, red rash and extreme itchiness. The most common of these are poison ivy, poison sumac, and poison oak. Perhaps the best advice we can give is, learn what these plants look like and avoid contact with them! Poison ivy is the most common of the three, but you should learn to identify each if you like hiking in the forest.

Typically, one develops poison ivy rash a day or so after an outing in the woods, especially near riverbeds, where poison ivy likes to grow; but poison ivy can also be found in open fields and even urban areas. The red rash shows up on the exposed body parts—the legs, hands, or whatever areas of one's exposed skin rubbed across the poison ivy. The intense itchiness, rash, and blistering can last up to two weeks, and the treatments your physician can offer will only alleviate the symptoms somewhat, not "cure" the poison ivy. Ice packs and cool wash-

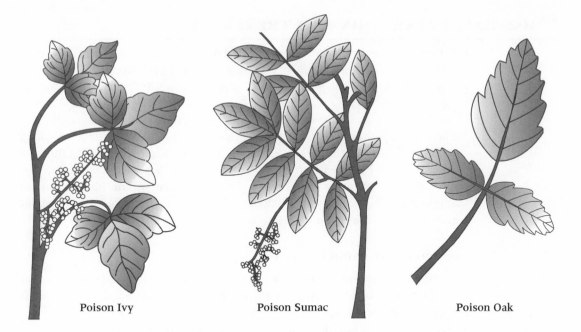

Poison Ivy   Poison Sumac   Poison Oak

cloths help to numb the skin somewhat and may give comfort. Lotions with 0.5 percent hydrocortisone can be bought at the drugstore without a prescription and may be applied to the affected skin three to four times a day. If your child is too young to understand the importance of not scratching, you need to make sure his fingernails are cut. After two weeks, all of the once open sores should be healing or healed. For the child who has widespread and severe facial involvement, consult your physician. A prescription of an oral anti-inflammatory steroidal called prednisone may be necessary to relieve the swelling and itching of these more extensive cases.

 ### Is poison ivy contagious?

Not in the sense that physicians use the term to explain, for example, "contagion of chicken pox." If you touch the oil of poison ivy, you will get the itchy rash. If your clothes or shoes (or dogs!) came in contact with the poison ivy oil and you subsequently touch them, you can still get the rash. Once you contract poison ivy, on the other hand, you are not contagious to others. The rash may weep and the fluid-filled blisters will seep fluid, but this carries no contagion. You will not spread the "poison ivy" nor cause a new case of poison ivy rash in anyone who comes in contact with you. Remember, however, to wash all of your poison ivied-child's clothing, shoes, and other objects that might have come in contact with the poison ivy oil. Another way to contract poison ivy is to throw some on a campfire; be aware that the smoke from burning poison ivy can waft the oil onto your skin and into your lungs.

POISONING: PREVENTION AND TREATMENT

Childhood injuries and deaths from accidental poisonings have, fortunately, been on the decrease in recent years. Educational campaigns directed at parents of young children, regional poison control hotlines, and safer means of packaging toxic substances have all played roles. Nevertheless, it is imperative for a parent to think carefully about the safe placement of household cleaners, chemicals, and medications. All these products appear interesting and, at first, edible to young children. Pills often are mistaken for candy, and bright-colored cleaning fluids or chemicals can be confused with a favorite beverage. If there is any possibility that your child may get into a substance in your house that will do him harm (and that possibility *always* exists for children under the age of six), then you must put it away in a place they cannot get into.

Common Household Poisons

1. Aspirin or other pain relievers, antidepressant medications, and cardiovascular medications (not surprisingly, these three types of medicines are among the most commonly sold medications in the United States)

2. Petroleum-based products, such as gasoline, kerosene, and similar products

3. Caustic chemicals such as lye, acids, drain cleaners, or bleaches, which can cause significant damage (in the form of chemical burns) to the gastrointestinal tract

4. Iron or vitamin tablets

Another significant source of poisoning is the inhalation of carbon monoxide, typically from automobile exhaust fumes or faulty heating systems. It is, therefore, important to never start up your car inside a closed structure (such as a garage with the door closed). It is also important to have your heating system checked annually for evidence of carbon monoxide leakage. Catalytic kerosene space heaters should never be used near children, not only because they can give off dangerous fumes in an unventilated area but also because of the risk of burn injuries *[see Fires]*.

Among teenagers, we see what is termed "intentional" poisoning, or attempts at suicide. The substances most commonly used for this type of injury include overdoses of aspirin and acetaminophen (Tylenol), benzodiazapines (e.g., Valium), alcohol, and antidepressants.

Tips for Preventing Accidental and Intentional Poisonings

1. If you use any medications, whether they are prescription or over-the-counter drugs, you must keep them far out of reach of your young children, preferably in a locked medicine chest. This also holds for leftover medicines once prescribed for your child. After a medication has been used for a specific purpose,

throw it away! Your physician will be happy to prescribe more medicine if it is needed *[see Medicines]*.

2. Do not keep large supplies of any medication in the house. This increases the chance that if a child gets into such a bottle, he might take a lethal dose. Some of the over-the-counter cold medicines have done such a good job of coming out in fun and tasty flavors that your child may be tempted to take a swallow of one of them. Store your extra medicines in an even better hiding place than those you take on a daily basis.

3. Always ask your pharmacist for child-proof safety caps on all medicines.

4. Eliminate caustic chemicals such as lye, battery acid, and other dangerous chemicals from households where young children live. If you must keep these substances, keep them far out of reach of children.

5. Store poisonous chemicals in their original, warning-labeled packaging. Never transfer them to an unmarked or another container that a child may confuse with a beverage container.

6. Promptly and properly dispose of all used auto batteries and small disc batteries. They contain acid and can be quite dangerous if ingested. Disc batteries are also a cause of choking, so there are two reasons not to have them in the same house as a young child.

7. Check your heating system on an annual basis for carbon monoxide and other toxic fumes.

8. Avoid keeping heating fuels such as kerosene and gasoline in the house with young children.

9. Keep the phone number of the regional poison control center for your area right near your telephone for use in the event of an emergency. It is also wise to keep a bottle of syrup of ipecac (a drug that induces vomiting) in the house, for use in the event your child does swallow something poisonous. *It is important to call the poison center before giving the ipecac (don't worry, you have time) as some chemicals, such as lye, are as dangerous coming up as they were going down.*

10. Call your local poison control center and then your physician, on an urgent basis, with any questions you have when confronted with a child who ingested something you think may be poisonous *[see also Injury and Accident Prevention]*.

Food Poisoning

Food "poisoning" refers to the contamination of food products, typically with disease-causing bacteria or viruses that cause a severe inflammation of the digestive tract (gastroenteritis). Symptoms tend to occur within two to twenty-four hours after the ingestion of the offending food. They include copious vomiting, diarrhea, belly cramps, exhaustion, and dehydration *[for care instructions see Diarrhea; Vomiting]*. If the symptoms are severe, you need to call your physician.

How to prevent food poisoning

• Refrigerate all perishable food properly.

• Do not thaw frozen products and then refreeze.

• Be scrupulously clean about washing meats, poultry, fish, vegetables, and so on before consumption.

• Look at the label information (e.g, date of packaging) and the quality of the product. If it looks badly packaged or stored, throw it away or return it!

• If you have leftovers, refrigerate them *before* they cool down. This significantly lowers the risk of bacterial colonization.

• Cream sauces, mayonnaise, and similar products are veritable playgrounds for bacteria—especially if left out in the summer's heat. Refrigerate these products and avoid leaving them out on warm summer days or allowing them to sit in a hot picnic basket.

• Honey can contain the microbes that cause *botulism*, a severe form of food poisoning. *Do not give honey to children under the age of one year. Corn syrup should be avoided for the same reason.*

• Apply these rules to your child's lunch box as well. Rarely are school lunches refrigerated, so pack wisely and avoid the perishables.

PYLORIC STENOSIS

Spitting up is a common activity for most newborns. There is, however, a more serious form of progressively worse spitting up and vomiting called pyloric stenosis. It classically begins in a baby's second to sixth week of life, when the baby starts to spit up with increasing force and frequency. This condition is caused by a thickening of the muscle tissue at the pyloric valve, which sits at the end of the stomach and just above the beginning of the small intestines. The thickened muscle prevents the free flow of digested food down the gastrointestinal tract and the result is forceful vomiting. In some babies we have examined, the baby's vomit literally projects across the room—much to the awe of all those present. More serious problems resulting from the frequent vomiting include malnourishment, dehydration, and severe constipation. Pyloric stenosis occurs about one out of every two hundred fifty children born in the United States; it is three to four times more common among male infants than female infants, and it may occur in familial clusters.

In the event that your newborn is vomiting frequently, you need to discuss this pattern with your pediatrician. A physical examination of the baby's belly can often diagnose pyloric stenosis. The enlarged muscle feels like an olive at the end of the baby's stomach. Ultrasound examinations can also be used to confirm the diagnosis. Pyloric stenosis is typically treated with a surgical operation *[see Abdominal Pain, Spitting Up, Vomiting].*

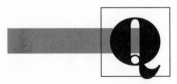

QUALITY TIME *[See Working parents]*

QUESTIONS MOST COMMONLY ASKED BY PARENTS

At the end of many of the entries in this book, we have included the questions that parents most frequently asked about various aspects of their children's health, safety, and behavior.

We, of course, welcome additional questions from our readers and encourage you to write your comments and questions to:

Drs. Howard Markel and Frank Oski
W. H. Freeman and Company, Publishers
41 Madison Avenue
New York, N.Y. 10010

If you have any immediate questions that have not been answered by this book, you should discuss them with your pediatrician.

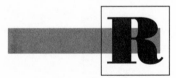

RASHES *[See Bites, insect; Chicken pox; Contagious and infectious diseases; Eczema; Eyes, allergic reactions; Fifth disease; Hand, foot, and mouth disease; Heat rash; Hives; Impetigo; Newborn appearance; Poison ivy, poison sumac, and poison oak; Ringworm; Roseola infantum; Scabies; Scarlet fever; Xerosis]*

RESPIRATORY SYNTICIAL VIRUS (RSV)

Respiratory synticial virus (RSV) is one of the most serious causes of upper respiratory infections during infancy. It is extremely contagious; in fact, germs can sometimes live on clothing or crib surfaces for hours. Adults, too, can contract RSV, although their symptom pattern is difficult to distinguish from that of influenza or other upper respiratory tract infections, unless a specific viral culture is performed *[see Influenza].* Each year, more than ninety thousand children are hospitalized with RSV; forty-five hundred youngsters die from its complications. Especially vulnerable to serious complications from RSV are those children who have serious lung diseases, congenital heart problems, or a history of prematurity with subsequent lung damage. No vaccine is presently available.

The symptoms of RSV can include a runny nose, low-grade fever, cough, and other cold-like symptoms. In some children, however, particularly small infants, these cold-like symptoms get far more severe. The cough becomes quite painful and difficult to stop, and the baby's breathing may become labored and difficult. Most babies and children who contract RSV, fortunately, do not require hospitalization and recuperate quite nicely in a week or so. Again, the care plan should be primarily comforting and supportive rather than medicinal. If for any reason you notice the baby having trouble with her breathing, you need to call the pediatrician immediately *[see Upper Respiratory Tract Infections].*

RINGWORM (Tinea Corporis)

The Rash

This pinkish-red, ring- or circle-shaped rash is caused by a fungal infection (despite its quaint name) and can appear anywhere on the body. It has a skin-colored center, scaly, raised borders, is somewhat itchy, and gradually grows in size if not treated.

Although most healthy children's immune systems will take of this unsightly infection within four months, there are several anti-fungal medicines that work to resolve the rash within a week or so.

Treatment

Once ringworm has been diagnosed, you can purchase an over-the-counter anti-fungal cream (e.g., Tinactin®), or your physician can prescribe a similar ointment. The cream needs to be applied twice a day to the actual "ring-shaped" rash and at least an inch or two of the healthy skin bordering the rash. This should be done for about a week. By this time, the skin where the ringworm was should be returning to its smooth, supple form. Remember to remind your child to avoid scratching the rash, since this only slows the healing process.

Ringworm of the Scalp

Occasionally, children get a ringworm infection of the scalp. The rash looks similar to those elsewhere on the body, but is more resistant to treatment than the skin variety. Your pediatrician will prescribe an oral medication (greisofulvin, available both as a syrup or a pill), which needs to be taken a day for the following four to six weeks.

 My daughter was just sent home from nursery school for ringworm. Is this a contagious disease?

No. It is not contagious to other children, and your daughter can return safely to school without fear of infecting others. Ringworm is a fungus that particularly likes to grow on the skin of puppies, kittens, and other domestic pets. Frequently (but not always) this is the origin of a child's bout with ringworm. If you do own a pet, you should check it for signs of ringworm and, if necessary, bathe it and apply an anti-fungal powder as directed by your veterinarian.

ROSEOLA INFANTUM ("Baby measles"; exanthem subitum; sixth disease)

This mild viral infection typically occurs in children under the age of two years. It is caused by the herpesvirus HH 6. The infection begins with a high fever, anywhere from 102° to 105°F, and can last three to five days. During this period the baby may act sleepy, fussy, eat less, and display other symptoms of fever *[see Fever]*. The fever suddenly passes and the baby appears happy but now has a lacy, pink-red rash over his belly, chest, neck, and arms. This rash does not itch, nor does it require treatment. The rash lasts anywhere from only a few hours to a day. Babies with roseola who are doing well and seem healthy do not need to see a doctor.

For those babies who appear to be ill—exhibiting crankiness, loss of appetite, more or less sleep than usual, or excessive, uncontrollable crying—a visit to the pediatrician's office is wise. In the overwhelming majority of cases, the physician will recommend acetaminophen for pain and fever relief. Plenty of fluids are also recommended. Incidentally, because roseola typically causes such a high fever, it is one of the most common "triggers" of febrile seizures *[see Seizures with Fever; Fever]*.

S

SAFETY ISSUES *[See Bicycle injuries; Bites; Car seats; Choking; CPR; Cribs; Cuts, scrapes, and minor bleeding injuries; Day care; Discipline; Drown-proofing; Electrical injuries; Eyes, emergency eye problems; Falls; Fires; Fractures; Guns; Head and neck injuries; Injury and accident prevention; Latchkey children; Medicines; Mouth injuries; Nosebleed; Poisoning; Smoking; Sprains; Strangers; Tooth injuries; Sunshine, sunscreen, sunburns, and sunglasses; Walkers; Walking injuries]*

SCABIES

Scabies is an extremely contagious skin infection caused by a mite called *Sarcoptes scabei.* The tiny female mite is less than a half a millimeter in length and likes to burrow into the uppermost layers of a child's skin, where it deposits its eggs and fecal material. Some four to six weeks after this infestation, the child will complain of unrelenting itchy skin that is often worse at night than during the day.

The Rash of Scabies

The characteristic rash of scabies appears as tiny bumps and blisters that may become raw with scratching. Sometimes you can see a tiny linear track along the skin where the mite has burrowed. The rash typically begins from the neck down, although younger infants may have lesions on their faces and scalps. Infants tend to get scabies often on the palms of the hands and the soles of the feet. In older children, the rash is especially prominent on the hands, especially the webs of the fingers and the wrists. It can also appear in the armpits, waist area, and even on the buttocks.

Diagnosing Scabies

The easiest way to diagnose a case of scabies is to have your pediatrician examine the rash and lightly scrape it in order to collect a specimen that contains the mite, eggs, or feces. The pediatrician will look at this specimen under the microscope in order to properly identify the cause of the rash.

Treating Scabies

Fortunately, treating scabies is quite easy. Your pediatrician will prescribe a shampoo-lotion that contains an agent called 1 percent lidane. Coat the child's entire body (excluding the head, unless it is involved) with the lotion and leave it on for about eight hours before bathing thoroughly. Sometimes the lidane lotion needs to be reapplied for more severe cases, but it should not be repeated for at least a week after the first application. The itchiness, incidentally, may take up to a week to resolve. As noted above, scabies is extremely contagious. All family members and friends who have had close contact with your child also need to be treated, even if they are not itchy or symptomatic. If everyone in the household is not treated, reinfection will almost certainly occur.

SCARLET FEVER

Scarlet fever is caused by the same organism that causes strep throat *(streptococcus)* but is accompanied by a bright-red (almost sunburned in appearance), sandpapery rash of the belly and chest that progresses to the rest of the body within twenty-four hours. There are areas of increased "redness" in the skin folds of the armpits, elbows, knees, and groin. The child will typically complain of a sore throat a day or so before the rash and will have a tongue that looks like a bright-red strawberry.

The rash of scarlet fever usually resolves within a week. In some children, peeling (or desquamation) of the skin occurs where the rash was at its reddest, such as the groin or between the fingers. This peeling—much like that experienced after a bad sunburn—usually resolves within a week or so and is harmless.

 Is Scarlet fever contagious?

Like strep throat, the disease is extremely contagious to others. The child suspected of having scarlet fever should see a physician, as should the children he has had close contact with. We treat scarlet fever with an antibiotic (e.g., penicillin) in order to prevent some of the long-term potential complications of a streptococcal infection, such as rheumatic heart disease. The antibiotic does little to make the sore throat or rash better, but needs to be continued for the prescribed ten days in order to prevent these serious complications. A few days after starting the penicillin, the child's fever or sore throat should be resolved and he may return to school without fear of infecting others [see Sore Throats].

SCHOOL PHOBIA OR AVOIDANCE

School phobia is more than the occasional ploy by a child who wants to avoid a conflict with the teacher or an upcoming test. Instead, children with school phobia are typically good students without specific academic problems who may fear leaving the protective home environment. The parents of these children are commonly excellent and loving parents, although some may be overprotective.

The school-phobic child may describe a variety of nonspecific physical complaints, such as a sore throat, headache, bellyache, upset stomach, dizziness, and other vague symptoms. In school phobia these symptoms last more than five days and do not appear to get better by the child's report, despite her looking well and not appearing terribly ill. The problems are typically at their most intense in the morning hours just before getting ready to go to school. By the afternoon, or on weekends and holidays, the child appears to be fine. These symptoms rarely appear during the summer months.

Your pediatrician can help assess whether the symptoms are psychosomatic rather than physical. This is not always an easy task, but you need to develop a plan to break such a cycle of school avoidance. Early intervention is the key, since the longer the child stays out of school, the more "intense" the symptoms become and the longer she is likely to stay home. This makes school progress next to impossible and will negatively affect the child's relationships with friends and family members. Because this is a difficult problem with serious potential complications, your pediatrician may suggest a consultation with a child psychologist in order to better define what is troubling your child.

A Plan to Resolve School Phobia

Make sure that your child does not have a more significant medical problem. Generally, children who are well enough to play about the house are also well enough to go to school. Information in this book and discussions with your pediatrician can help to differentiate between school phobia and other problems your child may be experiencing.

Once you have established that there is nothing physically wrong with your child, insist that she goes to school. Just as in the old adage about jumping back on the horse that threw you, children need to promptly overcome their fears of leaving home and going to school. The longer your child stays at home with school phobia, the longer she will continue to stay at home! These cycles can become incredibly difficult to break, so be calm and reassuring but firm. Your child *must* go to school, barring more significant illnesses, and that is not a point to be negotiated. *[See Discipline; Negotiating with Your Child]* Explain to your child that she will probably begin to feel much better once she returns to school on a daily basis. Try to involve her by making a chart that documents how she improves each successive day.

Some mornings your child may especially try your patience. Like adults, children can be quite creative in their methods of avoidance. Crying, screaming, accomplished acting jobs, and other techniques are not the easiest thing to face in the morning. Count to ten, be resolute but loving, and insist on her going to school. Do not engage her in a discussion of her complaints. In the event that your child missed the school bus, you should take her to school. A late appearance is far more therapeutic than no appearance. If the child comes home during the school day, you need to return her promptly.

After the child has actually spent a day or so back at school, talk openly with her about her specific fears or complaints. Try to engage your child after school is over for the day and discuss calmly what seems to bother her about going to school. Reassure her about her health. Agree to try to change any elements of the situation that are in your power to influence; for example, if your child feels that her teacher is "picking on her," arrange to have a meeting with the teacher to "clear the air," and make sure you tell your child about the meeting. Acknowledge that you have heard and understood your child's complaints, but be sure to conclude with your parental edict: she must go to school!

Discuss your child's school phobia with the teacher. School phobia is a common problem, and your child's teacher may have experience with it. Discuss the matter and develop a plan, especially if the child tries to feign illness during the school day and is commonly sent home.

Encourage your child to play with other children outside of the home. A good way to overcome a fear of leaving home is to have the child attend sleepovers and camp events—or simply an afternoon at a playmate's house—and then return to find that all is fine. This can help build a child's sense of independence. Many cases of school phobia may be prevented entirely by helping to socialize your child with other children. In the mad dash to raise the perfect baby, we often isolate ourselves from other family members, friends, and (most important for your child's social development) other children. There are many age-appropriate means of aiding your child's socialization skills. Beginning with infancy, reassure your baby about your absence *[see Separation Anxiety].* There are a number of activities with other toddlers that promote collective play, independence, and acquisition of social skills, such as play groups and child-safe playgrounds. See what is available in your local area and enroll your toddlers in these types of programs. Three- and four-year-old children enrolled in preschool tend to be better equipped for kindergarten and first grade than those who did not attend. Be reassuring and supportive as your child adjusts to each new experience.

SEA AND FRESHWATER ANIMAL BITES *[See Bites]*

SEIZURES WITH FEVER

Febrile seizures are involuntary jerking movements of the body associated with a high fever that rises rapidly over a short period of time. They typically occur in children aged six months to 5 years. These seizures are *always* associated with a high fever. During these episodes, the child may abruptly stiffen his body and roll his eyes up, followed by a jerking or twitching of the limbs and body.

Although febrile seizures are extremely frightening to anyone witnessing them (usually a parent), the good news is that they are generally harmless. Many times, the febrile seizure is the first indicator that the child even has a fever. If your child does experience a febrile seizure, here a few tips to help you through it.

1. Calm down!

2. Move the child to a bed or a carpeted floor so she does not hit any sharp or hard objects during the seizure.

3. Remember: children with seizures are not at risk of swallowing their tongues. Therefore, do not put anything in her mouth.

4. If the seizure lasts more than four minutes, call your pediatrician immediately; if the episode lasts less than four minutes, call your pediatrician AFTER you have made sure your child is comfortable and resting.

5. Children who have one episode of febrile seizure may be at risk for another. We suggest that the parents of a child who has experienced one febrile seizure be quite aggressive in administering fever-reducing medicines (such as aceta-minophen) at the first sign of fever and continue to do so every four to six hours until the child's fever has resolved *[see Fever: Measuring the Temperature and Fever-reducing Medicines]*.

6. Febrile seizures are not a form of epilepsy, a neurological condition that causes seizures. Children with febrile seizures are at no greater risk for developing epilepsy than those children who never experience febrile seizures *[see Seizures without Fever]*.

[See Fever; Roseola Infantum]

SEIZURES WITHOUT FEVER (Epilepsy)

Seizures are uncontrollable movements of the body caused by abnormal electrical impulses in the central nervous system. They can occur after injuries to the head, infections of the central nervous system, and number of other insults to the brain. This condition is called epilepsy and is rather rare among children. The overwhelming majority of seizures in children, about 99½ percent, are associated with fever *[see Seizures with Fever]* and are unrelated to epilepsy.

Seizures without fever can take on many different forms depending on the part of the brain that is experiencing this abnormal activity. They include jerking motions of body parts or of the entire body, a loss of stool or urinary continence, staring off into space, rolling up of one's eyes, twitches, body stiffening, and drooling. They are quite frightening to watch but are generally harmless. Most seizures last less than five minutes. If the seizure is lasting more than five minutes, it is a good idea to call your pediatrician. After more communication and observation, you may decide together when it is best to call 911 (Emergency Services) or visit the emergency room. Rarely does any damage occur to the person who has a seizure lasting less than thirty minutes.

What to do When your Child has an Epileptic Seizure

The first rule is to make sure that your child is comfortable, on the ground, and far from anything he can fall on or hurt himself with during the seizure. Because these are uncontrollable movements, you will not be able to stop them. Don't try.

As in any emergency, you need to make sure that your child's airway is clear of anything that might obstruct it such as food, gum, or an object. Place your child on his side or stomach so that in the event he does vomit or drool excessively, the liquid will drain out of his mouth rather than cause choking *[see Choking]*. Children with seizures are not in danger of swallowing their tongues. Mother Nature has made that anatomically impossible. If your child is breathing noisily or with great labor, however, his tongue may be in the way of his air flow. The best way to approach this problem is to:

• Stay calm

• Make sure he is not turning blue or has stopped breathing

• Do not put your hands in his mouth. Instead, gently pull the jaw and chin forward by placing your hands on the area of your child's tempero-mandibular (jaw) joint *[see Choking]*

• If there are still problems with airflow, call an ambulance

• After the seizure has ended, your child will experience extreme exhaustion and will typically fall into a deep sleep. Once this occurs and you have ascertained that your child is calm and safe, discuss the episode with your pediatrician. If the seizure is a new event, a medical examination for epilepsy and other illnesses of the central nervous system is indicated; if epilepsy has already been diagnosed, an initiation or a change in medications may be necessary. Epilepsy is a potentially lifelong condition that requires careful medical monitoring and antiseizure medication.

For more information on epilepsy, call or write:

Epilepsy Foundation of America
4351 Garden City Drive
Landover, MD 20785
(301) 459-3700

The Epilepsy Institute
67 Irving Place
New York, NY 10003
(212) 677-8550

SEPARATION ANXIETY

Beginning at about the age of six to eight months, many babies develop a "separation anxiety." Basically, whenever the parent leaves the sight of the baby, he becomes upset and cries. This may be provoked when the parents leave for work in the morning or when they leave the baby with a baby-sitter. This type of anxiety tends to be more severe at night.

Some ways to ameliorate this problem include:

• Spend as much time as you can, during the day, cuddling and holding your baby in order to reassure him of your presence and love. Studies have shown that extra loving parental contact can reduce the incidence of separation anxiety attacks and nightmares in infants.

• Check up on your infant during the night in a reassuring but nonengaging manner. This does not mean that you awaken a sleeping infant for a cuddling or play session. Instead, if he does awaken during the night in a fearful manner, check on his status, speak some reassuring words, and once you have ascertained that the situation is okay, exit gracefully. In the event that this does not work, an old pediatrician's trick may help. Most infants who are simply upset (but not ill) can be calmed down by speaking softly and placing your open palm on their belly.

• When you do use a baby-sitter, make sure your baby has had a chance to get used to and play with her before you leave. This is essential for new baby-sitters who have not yet had a chance to meet your child. As your child gets used to the new baby-sitter, this warm-up period will not be as necessary. We typically suggest that parents hiring a new baby-sitter arrange for her to come an hour early to facilitate this process. The extra hour you pay the new baby-sitter will be well worth it. Separation anxiety travels at warp speed when a baby awakens to find his parents gone and a "strange" baby-sitter present.

[See Day Care and Child-care Issues; Sleep]

SHOCK *[See CPR]*

SHOES FOR THE INFANT AND CHILD

Despite the gambler's plea, "Baby needs a new pair of shoes!", the fact of the matter is that babies rarely need to wear them. The major purpose of shoes is to protect one's feet from injury when walking over rocky or rough terrain. They also help keep one's feet warm and protected from the elements. Given that infants rarely do such walking, you can have plenty of time before rushing out to the store. Let us dispel a few common fallacies about shoes and children.

• Wearing shoes does *not* help a baby learn how to walk sooner. He will walk when he is ready to, not when you put shoes on him.

• Heels are *never* required for any child and may even lead to damage, such as falling injuries. Shoes with "ankle supports" are not necessary, either.

• Expensive or overpriced shoes are not necessary. Buy a good but inexpensive (as opposed to "cheap") pair of shoes when your baby is ready.

• Children with "flat feet" do *not* require special shoes or heels.

Fitting your Baby or Child with Shoes

The most reliable method of fitting a child for shoes is the age-old "pinch test." After your child has the shoe on stand him up and press with your index finger on the top of the shoe to find the end of the big toe. The length of the shoe should be about one-half inch beyond the big toe. To test the width, make sure there is room on either side of the child's foot by grasping the shoe at its widest point. There should be a little extra room at both sides. Remember, children's feet grow quite rapidly, and if the shoe doesn't fit, don't wear it!

What are "pigeon-toes"?

Pigeon toes (intoeing) refers to the condition of the child who walks with his feet turned inward. This is a very common problem that can be caused by a variety of factors. Infants, for example, may toe-in at the front of the foot. This condition is called metatarsus adductus *and is probably caused by the way the baby was positioned as a fetus in the uterus. It usually resolves within the first year of life. Most importantly, the feet are easily moved to the neutral position even though they seem to prefer to rest in the pigeon-toe position. Metatarsus adductus should not be confused with a condition called* clubbed foot; *this is a more fixed cause of intoeing. It is difficult to move a clubbed foot into a neutral position. A child with clubbed foot may need orthopedic splinting or surgery.*

Toddlers, typically during their second year, may develop intoeing because of a turning inward of the shinbone (tibia); pediatricians call this condition tibial torsion. *Children between the ages of three and ten may be pigeon-toed because of a turning inward of the thighbone (femur); we call this condition* medial femoral torsion. *Both of these problems are relatively harmless and tend to run in families.*

Most cases of intoeing tend to correct themselves as the child grows, without any treatment at all. In certain more severe cases, where the child is so pigeon-toed that it affects her walking or the condition begins early and persists well into the early school years, you may need to consult an orthopedic surgeon for advice regarding splinting, casting, or surgery. Your pediatrician will observe and assess your child's walking pattern at each visit and examination and will be able to discuss these findings with you.

What are bowlegs and knock-knees?

In reality, few children or adults have absolutely straight legs. Some children's legs, however, do seen to curve more than others. When a child's legs curve outward at the level of the knees, we call this bowlegs. Knock-knees *is a curving inward of the legs and the subsequent "knocking" together of the knees when the child walks. Most children grow out of this harmless condition, but if you have questions you should discuss them with your pediatrician. In rare cases, bowlegs and knock-knees can be a sign of more serious problems such as rickets (vitamin D deficiency), infections of the bones, arthritis, and fractures or broken bones at the level of the knee.*

What are "flat feet"?

Flat feet is the term used for feet with no (or very little) arch to them. Babies and small children may appear to have flat feet because of the way the bones are shaped and the fat and skin that surrounds them. By age six or so, the components making up the foot, such as the bones and cartilage, become less flexible and the arch develops. About two out of ten children do not develop arches at this age, but their feet remain flexible and no further treatment is needed. Corrective shoes, braces, and other paraphernalia will do little to cure flat feet and may actually cause harm.

Having said this, we must note that there are some rare causes of a fixed form of flat feet, such as tightened Achilles tendons (heel cords) and other orthopedic problems. Your pediatrician will examine your child's feet at each well child examination and will be able to assess them accurately.

SINUSITIS AND PURULENT RHINITIS

Sinuses—bone passages that are filled with air—exist in the human skull around and behind the nose, cheekbones, and forehead. They are lined with a moist mucous membrane that helps warm, clean, and humidify the air we breathe. Unfortunately, these passages are easily infected with viruses and

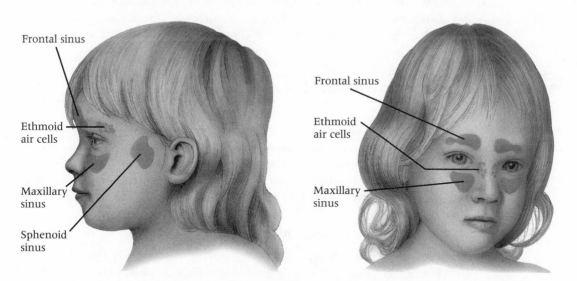

The ethmoid air cells and maxillary sinuses are present at birth. The frontal sinus begins to form at the age of two to four years and is mostly complete by four to nine years of age. The formation of sinuses in children is a slow, irregular process. All children are different! It is typically completed by the beginning of adolescence.

specific bacteria such as *Hemophilus influenzae, Streptococcus pneumoniae,* and other microbes.

Not surprisingly, *sinusitis* is frequently associated with an upper respiratory infection such as a cold *[see Upper Respiratory Tract Infections and Colds]*, long-standing hay fever *[see Allergic Rhinitis]*, ear infections, and other similar illnesses. More often than not it is a complicating feature of these primary problems. The child with sinusitis may or may not have fever. Typically, he will have a copious, thick, greenish nasal discharge, a persistent barking cough, headache, puffy eyes, possible tooth pain, and extreme pain above the sinus passages or when shaking his head from side to side. He is also likely to complain of pain when asked to jump up and down.

Your doctor should examine the child with sinusitis by tapping on the sensitive sinus passages to elicit pain, looking inside the nostrils and at the discharge, and reviewing previous problems that may be related, such as a cold, allergies, or another bout of sinusitis. For initial episodes of sinusitis, your pediatrician may elect to obtain an X ray of the skull and sinuses.

Most children with sinusitis are typically treated with antibiotics (such as amoxicillin) and pain relievers as needed, although the treatment regimen may vary depending upon your child's symptoms and medical history. More chronic and recurrent cases may require surgical intervention to reopen the clogged passages.

Purulent rhinitis refers to a similar infection of the nostrils and the air passages just above them. This causes a copious runny nose; the nasal symptoms are milder than those of sinusitis. It, too, is commonly caused by bacteria, it is easily treated with antibiotics.

SLAPPED CHEEK SYNDROME *[See Fifth disease]*

SLEEP AND SLEEP PROBLEMS

The battle of wills between child and parent is most frequently fought on the playing fields of the bedroom. Sleep issues perplex and worry parents. Too often they can be disruptive to the other members of the family.

Sharing a Bed with Your Child

Now is as good a time as any to bring up one of the relatively few "don'ts" of child rearing; specifically, it is *not* a good idea to let your child sleep in your bed. Recognizing that no rule can be absolute, you need to realize that once a baby or an older child has become accustomed to sleeping with Mommy and Daddy, it is extremely difficult to break the pattern. It is also risky, in that a slumbering parent can accidentally roll over on top of a sleeping baby, causing accidental suffocation, or the baby can roll out of the bed entirely *[see Sudden Infant Death Syndrome]*.

Having said this, we need to mention that in some cultures, sleeping with one's child is quite common. As long as both parents welcome this practice, have taken steps so that the child will not fall or be accidentally suffocated, and accept that their "marriage bed" will become something quite different with the presence of an extra guest, they need not worry about violating our "don't."

One of our colleagues, a child psychologist, suggested a healthy and reasonable alternative to this problem: when her small children are particularly frightened, say after a nightmare, they are allowed to come quietly into their parents' bedroom, with pillow and blanket, and sleep on the floor next to them. This compromise is a good one for many reasons. First of all, it allays the child's fears without letting her into your bed. It also builds a sense of responsibility in the young child; sleeping on Mommy and Daddy's bedroom floor is a privilege for special, specific situations. If the child abuses the privilege, exercising it every night or making excessive noise and waking both of you up, her option needs to be restricted.

Normal Sleep Patterns

The following information is provided to show what normal sleep patterns are for most children and to suggest how to avoid sleep problems before they occur. As any parent of a sleep-problem child can tell you, prevention is far easier than cure. Please note that the sleep times listed below are averages. Not all babies require the same amount of sleep. It is important to observe your baby's pattern of sleep, feeding, and other activities in order to adapt the information below to your own use.

The first weeks of life

During this period, the newborn spends a seemingly inordinate amount of time asleep—on average, about sixteen to seventeen hours every day. The problem is that newborns frequently sleep in spurts, waking up during the day and night depending on their cycle, their hunger, or comfort level. Most new parents attempt to work their schedule around the baby's until she becomes more "regular," i.e., her sleep patterns correspond to the rest of the family's!

Here are a few tricks that help your newborn form regular sleep habits and allow everyone in the family to get some sleep.

• The infant uses all sorts of cues, visual, auditory, and others, to orient himself toward falling asleep. For this reason, many pediatricians recommend placing the still awake—but drowsy—infant down for the night. In this way, the last thing that the baby registers are the cues of being drowsy in his crib.

• This doesn't mean he will fall instantly asleep. Many infants will move about a bit, try to make themselves more comfortable and so on before finally settling down to sleep. We usually recommend letting the baby settle to sleep herself, although some infants need a little extra, gentle rocking, cuddling, or holding.

• It is important to pick up or play with the baby, after the initial cuddling, only when the baby really needs your help. If you make a practice of picking up the baby every time she cries, she will soon figure out the payoff in that little scam and continue it *ad infinitum.*

• During the day you should restrict the baby's sleep time to less than three consecutive hours. The point of this exercise is to get the baby to sleep his longest during the night. Besides, infants are a great deal of fun to play and interact with, so what better time to keep your infant awake than during the daylight hours?

• It is best to give your baby her last feeding about the same time you get ready to go to sleep (e.g., 11:00 P.M.). This doesn't always work, particularly for breast-fed babies who sometimes require more frequent feeding than bottle-fed infants. Try eliminating the during-the-night feeding by altering the baby's schedule an hour up or back. Infants only require five to six feedings a day to grow and feed normally, and that doesn't necessarily have to interfere with sleep. This is usually accomplished by the time the baby is two to three months *[see Bottle Feeding Your Baby; Breastfeeding Your Baby].*

• There is no need to feed the baby more than every two hours during the daytime, and studies show that too frequent a feeding schedule can potentially interfere with an organized sleep pattern.

• During nighttime feedings or other encounters during the night, it is important not to engage your infant with entertaining games or play behaviors. Those merely signal the baby that it is time to awaken and interact. A sleeping baby need not be wakened during the night for a feeding; the one exception is the newborn who is a poor eater or who appears lethargic.

• There is no real need to change a baby's diapers while she is sleeping. Sleeping babies tend to tolerate wet diapers extremely well; they can be changed just as easily in the morning. It is rare that an infant has a bowel movement during sleep, although the infant with diarrhea may require an adjustment in this rule. Another exception is the child with diaper rash *[see Diaper Rash; Diarrhea].*

Three months

The average three-month infants sleeps about fifteen hours a day. By this point it is a good idea to place the infant's crib in his own room.

Four months

By this time, most infants have been trained by their parents to sleep through the night. Having said this, however, we realize that other babies may take longer to accomplish this important milestone. Fourteen to fifteen hours is the normal amount of sleep. If your child is still demanding a middle-of-the-night feeding, you need to work at removing this from his schedule or it will soon become extremely difficult to do so. The last meal should now be scheduled to a more tolerable 10:00 or 11:00 P.M. feeding. Sometimes these babies may continue to cry for a middle-of-the-night feeding; you should soothe the crying baby with gentle words and touching, but there is no need to feed. Eventually, the baby will receive the message. It is also a good idea not to let the baby sleep with a bottle. Drinking from a bottle in the lying-down position may be a risk factor for ear infections and tooth decay. *[See Ear Infections; Tooth Care, Tooth Decay, and Toothaches.]* More times than not, the baby drops the bottle from the crib and begins crying for that reason! Remember the importance of visual, auditory, and other cues of falling asleep; if the last thing a baby remembers before drifting off to sleep is being fed, then that will soon become the cue the baby seeks when falling asleep on subsequent nights. Continuing a nighttime feeding is, alas, an effective way to insure continued nighttime awakening during infancy.

Six to nine months

By this point, most babies sleep about fourteen hours a day. Babies between six and nine months sometimes develop a temporary fear of "strangers" and separation from their parents. It is important, therefore, if you are using a baby-sitter or helper to watch your infant that you introduce the baby to the sitter before the baby is put down to sleep. Otherwise, if the baby awakens to a stranger, she may be afraid and even more difficult to settle down. We suggest leaving the door of the baby's room open after putting her down; this, too, gives the baby a sense of security and makes sleep issues less of a struggle. New milestone achievements, such as crawling, may be associated with sleep problems. Some behaviorists recommend as many hugs and physical signs of reassurance as possible to better help your baby get over the fear of going to sleep alone at night. This seems excellent advice. We know of few babies who have failed to thrive in loving surroundings *[see Separation Anxiety]*.

One year

Babies at one year of age typically sleep about fourteen hours, including two naps. At this point, it is helpful to set up a typical, unchanging, and fun pattern of what many call "the bedtime ritual." These patterns can really start at any time during infancy, but by the age of one it is especially necessary. The ritual can include getting ready for bed, changing into pajamas, washing up, and cuddling up with your child as you tell her a pleasant bedtime story. Both parents should certainly participate. It should take about thirty minutes. Familiarity and repetition of this ritual breeds sleep! The important rule is to kiss the baby goodnight *before* she falls asleep. The baby needs to know that, once put to bed, she stays there until morning. Tantrums need not be indulged, and the parent must stick to a firm resolve to back this up. The crying one-year-old—or toddler—who simply wants to be allowed out of bed should be ignored. If you give in, the child will soon figure out how to manipulate bedtime issues even further. If your child leaves the bedroom on his own during such a struggle, you need to pick him up quietly and return him immediately to bed. Conversations invariably lead to bargaining, especially with older toddlers, and simply delay sleep.

Sometimes babies at this age and older have bad dreams and need reassurance. This is different from the manipulative behaviors described above, which are merely ploys to stay awake. It is perfectly reasonable to reassure the infant or toddler who complains of a nightmare. This will not always be easy to ascertain among younger children not yet able to talk. One word of advice: it is wise to avoid watching horror movies or telling frightening "ghost stories" just before bedtime—probably as wise for adults as it is for children and infants *[see Nightmares; Night Terrors; Television; Video Games and VCRs]*.

Eighteen months
By this point, most babies sleep about thirteen hours with only one nap.

Toddlers, two to four years
Although it may not always seem so, most toddlers sleep, on average, eleven to twelve hours a day and may not require a nap. it is important to recognize that children need less sleep as they grow older.

It is at this point that most toddlers are moved from the crib to a real bed. Although some developmental psychologists have timed this to about the age of two-and-a-half years, the real sign that it is time to get a bed is when the toddler can successfully and consistently climb out of the crib. Once the toddler learns this trick, she is not apt to forget it. Consider abandoning the crib after she first displays this skill.

It is a great idea to involve your child in the process of getting a "big kid's" bed. If you are taking the crib apart, let your child help. Similarly, bring her along with you to the furniture store to help pick out a new bed. A simple box-spring-and-mattress bed is suitable. You may want to move a large chair or a temporary railing next to the bed, to prevent the child from falling out. Other parents experiment with delaying setting up of the bedframe, so that the box spring-mattress is temporarily placed on the floor, but this depends on the child's feelings and fears of adjusting to a "big" bed.

Remember, this is a big event in a child's life and it should be thought of as an exercise in fun, accomplishment, and growing up.

Five years
Eleven hours of sleep per night is average. By this point in the child's life, a bedtime routine should be achieved. It is reasonable to expect "negotiations" over bedtime from your five-year-old. Making exceptions in the bedtime routine for special occasions, parties, or outings are one way of stretching his bedtime limits and evaluating if the child needs more or less sleep than you predict. Because

school is now a routine part of the child's life, however, you need to be sure that he is getting enough sleep at night. Evaluating his energy level in the morning by means of how long it takes him to get out of bed, ready for school, and so on are a good place to start.

 Our two-year-old son loves to wake up early and climb in our bed and play. However, we both work rather late and need to sleep beyond 6:00 A.M. Lately, ignoring his requests for early morning play has led to tantrums and noisy displays of temper. What should we do?

Most children obtain the amount of sleep they need and then awaken. Children who are "early-morning risers" typically need less sleep than the times prescribed above. This is perfectly normal. Think about your own sleep needs compared to your spouse's or some of your friends'. Frequently, the early-rising child has a parent who requires less than the standard "eight hours of sleep a night." If this rhythm does not correspond to your own, consider adjusting the child's sleep schedule. For example:

1. You might adjust the bedtime slightly later. If your toddler typically goes to sleep at, say, 8:00 P.M., try delaying bedtime to 9:00 P.M.

2. An early-rising child does not need an additional nap—although most toddlers do— and it is probably a good idea to experiment with eliminating them.

3. Set some rules about when it is acceptable to get out of bed and when it is not. You need to inform authoritatively your child that this is not a practice you encourage or appreciate. Conversely, when your child does succeed at not awakening you before the rooster crows, you should praise him accordingly. For the toddler in the crib this is easier than for the older child in a real bed. You can experiment with different toys that the child can play with until you awaken and come get him, tape players or radios that can be played (softly), access to a favorite videotape movie, and similar tactics. Remember, the key here is experimentation. No single "trick" works better than any other.

4. Close the drapes of your child's room before he falls asleep—the bright early morning sunrays can be as an "alarm clock" to the early riser.

5. Make sure that you make special arrangements for the weekends. An acceptable time to be awakened by your toddler on a weekday may be entirely different from that on a Saturday or Sunday morning.

For additional reading on this topic, consult:

Richard Ferber, M.D., Solve Your Child's Sleep Problems *(Boston: Little, Brown, 1985)*

SLEEPWALKING

This topic may seem more appropriate for a book about bad Hollywood movie plots, but sleepwalking actually does exist. It is typically seen among children who are between the ages of four and twelve years. The sleeping child walks with her eyes open and staring and shows poor coordination, but can act in ways that *seem* to have purpose, such as putting on or taking off clothes, making her bed or closing doors. During the event, which can last anywhere from a few to twenty minutes, it is all but impossible to awaken the child.

Like night terrors, sleepwalking tends to run in families. It appears among 15 percent of all children *[see Night Terrors]* and may have something to do with the number and level of "deep sleep" cycles your child experiences each night. Sleepwalking is entirely harmless and self-limited. Most sleepwalkers outgrow this strange habit by their teens. In the meantime, there are a number of things you can do to help the child with this problem:

• Try to lead the sleepwalking child back to bed or to the bathroom, if it appears that she needs to go there. The old myth of not waking up a sleepwalker is precisely that. It's very difficult to wake a sleepwalker, but if you do succeed in this task, no bad outcome will occur.

• As with night terrors and other conditions associated with sleep, overfatigue and lack of sleep can predispose to sleepwalking. Make sure your child gets the amount of sleep she needs and do not allow her to become overtired.

• Make sure that the bedroom area of a sleepwalker is "child-proofed" so that she doesn't run into sharp or dangerous objects and is kept from falling down a flight of stairs. Real danger can obviously occur if the sleepwalker leaves the house and starts down the street. Bunk beds are best avoided for all children, but especially for sleepwalkers and others who frequently awake during the night.

• If sleepwalking becomes a problem, awaken the child frequently during the night—as is done with night terrors—to prevent her from entering the deepest stages of sleep, where these events occur. Since sleepwalking typically occurs about two hours into sleep, try waking her up an hour and a half into her sleep. Keep her awake for at least five minutes and then let her go back to sleep. Try it for a week or two, it may break the sleepwalking cycle. It typically needs to be repeated.

SMOKING AND THE EFFECTS OF PASSIVE SMOKING

We began this book by saying that there are relatively few "don'ts" to child-rearing. Smoking, especially in the presence of your children, is one of these. Tobacco use is a leading cause of cancer, severe lung disease such as emphysema and asthma, heart disease, and a number of other problems. For your health, as well as for the future of your children who need you, *quit smoking!* Not smoking sets a good example for your child. Children of non-smokers are far less likely to smoke when they grow up, compared to those from smoking families.

Smoking can be dangerous to those who don't smoke but who live with a smoker. This is known as passive smoking. It refers to a nonsmoking person who is in the same room with and breathing the same air as someone who is smoking.

There are two major ways a nonsmoker may be exposed to cigarette smoke: 1) secondhand smoke, the actual smoke one exhales after puffing on a cigarette; and 2) sidestream smoke, the smoke that comes off the end of a burning cigarette. Sidestream smoke is far more dangerous than exhaled smoke, because it has not gone through the cigarette filter or the smoker's lungs and thus contains about two to three times the undesirable toxins that the smoker inhales. It doesn't take long for a smoker to fill a room with his or her presence and most of this "smokey" atmosphere is caused by sidestream smoke.

Passive smoking can even harm a child in the womb. Medical studies have confirmed that mothers who smoke give birth to smaller babies, as well as infants who have a greater chance of dying from sudden infant death syndrome *[see Sudden Infant Death Syndrome]*. In addition, children of smokers tend to suffer more frequently from asthma, pneumonia, ear infections, upper respiratory tract infections, sinus infections, sore throats, and accidental cigarette burns to the skin.

How can I protect my child from the harmful effects of passive smoke?

The best way to protect your child from passive smoke is to insist that every member of the household (including baby-sitters) stop smoking. As noted above, this is an excellent idea for many reasons beyond your child's immediate health. Tobacco (and its active ingredient, nicotine) is an addictive substance that most people have a hard time giving up. If you need help quitting, and most people do, ask for it. Perhaps the best source of help and information is the toll-free telephone help line of the American Cancer Society; call (800) 4-CANCER for advice and smoke-ending programs in your area.

Some people, of course, simply will not stop smoking. You need to set clear guidelines for them, that restrict smoking in your home and car, especially in the presence of your children. Smokers should be shown the patio, garage, or other suitable outdoor location as the place to satisfy their need for a cigarette without harming your children. This includes smoking parents! A spare room with a tightly shut door and adequate ventilation to air out the room well before a child enters, may also be an option. This may seem harsh, but it is important to remember the risks of passive smoking to your child.

Is it true that the toxins from cigarettes can enter my breast milk?

Absolutely true, if the nursing mother is a smoker. If you are breastfeeding, you should never smoke. Because breakdown products of nicotine find their way into breast milk, nicotine patches are not recommended to breastfeeding mothers for the same reason [see Breastfeeding Your Baby]. Even if you are bottle feeding, however, you should still never smoke in the presence of your child because of the effects of passive smoke.

SOFT SPOTS ON A BABY'S HEAD *[See Newborn appearance]*

SORE THROATS AND "STREP THROAT"

We all get them and sore throats are a particularly big problem among children from two years of age on to the teen years. Most sore throats are caused by viruses, but for those children who are between the ages of two and eighteen, there is a risk of "strep throat." Caused by streptococcus bacteria, they are more dangerous not because of the sore throat itself, but because of subsequent problems that may develop from the infection, such as rheumatic fever (and heart disease) and, rarely, kidney problems. It is imperative, then, for the child with a strep throat to be seen by a physician. Even though there is a somewhat characteristic appearance to a strep throat, the only definitive way to diagnose it is with a throat culture or one of the newer rapid strep antigen tests. The risks of rheumatic heart disease can be completely prevented with a course of antibiotics such as penicillin. The rare kidney disease that results from a few strains of streptococcus, on the other hand, is not prevented by antibiotics.

Another useful thing about early treatment for strep throat with antibiotics is that it will prevent the affected child from being contagious to others within twenty-four hours of beginning the course of medicine. This is especially important if there are other children in the household or in determining when it is safe (to others) for the child to return to school.

 Do I have to call the doctor every time my child gets a sore throat?

You should always feel free to call your pediatrician whenever you are concerned about your child's health. Listed below are the types of symptoms associated with a sore throat that require immediate medical attention. They include:

- *Drooling or great difficulty swallowing in association with a sore throat*
- *Extreme sore throat pain that will not let up*
- *The child has difficulties in opening her mouth or in breathing*
- *Your child appears seriously ill*
- *Your child experiences frequent infections of the tonsils [see Tonsils and Adenoids]*

On the other hand, there are circumstances that require medical attention but do not have to be handled on an emergency basis in the middle of the night. These include:

- *A fever greater than 101.5°F*
- *Sore throat continued beyond one or two days*
- *Rashes along with a sore throat, especially one that looks like sandpaper or red "goose bumps"*

- *Complaints of belly pain*
- *Recent contact with another child who was diagnosed with either impetigo or strep throat*
- *Tongue that is bright red like a strawberry ("strawberry tongue")*
- *Pus or greenish-yellow discharge seen in the back of the throat*
- *Large, rubbery lymph nodes in the neck region*

These situations require a physical examination and a throat culture by a doctor in order to rule out a bacterial infection and, if necessary, to prescribe an antibiotic.

Are there any good remedies for simple, nonserious sore throats?

Hot fluids such as soup or tea can alleviate some throat soreness, as can cold fluids, ice chips, ice cream, and popsicles. Anesthetic-containing candies, on the other hand, can cause serious problems if too many are ingested—which seems to be a common problem when combining the issues of childhood illness and candy posing as a "medicine."

My daughter is always getting sore throats. Wouldn't it be a good idea to have some antibiotics on hand so I can just treat her whenever this problem occurs?

No! First of all, antibiotics do not have a very long shelf life, so the stockpiled antibiotic that has been sitting in the medicine cabinet for more than a couple of weeks is often no longer effective. More importantly, given that only 10 percent of all childhood sore throats (fewer in teens or adults) are caused by a strep infection, antibiotics are not needed in most cases. Antibiotics do not treat viruses! In fact, the inappropriate use of an antibiotic can cause more harm than good, such as upset stomachs, rashes, allergic reactions, and diarrhea. The overuse of antibiotics leads to bacteria that are resistant to antibiotics, and this can make treating future infections more difficult. Your child should only take the antibiotics prescribed for her by the physician. Borrowing medicine from others is never a good idea [see Medicines, Antibiotics].

SPEECH AND HEARING DEVELOPMENT: A PARENT'S CHECKLIST

As your child grows, she will become increasingly adept at indicating her needs. Acquiring these communication skills is tied to the development of speech, vocabulary, comprehension, and hearing. You can begin to assess how your baby hears and speaks (or attempts to speak) rather early in her life. One part of your child's pediatric examination is a rough assessment of her hearing *[see Well-Child Pediatric Examination Schedule]*. If you have concerns, a more definitive examination should be performed by a hearing and speech professional.

The following checklist will help you to assess your child's language and hearing abilities.

SPEECH AND HEARING DEVELOPMENT: A Parent's Checklist

Age	Hearing/Understanding	Language Development
Birth	Does the baby listen to you speak? Does the baby cry or startle at noises? Does your baby awaken at loud sounds?	Does the baby make pleasure sounds? When you play with your baby does he/she look at you, look away, and then look again?
1–3 months	Does your baby turn to you when you speak? Does your baby smile when you speak with him? Does your baby recognize your voice and quiet down?	Does your baby repeat certain sounds (e.g., cooing, goo-gooing)? Does your child cry differently for different needs? Does your baby smile when he/she sees you?
4–6 months	Does the baby respond to changes in the tone of your voice? Does the baby respond to "No"? When hearing a "new" sound (e.g., a doorbell), does the baby look for the source? Does your child notice toys that make noise?	Are the baby's babbling sounds taking on a speechlike pattern? Is the baby exploring new sounds (e.g., p, b, m)? Does the baby indicate with sound or gestures his/her wants? Does the baby make gurgling sounds when alone? When he/she is with you?
7 months–1 year	Does your toddler understand simple common words such as "juice," "water," "cup," "shoe," etc.? Does your child respond to your verbal requests, such as "Come here," "Do you want more?" etc.? Does your baby like to play "peek-a-boo" or "pat-a-cake"? Does your child look up or about when you call his/her name?	Does your child speak one or two words which are clear only to parents as long as they are consistent? Does the baby's babbling pattern include long and short groups of sounds (e.g., "baba," "mama," "dididi")? Does your child use specific sounds, other than crying, to get your attention?

Age	Hearing/Understanding	Language Development
1–2 years	When you are reading to your child, can he/she point to pictures of objects in the book as you name them? Can your child point out some of his/her body parts when asked? Does your child follow simple commands? Does your child enjoy listening to songs, stories, nursery rhymes?	Most children this age begin to say more recognized words each month. Does yours? Can your child phrase a two-word question such as "Where daddy?" "Go bye-bye?" etc.? Can your child phrase a two-word declarative statement such as "More juice." "No bath!" Is your child using different consonant sounds at the beginning of words?
2–3 years	Can your child distinguish the difference between opposite words, such as "go–stop", "up–down", "big–little"? When a doorbell rings or you turn on the television, does your child notice the new sound? Can your child follow a request with two parts such as "Get the book and put it on the couch?" Does your child notice toys that make noise?	Does your child have a word for almost everything in his/her world? Can your child use two-to-three word sentences to ask for and talk about things? Can you understand your child's speech most of the time? Does your child use words to identify objects (as opposed to gestures)?
3–4 years	Can your child hear you when you call him/her from another room? Does your child listen to television at the same volume as other members of the family (as opposed to louder)? Can your child answer simple "Why," "Where," "What" questions?	Does your child talk about his/her activities, friends, or school? Can your child pronounce most sounds, activities, friends, or school? Can your child speak easily without repeating sounds, syllables, or words? Can people outside your immediate family understand your child when he/she speaks? Does your child use sentences that contain more than four-to-five words?
41/2–5 years	Can your child understand most of the converstation he/she hears at home and in school? Does everyone who knows your child think he/she hears well? Can your child listen to a simple story and then answer simple questions about it?	Can your child communicate easily with other children and adults? Can your child pronounce most sounds correctly? (Some children this age may still have difficulties pronouncing one or two sounds.) Does your child use the same grammar and sentence structure as the rest of the family?

How to Score the Checklist

• If you answered "Yes" to all of the questions for your child's age, then everything appears to be normal

• If you answered "No" to one or two questions for your child's age, you need to discuss these potential signs of delayed hearing or speech development with your pediatrician

• If you answered "No" to more than two questions for your child's age, then your child requires a professional speech and hearing assessment

[See Stuttering]

SPIDER BITES *[See Bites]*

SPITTING UP (Regurgitation)

About half of all babies will "spit up" or regurgitate their food during the first weeks and months of life. This "spitting up" is different from vomiting in that it is not forceful and usually results from overfeeding. Remember, the newborn baby's stomach is about the size of a golf ball and can only hold an ounce or two of breast milk or formula. Adding more only increases the chances of the baby spitting up.

Spitting up or regurgitation is probably caused by an immature gastrointestinal system. Specifically, the muscles at the inlet of the stomach do not close completely, and the result is a reflux of food: spitting up. In order to justify our medical degrees, physicians call this syndrome gastroesophageal reflux.

Some babies spit up more than others. However, the good news is that most babies resolve this problem as they grow. Many babies improve at six to eight months, when they begin sitting up; others improve as they begin to walk. If your baby's spitting up does not appear to resolve with time, you need to discuss this with your pediatrician. Listed below are some helpful hints.

Try Feeding Your Baby Smaller Portions of Formula (Don't Overfeed the Baby)

Stuffing your baby with too much formula increases the chances that he will spit up. Decreasing the feeding portions, then, is the best way to attack this problem. Try reducing the amount of the feeding by one ounce, and restrict the bottle-feeding time to about fifteen or twenty minutes. If you are breastfeeding, give the baby a chance to nurse at one breast but pump the other breast for a future feeding (and to keep your breast milk supply up). Increase the time between breast-feedings to about three hours.

Do not put Pressure on the Baby's Belly

It is important not to use tight clothing or diapers that may place pressure on the baby's stomach—which will only increase the likelihood of spitting up. It is also important that you make sure that friendly uncles and other vigorous relatives do not roughhouse the baby right after a feeding. They may wind up with more than a smile!

Burp Your Baby Regularly During Feeding

You should try to burp the baby at least three to four times during a feeding. To prevent the now-shortened feeding from becoming simply a burp-fest, try to burp the baby as she takes a rest from the bottle, and try to make sure that burping takes less than a minute. If your baby uses a pacifier, try to reduce the time she uses the device. Sucking on a pacifier can cause more air to enter the stomach and create a sensation of fullness *[see Burping Your Baby]*.

Think Carefully About how You Position the Baby after Feeding

Placing a baby who spits up requires some extra thought and care. You want to make sure that right after a feeding, the baby is placed in an upright position. If you are unable to hold the baby in this position, try placing her in a baby swing or a Snugli-type baby pack. This will enable the formula to be held down somewhat by gravity and should help reduce the chance of spitting. Infant seats, on the other hand, place the baby in a lying down or angled position and only increase the pressure on the stomach contents and the chance of regurgitation. If your baby has long-term problems with spitting up, you should discuss them with your pediatrician.

There are some circumstances, however, where the baby's gastroesophageal reflux is more severe than merely spitting up. Make sure that your infant is not experiencing the following serious warning signs.

• The baby has lost rather than gained weight over a given period when he has been spitting up

• You notice blood (material that looks like wet coffee grounds) in the regurgitated material

• The spitting up is associated with coughing *[see Pyloric Stenosis]*

SPRAINS

Sprains are common injuries that cause the tearing or extreme stretching of a ligament. Ligaments are the stretchy bands of connective tissue that hold the muscles and bones together to form a joint. Sprains typically occur after a particularly hard fall or collision (such as one child running into another, followed by a fall).

Fortunately, children tend to suffer from sprains less frequently than adults. The most common sites for sprains are the ankles and knees. One good way of avoiding these injuries is to child-proof your child's play activities. In other words, make sure that your child plays on a forgiving surface (grass is a kinder surface than harder surfaces such as a cement sidewalk) and avoids more hazardous play activities such as climbing tall trees, monkey bars, and similar high perches *[see Falls]*.

If your child does fall, you want to look at the injury to assess how *red* it is; how *swollen* it is, and how *painful* the injury is. Most sprains hurt a great deal!

For Serious Sprain Injuries

In the case of a more serious sprain, where the ligament may have torn, the affected joint is quite loose or floppy. For these sprains, or if you notice that your child is in severe pain or that there is bleeding into the injury itself, it is best to call your physician *immediately* to assess the problem.

For Mild Sprain Injuries

If the sprain is obviously mild, or your physician has examined the sprain and agrees no emergency or surgical intervention is needed, the major treatment for sprain injuries is best remembered with the mnemonic "RICE"; it stands for the following treatments.

R = REST. Do not walk or bear weight on the sprained joint. Rest it. Avoid using it for the next several days to weeks.

I = ICE. After the initial injury, place an ice pack on the injury. This helps to reduce swelling, inflammation, and pain. If the sprain appears to be healing and is not as painful on the second day, you may replace the ice packs with a heating pad. Be careful to use the heating pad at low or medium levels. Never let your child fall asleep with the heating pad turned on. Skin burns can result from overuse of a heating pad.

C = COMPRESSION. You should wrap a supportive, compressing bandage (such as an ACE® bandage) around the joint affected by the sprain injury. Wrap it tightly but not too tightly that you prevent blood flow to the affected area. If your child complains of tingling sensation, numbness, or you notice a blue discoloration of the bandage area, you need to loosen it and readjust it. Giving the child a mild pain reliever such as acetaminophen can also be helpful *[see Fever]*.

E = ELEVATION. Elevate the sprained joint, such as an ankle, by placing it on one or two pillows. Adjust for comfort.

SNAKE BITES *[See Bites]*

STORK BITES *[See Newborn appearance]*

STRANGERS: WHAT PARENTS NEED TO TEACH THEIR CHILDREN

No matter how carefully you raise your child in a safe, loving, and healthy environment at home, eventually she will interact with a much larger world, be it a preschool day care center or even playing outside with friends. It is possible that she may come in contact with people who, for whatever reason, desire to hurt, abuse, or molest her.

All toddlers need to be taught calmly but authoritatively that they should *never* talk to strangers and that they should avoid going *anywhere* with someone who has not been clearly identified or introduced to them by their parents. The purpose of these discussions with your child is not to frighten her, but, instead to teach her an important safety measure. Remember that, although you can begin this instruction with a child as young as two years of age, these discussions should be repeated from time to time throughout early childhood.

Most importantly, the child should be taught never to allow anyone besides her mother or father or the child herself to touch her "private parts" (i.e. the sexual organs). The child should also be taught to report anyone requesting such "touching" immediately to her parents. One caveat to this approach is that you may want to mention to your child that doctors often examine "private parts," so that such an examination—in the presence of a parent—is okay.

STUTTERING

What is Stuttering?

True stuttering or stammering is the repetition of sounds, phrases, syllables, words, or phrases. It can include long pauses or hesitations that make the speech pattern hesitant and unnatural. Stuttering is four times more common in boys than in girls. When the stuttering child is tired, nervous, or excited, the stammer typically gets worse. The child with a true stutter may become nervous before speaking, and you may notice a tightening of his facial muscles or hear changes in the tone of his voice. The child often visably struggles to get out certain sounds or words. He may avoid troublesome sounds or words.

Some similar speech problems include normal dysfluency (pseudo-stuttering). The features of this speech pattern explain the child who repeatedly interjects meaningless or needless words into the sentence. It is relatively common in the child age eighteen months to five years and is a function of the child's mastery of speech and language. An example might be the child who speaks very fast and tumbles over words and sounds; another is the child who fills his sentences with "like" and "um": "Like, I, like, I want to, like, be a cowboy" or "um-um-um, Can I, um, um, go, um to the bathroom?"

A similar problem is *dysarthria*, which is a way of describing the speech patterns of children younger than the age of four years. As a child is learning to speak, she will experiment with different pronunciations and sentence structures; sometimes sounds are left out of the toddler's words, making her difficult to understand (parents universally understand their toddler's "baby-talk"). Almost all children outgrow these learning-to-talk problems by ages four to six.

What can I do to help my stuttering child?

It is important to remain calm and patient. The stuttering child is not doing it on purpose and does not need to feel worse about something that may already embarrass him. Love your child, treat the problem with constructive optimism, and try to place yourself in his situation. When your child speaks, allow him to finish his own sentences (as opposed to your filling in the words). Do not look expectant or bored. Try not to correct him. Don't make fun of his speech impediment. Encourage his progress. Learn to listen at a slower speed. If there are other children in the home, do not let them interrupt a conversation with the stuttering child. He needs to talk to his parents, too!

When should I seek out professional advice?

*If your child has true stuttering rather than normal dysfluency or dysarthria, you should consult a speech pathologist. These professionals help children with speech problems. If the child is over five years of age and is still having problems, discuss them with your pediatrician. Notice the child's speech patterns and discuss them with your pediatrician at the two-, three-, and four-year-old well-child examinations [see **Well-Child Pediatric Examinations Schedule**].*

STYES (Infections of the eyelids; hordeolum)

Styes are exquisitely tender bumps that occur at the end of the eyelid or near the edge of an eyelash. They are caused by the infection of a hair follicle. The offending infectious culprits are bacteria known as staphylococcus. Styes look a great deal like pimples and can be swollen as well as painful. The area around the stye should be kept clean. As difficult as it may sound, it is important that you try to keep your child from rubbing his eyes and irritating it further. In fact, the most common cause of styes is excessive rubbing of the eyes. Unfortunately, we all do this—regardless of age—many times a day.

The best way to help open these styes up and relieve the pain is to apply warm compresses to the area for twenty-minute periods four times a day and then cleansing it with soapy water. The prescription of antibiotic ointments has been gaining popularity recently; however, these ointments do little to treat the stye. Most staph germs that live on human skin are resistant to antibiotics *[see Medicines, Antibiotics]*. However, some reports suggest that these medicines may help prevent the stye from spreading to other sites, along the eyelid and lash.

With the compress treatment discussed, the stye should begin draining or improving within three days. Styes are usually gone in a week to ten days. Styes lasting longer or not appearing to get better need to be looked at by a physician.

SUDDEN INFANT DEATH SYNDROME (SIDS)

Sudden Infant Death Syndrome (SIDS)—or more commonly, crib death—is defined as a sudden, unpredictable, and inexplicable death of an infant under the age of one year. The cause of death remains unexplained even after a thorough medical investigation, autopsy, examination of the scene of death, and a complete review of the clinical history.

Doctors and other health-care professionals do not know the exact cause of SIDS, although it remains one of the leading causes of death among babies between the ages of one month and one year of age. Each year in the United States, for example, about 6,000 infants die of SIDS (this number works out to about one in every thousand infants). The majority of these unfortunate babies are between the ages of one and four months. Boys are victims more frequently than girls. The majority of the cases occur during the fall, winter, and early spring months.

Although no one is quite sure what causes SIDS, there are a number of things you can do as a parent to help reduce the risk for your baby. Before we discuss the specifics, we will begin with the most important advice we can offer: although the risk of SIDS is real and frightening to most parents, fortunately it is a relatively *rare* problem. Relax and enjoy your baby! Don't let your worries about SIDS (or other health problems that you read about but which have not occurred in your own child) interfere with the joy and pleasure of having a baby.

In addition to that simple, but important, reminder, here are a few other suggestions we can offer to help reduce the risk of SIDS.

Sleeping Position of Your Infant

Pediatricians have found that babies who are put down to sleep on their backs or on their sides with a lower arm forward as a means of preventing them from rolling over (with a rolled-up blanket as a support) are at much lower risk for SIDS than babies who sleep face down on their stomachs.

Some babies may not adjust well to sleeping in these positions. For example, those babies with specific birth defects or breathing, heart, or gastrointestinal

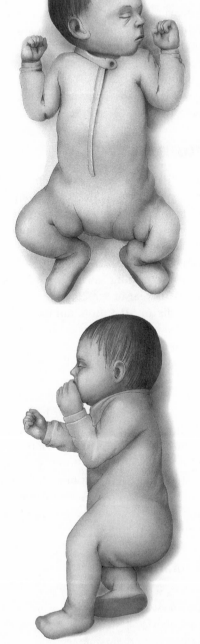

These sleep positions are recommended to lower the risk of SIDS.

problems may have a more difficult time adjusting to sleeping on their backs than other babies *[see Spitting Up].* If this is the case with your baby, talk with your pediatrician about alternate sleep positions to try. Incidentally, babies sleeping on their backs are *not* at higher risk for choking than those who do not. *[see Choking].*

Bedding

It is important to make sure that your baby sleeps on a firm mattress in a child-approved crib with proper safety features *[see Cribs].* Avoid placing the baby on or under thick blankets, comforters, or "covers." She can easily get tangled up in these thick blankets, which puts her at risk of suffocation. Other fluffy, full, or plush bedtime items to avoid include waterbeds, pillows, sheepskins, beanbags, and stuffed animals. These crib accoutrements may make the nursery beautiful, but they can be the cause of smothering in some babies.

Temperature of the Baby's Room

Newborn babies need to be kept warm, but they do not need to be roasted! Most babies over two months of age have little difficulty in regulating their body temperatures and do *not* need to be bundled, swaddled, or wrapped. A good rule of thumb is that if the temperature of the baby's nursery is comfortable for you, it is comfortable for the baby, as well.

Keep the Baby's Environment Smoke-free

It is extremely important to keep the baby's environment smoke-free *[see Asthma and Wheezing, Smoking and the Effects of Passive Smoking, Upper Respiratory Tract Infections and Colds].* If you must smoke, do it outside and away from your baby or child. Infants who are exposed to secondhand smoke are at increased risk not only for SIDS but also asthma and upper respiratory tract infections. The risk of SIDS is also increased for babies whose mothers smoked during pregnancy. Do yourself and your family a huge health favor: *quit smoking!*

If you have questions about SIDS or desire more information on how to prevent it, you can all or write the "Back to Sleep" Campaign to Reduce the Risk of Sudden Infant Death Syndrome at:

(800) 505-CRIB
Back to Sleep
P.O. Box 29111
Washington D.C. 20040

SUNSHINE, SUNSCREEN, SUNBURNS, AND SUNGLASSES

We all need to monitor how much sun we get during the summer months. Although a deep tan has often been associated with the appearance of health, we are learning more and more about the dangerous aspects of sun exposure. These dangers range from minor but annoying sunburns to the risk of sun-related skin cancers.

An Ounce of Prevention

Babies under the age of six months: In general, babies under the age of six months should be exposed to the sun as little as possible. Trips to the tropics are not a wise vacation choice during infancy. This does not mean you cannot take your baby out during the summer. Just be sure to avoid direct exposure for long periods. For example, if you go on a picnic or an outing, make sure to find shady, well-ventilated spots. Another useful tip is to plan the timing of the outing. The sun is at its strongest between 10:00 A.M. and 3:00 P.M. in most parts of the United States. These are good "peak times" to avoid with your baby. At present, most pediatricians do not advocate using sunscreen lotions on infants under the age of six months because they are absorbed differently by different infants with inconsistent results. Talk with your pediatrician about these products.

Other techniques you can use for your small baby, aside from choosing shady places include:

• Avoid taking infants to the beach. The sunlight is always at a peak near the beach because the sun reflects off the water and sand. This can cause serious sunburn even when precautions are taken.

• Put a hat on the baby's head when going out in the sunlight, even for brief periods. A light, long-sleeved T-shirt or "body suit" can be useful in sun protection. The trick here is to find a garment that is light-textured enough to prevent the baby from overheating. An umbrella as a sunshade is also a good idea.

Remember, after a month or two of age, the baby's temperature regulation system is very similar to your own. If you're too hot, so is she!

• Dress the baby in light-colored rather than dark-colored clothing. Dark clothes absorb more sunlight and heat.

• Cloudy days do not mean that there is no sun out. Indeed, even on the most cloudy of days, 60 to 80 percent of the sun's ultraviolet radiation can still reach humans.

Toddlers and children: As your children get older and more mobile, they are going to want to play more outside. They will, consequently, be more exposed to the sun. In general, the best means to avoid much of the harmful effects of sunshine is to play indoors during the sun's peak time (10 A.M. to 3P.M.) and to use sunscreen when playing outdoors.

Sunscreen lotions with a sun protection factor (SPF) *greater* than 15 are a good idea for anyone spending more than thirty minutes out in the sunlight. These sunscreens help reduce the more dangerous aspects of the sun's ultraviolet (UV) radiation. When buying a sunscreen, make sure you understand what you are buying. For example, a product with an SPF rating of 15 protects one against 93 percent of the sun's ultraviolet rays. This is generally sufficient for most children and adults, although some people with light-colored hair or fair skin are even sensitive to this reduced level of sunshine and may suffer sunburns. Higher SPF-rated products (30 or greater) are available if needed. Apply the sunscreen to all exposed areas of the skin. If you are going swimming, there are a number of waterproof products on the market. Even these products need to be reapplied every three to four hours.

Each day, in most major newspapers and on most television news programs, the weather section includes a prediction of the amount of UV radiation that will be present for the following day. This index is on a scale of one to ten, with ten being the most intense UV radiation exposure. This information should help you make even better decisions regarding sun exposure. Common sense is also an important factor. Be sure to watch and monitor how much sunshine your children are exposed to, and set a good example for them: if you don't take these precautions seriously yourself and you spend hours worshipping the sun, chances are your children will, too!

Sunburns

Sunburns are caused by too much exposure to the ultraviolet radiation of the sun. They are painful and annoying. Generally, we don't even realize when we are experiencing sunburn until the damage has already been done. Pain or redness typically does not begin until two to four hours after sun exposure; pain, soreness, reddening of the skin, and swelling reach their peak after twenty-four hours. Most cases of sunburn are considered first-degree burns because they are limited to the outmost layer of the skin. With prolonged exposure, one can develop a more severe (second-degree) burn, with blistering and more serious symptoms. Remember, prolonged exposure to the sun and repeated bouts of sunburn (especially second-degree burns) increase the risks of developing skin cancer. They also lead to premature wrinkling and other forms of skin damage.

Some Home Remedies

Although prevention is *always* preferable to treatment, listed below are a few tips to provide some relief for your sunburned child:

• Pain relievers such as acetaminophen (Tylenol®) may bring some pain relief *[see Fever]*.

• Drinking plenty of fluids helps to prevent dehydration from too much sun exposure.

• Applying a 0.5 percent hydrocortisone lotion to the especially sensitive spots may also help. This lotion is available at your local drugstore and does not require a prescription.

• Showers—especially if they are hot—can actually cause more pain than relief because of the jets of water spraying down on the sensitive skin. Instead, try cool washcloths and cool baths, several times a day. Adding a few tablespoons of baking soda to the bath water is also a time-honored technique.

• Avoid soap, butter, lotions, numbing medicines such as lidocaine or benzocaine, perfumes, sprays, insecticides, and anything else that might irritate the skin further.

Within a week or less after the sunburn, expect your child's skin to peel in the affected spots. This can be sensitive and itchy. Again, try applying some 0.5 percent hydrocortisone cream to the sensitive spots. Have patience; this, too, shall pass.

Some cases of sunburn are more severe than others. If you notice any of the following problems in your sunburned child, you should call your pediatrician.

• The sunburn is especially severe or all over the body

• The child develops a fever greater than 102°F, without a clear source of infection

• There is evidence of a skin infection at the site of the sunburn (i.e., drainage of pus at the site, severe blistering, red streaks emanating from the burn, and so forth)

- Your child refuses to look at lights (natural or electric) because it hurts his eyes
- Your child appears ill, unsure of his balance, dizzy, or confused
- You are concerned about your child's health and have questions

Sunglasses

Recent studies have shown that the sun's ultraviolet radiation can be harmful to the eyes. Consequently, it is important to protect them with proper sunglasses that absorb at least 99 percent of UV radiation. Purchase only those sunglasses that are labeled: "Blocks 99 percent of ultraviolet rays"; "UV absorption up to 400 nm"; "Special Purpose Sunglasses"; or "Meets ANSI (American National Standards Institute) requirements." Make sure the sunglasses you purchase are appropriately labeled; the darkness of the lens is *not* related to its ability to block out UV radiation.

When purchasing a pair of sunglasses for your child, you also need to make sure that they fit. Choose a pair with large lenses and frames that are well fitted and close to the surface of the eye. Glasses with side-shields are best, since they also block out the peripheral UV light that is not screened out by conventional frames. Make sure that the lenses and frames are made of nonbreakable plastic. And above all, if your child is old enough, allow him to participate in the selection process. We are all likely to wear something we like rather than dislike.

Sunglasses should not be considered a substitute for sunscreen, protective clothing, or hats. They protect only the eyes. It is a good idea to teach your child never to look directly at the sun. Sunglasses do not protect against serious injuries to the eyes that can result from prolonged, direct, sun exposure.

SURVIVING SHOPPING WITH YOUR CHILD

Bringing your young children with you when you shop for food or other commodities is a difficult but often necessary task. The impulsivity of toddlers, combined with the "American" disease of "I-want-itis," requires patience, thought, and some strategy. Marketing experts who study "kid-influenced spending" estimate that children played a direct role in American families' purchasing over $157 billion worth of goods and services in 1993; this figure should double by the year 2001! To help you avoid succumbing to the "nag factor" and economic disaster, we pass along several helpful hints recently received from one of our favorite child psychologists (and the mother of three), Dr. Eileen Mollen of the University of Michigan.

- You need to rehearse with your children these important rules for store behavior *before* you leave your car to enter the store.

• The child must either stay in the shopping cart (with his bottom on the seat of the cart and his hands to himself) *or* the child must stay close to the shopping cart. No hunting expeditions are allowed!

• Be clear (and honest) with your child about what will be the reward for good behavior (e.g., riding a coin-operated ride; receiving a coloring book; getting to look at the toy aisle for a few minutes at the end of the shopping trip, etc.).

• As the parent, you need to anticipate your child's needs once he arrives at the store. This will allow you to keep your child occupied and happy during the shopping trip. This includes the following:

1. **Food:** If you are going to the grocery store, begin the trip by buying the child a bagel or a box of crackers that he can eat and enjoy; if you are shopping elsewhere, bring a small bag of "snacks" (e.g., crackers, fruits, cereal, or similar food) with you.

2. **Toys:** Bring a small bag of toys with you that can be played with in the shopping cart. You need to make sure the toys selected are big enough not to slip through the grid of the shopping cart. It is helpful to designate a particular toy (or set of toys) as "special" toys used only for shopping trips. This helps keep the appeal of these particular toys for a longer period of time.

3. **Involvement:** As toddlers get older (e.g., over two years), they need to be more involved with the shopping trip. Talk with your child as you pick out your grocery needs. Let your child, for example, choose some of the oranges you are about to buy, or the cereal, or whatever. Keep your child amused with a running commentary on what you are doing, why you are buying certain things and not others, what you might prepare from these groceries, and so on. This may take some time, but is far more productive—and in the long run easier—than dealing with a temper tantrum.

4. **Distractions:** Perhaps the most difficult part of a shopping trip is waiting in the checkout lines. This period of time may seem like hours to an adult; it often feels even longer to young children. You need to be especially creative as a parent in these situations. Singing ("Row, Row, Row Your Boat," "The Wheels on the Bus Go Round and Round," or whatever tunes your child enjoys) sometimes works, although people around you may give you funny looks. Playing games such as "Identify the body part," "Finding colors," or comparing the size and shape of different objects in the cart often works with young toddlers. For older children, quiet interactive games such as "Guess the number" can be helpful.

5. **Bathroom breaks:** This is especially important for the newly toilet-trained toddler. Know where the public restrooms are and use them!

• For especially long shopping trips, you may want to leave your young toddler at home with a baby-sitter. Another option is to simply shop alone in the evening if your spouse is at home and is available to care for the children.

SWALLOWING PROBLEMS (Dysphasia)

Although there are several causes for what physicians term dysphasia, there are a few extremely serious conditions that require immediate attention. For example:

- The child who complains of a sore throat and cannot swallow or is drooling
- The child who can't swallow and has croup
- Recent ingestion of a food that the child is allergic to, or being bitten or stung by an insect
- The child who swallows a foreign body or, worse still, some type of poison or corrosive liquid (e.g., lye)
- The child with any type of mouth problem that prevents him from opening his mouth
- Refusing to drink for more than eight hours
- The child who appears very ill

TEETHING

The infant's first tooth is both a source of pride and concern for new parents. Most babies develop the first tooth at the approximate age of six months. The word "approximate" is used advisedly, since it can vary from child to child; some can begin teething as early as four months, others take as long as ten to twelve months for this event. Teething delayed much longer than the first year to eighteen months of life can, however, be a telling sign of delayed bone growth or other metabolic conditions such as rickets or hypothyroidism. Incidentally, the first tooth to erupt is typically the central lower incisor, with the rest of the incisors, first molars, cuspids, and molars to follow.

 My infant has just begun teething and appears to be in pain. What can I do?

Teething generally causes local temporary discomfort and irritation at the site of a slowly growing tooth. Painful episodes of teething may even run in families. Things you can do to help include:

1. Massaging the area of inflamed gum in the baby's mouth with a clean finger for one to two minutes. Ice can also aid with this method.

2. Some babies prefer massaging their own gums by chewing on a hard, and often cold, teething ring. Similarly, a cold, wet washcloth or even a popsicle will bring comfort.

3. Some babies may require a dose or two of acetaminophen (Tylenol) for pain relief.

4. Avoid giving the teething baby hard foods, such as raw carrots, or foods with a high acid content, such as orange or pineapple juice.

5. "Numbing" or anesthetic gels and jellies are probably best left on your pharmacist's shelf. Their effect is swept aside almost as quickly as the baby licks the jelly off the affected area. Excessive use of these products can cause severe drug reactions including cardiac arrest.

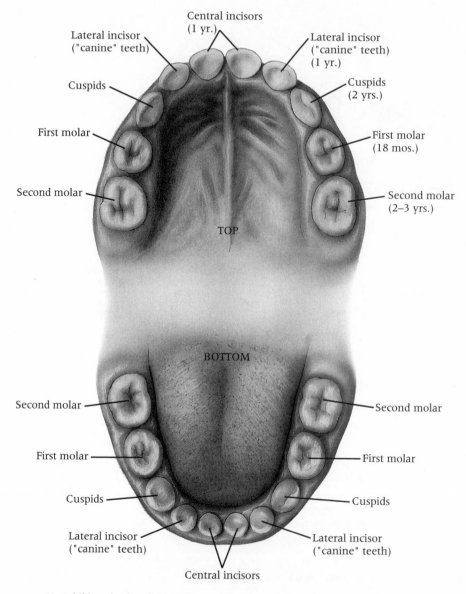

Central incisors
(1 yr.)

Lateral incisor
("canine" teeth)

Lateral incisor
("canine" teeth)
(1 yr.)

Cuspids

Cuspids
(2 yrs.)

First molar

First molar
(18 mos.)

Second molar

Second molar
(2–3 yrs.)

TOP

BOTTOM

Second molar

Second molar

First molar

First molar

Cuspids

Cuspids

Lateral incisor
("canine" teeth)

Lateral incisor
("canine" teeth)

Central incisors

Most children develop all 20 "primary teeth" between the ages of two and three years.

I heard that teething can put the baby "out of sorts" and cause other problems such as irritable behavior, fever, or diarrhea. Is this true?

Teething can make a baby uncomfortable or slightly "fussy" or difficult to feed. It is safer to assume that the teething baby who develops irritability, elevated temperature, diarrhea, vomiting, rash, or inflamed throat, however, may be ill for other reasons and requires just the same attention as the ill baby with the same complaints who is not teething.

TELEVISION

We are surrounded by the influence of television and the media. With the technological means to bring entertainment, information, and other events into our homes increasing at such a rapid rate, one can only wonder what further effect the television and its electronic relatives may have on our children.

How Much TV do Children Watch?

Here are a new numbers from a 1992 Nielsen Ratings report on television that startled us. In the United States alone:

• The average two-to-five-year-old watches over twenty-seven hours of TV a week (about four hours a day).

• The average six-to-eleven-year-old watches over twenty-three hours of TV a week (about three and a half hours a day).

• The average teenager watches over twenty-one hours of TV a week (about three hours a day).

• By the time a child graduates from high school, he or she has spent about twelve thousand hours in school; during this same period, that child has logged in over fifteen thousand hours watching television.

Anything that takes up this much time in a child's life is bound to have an influence on them. Some of these influences, of course, are good ones. On the other hand, TV provides many negative influences that must be considered by parents.

What has Research Found out about the Effects of Television Viewing?

Television violence and aggressive behavior: There are thousands of scientific studies confirming that exposure to heavy doses of television violence increases the likelihood of aggressive behaviors, especially in males. These behaviors, of course, are over a large range, from play-fighting or wrestling among younger children all the way to violent behaviors including homicide and suicide during the teen years. To call current television programming violent is an understatement of laughable proportions. For example:

• Between 1982 and 1988, the cartoon shows devoted to military or war stories increased from ninety minutes of airtime per week to twenty-seven hours per week.

• Movies of the horror, thriller, and "shoot-em-up" genres frequently contain up to hundreds of graphically portrayed fatalities. These films are inappropriate for children under the age of twelve years of age. These horror films are especially frightening to the toddler and young child (six years or younger) who cannot discern the difference between fantasy and reality.

• About 80 percent of all children's programming on network and cable television portrays some violence.

• On cable television the average child watches seventeen violent acts per hour; on the networks, it's thirty-two violent acts per hour!

It is not possible to blame all violent behaviors in our society simply on television; it's far more complicated than that. Nor are all so-called "violent" or aggressive acts the same. For example, toddlers and young children often show a natural aggression and exuberance in their play and interactions. Childlike aggressive behaviors such as pushing others, wrestling, and toy-gun play are common among children regardless of television exposure. It's just that those children who do watch a lot of TV tend to behave more aggressively *[see Aggression]*.

Research on TV and children has suggested that television depiction's of violence, where no one is really hurt and nothing "bad" seems to result, contributes to an unreal sense of violence in children (whereas in real life, people actually get hurt). In a way, children may be desensitized to the true effects of violence by witnessing it so frequently in these unreal fantasy shows. Consequently, they may be more likely to use violent or aggressive gestures when interacting with others.

Commercialization of television and consumerism: Television is the best salesperson in the history of humankind. Companies that manufacture products geared for children have taken advantage of this to improve the sales of their products. For example, toy manufacturers spend approximately fifty million dollars a year advertising their wares to consumers who are too young to understand a potentially deceptive commercial. Teenagers are an even better target for advertisers; last year more than seventy-one billion dollars were spent by American teens!

Many television shows, particularly cartoons and commercials geared toward children, create characters or formats that lead to larger sales of associated toys, books, and other consumer products. As a parent, you need to be careful about the effects of this not-so-benign influence. Sitting down and discussing the realities of receiving toys and spending money are essential if you hope to avoid confrontations with the child fresh from a Saturday morning of television-watching, wailing, "I want . . . "

You need to keep abreast not only of the television shows your child watches but also the commercials. Again, this is especially true of toddlers and younger children (under six years), who have difficulty distinguishing reality from fantasy as well as distinguishing the actual show from the commercial. Advertisers take extreme advantage of a young child's developmental reasoning abilities. Some commercials are quite graphic or violent, as well.

School performance: There is good evidence to suggest that a child's school performance begins to drop with more than two hours of television per day. This is particularly true for reading skills. At the very minimum, more than two hours a day of television take time away from homework and reading for pleasure. Schoolwork needs to take precedence over television, without exceptions. It's a simple rule that often takes many different negotiations, but well worth the battle. Restrict your child's television viewing to under two hours a day.

Stereotyping of race, religion, nationality, and ethnicity: A recent survey of American children's television programming revealed that white males represent between 75 and 90 percent of all the characters portrayed. Cartoons especially are rich in stereotypes and often portray villains or clownish figures as foreigners with accents, non-Caucasian features, and anti-social behaviors. One can find untoward stereotypes of Jews, African-Americans, gays, women, and any number of other social groups in a typical evening's worth of television. This is another reason parental monitoring is essential: in order to explain to children the difference between stereotypes and reality.

Obesity: There are several studies that implicate heavy television watching as a possible cause of obesity in children and teenagers. While this is clearly not true for all children who watch TV, one can understand the risk that the absorbing passive activity of TV-watching poses when combined with snacking. Couch potato behaviors—whether in children or adults—may include hoisting large quantities of tasty snack foods into one's mouth and a distinct lack of physical exercise. A frequent result is gaining excess weight. Studies show that behaviors learned in early childhood, such as excessive eating and television viewing, are commonly practiced throughout one's adult life. For your child's physical as well as his intellectual health, insist on limiting the hours spent staring at the television.

Sex and sexuality on television: Sex is as ubiquitous on television as violence. Commercials use sexual innuendo and explicit sexual references to sell a variety of products, even to children and teenagers. Explicit sexual activity is not appropriate viewing for small children and needs to be removed from their media universe. Small children typically exhibit a curiosity about body parts, gender difference, and the like, but interest in actual sexual activities is *not* part of that curiosity.

Teenagers, on the other hand, show a great deal of curiosity about sex and sexual activity. One survey of teenage television watching revealed that the average American adolescent views more than fourteen thousand sexual references on TV annually; of these, only one hundred seventy-five deal with human sexuality in a responsible manner. It is hard to estimate the exact influence of "television sex" on teenage sexuality. It probably plays some role in our alarming rates of teenage pregnancy, sexually transmitted disease cases, AIDS, and similar problems.

There is one positive side to the many television shows that include sexual scenes or discussions of sexual issues: many parents have used these shows as a "springboard" for their own discussions on these topics with their adolescent children. Studies consistently show that the best and most successful instruction on sexual matters for adolescents comes from their parents.

Cigarettes and alcohol: Cigarettes are currently banned from advertising on American television, as are hard liquors. But beer and wine manufacturers, on the other hand, spend more than nine hundred million dollars advertising their products. Cigarettes and alcohol are the most commonly abused drugs among teenagers in the United States. Characters on television shows are allowed to drink alcohol, smoke cigarettes, and, at times, use illicit drugs. More often than not, the use of cigarettes and alcohol is made to appear glamorous rather than a potential health problem.

The negative images produced by commercials portraying beer drinking he-men at swinging parties are obvious to most adults. Adolescent boys, however, do not see these scenarios as anything but a noble aspiration. Similar advertising games have been played on young children by the tobacco industry. Cartoon characters hawking cigarettes are cynically designed to appeal to young (eight-to-twelve-year-old) potential smokers. These campaigns offer great "prizes" if you buy their product, such as T-shirts, jackets, and the like—all emblazoned with the cartoon character and the cigarette logo. Currently, the tobacco industry spends over 3.2 billion dollars a year advertising their products in newspapers, magazines, and other print sources easily available to children *[see Smoking]*.

 What should I do as a parent to help my child use television responsibly?

We must confess that we recall many wonderful hours seated in front of a television set. Nor will we wax nostalgic about a kinder, gentler television with wonderful children's entertainment programming in past eras. Some positive features of television do exist, such as those programs that expose young viewers to music, entertainment, instruction for toddlers on learning the alphabet and simple arithmetic, as well as ideas about kindness, cooperation, and racial harmony. Similar shows produced for older children and teens have intelligently discussed issues such as AIDS, alcoholism, drug abuse, teenage pregnancy, divorce, and other social issues. How many of these positive programs are produced, as opposed to shoot-'em-up-beat-'em-up shows? That depends largely upon the collective responses of you and your fellow parents. Never forget, networks respond to their viewers. An essential mission of network and cable television is to generate the greatest amount of money from their advertisers. Are you dissatisfied by a particular show that is inappropriate for your child? Chances are, so are other parents. Discuss these issues with your friends and write to the local station affiliate or to the President of Entertainment at the network offices listed below.

Broadcast networks

ABC: 2040 Avenue of the Stars, Fifth Floor, Los Angeles, CA 90067
NBC: 3000 West Alameda, Burbank, CA 91523
CBS: 7800 Beverly Blvd., Los Angeles, CA 90036
FOX: 10201 W. Pico Blvd., Los Angeles, CA 90035

Warner Brothers Network (WB): 4000 Warner Blvd., Los Angeles, CA 91522

UPN (Paramount) Network: 5555 Melrose Ave., Los Angeles, CA 90038

Public Broadcasting System (PBS): 1320 Braddock Place, Alexandria, VA 22314

Cable networks

Arts and Entertainment Cable Network: 235 E. 45th St., New York City, N.Y. 10017

American Movie Classics (AMC): 150 Crossways Park West, Woodbury, N.Y. 11797

America's Talking/CNBC: 2200 Fletcher Ave., Fort Lee, N.J. 07024

Black Entertainment Network (BET): 1700 N. Moore St., #2200, Rosslyn, VA 22209

Bravo: 150 Crossways Park W., Woodbury, N.Y. 11797

The Cartoon Network: 1050 Techwood Dr., NW, Atlanta, GA 30318

Cinemax: 1100 Avenue of the Americas, New York City, N.Y. 10036

Comedy Channel: 1775 Broadway, New York City, N.Y. 10019

The Discovery Channel: 7700 Wisconsin Ave., Bethesda, MD 20814-3522

Disney Channel, 3800 W. Alemeda Ave., Burbank, CA 91505

Encore: 11766 Wilshire Blvd., Suite 710, Los Angeles, CA 90025

Family Channel: 1000 Centerville Turnpike, Virginia Beach, VA 23463

Home Box Office: 1100 Avenue of the Americas, New York City, N.Y. 10036

The Learning Channel: 7700 Wisconsin Ave., Bethesda, MD 20814

Lifetime: 309 W. 49th St., New York City, N.Y. 10019

The Movie Channel: 1633 Broadway, New York City, N.Y. 10019

MTV: 1515 Broadway, New York City, N.Y. 10036

Nickelodeon: 1515 Broadway, New York City, N.Y. 10036

Science Fiction Channel (Sci-Fi): 1230 Avenue of the Americas, New York City, N.Y. 10020

Showtime: 1633 Broadway, New York City, N.Y. 10019

Turner Broadcasting Network

   CNN: 1 CNN Center, 7th Floor, North Tower, Atlanta, GA 30348

   TBS and TNT: 1050 Techwood Dr., NW, Atlanta, GA 30318

USA: 1230 Avenue of the Americas, New York City, N.Y. 10020

VH-1: 1515 Broadway, New York City, N.Y. 10036

If you do not receive an appropriate response from these companies, you should write to:

Federal Communications Commission
Bureau of Mass Media, Division of Enforcement
Room 8210
2025 M Street
Washington D.C. 20554

On the next page we have listed a few more tips to use in helping your child enjoy television in a responsible and appropriate manner.

• Television is not an appropriate baby-sitter. Human interactions and play are infinitely superior to any electronic version. Instruct your sitter or day-care worker to limit the television, video games, computer play, and VCR programs as special activities rather than daily ones.

• Toddlers, especially, have difficulty differentiating fantasy from reality and are likely to become frightened or upset about a particularly frightening or intense television program.

• It's a good idea to limit your child's television viewing to less than two hours a day. This includes videocassette tapes and movies. Remember that the child's development of other recreational skills, conversation, social skills, reading skills, school performance, exercise, and eating habits are likely to be negatively affected by too much television watching.

• Parents need to monitor what television shows and commercials their children and teenagers are watching. Think of it this way: if we offered you a teaching service, where complete strangers whom you had no way of interviewing or rejecting were going to come in your house and spend three or more hours with your child every day, you would probably decline. Your television, potentially, plays that same role. You need to watch on a regular basis the television programs (including commercials) that your child watches. This is essential if you are going to properly supervise your child's television viewing habits and prevent her from watching programs that are not appropriate for children.

• When you set a bedtime for your children, do not allow routine television shows to interfere with that rule. There will be times, of course, that a particularly special event is being televised after bedtime, and rules can be broken on such occasions. But for the most part, it is not a good idea to let a school-aged child stay up with you watching the Late Show. Children who lack sleep often do poorly in school.

• Make a firm rule of no television during meals. Mealtime is probably the only time your family has to see and interact with one another. Television prevents any such social process.

• Discuss fantasy versus reality with your child; this includes television shows and commercials. Teach them that the TV world is not real.

• Explicit, sexual, or violent television shows, movies, and other forms of entertainment are *not* appropriate for children. You need to specify to your younger children what is and is *not* okay to watch. Some older children like lists of what they can or cannot watch. Many children under the age of fourteen experience nightmares after watching particularly scary movies *[see Nightmares]*. Feel free to discuss the real impact of violence (i.e., if you shoot a gun at people, they really do die) *[see Guns and Firearms]*.

• Encourage your child to watch shows that present information or teach valuable lessons or concepts. Some parents employ responsible television shows on subjects such as sex education, AIDS, drug abuse, or other difficult-to-discuss subjects as a springboard to open up a discussion with their child. (This is especially useful in middle childhood eight-to-eleven-year-olds and with teenagers.)

• If you subscribe to an adult-video cable channel or rent adult or R-rated movies, remember that these are easily available to children unless you take specific precautions to prevent it. Obtain a cable-lock for the channels you do not want your children to watch, and be careful with the videos! Channel blocking "V-chips" may soon be available for all new television sets by a recent order of Congress.

• Most importantly, be a positive role model. Cough potatoes beget coach potatoes. If you spend all of your leisure time channel-surfing and watching the tube, so will your children. It is also not a good idea to get into the habit of leaving the television or radio on all day and night as "background noise." There is no such thing as television acting *only* as background. Eventually it draws in even the most disdainful observer.

 My five-year-old boy is wonderful and well behaved except after watching a particular television show that involves a great deal of violence— karate-style fighting with monsterlike creatures and weaponry. What should I do?

This is a tough one, because chances are the more violent and worrisome the show, the more your child and all of his friends will want to watch it. Peer pressure to know every detail about a "cool" or favored television show is intense among young children. On the other hand, these violent shows are not really appropriate for them, even though they may have been carefully geared toward their mentality and level of understanding.

For example, many children's shows feature "superheroes" who have the ability to transform themselves into a weapon, a monster, or anything else they fancy at the time. Such a skill is especially appealing to the preschooler and early-school-aged child (three to seven years) because of the "magical thinking" patterns—most children this age fantasize about transforming themselves into another person, a larger person, or even an object. Television writers exploit this facet of child development in these shows.

A good sign that the show in question is too violent, as you suggest, is when your child is suddenly kicking his little sister after an episode of the Mutant Dirtbike Whatever Rangers. We suggest that you sit down with your son and explain why you feel this show is not appropriate for him. Emphasize that the scenes on the TV are not real and that there are many positive means of solving conflicts far superior to nuking your enemies. Find a different format of entertainment for him [see Computers and the Internet; Video Games and VCRs].

THRUSH (Candida)

This common yeast infection of infants, with its quaint name, appears as thick, furry white patches inside the baby's mouth. Babies are especially prone to this infection because the yeast organism likes to grow in the lining of a mouth that is damaged or sore from frequent sucking—a definite risk factor for babies! Too much sucking on a pacifier or your giving the baby a bottle at bedtime and leaving it with her all night can worsen the risk of thrush.

Once you see thrush, you will not forget it. As noted above, its hallmark is thick, whitish, almost "furry" irregular patches on the baby's gums, inside the mouth, and sometimes on the tongue. This is not to be confused with the whitish debris and coating of the baby's mouth and tongue after bottle- or breastfeeding. Thrust patches do not wipe away like partially digested milk curds.

Thrush is painful to the baby but is not contagious to others. It is easily treated with an antifungal medication. Many pediatricians may want to see the baby before prescribing the medication. It is given orally three to four times a day until *three days after the thrush has disappeared* (in most cases this occurs on day three or four of treatment). Place the liquid medication on a washcloth or cotton ball and wipe the tongue, gums, and inner lining of the mouth with it. Hold off on feeding the baby until thirty minutes after administering the medication.

For mothers who are breastfeeding, there is a risk that your nipples may become irritated and infected with thrush. Consequently, your pediatrician will suggest that you apply a small amount of the antifungal medicine to each nipple four times a day for the same period. For bottle-fed babies, make sure all nipples are washed in the dishwasher before reusing.

During the baby's experience with thrush, she may find it painful to suck. Be patient and remember that thrush does hurt. Gradually, as the medication takes effect, you will see a return of the baby's normal sucking and feeding activities. In any event, you may want to restrict the baby's sucking only to feedings that are fifteen minutes or less. Pacifiers ought to be restricted, for obvious reasons. For those infants, however, who demand the pacifier you need to make sure to use a small one that has been soaked in medium-hot water (about 120° to 130°F) for about fifteen minutes. Make sure to cool it before use. The larger the pacifier, the more the baby struggles to master it with her mouth—hence the more potential for irritation of the sensitive and sore mouth.

Finally, it is not uncommon for the baby with oral thrush to also develop a candidal (yeast-infected) diaper rash. This, too, is easily treated with an antifungal ointment, four times a day for a period of seven to ten days *[see Diaper Rash]*.

THUMB SUCKING AND PACIFIERS

For many years, adults interpreted a child's thumb sucking as a sign of insecurity or immaturity. In point of fact, it is a harmless activity that many infants and toddlers find soothing, comforting, and enjoyable. Remember, a small child explores the world through his mouth and finds great pleasure in the sensations surrounding activities such as eating or sucking. Indeed, the "original" source of oral gratification is sucking at a mother's breast.

For children under the age of four, thumb sucking is to be expected, is entirely normal, and in the majority of children will be dropped for other habits as they grow older. While previous generations of pediatricians and parents used to discourage children from sucking their thumbs as soon as the habit developed, most child psychologists, pediatricians, and pediatric dentists suggest that there is no need to be so aggressive.

For the statistically minded, about 50 percent of all children will, at least occasionally, suck on a thumb or finger during the first year of life. This figure drops significantly to about 15 percent of all children by the age of six and even more drastically between the ages of nine to fourteen, when less than 5 percent of children continue to suck their thumbs.

Aside from the unsightly vision of a teenager still sucking his thumb and the intense teasing that will result from such a behavior, there are other reasons the habit should stop at the age of four. The major reasons include potential long-term changes in the child's teeth and in thumb or finger itself.

An Orthodontist's Dream!

Long-term thumb sucking (beyond the age of four years) will alter the child's teeth markedly. The most common change is what has been nicknamed "buckteeth," the protrusion of the front teeth caused by the constant pressure of a thumb in the mouth. Another problem that can be caused by chronic thumb sucking is the "open bite"; specifically, there exists an open gap between the top and bottom set of incisors that is large enough to allow passage of a toothbrush, tongue, or even the thumb while the teeth are still clenched. Finally, there is "cross-bite," which is caused by long-term sucking: the roof of the mouth becomes narrowed and the development of the upper jaw is impaired, leading to serious speech impediments, such as lisping. The bottom line, alas, is that corrective braces and orthodonture costing up to several thousand dollars are often needed to correct the misalignment problems caused by thumb sucking.

Physical Damage to the Thumb

Long-term thumb sucking can cause a variety of problems in the thumb itself, such as chapping and cracking of the skin. This problem is best treated by placing some petroleum jelly on a bandage over the damaged skin for a few days.

Another problem that can result from thumb sucking is an infection of the fingernail called a *paronychia*. When your child develops a raised area of pus, redness, or swelling right at the nailbed, between the cuticle and the fingernail, it can be quite painful. This needs to be seen by the pediatrician, who will open up the area with a lance and prescribe an antibiotic to ensure its proper healing.

The rarest complication of long-term thumb sucking is the possible bone malformations that can result; at times, we have seen thumbs bent sideways at the area of the first line, or joint, of the thumb—which can only be corrected by surgical intervention.

My five-year-old daughter is still sucking her thumb. All of her friends are making fun of her, calling her a "baby," yet she still persists in thumb sucking. What do I do?

There are a variety of approaches to helping your child "kick the habit" of thumb sucking. The most important principle is not to turn it into a major battle or issue. Such an approach is destined for failure. She must be convinced that stopping is the right thing to do. No child ever stopped a favorite habit simply because it annoys her parent. We suggest that thumb sucking be ignored until about the age of four to six, with the understanding that it is a natural means of comfort for the toddler and, in most cases, will be dropped by the child on her own.

    For the four-year-old or older who continues to thumb suck, it is best to begin by gently showing the child what all the thumb sucking is doing to her. For example, show her, carefully, the "pruny" and chappy skin changes that may exist on the thumb. It is also a good idea to get a mirror to show the child the changes in her teeth caused by the habit. Once this has been done, you need to make sure the child agrees with you and senses a need to stop thumb sucking. A gentle game to help this process involves placing cartoonlike bandages on the thumbs during the day, as a reminder to not suck, while substituting a pleasing, colorful glove or mitten at night, to prevent a recurrence of the problem. At all times, the child needs to be actively involved in the process. Encourage and reward her with immediate gratification such as stickers or a treat that she especially enjoys; always use kind words to keep the process going. Constructing a chart that marks the child's progress, with the promise of a special prize for the ultimate goal, is a great way to teach the child about working toward a goal and to stop thumb sucking. Remember not to make a big deal out of failures and to keep encouraging the child in her attempts. We find this approach far more gentle, helpful, and fun than older methods of painting thumbs with awful-tasting substances or getting into shouting matches with the child.

Are pacifiers a good idea?

If you start immediately with a rubber-plastic pacifier, you may prevent the habit of thumb sucking in the first place. Generally, we suggest offering a pacifier to the baby at the age of two months or so. The best time to start "weaning" the baby from the pacifier is about the time he becomes more mobile (e.g., starts crawling, or at six months) in order to prevent the pacifier from becoming a habit that needs to be broken. It may take some time to actually remove the pacifier from the baby's routine, so do it gently and gradually. For example, at the age of six months, once the baby is asleep, remove the pacifier from her mouth. On certain occasions, such as family outings, you may choose to "forget" to bring the pacifier along. You should also restrict the use of the pacifier, once this process has begun, to naptime and nighttime. Finally, as the child becomes less dependent upon it, encourage the child to throw it away. This goal can generally be achieved, if you are patient and gentle and quick to praise the child, by the age of four. Remember: if the child becomes upset over the removal of a pacifier, do not force the issue. *No child ever gives up anything he enjoys because his parent is yelling at him or humiliating him by calling him a baby. As in any issue of child rearing, you need to pick your battles wisely.*

The advantages the pacifier has over a thumb is that it is made out of a pliable soft substance that does not change the configuration of the teeth and, obviously, avoids skin or bone damage to the thumb. Moreover, unlike a thumb—which the child handily carries about with him—the pacifier is easily left behind at home when you start the "weaning" process.

Substituting a pacifier for a thumb that is already in use, on the other hand, is not nearly as easy a task. Generally, once a child has begun to enjoy the comforts of real thumb sucking, he is less likely to give it up for a pacifier. It is also important to remember not to make the pacifier, or the thumb for that matter, into a substitute for old-fashioned attention to your baby. Talking to him, playing, holding and hugging him, especially during stressful moments when the child may seek the comfort of a pacifier—or a thumb—are far better sources of comfort than any piece of plastic could ever be!

A Few Rules about Pacifiers

1. Remember to select the pacifier carefully. Do not make your own pacifier. Instead, choose one at the store that is constructed in one piece (to avoid a piece breaking off in the baby's mouth and potentially causing suffocation); you also should avoid any product with a string around it to hang over a baby's neck, like a necklace. The risk in such a product is, again, suffocation—this time by strangulation with the string.

2. Never buy the type of pacifier that has a liquid center, because of the risk of bacterial infections; never coat the pacifier with sugar, syrup, or honey. This will promote tooth decay and, in the case of corn syrup or honey, can be the cause of a disease called botulism in the baby under one year of age. Always clean the pacifier frequently, particularly if it falls out of the baby's mouth onto the ground. Finally, inspect the pacifier frequently to see if it is still intact. If it is broken, damaged, or about to break, get rid of it and buy a new one.

Tics

Tics are repetitive movements, noises, and involuntary muscle movements. They can sometimes be expressed as exaggerated coughing, blinking, sniffing, or sneezing. Barking, mouth twitching, and head jerking are other forms of tics. They can be seen in children as young as one year, but they are more commonly seen in children over seven or eight. Most childhood tics are temporary and only last a few weeks to a year; classically, they are repetitive winks or nose twitches that may appear and disappear over a few weeks or months. The more chronic or life-long form of tics is referred to as *Tourette's syndrome*. This syndrome includes multiple ticks, muscle jerks, vocalizations, barking, and sometimes repetitive profanities.

If you notice any type of tics in your child, feel free to discuss them with your pediatrician. Tics are quite common and occur at some time in almost 20 percent of all children. The exact cause of tics and its more severe form, Tourette's syndrome, is not known, but the sometimes odd behaviors are not done on purpose. Do not become angry; be patient, and remember that it is *not* your child's fault. We rarely prescribe any medications for tics because there are few medications that do anything to reduce them and the side effects they can cause such as extreme sleepiness. Severe tics may require a consultation with a pediatric neurologist.

TIME OUT *[See Discipline]*

TOILET TRAINING

One of the most needlessly embattled areas of child rearing is toilet training. There is little wonder, in the parent's mind, why such a goal is to be devoutly wished for. Yet not all children desire to be toilet trained at the same time or in the same way. For example, at the beginning of the twentieth century, many pediatricians instructed mothers to attempt toilet training as early as four to six months of age! Fortunately, we have evolved somewhat and allow a more permissive approach to the process. Rest assured that all normal children eventually do become toilet trained. Patience is the most important factor. The typical time to begin such training is anywhere from two to three years of age, although some children will learn earlier.

Three important developmental milestones need to be achieved *before* a child can be successfully toilet trained:

1. **Body control awareness:** the child needs to learn the feeling of a full bladder or bowels: the sensation of "having to go to the bathroom."

2. **Language skills:** the child needs to be able to articulate his awareness of "having to go to the bathroom" in an understandable manner.

3. **Motivation:** if the toddler is not yet interested in achieving toilet training, no amount of yelling, taunting, or insulting will do much to ameliorate the problem.

It is important to think of toilet training in the context of what the toddler can do, physically and mentally. Going to the bathroom is a complicated, many-stepped process that requires a great deal of learning. On a purely mental level, the child needs to learn a little bit about advance planning—something most toddlers are notoriously bad at! He needs to begin to think about what is happening in his body and respond accordingly. For example, on a purely physical level, the child needs to learn bladder muscle control to hold and release urine—as opposed to doing it spontaneously when wearing a diaper. The same goes for holding bowel movements. He also needs to learn the feelings of a full bladder and bowels and respond by announcing a need to "visit the potty" or, later, make that trip on his own. Finally, he must be able to relax enough to allow "nature to take its course."

Some children express a distinct fear of the toilet. While this seems amusing at first glance, it is easy to understand. The toilet is a big device, often seemingly larger than the child, with swirling water that carries things away at the pull of a lever. Many small children—who still think very concretely and egocentrically—fear that they, too, will be flushed down the toilet, or that a monster may emerge out of the bowl, or a number of similar fears. You need to be reassuring during this entire process to avoid such fears taking over.

Perhaps most importantly, you need to reassure the child that she will, indeed, master toilet training—when, and only when, her body is ready. Such an explanation removes blame from accidents (and they will happen) and allows the child to reason through the process with confidence. With due respect to Sigmund Freud, you do not have to worry about permanently scarring your child with every aspect of the toilet-training experience. Avoid getting into fights or shouting matches with the toilet-training child—but only because they interfere with the process of getting the child toilet trained, *not* on account of the risk of some future psychological problem developing because of the experience. A difficult round of toilet training does not brand your child as psychologically disabled. On the other hand, you do want this process to be a positive learning experience, filled with a sense of accomplishment and—if possible—enjoyable rather than a battleground. As with so many issues in child rearing and parenting, if at first you don't succeed, keep trying and be patient. The outcome, in this case, is almost always rewarding for both the parent and the child.

A Step-by-Step Approach to Toilet Training

1. Be positive, persistent, and reassuring! Remember, your child did not immediately learn how to walk or talk. These events took time, trial, and errors. A level of calmness, understanding, and patience is essential. Battles over the toilet are heavily weighed in your child's favor; if you do enter into such a process, you will most likely lose. You and your child *will* succeed in this task, even though it may not always seem obvious during the early stages of the process.

2. Before the child is actually ready to learn this task, it is perfectly permissible to discuss the topic with him. He should know what bowel movements and urine are (we will allow you to select the "term" of your choice to refer to these activities!). He needs to learn when a diaper is wet or soiled. He will also learn some aspects of delaying the event, even while still in diapers, and it is reasonable to discuss this issue with a small child. It is perfectly reasonable for your toddler to see what goes on in a bathroom—if it does not embarrass you—so he gets used to the concept of what that place is actually for.

3. A good place to start is by purchasing one of the "potty chairs" (available at any department or toy store). Talk with your child about getting her own "special potty." She should be part of this selection process. A favorite color or character on the device is a nice way of personalizing the potty chair for your child. Issues

of the size of the potty or toilet and the fear of falling in frequently come up during this conversation. You can reassure your child that you would never let such a thing happen, which is why you purchased the special potty chair. It is important to listen to your child's fears and to address them specifically and gently, as opposed to dismissing them as "childish fears." They are very real to the child and can be far more easily taken care of with gentle discussion than by ignoring or laughing at them. Let your *child* bring up any fears; don't raise them yourself simply because you read about them here! Some children may have no fears at all, and there is no reason to put frightening ideas into their heads. Explanations about developing into a "big girl" or a "big boy" are often helpful, especially if the child has an older sibling or friend who has already mastered the transition. In a way, this is one of the child's first "rites of passage" into a more grown-up world. You should emphasize this positive and important step.

4. The potty chair may be initially placed in the child's bedroom or playroom rather than the bathroom, if you wish, but eventually it needs to be in the bathroom. If your child has a favorite doll or stuffed animal, she can role-play the experience with that object and the special potty chair. However you manage it, the process should begin slowly, gently, and reassuringly over two or three weeks.

5. During this period, it is a good idea to explain the concept of tightening and relaxing muscles. After all, muscle control is the essence of toilet training. Begin by showing your child what a tensed fist or arm is like and have her imitate it. Slowly graduate to the muscles in her urinary and rectal area. If she learns how to practice tensing and relaxing these muscles, you have made great steps toward her success. Remember, these are not easily learned concepts. They may take a while to master.

6. Some children are hesitant to learn so many aspects of the process at once; you may need to break it down into understandable and manageable steps. Merely sitting down on the potty may be a difficult task. Muscle control is almost always difficult. Learning when to say "I have to go to the bathroom" in a timely manner is another. Most toddlers can easily learn the feeling of a full bowel or bladder; it's the *response*—saying "I need to go to the bathroom"—that takes some time. Gentle, but not nagging, reminders often help. Don't hesitate to ask your child now and then if she needs to use the potty—particularly if she begins to squirm in a meaningful or recognizable manner. Most important, allow your child to feel comfortable with each and every step of the process at his or her own speed.

For example, you might allow your child to sit on the potty at scheduled times during the day while he is still protected by diapers and have him "go to the bathroom" that way. Slowly move both the potty chair and whatever toys have become involved in the process closer to the bathroom over the weeks, with the eventual goal of moving the chair into the bathroom itself. In this way, the child still has the security blanket of the diaper but is "going to the bathroom" like a "big person." So-called "practice runs" are a useful step. Remember, however, never to force your child onto the "potty" or hold him down on it. Such efforts are doomed to fighting and failure.

7. As things progress, you might try having your diapered child sit on his potty chair (placed on top of the *closed* toilet) and go through the same process. Eventually you can loosen the diaper or take it off completely, so that he is actually using the potty rather than the diaper as the final receptacle. Be reassuring and expect this not to go in the simple, step-by-step manner described here!

8. The next step needs to be gradually introduced at whatever speed your toddler allows. When your child appears ready, open the toilet lid and allow the child to sit on the toilet seat in an attempt to use "the real potty." Most potty chairs today have a false bottom, allowing them to adapt to the adult toilet seat. This gives a sense of security not commonly found with a large, adult-size seat.

The toilet should never be flushed while the beginning potty-trainee is sitting on it. It frequently frightens the child. Make a game about flushing—once the child is standing on firm ground—is one approach. For those children who express a particular fear of flushing, simply don't push the issue. Flush the toilet *after* she leaves the bathroom.

Don't be afraid to back off if your child is having difficulty, and remember not to get upset. As explained above, the real reason for any temporary failures is not that your child is "bad," but simply that his body is not yet ready for toilet training. As the child gains more mastery of the toilet, applaud his efforts and make sure he knows that you are pleased with his progress. You should also remember that "accidents" are to be expected. They can be embarrassing, even for a toddler, but loving reassurance and prompt diaper-changing can quickly dispel negative experiences.

How long should I expect the toilet training process to take?

Typically, it can take anywhere from two or three weeks to two months. Having said that, we will again remind you that all children are different. The length of training time is far less important than the end result. Remember that accidents can occur even after toilet training mastery; you should expect them and handle them with calming reassurance. A typical example is the long-trained four-year-old who is outdoors playing. He may know he has to go to the bathroom, but because he is having so much fun or the bathroom seems too far away, he simply forgets and has an accident. Be calm, reassuring, and forgiving.

My three-year-old daughter is a delightful little girl, intelligent, independent, and happy. Yet whenever we attempt to discuss the issue of toilet training, she resolutely says "No!" and a battle ensues. What should I do?

First, you need to take several deep breaths and remember that battles over toilet training are best avoided, as are punishments, reprimands, or ridicule. Any toddler worth her salt will respond to such tactics with a resounding "No!" Explain to the child that you understand that her body is not yet ready for toilet training, and put the potty away for a few weeks. Try again at that time, provided the child is willing, and initiate the process all over again.

Children who are older than two and a half years but remain non-toilet trained are called "resistant" to the experience. Frequently, the issue has been discussed at great length in these households and a number of "lectures" have been presented to the toddler on the topic, to no avail. Try not to get upset about the resistance, although we agree it is a difficult task. If less focus and attention are given to the topic, it is likely that she will tire of being soiled or wet—and of the accompanying social stigma of having a full diaper in a public setting, such as preschool or day care.

Try to resist the temptation to remind your toddler about going to the bathroom all the time. (Having said that, we acknowledge that few parents succeed in this restraint.) Resistant children at this age do know what feeling a full bladder or bowel is about; they really do not need additional parental pressure. Pressure—whether by nagging or forcing the child onto the toilet—is a waste of time.

Rewarding the child for progress—whether it is earlier warnings about "having to go" or actually using the potty chair—is essential. Devising a chart of progress, with stars and similar stickers, is always a good place to start. You might create an ultimate goal or reward based upon success as an excellent means of positive reinforcement, to show the child what rewards hard work can bring **[see Negotiating with Your Child].**

It is important to add a note about the child who has physical or psychological reasons for not being dry or clean. Bouts with diarrhea, either because of a gastrointestinal infection or as the side effect of particular medicines such as antibiotics, can cause even the best toilet-trained child to have an accident *[see Diarrhea and Dehydration].*

Other children are chronic stool-holders and become constipated or stretch out their colons to a point where it is difficult to receive the message that their bowels are full. This can result in leakage and fecal soiling *[see Constipation; Encopresis].* Similarly, some children cannot stay dry because of anatomical problems in the urinary tract—although this condition is not as common as toilet training resistance. Still others over the age of six years do not stay dry at night, perhaps because they sleep too soundly *[see Bedwetting].* These, however, are markedly different problems from those of fundamental toilet training and may require additional consultation with your physician.

TONSILS AND ADENOIDS

As recently as the 1960s, it was rare to find a child older than five who still had his tonsils or adenoids. At one point or another, these small pieces of lymphoid tissue have been named as the cause of everything from ear infections to bedwetting to tuberculosis to hyperactivity. First, let's discuss the medical indications for removal of the tonsils and adenoids—which remains the most commonly performed operation of childhood—followed by a discussion of problems that probably will not become better with their removal.

It is important to realize that the procedure to remove the tonsils or adenoids is not a simple one without risks. To begin with, there exists a small but very real

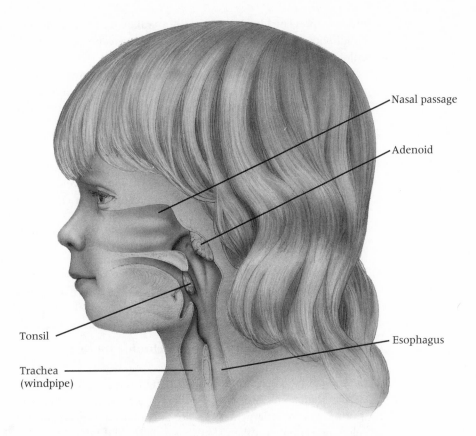

Nasal passage

Adenoid

Tonsil

Esophagus

Trachea
(windpipe)

The tonsils are in the back of the throat on either side. The adenoids are not visible during ordinary examination. They sit in the rear of the throat beneath the palate and near the rear nasal passages.

chance of death whenever you place a patient under general anesthesia (a process that renders someone unconscious to pain and sensation, using specific medications). Secondly, there is also a small risk of bleeding to death from the surgical site about five to seven days after the operation. In short, one out of every fifteen thousand tonsillectomies results in death. Naturally, this is not a great risk—particularly if the procedure is needed. But on the other hand, given that some 95 percent of all the tonsillectomies performed in this country do not meet the criteria for the operation discussed below, it is a risk that is not necessary to take with a healthy child. The procedure is also an expensive one. You should mull over all these factors before subjecting your child to a procedure he may not even need.

Specifically, the procedure involves putting the child to sleep, using a general anesthetic; then the offending tissue is removed with a scooplike instrument in order to prevent bleeding. The child wakes up to one of the greatest ironies of childhood; at last, he has all the ice cream he can eat, but his throat is too sore to enjoy eating it!

Listed below are some of the signs and symptoms physicians look for when recommending a child undergo a tonsillectomy and adenoidectomy. If you notice these problems before your doctor does, you should set up an appointment to discuss them.

Is your child a chronic mouth-breather?

These children rarely use the nose to breathe and have a characteristic open-mouthed appearance. Frequently, these children develop facial bone changes as well that may require dental braces. Don't forget that children with colds or nasal allergies often breathe through their mouths during the acute episode. This is not a problem as long as they return to their normal nose-breathing pattern once the cold or allergic event has ended.

Does your child have a "hot potato" voice?

Some children speak in a tone that suggests they have a hot potato in the mouth. The distortion comes from overly large tonsils blocking the nasal passages and preventing the voice from resonating in a more normal fashion.

Does your child display loud and chronic snoring?

Few people admit to it, but almost everyone snores at one time or another. There can be many causes for snoring, ranging from sleeping with one's mouth open to enlarged adenoids. When the adenoids are especially enlarged, so is the child's snoring. Severe enlargement of the adenoids and tonsils can lead to the child developing a problem called *sleep apnea*. This child typically snores loudly and temporarily stops breathing at irregular intervals during sleep. Because this can cause a variety of serious problems from lack of oxygen to right-sided heart failure, the snoring child needs to be evaluated to see if enlarged adenoids are, indeed, the problem.

Does your child suffer from abscesses of the tonsils or lymph nodes near the tonsils?

If this becomes a chronic or frequent problem, your pediatrician needs to take a good look at your child's tonsils and adenoids to evaluate the need for their removal.

Is your child unable to swallow properly?

Although a child's tonsils can become quite large, especially after an infection, it is the entity of "kissing" tonsils that causes chronic swallowing problems. In short, kissing tonsils are so large, even when not infected, that they touch each other and can block the passage between the mouth and esophagus. Rarely, children develop tumors of the tonsil: in these cases, the diseased tonsil is almost rock-hard and is accompanied by enlarged lymph nodes. This condition requires surgical removal.

Some other problems commonly associated with the tonsils that *do not* require a surgical approach include:

1. **Enlarged tonsils:** as noted above, a child's tonsils can become quite large before they start to shrink in size at eight to twelve years of age. As long as they do not "kiss" (touch each other), this is completely normal and will take care of itself.

2. **Frequent upper respiratory tract infections (URI's):** It was once thought that enlarged tonsils were a factor in the child who developed frequent viral infections of the throat. In fact, because the tonsils produce valuable antibodies that help to fight off infection, their removal probably does more harm than good. Remember, most young children have frequent colds. As long as the URI's get better each time and have no serious complications, there is really nothing to worry about.

3. **Frequent strep throats:** This, too, was a problem thought to be caused by the innocent tonsils and adenoids. Rarely do strep throat infections become less frequent after the tonsillectomy. Although some ear, nose, and throat surgeons continue to recommend tonsillectomy for the child with seven or more culture-positive strep throats a year, recent studies have shown that a daily dose of penicillin over a period of six months is equally effective. Many normal children carry the streptococcus bacteria in their throats but suffer no effects of illness. This carrier state is relatively harmless and, again, does not require surgery.

4. **Frequent ear infections:** This clinical problem is rarely helped by surgical procedures such as a tonsillectomy. Rarely, the child with enlarged adenoids, mouth breathing, and chronic nasal blockage may experience some relief with a tonsillectomy and adenoidectomy.

Other problems that will *not* go away with removal of the tonsils include problems of behavior, allergies, asthma, or seizures.

Unless your child suffers from one of the rare conditions noted on the previous page, let your child hold on to his or her tonsils as long as possible! The tissue may help actually fight off throat and upper respiratory infections and will ultimately shrink to an extremely small size by the age of twelve or so.

TOOTH CARE, TOOTH DECAY, AND TOOTHACHES

Caring for Your Child's Teeth

Brushing and flossing

While all children are different, most dentists recommend that children begin brushing their teeth all by themselves at about the age of six. Indeed, many children simply don't have the coordination or desire to brush their own teeth before then! Consequently, the parent of a child under six needs to help him with this chore—probably as soon as the first teeth erupt (age six months to one year). The best way to do this is either to put a small amount of fluoride-containing toothpaste on a washcloth and, literally, scrub them clean, or—for the braver parent—

to try the same maneuver with a small toothbrush with soft bristles. There do exist special broad toothbrushes with a wide handle specifically made for the purpose of an adult helping a child to brush his teeth; they are available at most drug stores.

It is important to brush after every meal in order to rinse off food debris and plaque, a sticky substance that adheres to teeth. Plaque attracts a type of bacteria that destroys the hard enamel of the teeth, making them susceptible to decay and cavities. Indeed, many dentists encourage brushing within ten or fifteen minutes after every meal to prevent this bacteria from growing and harming the teeth.

Remember to brush each and every tooth. It is difficult, especially when brushing someone else's teeth, to reach in the back of the mouth to clean the back molars. Unfortunately, the molars are most sensitive to plaque formation and decay, so their cleaning is essential to good dental health. Some of the newer, long, angled toothbrushes may help. Another useful "trick" is to have your child rinse out his mouth with water and some fluoride-containing liquid tooth cleaner after meals.

Remember, if you make an enjoyable experience out of brushing teeth, your child is more likely to look forward to this important aspect of hygiene than if it becomes a struggle over power and control. Another popular way to clean teeth after meals, incidentally, is chewing sugar-free gum. This encourages the mouth to produce saliva, which contains an acid that kills tooth-decaying bacteria.

While parents can help with brushing at an early age, flossing is best learned after the age of six, since most children under this age have wide spaces between the actual teeth and debris is removed easily.

Visiting the Dentist

The American Dental Association currently recommends that semi-annual dental examinations for your child begin at the age of three, unless you notice that the teeth are developing in an abnormal manner. Your pediatrician can recommend dentists who specialize in children's dental health issues in your area. New techniques with fluoride treatments and teeth sealing, available through most dentists, can markedly reduce the number of cavities your child experiences, not to mention the dental bills you have to pay!

Fluoride Supplements

Fluoride helps to build tough enamel coatings over the teeth that prevent bacteria from eroding them and causing cavities. Many water supplies in the United States are treated with fluoride for just this purpose (approximately 1 part fluoride per 1 million parts water). Studies have shown that fluoridated water can help decrease the number of cavities by more than 70 percent.

Not all children drink enough water each day to receive the full benefits of this fluoride protection—about one pint a day is suggested. Others may drink non-fluoridated water because their family drinks bottled water, well water, or because their city does not add fluoride to its water supply. For these children, dentists recommend that additional fluoride be added to the child's drinking water as a means of extra protection. Your pediatrician can prescribe fluoride tablets or drops that dissolve in water and are both tasteless and colorless. This is only necessary if the water supply contains less than 0.3 parts per million (mg/L) of fluoride. The recommended dosage of fluoride is typically 0.25 mg per day for a child between the ages of six months and three years; increase the amount to 0.5 mg per day for the child between three and six years; and 1.0 mg per day for the child older than six years. You can find out how much fluoride is (or isn't) added to your water supply by calling your municipal water department. Incidentally, fluoride should never be added to milk, since milk decreases the absorption of fluoride by about 70 percent. Mix the tablets or drops only with water.

Fluoride is entirely safe—as long as one does not overdo it! Remember, more is not necessarily better. So it is not wise to add more fluoride to the drinking water than is prescribed. Indeed, too much fluoride can cause whitish spots on the teeth, a condition called *fluorosis*. These white spots are harmless but may be considered unsightly by some. They are especially common if the child is ingesting more than 1 mg of fluoride per day. Incidentally, it is nearly impossible to develop fluorosis from fluoridated municipal water supplies.

Fluoride-containing toothpastes typically contain about 1 mg of fluoride per squeeze, providing an additional means of coating the teeth with protective fluoride. This can become a problem, however, if the child swallows the toothpaste every day or starts to eat it for other reasons. Use fluoride-containing toothpaste sparingly and discourage your child from swallowing it.

Tooth Decay and Toothaches

For some reason a toothache is one of the most memorable and excruciating types of pain suffered by children and adults alike. The continuous throbbing, swelling, and pain with eating (especially hot or cold foods) can turn even the most agreeable child into a holy terror. For children, the most common cause of toothaches is tooth decay. Baby (temporary) teeth are especially prone to tooth decay, largely because there is little hard tooth enamel surrounding each tooth. Although permanent teeth are far better coated with this protective layer, they too can decay without proper care. To protect your child's teeth, make sure she brushes with a fluoride-containing toothpaste and flosses after each meal and before bedtime.

Tooth decay can cause a cavity, an actual hole in the tooth itself. If it occurs below the gum line, it can cause an infection, known as gingivitis, of the sensitive gum tissue. Without any serious tooth decay or toothache, one can also suffer from a swollen cheek, swollen lymph nodes in the neck, and tenderness or excruciating pain around the affected area.

Do I need to have my child see the dentist for a toothache or cavity of her baby teeth, since they are going to fall out anyway?

Yes. Tooth decay to a baby tooth can easily spread upward to where the permanent tooth is in the jaw and cause damage to both structures. Your child should see the dentist every six months for a checkup and, if necessary, filling of cavities beginning at the age of three. If, on the other hand, the pain is intense or present for longer than one day, or if you can see a tooth that has an obvious blackish-brown hole or cavity, or if there is a swollen, tender, raised area on the gumline, you should call your dentist for an appointment. Children with the above symptoms and the presence of fever (greater than 102°F), a swollen jaw, or both, need to be seen by the dentist that day for treatment.

Is the removal of all sugar from my child's diet necessary to prevent tooth decay?

Not really. Poor sweet, delectable sugar has been alternatively blamed for just about every problem in childhood ranging from cavities to hyperactivity. Some common sense and moderation can make everyone's life more tolerable and healthy.

Specifically, you should encourage a healthy diet for your child for a variety of reasons. Avoiding sticky, sugary foods or candies that adhere to the teeth and may cause decay is a good idea. Further, it is unwise to allow your infant to go to sleep sucking on a bottle containing milk or sweet drinks. This can cause dental cavities and, some physicians believe, may promote ear infections, since swallowing in a lying-down position may cause the liquid in the mouth to reflux into the Eustachian tube of the ear [see Ear Infections]. We realize that a crying child often settles down with a bottle, but if you must give the baby a bottle, choose water and remove the bottle once the baby has fallen asleep.

Frequent snacks and soft drinks are best avoided for nutritional reasons in addition to dental hygiene. But nothing can compare, in terms of keeping teeth clean, to old-fashioned brushing!

Tooth Injuries

Clearly, trauma to the temporary or "baby" teeth, is not nearly as serious as damage to an adult or permanent tooth. Although baby teeth can be loosened or slightly moved about during a trauma, they usually either heal and "firm up" or fall out with an adult tooth to follow. Similarly, teeth—especially baby teeth—can be slightly displaced or pushed inward after a fall or blow to the mouth. Again, these generally will heal and straighten out without any serious intervention. If, however, your child continues to complain of pain over the next few days, develops a dark or blackened tooth, or becomes extremely sensitive to hot or cold foods, a trip to the dentist is necessary.

When a tooth is actually broken or chipped, such as when biting on a particularly hard object, a dentist must be called to assess the damage and, if necessary, treat it. This is particularly important if the tooth is actually broken in half and you can see the reddish pulp or center of the tooth.

Perhaps the most serious injury to teeth is an *avulsion injury* of the permanent tooth, which literally means the adult tooth has been knocked out. While baby teeth are not reimplanted by dentists, there is a considerable success in reimplanting avulsed permanent teeth. Such procedures are most successful when done within twenty minutes of the injury and are rarely successful beyond two hours after the injury.

 My son's front tooth (a permanent one) was just knocked out by a baseball. What should we do?

Before you order a crown, find the knocked-out tooth and carefully wash it with water. Then you must carefully, and gently, try to place the tooth back into its socket exactly as it once was. Place a piece of gauze on the tooth and have your child bite down, again gently, on the tooth in question—or hold it in place with his finger—while you get to the dentist immediately. If you cannot replace the tooth in this matter, place the tooth in a cup filled with your child's saliva or with milk and bring it with you. Remember, however, that in the grand scheme of things, it is only a tooth—not worth driving recklessly for or getting into an accident.

TOYS *[For prevention and safety information, see Allergies; Choking; Injury and accident prevention]*

TRANSITIONAL OBJECTS

Many children reach to soothing and comforting objects, especially in times of stress. These objects may include a favorite stuffed animal, doll, blanket, pacifier, or thumb. Many children begin to choose a transitional object between the ages of ten and twenty-four months. They tend to seek out this object when experiencing a transition, such as a parent leaving for work in the morning. The child will clutch the object for comfort, and she learns to become rather attached to her particular transitional object. Don't try going on a vacation with a toddler and forget to bring her favorite toy or blanket!

The child begins to tire of the transitional object beginning at the age of three years, although subsequent bouts of developmental stress can cause her to look for her transitional object long after having given it up. Gradually, the child will desire it less and less. Transitional objects are entirely harmless. Developmental psychologists suggest that they may be a sign that the child is developing self-reliance techniques. We recommend using a clean, non-allergic toy or doll; however, there will always be those who prefer the traditional security blanket.

TUBERCULOSIS *[See Immunizations]*

UMBILICAL CORD CARE (The belly button)

The umbilical cord provides the essential link for nourishment, oxygen, and blood flow to the unborn baby. Once the infant is delivered, however, the doctor cuts the cord, leaving a small stump. The umbilical stump is "painted" with an antiseptic solution (either "triple-dye" or Betadyne®) that makes the stump appear a dark blue or orange in color. The stump eventually dries up and falls off, leaving behind the navel or "belly button." This usually occurs during the first week or two of life, although in some babies it can take as long as three to four weeks. The remaining area may initially appear somewhat raw and is called "granulation tissue" by doctors. Umbilical cord stumps that remain attached longer than four weeks can be a sign of an immune problem and should be examined by a physician.

Cord Care Tips

• The navel and umbilical cord stump should be kept clean. In most cases this can be accomplished by wiping the area with a piece of sterile cotton and some rubbing alcohol.

• Make sure to use rubbing alcohol at the base of the stump as well as the top of the dried-up cord!

• This cleansing, combined with keeping the cord out of the diaper area, helps the drying process along and facilitates the stump's falling off.

• One way to keep the cord away from a wet diaper is to roll the top of the diaper over, like the cuffs of pants (as shown on the facing page); another is to cut away a small wedge from the front of the diaper with a scissors so that the cord sticks out. Repeat these "cord care tips" each time you change the diaper.

• Occasionally the area may bleed a bit, especially as the cord stump is about to fall off; as long as the bleeding stops with mild pressure, there is nothing to worry about.

• If the tied off area becomes loose and bleeding is excessive or persists more than ten minutes, you need to consult your baby's physician.

• Sometimes a clear discharge may come out of the cord area; again, careful cleansing with cotton-tipped swabs and rubbing alcohol usually takes care of the problem. Those babies with a lot of umbilical cord oozing may need as many as

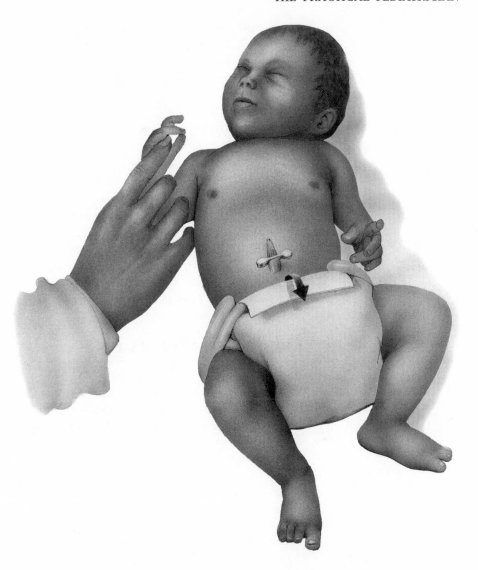

six or more such alcohol cleanings a day. Be patient and careful. Continue to rub the area; since the region has no sensation, you will not hurt the baby. Eventually the cord will fall off.

When to Call the Pediatrician

1. **Infection (omphalitis):** If you observe that the cord area of the skin around it becoming red, inflamed, surrounded by red streaks or oozing pus, or notice a foul odor from the stump, you need to be concerned about an infection. You need to call the doctor immediately.

2. **Granuloma (a benign skin lesion):** If the raw region left after the cord falls off appears especially rough or an extremely reddened button of tissue is forming, you should call your physician, on a non-emergency basis, for an office visit. Granulomas are treated and removed with a chemical called silver nitrate.

 My baby has an umbilical hernia. Does it need to be surgically corrected?

Probably not. Umbilical hernias are caused by a small part of the baby's intestines being pushed through the same hole that the umbilical cord and its associated blood vessels passed through when the baby was still a fetus. When the baby is crying or straining, a bulge appears at the navel. This is not painful, and serious complications are extremely rare. In the overwhelming majority of cases, the ring closes and the umbilical hernia disappears by the time the child is five or six years of age. For those umbilical hernias still present after the age of seven years or those that are especially large (greater than one inch in diameter), a minor surgical procedure can be performed on an outpatient basis that corrects the defect. Special bands, trusses, or other devices constructed to "hold in" the hernia, on the other hand, do nothing but make the baby uncomfortable. They are best relegated to medical museums.

UPPER RESPIRATORY TRACT INFECTIONS AND COLDS

Pediatricians know that winter has arrived not by mere measures of snow but by the steady increase of children with coughs, runny noses, and other symptoms of upper respiratory tract infections ("colds") walking into their clinics. We all get colds, typically in the winter months when many upper respiratory viruses are at their peak incidence, but babies and young children are especially prone to these infections and their potential aftermath. Colds are extremely contagious and easily spread from person to person. Although good hand washing helps to reduce the spread of cold germs—which can live on inanimate surfaces such as toys, tables, and cribs for hours—few toddlers exhibit that skill! Coughing in one's face, kissing a sick person, and sneezing on others are other good ways of spreading the cold around. The viruses that cause the majority of upper respiratory tract infections (URIs) enter the body through the mouth and nose. They infect cells lining the airways and do their all-too-familiar work from there. The major features of URIs (colds) are well known:

- Runny nose
- Watery eyes
- Sore throat
- Fever
- Coughing
- Swollen lymph nodes *[see Lymph Nodes]*
- Hoarseness

Colds can last anywhere from a few days to a week. The cough is frequently the last symptom to go away and may be present as long as two or three weeks after the cold. You need to observe your child carefully to make sure he is getting better. Some children develop a secondary infection of the ears, chest, or eyes— to name a few sites—as a complication of the URI.

Precautions to Take with Infants with Colds

When a small baby, especially under six months of age, develops an upper respiratory tract infection, it can be worrisome for many reasons. One reason for concern is that small infants can become ill rather quickly, and a viral infection can lower the baby's resistance to secondary infections such as lower respiratory infections.

Viruses that attack the lower respiratory tract are an especially dangerous problem for the small infant. The infant's airway and breathing tubes (the trachea, the bronchi, and the bronchioles) are considerably smaller than the older child's and still developing. These tiny airways are more easily affected and narrowed by inflammation (which viruses cause) and excessive mucus production. This can affect the baby's normal breathing patterns. Pediatricians call this inflammation of the airways *bronchiolitis*. A common and potentially serious cause of bronchiolitis is Respiratory Synticial Virus or RSV *[see Respiratory Synticial Virus]*. Listed below are some suggestions on what to look for in a baby's breathing pattern during a cold.

How to assess your baby's breathing patterns

Babies who are getting enough oxygen are "pink" in skin color and around the lips and mouth; babies who are having difficulty getting enough oxygen appear to be "blue" in these areas. (For babies of color, skin tone is less helpful in assessing the baby's oxygenation, but you can use the color of the lips, mouth, and fingernail beds to make this judgment.) Another excellent but indirect sign of a baby's getting enough oxygen is to note whether the baby is eating normally. Babies expend a great deal of energy sucking from a bottle or nursing; if they cannot breathe well, they will not feed as long. Babies who are having some difficulty with breathing do not sleep well, either.

Another helpful sign of a baby's breathing is the pattern of the breathing itself. Does it appear as if your baby is working very hard to breathe? Are her chest, abdomen, or neck muscles moving in exaggerated or labored movements? Is she grunting, or wheezing, or making any sounds during breathing? If these signs exist, or if for any reason you are concerned about your baby's breathing pattern, call your pediatrician immediately.

When to call the pediatrician

If the baby's symptoms appear to worsen; if he is having a difficult time breathing; if his fever is increasing; of if you simply have a question, call your pediatrician. If you have a concern, you probably have good reasons!

Toddlers and Children with Colds

For the majority of babies and young toddlers who contract URI's, runny noses, low-grade fevers, watery eyes, aches and pains, and general feelings of "blah" rule the day without serious complications or problems. Since the majority of these URIs are caused by viruses, we do not have any specific medicines that "knock out" a cold. If, on the other hand, your baby develops a secondary ear infection, for example, you will need your doctor to prescribe an antibiotic for that particular problem. Cold remedies are not helpful and are potentially harmful. They are typically a stew of over-the-counter medications that do little (other than make one especially sleepy or, at times, hyperactive) and cost much. Leave them on the shelf of the drugstore! *[see Medicines, "Over-the-Counter" or "Patent" Medicines].* The primary recommendation we make is for good, old-fashioned supportive care of your child. Make her comfortable. Make sure she is drinking enough fluids to continue urinating and has moist lips and mouth. Use fever reducers if needed, warm fluids and hard candies (only for children older than four years) for throat discomfort, and lots of tender, loving care and parental patience.

URINARY TRACT PROBLEMS

Painful Urination

Pain upon urination (*dysuria*) is always an abnormal symptom and needs to be addressed immediately by a pediatrician. It is, more specifically, the burning, stinging, or pain upon urination; increased urgency (i.e., the child cannot wait to urinate); increased frequency; and urinating smaller-than-usual amounts. Infants who cannot yet speak will consistently cry with each episode of urination.

Causes of painful urination

Infections: One of the most serious cause of problems with urination is that of a bladder or urinary tract infection. Little girls and, less frequently, boys are prone to this type of infection. Unlike in adults, however, the infection can easily pass from the bladder up the ureters to the level of the kidneys, where a far more serious infection (pyelonephritis) can result unless rapid diagnosis and treatment with antibiotics intervene. Moreover, the kidneys of children are far more susceptible to scarring and damage as a result of a urinary tract infection than those of adults. Fortunately, these problems can be avoided with quick response to the child's complaint of painful urination and rapid treatment.

Warning signs of a serious urinary tract infection brewing include a high fever (generally over 101°F), severe belly or back pain, tea- or Coca-Cola-colored urine or urine that appears to have blood in it, and difficulty or pain in urinating. The child, moreover, simply appears to be ill. A recent onset of bedwetting, either during the night or day, previous history of a urinary tract infection, or a suspicion of pinworms is also important to note when speaking with your physician.

Chemical urethritis: More commonly than infections, we see forms of vaginal, penile, and urethral (the opening where urine comes out) irritation. In a little girl, this irritation can "spread" to the sensitive inner lining of the vagina, becoming vaginitis.

A number of things can cause such irritation, including bubble baths, residual soap or shampoo in these sensitive areas, and wearing occlusive "non-breathing" undergarments made of nylon or polyester. Improvements in the child's personal hygiene, more frequent underwear changes, and avoidance of the offending soap product and polyester underwear are usually quite adequate. We generally recommend that the child with non-infectious urethritis take several warm-water baths *without* soap daily for the first week and at least once daily when the condition improves.

There are other precautions that need to be taken to prevent this problem from recurring.

1. Use only cotton underwear.

2. Throw away the bubble baths and shampoos that may be the offending cause; wash your child's genitals with a clean washcloth dipped in warm water only. Remember that the skin lining the opening of the penis or vagina is quite sensitive to chemicals. The rest of the bathing process should take place in water only, with soap used only at the end of the bath. Baths should be limited to ten to fifteen minutes. Rinse the child off before taking her out of the tub.

3. Teach your children, especially little girls, to wipe themselves from front to back. A reverse process of hygiene can introduce bacteria from bowel movements into the urinary tract.

4. Encourage your child to drink plenty of fluids during the day to "flush out" the bladder and prevent infections from taking hold. Three or four eight-ounce glasses of his favorite beverage is a reasonable goal. A good way to gauge this progress is to ascertain what color the child's urine is. A child with golden or dark urine is dry and at greater risks for problems; the child with clear urine is well hydrated. As a corollary to this point, ask your child if she needs to go to the bathroom during the day. She should be encouraged to do so, as opposed to "holding it" for long periods of time. Schoolteachers, too, should be alerted if a problem exists, so that the necessary permission to go to the bathroom during school is granted freely. Again, frequent urination, or at least urinating when nature first calls, aids in "flushing out" the bladder. The longer urine is retained, the better "soil" it makes for a urinary tract infection.

My daughter's urine smells really bad. Is this a sign of a urine infection?

Probably not. Urine is not a terribly delightful fluid to smell in the first place. For most people, including children, stronger-smelling urine may be a sign of being dehydrated. Another cause of really bad-smelling urine can be specific foods, like asparagus, or drugs, such as penicillin. If, on the other hand, your child's urine has consistently been strong in odor since birth, you should consult your physician. Rare metabolic disorders of infancy can be heralded by foul-smelling or funny-smelling urine. Finally, if the child's urine has suddenly become distressing to your nose and remains so for at least twenty-four hours despite attempts at rehydration, you should also consult your physician.

Blood in the Urine

Many things can make one's urine *appear* red, pink, or otherwise "blood" color, including eating beets and drinking sodas or juices artificially colored with red dye. We shall discuss in this section the presence of actual blood in the urine.

When noticing urine that is frankly bloody—red, Coca-cola-colored, tea-colored, or pink-tinged—it is a good idea to discuss the finding with a pediatrician. Bringing the soiled diaper, if one exists, or a specimen of the child's urine is a good idea. You also need to take a good look at the child and note if he appears ill; has swollen eyelids or other swollen facial features; has recently experienced a traumatic injury or has pain in his side (flank) or back; complains of headache; or is having difficulty in actually urinating. All of these symptoms suggest a more serious cause for the blood and require investigation.

Video Games and VCRs

As television was technology's gift to our childhood, it's gifts to today's child are the video game and videocassette recorder (VCR). We were recently watching a network rerun of a classic movie with a six-year-old boy named Jason who became terribly frustrated when he could not "fast-forward" the commercials! As with television, *you* need to be in control of these devices. Moderation of your child's activities including watching television and videos or playing video games, rather than their strict prohibition, is the key.

Video Games

Since their introduction in the early 1970s (does anyone remember PONG?), video games have become an integral part of the American child's leisure time. There are cartridge-style tapes that can be plugged into one's television set, portable game devices one can carry along to school, and video game arcades at the mall—every means of computerized play that toy manufacturers can dream up! The fact is, if your child is anywhere from four (and perhaps even younger) to sixteen, he or she has probably spent considerable time playing video games.

There have been several studies which suggest that video games are somewhat preferable to passive television watching in that they are more mentally interactive. For example, the child playing a video game needs to be able to concentrate, pay attention to the details or intricacies of the game, exercise learning strategies such as sequencing events, and use his memory. Video games probably enhance a child's hand-eye coordination and his awareness of perception and spatial relationships.

So what are the negative points? Well, the child can spend an excessive amount of time playing video games (more than two hours a day), to the exclusion of his homework. Video games are often far more intriguing than a spell of arithmetic. Moreover, video games are typically a solitary activity, which can hamper a child's development of social skills.

Some video games are extremely violent or graphic. As with violent television shows, there is ample evidence that violent games promote violent or aggressive behaviors in children. You need to preview the video games you purchase or rent for your child, just as you would a movie or television show. The same goes for the tapes or games your child may borrow from a friend. Don't let "strangers" into your house!

Like other forms of entertainment, video games need to be controlled by the parent, rather than giving the child carte blanche. A general rule of thumb is to allow a total of two hours per day total spent playing video games, computer games, and watching television and videotapes. This is not an inviolable rule. For example, today there are many single-parent families and households where both the mother and father work, such that the family's "quality time" is more limited than that of other families. In such a case, you should make sure that the "entertainment" or "video" time is, proportionally, a small part of the total time the family gets to spend together. Video games and similar distractions particularly need to be restricted on school nights and until after homework is completed. As with television, do not allow your child to delay going to bed in order to continue playing video games.

Home computers, incidentally, are capable of playing many video-type games. An added benefit to computer-based games, however, is that they encourage the child to become computer-literate. Some computer games created by educational companies, for example, are especially good at combining learning with fun. Also widely available are multi-media CD-ROM editions. Ask your child's teacher for possible recommendations. There are, however, negative features to computers. Some computer games are too explicit or graphic for children, as are specific bulletin boards on the Internet. As with videos and television, be aware of what your child is viewing at the terminal *[see Computers and the Internet]*.

Video Movies and VCRs

Since most Americans frequent their local video store in search of entertainment on a daily or weekly basis, we will remind you that many movies today are inappropriate for children's viewing. A great many graphic and violent films are released and viewed each year. Naturally, many of these viewers are bound to be children. Unfortunately, a child's ability to discern reality from fantasy (especially for the child under six) is poor. Violent films frequently inspire nightmares, difficulty in going to bed, daytime worries, and fearful responses among this younger audience. Worse still has been the chronic desensitization to violence and suffering that these films engender among us all, but especially children *[see Television]*. Each year we read in the newspaper about a child who tried to imitate a particularly violent television or movie character—often with disastrous results.

As a parent, you need to follow some simple rules to help prevent your child's overexposure to violence and other objectionable material.

1. R-rated movies should *not* be viewed by children under the age of thirteen. Not all R-rated movies are the same; some contain profanity, some have nudity, portrayals of sexual and violent acts—some have all four. You need to preview

the films and decide, based upon your own moral code, what is or is not objectionable. Most people agree that graphic violence or sexual violence are never suitable topics for young children and teens.

2. Pick the movies your child is going to watch. Just because your neighbor's kid loved the slasher-horror film playing down the block doesn't mean your son must watch it, too. Read movie reviews and watch the movies yourself, with your child. The same goes for the vast sources of movie entertainment available on cable and network television. Even the news can be alarming and worrisome to some children.

3. If your child is troubled about something he may have seen on television, open up a discussion to explore his fears. You need to explain the differences between TV and real life and offer reassurance and love to your child. Remember, these "fake" events really do scare and upset children.

4. Make specific rules about what your child can watch, play, and so on, outside the home. Scary movies are a particular problem around Halloween and at sleepover parties. It is becoming increasingly difficult to protect your child from the world once he leaves your home, but every parent tries.

VITAMIN SUPPLEMENTS *[See Bottle feeding your baby; Breastfeeding your baby]*

VOMITING

At some point in your infant's life, the infant will vomit. Vomiting is defined as the involuntary, forceful expulsion of the stomach's contents through the mouth. And as any experienced parent can tell you, forceful is the operative word! Vomiting is different from the more common "spitting-up" *[see Spitting Up]*. Vomiting generally involves all of the stomach's contents. Spitting up is the expulsion of small amounts of fluid or food without any evidence of forceful projection. Spitting up resolves as the infant learns to swallow and her gastrointestinal tract matures. Vomiting, on the other hand, can occur at any time during life and can be caused by a large number of different medical problems.

Perhaps the most common cause of vomiting during infancy and childhood is infectious viruses that attack and irritate the lining of the stomach and gastrointestinal tract. Sometimes these same viruses also produce diarrhea *[see Diarrhea and Dehydration]*. Vomiting caused by a viral infection typically resolves within twelve to twenty-four hours. If, after this period, your child is still vomiting without any resolution, consult your pediatrician.

Our Tried, Tested, and True Method of Feeding a Vomiting Child

It seems somewhat obvious that you need to feed even a vomiting child, yet many parents are afraid to do this lest they cause more vomiting. But food is far less important than fluids. Your child will not starve if she does not get in a lot of calories, but she will suffer serious consequences if she becomes dehydrated. Fluids, not calories, are the key! When faced with a vomiting child, you need to strengthen your resolve, put on some old clothing, and remember to be patient, patient, patient!

We begin by changing the diet from its regular constituents to "clear fluids"—liquids that appear clear against the light and contain no formed elements (e.g., food). For example, oral electrolyte solutions, ginger ale, and plain broth are considered clear fluids; chicken rice soup or milk are not. Soda pops such as ginger ale are helpful since they taste good, but you need to let them sit for awhile so the bubbles dissolve. Air bubbles expand the stomach and may increase the chance of vomiting. Plain water should be avoided at first to prevent causing electrolyte abnormalities in the blood.

Offer your child the clear fluid in small amounts until she has gone eight hours without vomiting. For children between one and six years, you can give the clear liquids at the rate of one tablespoon several times per hour when the child is awake. For school-aged children, try one ounce of clear liquid every ten minutes. If your child succeeds with this regimen by not vomiting for over four hours, you can try doubling the amount of fluid given every ten minutes. If your child *did* vomit during this refeeding session, clean her up and reassure her, then let her sensitive stomach rest for about an hour. Start again, but with smaller amounts of fluid. This slow, one-swallow-at-a-time approach rarely fails.

After your child has gone for more than eight hours without vomiting, she can advance to a plain diet such as crackers, boiled rice, mashed potatoes, gelatin, and bland soups. The following day you can begin to introduce her regular diet. Remember, the loss of a few hundred calories will not hurt your child as long as she gets the necessary fluids.

The secret to success in this endeavor is to remain calm, patient, reasonably clean, and to refeed—slowly, slowly, slowly!

Important Points to Remember

1. For the vomiting child—give clear fluids only for the first eight hours (no solids or milk).

2. Give bland foods after eight hours without vomiting.

3. For infants under the age of one, offer oral electrolyte rehydration solutions as the clear fluid of choice. (These products include Pedialyte®.)

4. For breastfed babies, don't stop the breastfeeding; simply give less breast milk to the baby. You may have to use a bottle if the baby does not wish to nurse. (Breastfed babies rarely develop the vomiting and diarrhea associated with gastrointestinal viruses.)

5. If a virus caused your child's vomiting, there is no medicine that will cure it. Only time and many, many spoonfuls of clear liquids make it "go away."

6. Call or see your physician if:

- Your child is less than one month of age and has vomited
- Your child is vomiting and has not urinated for more than six hours
- Your child has been vomiting and is no longer crying with tears
- The vomit is especially projectile (i.e., it literally shoots across the room)
- The vomit appears greenish in color (bile-tinged)
- The vomit has blood (or a substance that looks like used coffee-grounds) in it that is not associated with a recent nosebleed
- Your child is vomiting for more than twelve hours without any respite or improvement
- Your child is complaining of abdominal pain
- Your child is unresponsive or difficult to awaken

Walkers

Walkers allow a young infant to ambulate before he can actually walk. They are, however, best left at the department store, because they are truly accidents waiting to happen. Simply put, the infant who has not yet learned to walk lacks both the judgment and the coordination to safely move about in a wheeled object. Indeed, it's almost like giving an eight-year-old the keys to your car—he may be able to turn the wheel and possibly even reach the pedals, but he clearly will not know what he is doing!

Each year, more than one million walkers are sold in the United States. Unfortunately, each year there are over twenty-five thousand walker-related injuries. Of those infants who use a walker, 30 to 40 percent will have some type of accident! Most often these accidents are relatively minor ones, such as tipping the walker over or entrapping the infant's fingers or extremities, but more serious injuries, such as falling down the stairs, running into the sharp edges of furniture, or pulling objects down onto themselves occur with frequency. Stairwell walker injuries are especially serious and can result in closed head injuries, broken bones, dental trauma, cuts, bruises, and other wounds.

Finally, there is absolutely no evidence that using a walker will promote "real" walking. Indeed, one of the more common, although fortunately benign, complaints that pediatricians see in those infants who use walkers is one in which the infant holds his feet "pointed out," like a ballerina. This "pointing out," in the absense of any real muscle or bone problem, is caused by the baby spending a lot of time in his walker and manipulating the device by standing on his "tip-toes" in order to push off and move across the floor. This condition is almost always "cured" by simply returning the walker to its box—or a nearby closet—and allowing the infant to resume crawling or cruising until he begins walking on his own.

Children have been learning to walk for far many more years than there have been walker devices. Your child can easily learn this task—sans walker—as well!

[See Injury and Accident Prevention]

WALKING INJURIES

After automobile injuries, pedestrian-related accidents make up the next largest category of motor-related deaths. Unfortunately, the scenario of a child being hit by a car is an all too common one in the United States. Not surprisingly, these accidents occur most frequently at busy intersections and in urban areas, but all children need to be taught a healthy respect for moving vehicles and the importance of safety.

Whenever possible, you should keep your children physically separate—especially small ones—from moving traffic. This includes supervising their play so they do not stray into the street, putting up fences around your yard, and carefully teaching them the importance of "holding hands" and looking both ways before crossing the street. No young child should ever be allowed to cross or play in the street alone. In general, it is wise for *all* children to play only in yards and parks, not in the street. Clearly, different children become more responsible in this regard at different ages, but the child under the age of eight needs to be watched with extra care.

One good way to promote street safety is to have your child wear reflective outerwear when walking to school. This is especially important in those parts of the country that have little sunlight during the early morning and the late afternoon hours of winter.

Encourage your neighborhood and city government to install clean, safe, and effective sidewalks to provide a safer route for your children than walking in the street.

When driving near a school bus, be sure to follow the safety laws regarding stopping and speed control; similarly, when driving near areas where children are at play (e.g., schools, playgrounds, and so on), slow down!

Teach your child to always look "to the left—to the right—and to the left again" when crossing a street. Help him plan a safe and direct route to and from school, if he walks, and insist that he crosses the street with the crossing guard's instructions.

WARTS

An old dermatologist once told us that the Bible was really referring to warts when it intoned, "Be fruitful and multiply." Warts are round projections of almost gnarled, roughened skin, which can appear almost anywhere on the body, although they are most commonly found on the hands and feet. They are typically the color of the skin but may appear pink. They do not hurt when pressed with one's finger, although you should *not* touch warts (see below). Warts on the sole of one's foot (plantar warts) can be tender to the touch.

Warts can be easily removed with relatively little pain by using liquid nitrogen. This is an extremely cold substance that actually freezes the wart off as it numbs the healthy skin with its sub-zero temperature. Most physicians have this medicine at their offices or can advise you where to obtain this treatment. Home remedies and acid-containing over-the-counter medications exist, but as a rule we rarely recommend them. These chemical agents eat away at the wart but are also abrasive to healthy skin. Shaving the wart away with a razorblade is also another common but rather dangerous approach that we do *not* recommend.

What causes warts?

A variety of viruses are responsible for these annoyances. Although most warts are not terribly contagious from person to person, you can transmit a wart from one part of your body to another. The most common way is the child who picks at the wart with his fingers or bites at the wart. This can cause the warts to spread to other parts of the child's hand, body, and face. Therefore, you need to explain to your child the importance of not picking at or biting the warts. If he has problems with self-control, try wrapping the offending wart with a bandage.

What are genital warts?

These warts, also caused by a virus, tend to be sexually transmitted and are a common problem among sexually active teenagers and adults. Rarely, a child will get a garden variety, non-sexually transmitted wart in the genital area. More commonly, alas, in our modern times, genital warts can be a sign of sexual abuse. If you notice warts in your child's genital area, you should have them examined by a pediatrician.

WELL-CHILD PEDIATRIC EXAMINATION SCHEDULE: WHAT TO EXPECT WHEN YOU VISIT THE PEDIATRICIAN

A Visit-by-Visit Guide to Your Child's Health Supervision Examinations

Your pediatrician follows a specific schedule of well-child health supervision visits and immunizations that has been developed by the American Academy of Pediatrics. We have adapted this schedule so that you, as a parent, can know what to expect at each visit in terms of

- Questions you may have
- Questions your pediatrician may ask

- Physical examinations
- Developmental assessment of your child
- Immunizations
- Other pertinent topics for discussion

Using the well-child charts as your child's personal medical record

You should feel free to use the following well-child charts as checklists to organize your visits to the pediatrician and to record important information. In order to provide you with a complete checklist for these visits, we begin with a chart that outlines what to expect during your first (prenatal) conference with your pediatrician. The charts that follow outline what to expect during each well-child health supervision visit from your child's first (newborn) visit through age eight. We have designed this section so that you can record the date of each immunization, the examination she underwent, and the topics you discussed with your pediatrician. If any major health problem comes up, regardless of what it was, you should make a note on your child's "personal medical chart."

We have also provided growth charts so that you can record the head circumference of your baby from birth to three years of age, and weight and height for your child from birth to three years old and again from two to eight years of age. These growth parameters are based on the head circumferences, weights, and heights of tens of thousands of children. They are rough guidelines—no more, no less—for normal weights, heights, and head circumferences in most babies and children. Your pediatrician will measure these growth parameters at each examination.

Use the growth charts to record information on your child's head circumference, weight, and height and see how your child is growing with respect to other children. Each of the growth charts contains five dark curves. These curves show the normal range, from the fifth percentile to the ninety-fifth percentile. The darkest (center) curve shows the fiftieth percentile. Percentiles are a fancy way of saying the following: If, for example, your child is in the fiftieth percentile for his weight and height, it means that if you took 100 normal, healthy children, your child would be heavier and taller than 50 percent of this group. If you are a pessimist, we suppose he would be lighter and smaller than 50 percent of them!

At each visit, ask your pediatrician for information on your child's weight, height, and (during infancy) head circumference. Then record them on the appropriate growth chart. To record this information accurately, simply find the intersection between the child's age and the growth parameter you are recording and mark the chart accordingly.

WELL-CHILD HEALTH SUPERVISION VISITS: Prenatal Conference

Common Questions Parents Have	Questions your Pediatrician May Ask	What Are the Pediatrician's Practice/Arrangements?	Topics for Discussion
Should we breast feed or bottle feed?	How has the pregnancy gone thus far?	How you may reach the doctor	Prenatal classes
If we bottle feed, which formula is best?	Who is your obstetrician? His/her hospital affiliation?	What are the on-call arrangements; in emergencies?	Baby care information
Can your practice offer advice and support for breast feeding mothers?	Information regarding prenatal/child birth courses	Are there specific telephone hours?	Information on the preparations for the nursery, baby furniture, etc.
Circumcision issues	Information regarding your experiences as a child and how you plan to rear your baby	Schedule of visits	Discussion of the changes in family relationships with the addition of a baby
	What is your previous experience as a parent or with child care?	Office hours	Smoking
	Does the mother work or intend to return to work?	Fees and insurance arrangements	Circumcision issues
	Any special concerns the parents may have?	Hospital affiliation?	Feeding
			Help for the new mother at home; how to set up "support systems"
			Smoke detectors and fire extinguishers need to be installed

WELL-CHILD HEALTH SUPERVISION VISITS: Newborn Visit

Physical Examination	Immunizations	Anticipatory Guidance your Pediatrician Will Offer
The pediatrician measures the baby's head circumference, length, and birthweight to assess normal growth	HBV #1	Method of feeding (bottle or breast)
The baby's consolability and self-quieting abilities are assessed		Addition of Vitamin D for breastfed babies
Physical examination of the skin, eyes, heart, chest, pulses, hips, feet, genitals, rectum, and abdomen are performed		Umbilical cord and circumcision care issues
		Possible vaginal discharge in a baby girl
		Enlargement or engorgement of the baby's breasts
		Jaundice (Hyperbilirubinemia)
		Crying and jittery movements
		Sleeping
		Hiccups; sneezing
		Spitting up
		The fontanelle (the soft, bulging spot at the top of the baby's head)
		Stools: what they look like; differences between babies
		Bathing and skin care
		Pacifiers
		Colic
		Individual temperments of infants
		Importance of close interactions
		Sibling issues
		Potential maternal depression
		When to call the doctor (e.g., fever, vomiting, diarrhea)
		Accident prevention advice
		The change in relationships that occur with a new baby
		The mother and father's need for rest and help

The pediatrician will examine your child, inquire on how the delivery went, and ask about the preparations at home for the baby's arrival. This visit typically takes place in the hospital.

WELL-CHILD HEALTH SUPERVISION VISITS: 2–4 week Visit

Questions your Pediatrician May Ask	Developmental Milestones	Physical Examination	Topics for Discussion
Do you have any concerns?	Baby can raise head when lying prone	The pediatrician will measure the baby's head circumference, weight, and length to assess normal growth and development	*Nutrition Issues:* Breast- or formula-fed; fluoride and Vitamin D supplements, if indicated; when are solids introduced?
Is the family adjusting well to the baby? Any stresses?	Baby will fix his or her eyes on a face or object and follow it as it moves	Physician examines the baby's umbilicus (belly button), circumcision, eyes, hips, heart, chest, hearing, abdomen, rectum, skin	*Accident Prevention Issues:* Car seats; do not leave infant unattended on a surface from which he may fall
How are you enjoying the baby?			Sleep issues
What is his or her personality like?			Stools; urine
Have you or your husband had adequate rest or respite since the baby's birth?			Crying; colic
Are you planning to return to work?			Importance of holding, cuddling, talking to, and enjoying your baby
Are there any signs or symptoms of the mother being over stressed, fatigued or depressed? Signs of stress, etc. in the father?			Advice for new parents, baby-sitter issues, time for themselves, etc.

WELL-CHILD HEALTH SUPERVISION VISITS: 2-month Visit

Questions your Pediatrician May Ask	Developmental Milestones	Physical Examination	Immunizations	Topics for Discussion
How is everything going at home? Any new stresses, concerns or questions?	The baby will recognize or acknowledge a face in his or her direct line of vision	The pediatrician measures the infant's weight, length, and head circumference	DPT #1 HBV #2 HIB #1	*Nutrition Issues:* Breastfeeding issues Need for supplementing Vitamin D (for breastfed babies) or iron (for preterm babies) Introduction of solid foods at 4–6 months
What is your baby doing in terms of development, awareness, hearing what you say, interacting, etc.?	When given a rattle, the baby grasps it with his or her hand	The pediatrician examines the baby's eyes, ears, mouth, chest, heart, hips, legs, genitals, rectum and skin	TOPV #1	*Accident Prevention Issues:* Avoid leaving the baby unattended on beds or tables, care with hot liquids, cigarettes, advice against walkers
Feeding issues	The baby exhibits a social smile			Sleep issues
Are you working?	When you coo to the baby, he or she responds with a vocalization			Issues that might come up if both parents work outside of the home
				Importance of playing with, talking to, holding and loving your baby

WELL-CHILD HEALTH SUPERVISION VISITS: 4-month Visit

Questions your Pediatrician May Ask	Developmental Milestones	Physical Examination	Immunizations	Topics for Discussion
How are things going at home? Any new stresses, concerns, or questions?	The baby holds his head erect and will raise his body on his hands in the prone (or lying-down on his stomach) position	The pediatrician measures the baby's head circumference, weight, and length to assess the infant's growth. The weight-to-length ratio is especially helpful in making sure the baby is getting adequate calories to grow properly	Mention any previous reactions to your doctor	Continue Vitamin D supplements if the baby is breastfed
If both parents are working outside of the home, what substitute care has been arranged?	The baby displays steady head control when held in the upright position	The pediatrician examines the baby's eyes, ears, and mouth, neck, chest, heart, genitals, rectum, legs, and skin	DTP #2 OPV #2 Hib #2	Fluoride supplementation
Does the baby hear well?	The baby displays no head lag when being pulled up to the sitting position			Iron supplementation
	The baby can roll from his stomach to his back; displays symmetrical posture			Solid-foods should be introduced, one at a time, between 4–6 months
	The baby will play with his hands (e.g., pat-a-cake); hold a rattle; bring hands to his midline			Sleep issues
	The baby will be entertained by a mobile; he may wave his arms			Concerns about thumb sucking
	Baby will follow a visual object 180 degrees			The importance of talking to the baby and responding to his vocalizations
	The baby smiles, coos, squeals, laughs, and initiates social contact at this age			Accident prevention (e.g., car safety, protection against falls, keeping dangerous chemicals, powders, and small objects out of reach, tub safety, baby-sitters)

WELL-CHILD HEALTH SUPERVISION VISITS: 6-month Visit

Questions your Pediatrician May Ask	Developmental Milestones	Physical Examination	Immunizations	Topics for Discussion
How are things going for you and your family?	The baby can easily roll over on her own	The pediatrician measures the baby's weight, length, and head circumference to assess baby's growth and development	Any reactions to the last "shots"?	*Nutrition Issues:* Milk or juice bottles should not be substituted for pacifiers Use iron-fortified cereals, include plenty of fruits and vegetables in the diet Fluoride supplements; adding solid foods to the diet
Are there any new questions or concerns about the baby?	The baby will sit, erect, with support when placed in the sitting position	Full physical examination as described for previous visits including check-ups for normal hearing and vision	DTP #3 OPV #3 HIB #3 HBV #3	*Accident Prevention Issues:* Make a home checklist for hazards Information on car seats and safety Protection against hot liquids, plates, pots Protection from falls; avoiding walkers, the importance of staircase-gates Water safety (e.g., tubpools, never leave an infant near water unattended) Electrical outlets, plugs, cords
Have any new stresses developed?	She can bear weight when placed in the standing position	Assessment of parent–infant interaction		Sleep issues; resistance
What's a typical day for your baby and your family?	She can transfer objects from hand to hand (by the end of the 6th month)			Stranger-anxiety issues
What has the baby learned to do since our last visit?	She will use her hand in a "rake" pattern to get hold of objects			Thumb sucking; masturbating
	She laughs and babbles			Teething
	Baby may turn to sounds; she may imitate sounds			Shoes
	The baby may begin to show early "stranger-anxiety"			Day care
				Importance of playing games with your baby

WELL-CHILD HEALTH SUPERVISION VISITS: 9-month Visit

Questions your Pediatrician May Ask	Developmental Milestones
How are things going for you and your family?	The baby sits well on his own
Any new questions or concerns or stresses?	The baby crawls, creeps, or hitches on his bottom
What new things has the baby learned to do since our last visit?	He begins to pull his body to a stand and cruises (walking from one object of furniture to another while continually hanging on for support)
What's a typical day for your baby and your family?	He can poke, use his fingers to form a pincer grasp with his thumb, and use his thumb with his hand in a raking motion
	The baby bangs two toys together and exhibits unilateral (one-armed) reach
	He begins to finger-feed himself
	Baby babbles with polysyllable sounds
	He may speak one or two meaningful vocalizations
	He will respond to his name; can articulate "No"; will point to where Mama or Dada is
	Understands a few words such as "No"
	Will use "dada" or "mama" nonspecifically
	Likes to play games such as "peek-a-boo" and "pat-a-cake"
	Displays stranger-wariness or anxiety

Physical Examination	Immunizations	Topics for Discussion
Weight, height, and head circumference	None	*Nutrition Issues:* Table food; self-feeding Using toast to encourage self-feeding Begin to wean from the bottle Encourage the use of a cup Anticipate the baby to decrease dietary intake over the next few months Supplement with Vitamin D, if breastfed; fluoride supplements
Physical examination as described in earlier visits, including hearing and vision checks		*Accident Prevention Issues:* Guard the stairs and windows with special barriers Discuss poison control issues Do not feed the baby small objects such as peanuts, raisins, popcorn, etc Auto and auto seat safety information Water safety issues
Assessment of parent–infant interaction		Sleep issues; (e.g., night and early morning awakening)
		Social games
		Shoes
		Day care
		Encourage the baby's vocalization, imitation, and communication
		Discuss autonomy, the setting of limits and discipline issues
		Importance of playing games with your baby

WELL-CHILD HEALTH SUPERVISION VISITS: 12-month Visit

Questions your Pediatrician May Ask	Developmental Milestones	Physical Examination	Immunizations	Topics for Discussion
How are things going for you and your family?	The baby can pull herself to a stand and cruises	Weight, height, and head circumference	Tb test	*Nutrition Issues:* Plan to wean the baby from the bottle The baby may decrease her food intake Fluoride
Are there any new concerns or stresses?	She may walk with support and take a few steps on her own	Physical examination as described		*Accident Prevention Issues:* Know the number of your regional poison control center and have syrup of ipecac in the home Make the kitchen child-safe Water should not be heated above 120° F Poison-proof your home Protect stairs with gates Auto and car seat safety Water safety
Are both parents working outside of the home? Who takes care of the baby while you work?	She exhibits a precise pincer grasp, with the thumb and forefingers, when picking up small objects	Assessment of parent–infant interaction		Sleep problems
What new things is the baby doing since our last visit?	She will point			Encourage the baby to develop speech by talking to her
	The baby speaks 1–3 words or meaningful sounds (e.g., "wa-wa" for water)			Pick up, play with, hold, cuddle, and enjoy your baby
	The baby uses "mama" and "dada" correctly (i.e., only daddy is called "dada" as opposed to everyone a few months ago)			Begin reading stories and playing games
				Discuss discipline issues, the setting of limits and the baby's need for autonomy
				Practice praising your baby —particularly when she exhibits desired behaviors

WELL-CHILD HEALTH SUPERVISION VISITS: 15-month Visit

Questions your Pediatrician May Ask	Developmental Milestones	Physical Examination	Immunizations	Topics for Discussion
How are things going for you?	Walks alone	Weight, length, head circumference, weight-for-length	MMR HIB #4 OPV #4, DPT #4	*Nutrition Issues:* Phase out bottle by 18 months No bottles in bed Avoid giving baby juice or carbohydrate drinks in bottle as a preventive for tooth decay Fluoride supplements, if necessary
How is your family?	Crawls up stairs	Physical exam as described above		Toilet (bladder and bowel) training
Any questions, concerns or stresses?	Self-feeds with finger			Discipline issues
Any concerns about your child's developing independence?	Begins to develop fine-motor coordination (e.g., can pick up a small object such as a raisin and put it in a cup)			Discontinuing the pacifier
	3–6 word vocabulary; still uses jargon or gestures			Play, read, talk with, and sing to your baby Show affection
	Can point to 1 or 2 body parts when asked			Day care issues
	Searches for and frequently finds "hidden" objects			*Accident Prevention Issues:* Toddler car seats Falls Child- and poison-proofing the home Burns, scalds, electrical injuries Gates and stairs Water safety
	Gives and takes a toy			
	Understands simple commands			
	Removes clothes			

WELL-CHILD HEALTH SUPERVISION VISITS: 18-month Visit

Questions your Pediatrician May Ask	Developmental Milestones	Physical Examination	Immunizations	Topics for Discussion
How are you? Your family?	Child can walk up stairs while holding someone's hand	Weight, length, head circumference. Observe child walking	None	Nutrition
Any stresses?	Child sits in chair	Physical exam		Accident prevention
How does your family interact?	Child can kick and throw a ball			Sleep issues
	Child speaks 4–10 words and may express two (and often more) wants			Toilet training
	Child can feed him/herself and can use spoon			Play activities
	Child imitates crayon or pencil stroke			Discipline
	Child will pucker lips and kiss when asked by an appropriate person			Thumbsucking
				Masturbation
				Favorite toy

WELL-CHILD HEALTH SUPERVISION VISITS: 24-month Visit

Questions your Pediatrician May Ask	Developmental Milestones	Physical Examination	Immunizations	Topics for Discussion
How are you? Your family?	Child climbs up and down steps holding rail or hand	Length, head circumference, weight	None	Accident prevention
Any stresses?	Child jumps and runs	Hearing check		Play issues
How does your family interact?	The child's vocabulary is about 50 or more words; uses 2-word phrases; pronouns such as "I, me, you"; refers to self by name	Full physical		Television issues
	Speech should be intelligible to parents			Story books
	Child is able to understand and respond to a 2-part verbal command (e.g., "Go inside and sit down!")			Sleep issues; when to move to a regular bed
	Child will draw or imitate horizontal and circular strokes			Nutrition Snacks; struggles over eating
	Child frequently asks the charming question "What's that?"			Toilet training
				Positive reinforcement
				Brushing their teeth

WELL-CHILD HEALTH SUPERVISION VISITS: 3-year Visit

Questions your Pediatrician May Ask	Developmental Milestones	Physical Examination	Immunizations	Topics for Discussion
How are you? Your family?	Child can jump in place; kick a ball; stand on one foot for a brief period	Height, weight, head circumference, weight-for-height, blood pressure, vision test, speech test, hearing test, full physical	None	Nutrition; balanced diet; vitamins
Any stresses?	Child can pedal a tricycle			Accident prevention (traffic safety, animals)
How does your family interact?	Child alternates feet while ascending stairs			Play activities
	The 3-year old should speak in understandable phrases and sentences; if no sentences or intelligible speech to strangers has been exhibited, the child needs to be evaluated			Discipline
	Child is able to understand and respond to a 2-part verbal command (e.g., "Go inside and sit down!")			Dental appointments
	Child can give full name, knows age, gender, numbers to three (or more)			Toilet training
	Child will copy a circle and cross			Nursery school; day care; baby-sitting
	Recognition of colors			
	Child enjoys "pretend" play			

WELL-CHILD HEALTH SUPERVISION VISITS: 4-year Visit

Questions your Pediatrician May Ask	Developmental Milestones	Physical Examination	Immunizations	Topics for Discussion
How are you? Your family?	Child will alternate feet while descending stairs; can jump forward; hop; can climb a ladder	Full physical exam		Accident prevention
Any stresses?	Child rides tricycle	Hearing check		Behavioral issues
How does your family interact?	Child has the "fine motor" coordination to cut and paste	Vision check		Toilet training
	Child counts to 10	Measure weight and height		Parenting issues
	Child uses "I" correctly			Nursery school; day care; baby-sitting
	Child names and matches three or more colors			
	Child dresses and undresses with supervision			
	Child engages in make believe play			
	Child will copy a cross, circle, and possibly a square			
	Child can draw a person with face and arms or face and legs			

WELL-CHILD HEALTH SUPERVISION VISITS: 5-year Visit

Questions your Pediatrician May Ask	Developmental Milestones	Physical Examination	Immunizations	Topics for Discussion
How are you? Your family?	Child skips, walks on tip toes, can "broad jump"	Full physical exam	DPT/OPV MMR booster	Accident prevention
Any stresses?	Child knows age; may name five colors; identifies coins	Vision		Learning home address and telephone number; "911"
How does the family interact?	Child can define at least one word such as ball, shoe, chair, table, dog	Speech		Saying "No" to strangers
School?	Dresses and undresses without supervision	Hearing		School readiness
TV issues?	Child can copy triangle and can draw a person with a head, body, legs, and arms	Blood pressure		Dental care
Friends?	Child exhibits sexual curiosity			Discipline
	Child dresses and undresses with supervision			Behavior
	Child engages in make-believe play			
	Child will copy a cross, circle, and possibly a square			
	Child can draw a person with face and arms or face and legs			

WELL-CHILD HEALTH SUPERVISION VISITS: 6-year Visit

Questions your Pediatrician May Ask	Developmental Milestones	Physical Examination	Immunizations	Topics for Discussion
How are you? How is your family?	Child can ride a bicycle	Weight, height, weight-for-stature		*Acquiring Good Health Habits:* Balanced diet Junk food Weight issues Cholesterol and fat Regular physical activity
Are there any specific concerns?	Child can tie shoelaces	Vision		*Accident Prevention:* Bicycle safety seat belts Swimming lessons
Any family stresses?	Child has mastered the learning tasks of counting to10, printing first name and numbers up to 10	Hearing		Television
How is school? Friends?	Child knows right from left	Speech		*Activities with Parents:* Establishing rules Spending time with your child Showing interest in your child's daily life (e.g., school) Adult supervision Encouraging and praising your child The parental role model
What aspects of your child are you most proud of?	Child can draw a person with six body parts and clothing	Blood pressure		Discipline
How is the family communicating and interacting with one another?	Child is expanding circle of social interactions (new friends)			Behavior
Is supervision of your child an issue?				
Do you have any school reports I may review?				

WELL-CHILD HEALTH SUPERVISION VISITS: 8-year Visit

Questions your Pediatrician May Ask	Developmental Milestones	Physical Examination	Immunizations	Topics for Discussion
How are things going for you and your family?	Child can tell time	Physical examination		*Good Health Habits:* Balanced diet (including information on fat and cholesterol) Avoid junk food Physical activity Dental care
Are there any new questions, concerns or stresses?	Child reads for pleasure	Weight, height, weight-for-stature		Television and video games
How's school going?	Child exhibits sense of humor and play	Vision		*Accident Prevention Issues:* Bicycle safety Swimming safety Seat belts Drug and alcohol prevention
How does your child play and interact with other children or family members?	Child understands concept of rules	Hearing		*Parental Interaction:* Establishing fair rules Communicating and interacting with your child Showing interest in child's daily activities Allowances The importance of love, praise, and encouragement Adult supervision Parental role model
Have you thought about teaching your child information regarding sex and substance abuse?	Child is able to take care of his or her belongings	Speech		
	Child is expanding circle of social interactions (new friends)	Blood pressure		

Adapted from the American Academy of Pediatrics, Health Supervision Visits, 1994.

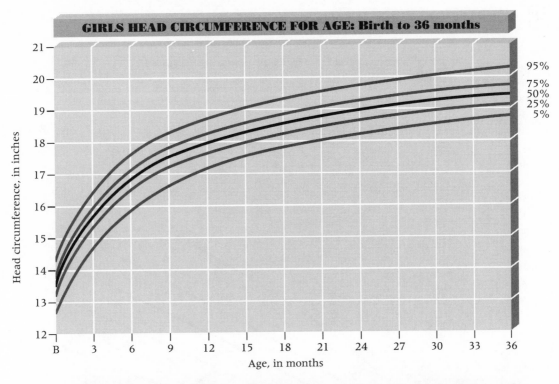

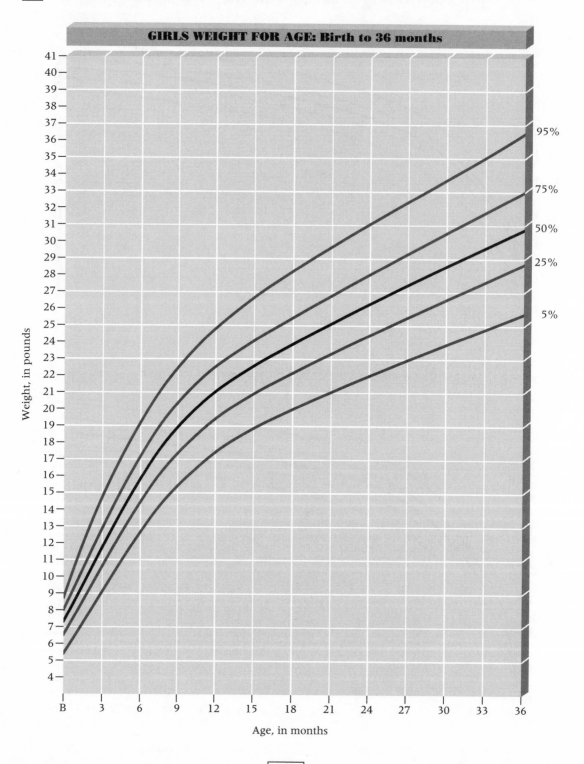

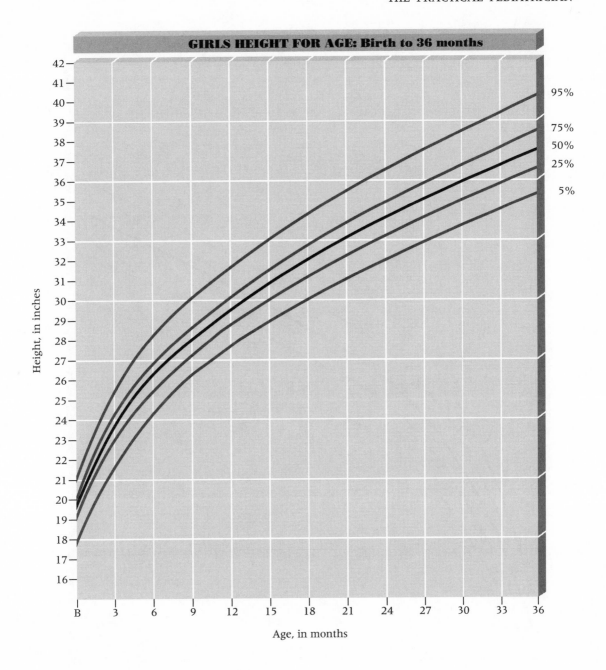

GIRLS HEIGHT FOR AGE: Birth to 36 months

Height, in inches

Age, in months

95%
75%
50%
25%
5%

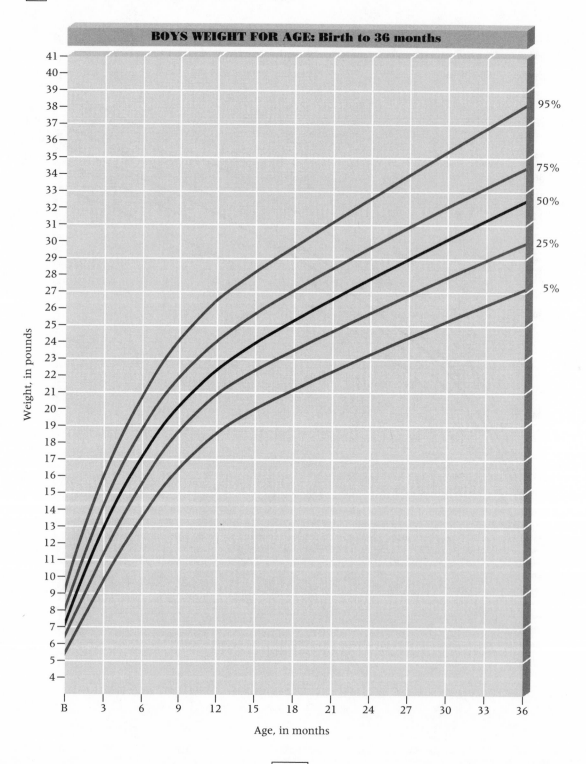

BOYS WEIGHT FOR AGE: Birth to 36 months

Weight, in pounds

Age, in months

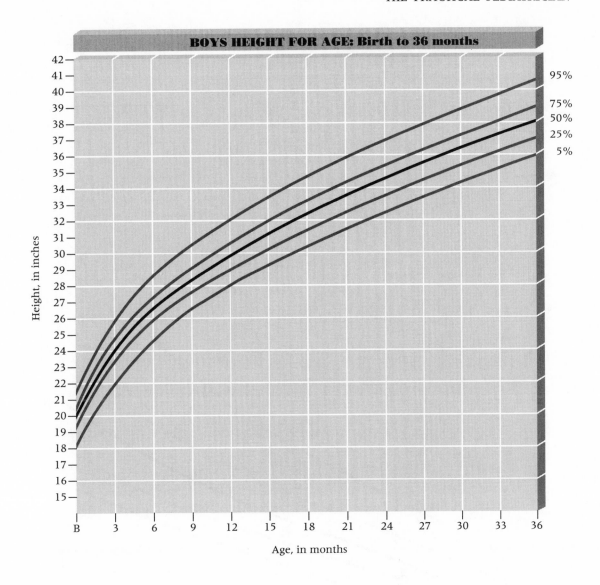

BOYS HEIGHT FOR AGE: Birth to 36 months

Height, in inches

Age, in months

95%
75%
50%
25%
5%

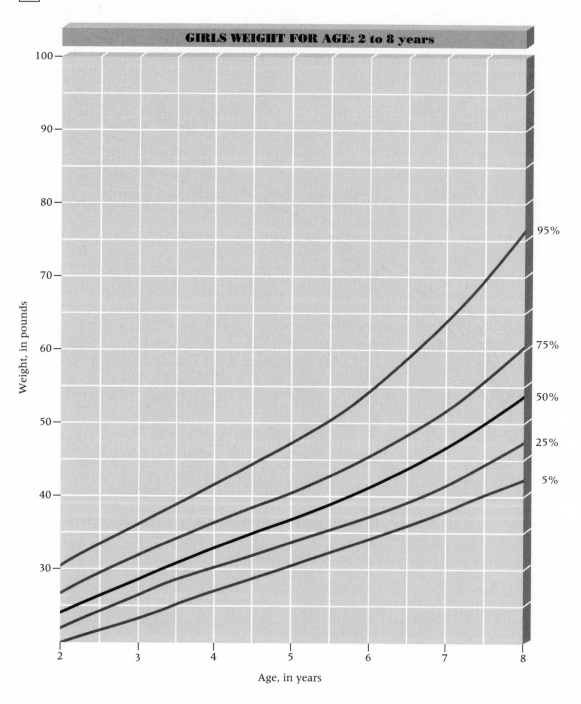

GIRLS WEIGHT FOR AGE: 2 to 8 years

Weight, in pounds

Age, in years

95%
75%
50%
25%
5%

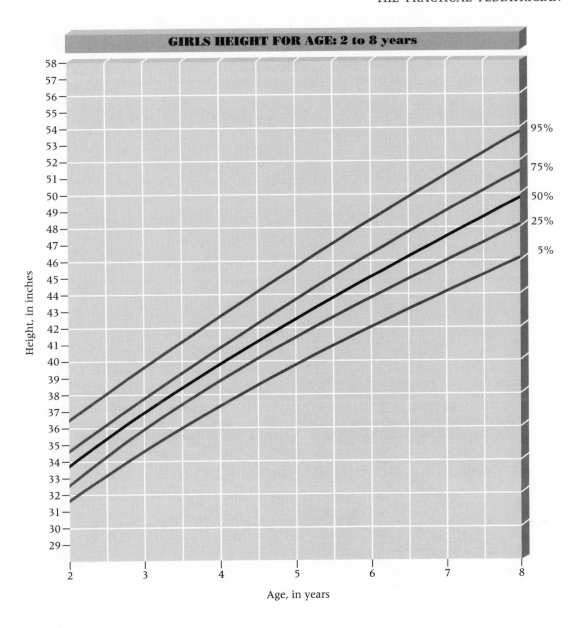

GIRLS HEIGHT FOR AGE: 2 to 8 years

Height, in inches

Age, in years

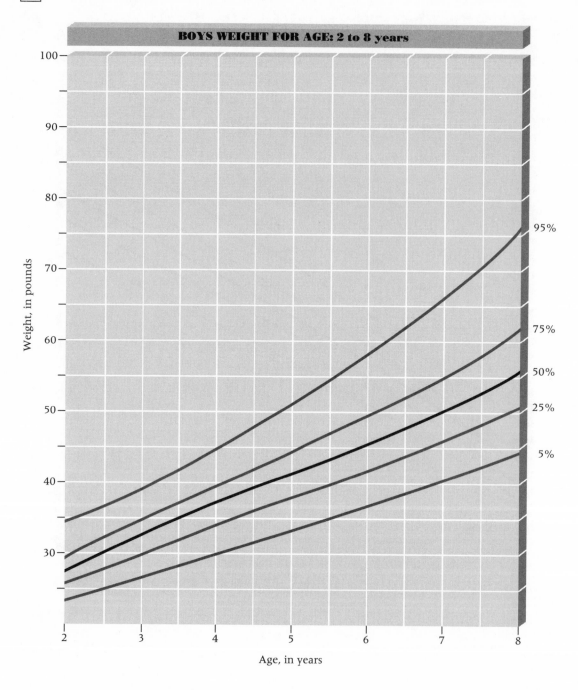

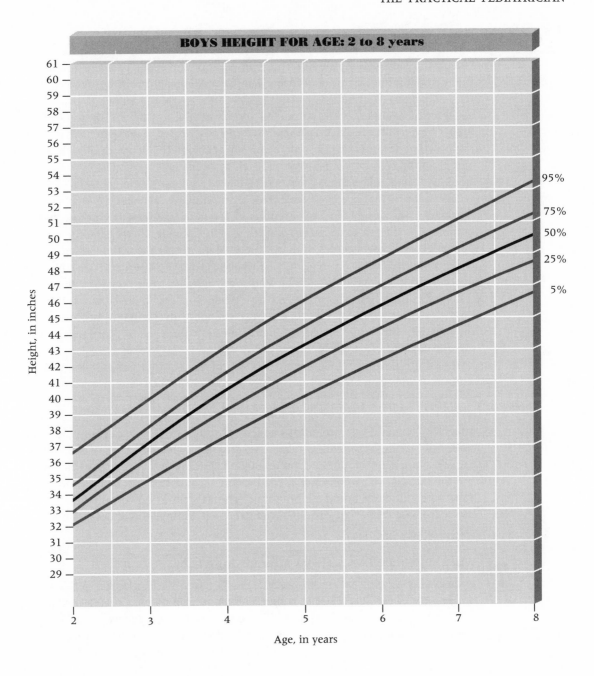

WORKING PARENTS

One of the most striking social changes in parenting over the past few decades is the increasing number of dual-career families and single-parent households. For reasons ranging from necessity to individual career goals, more than 50 percent of all American mothers work outside of the home, and less than 15 percent of all homes have a full-time stay-at-home mom. In other cases, single parents have full responsibility for their child's welfare and struggle with the demands of both work and parenting. No one can (or should) tell a parent how to settle this issue. Instead, we congratulate those parents who manage so many different tasks so well.

The reality is that it is impossible to do everything. Pace yourself. Exhaustion is one of the biggest problems of parenthood. Try to do as much as you can that is important, and learn to delegate what is not. For example, if you have the choice of playing with your toddler or doing a load of laundry, choose the toddler. Most children love to spend any type of "quality time" with their parents. You'd be surprised what they may enjoy doing with you, ranging from preparing meals to simply spending time chatting—perhaps while you get to that laundry! Daily time spent with your child is, perhaps, the soundest investment in his future. In the end, all of us remember these interactions with our parents far longer than their professional accomplishments.

If you are having trouble coping with all of your varied responsibilities, talk about it. If you are married, discuss your concerns with your spouse, and consider new divisions of labor in the home. For example, make a list of the household duties you and your spouse carried out *before* the baby was born; then make another list containing the new tasks added by your baby's arrival. These may include baby-sitting, changing the baby, feeding the baby, taking the child to the pediatrician, child-proofing the home, buying clothing and supplies for the baby, and similar tasks of parenting. Make a division of these labors of love as you have done with the more mundane household chores such as grocery shopping. Get advice from other working parents. And keep persevering. You're doing far better than you give yourself credit for!

When should I return to work after having a baby?

We commonly suggest a maternity leave of six to eight weeks after childbirth. In this manner, both the mother and the child recuperate from the delivery process and a routine of feeding, sleeping, and so on is established between them. This is a minimal period of time when you think about the average length of one's working career. In some countries, maternity (and paternity) leave is far more generous and, we think, productive for the child's welfare. When you check with your employer about your benefits with respect to maternity leave, you may also want to inquire about options such as job sharing, "flextime," part-time hours, or work-at-home programs.

[See also Bottle Feeding Your Baby; Breastfeeding Your Baby; Day Care and Child-Care Issues; Separation Anxiety]

Worms

Perhaps the greatest advantage of arranging a volume on baby and child care in alphabetical format is that it allows one to place this section at the back of the book! Although it is not a particularly appealing topic, children do commonly suffer from parasitic intestinal infections caused by worms. Indeed, if you took all the human beings in the world, the most common type of infection would be parasitic worms, although this problem is most serious in underdeveloped and impoverished areas of the world. We will discuss the most common types of worm infestation for children living in North America. They include pinworms, roundworms, and hookworms.

Pinworms

Humans become infected with pinworms by swallowing their eggs. Pinworm eggs may be in contaminated foods, drink, or on the hands of other children. The infection is further spread when the infected child scratches her rectal area, where she invariably picks up some more eggs to swallow or pass on to others. Clothing, especially underwear, can be laden with pinworm eggs.

The eggs travel to a person's small intestine, where they hatch and develop into larvae. Approximately one month later, these immature worms travel to the large intestine and rectum, where they live. A particularly disgusting feature of the pinworm's life cycle is that it likes to travel out of the anus, especially at night.

Perhaps the most notable symptom of this worm infestation is an intense itching sensation in the rectal and genital areas. In some children, it may be confused with or complicated by a urinary tract infection *[see Urinary Tract Problems, Painful Urination].* Other symptoms include fussiness, sleep disturbances, belly pain, and a loss of appetite.

Diagnosing pinworms

If your child complains of itchiness in the rectal area, your pediatrician will examine her for evidence of worms or worm eggs. The easiest clue to this condition is obtained by placing a piece of cellophane tape over the child's anus first thing in the morning, before she has had a chance to use the bathroom. Peel it off and look on the sticky surface for evidence of eggs or worms. Wrap it up carefully in a piece of tissue paper or plastic wrap and bring it to the doctor; he or she will examine the tape under the microscope for evidence of the infection. The pinworms may be visible to the eye; they look like white strands of thin silk. But they are far easier to see with the aid of a microscope.

Treating pinworms

Your doctor will prescribe a medicine called an anti-helminthic agent. These medicines kill the living worms but not the unhatched eggs. Sometimes, the medicine needs to be prescribed more than once. For pinworms, the whole family needs to be treated.

Roundworms

Like pinworms, roundworms are intestinal parasites that are primarily spread by fecal contamination. Sometimes food or soil can be contaminated with roundworms. Roundworm eggs hatch in the child's intestine, and the larvae then travel into the bloodstream and into the lungs. The person infested with roundworm subsequently coughs these larvae up and swallows them once again. They then mature in the small intestine. These parasites may live in the intestinal tract for as long as a year before discovery.

Unlike pinworms, roundworms are a serious and potentially damaging infection and can lead to obstructions of the digestive tract or to malnutrition. Roundworms can be difficult to diagnose in a child without clear symptoms; in general, the child with roundworms may complain of breathing disturbances (e.g., coughing, wheezing), belly pain, nausea, cramping, and other abdominal problems.

Diagnosing roundworm

You should suspect roundworm if you see worms in either your child's vomit or stools, especially when associated with the symptoms noted above. Roundworms are especially difficult to see with the naked eye. Your pediatrician will examine the stool under the microscope to confirm the diagnosis.

Treating roundworm

The child, but not the other family members, will be prescribed an antihelminthic medication.

Hookworm

The hookworm has a life cycle similar to that of roundworm, although it typically enters the body through cuts or breaks in the skin. One of the most common ways to contract hookworm in the United States is to walk barefoot along farm land or pastures where there are animal or human feces infected with the hookworm eggs. Wearing shoes whenever walking outside is always a good idea.

Hookworm infections cause chronic or long-term bleeding from the gastrointestinal tract. This loss of blood eventually leads to a condition called iron deficiency anemia, which causes pale skin, lack of energy, restlessness, and may interfere with your child's intellectual development *[see Iron Deficiency Anemia]*. Hookworm may also be associated with an intensely itchy rash, dry skin, diarrhea, cough, wheezing and other breathing disturbances, appetite disturbances, and a generalized lack of energy.

Diagnosing hookworm

As with roundworm, the stools of the child need to be examined under a microscope.

Treating hookworms

The child, but not the other family members, will be prescribed an antihelminthic medication.

The Last Word on Worms

It is always a good idea, when discovering that one family member has any type of worm infestation, to have everyone else checked out for worms. Above all, teach your child the importance of washing her hands after using the bathroom, before eating or touching food products, and after play *[see Contagious and Infectious Diseases].* (Please note that "ringworm"—which is discussed elsewhere—is *not* a worm infestation. It is caused by a fungus *[see Ringworm].*)

XEROSIS (Dry skin associated with winter and artificial heat; winter eczema)

Many children (and adults) experience dry, flaky skin during the winter months. The more time we spend indoors with the heat on, the more dehydrated and dry our skin becomes. Washing with harsh or drying soaps and bathing too frequently may also contribute to this problem. In extreme cases, the skin may be scaly, rough, and quite itchy. With extensive dryness, the skin can become cracked and tender. We generally recommend using emollient creams that rehydrate the skin (available at most drugstores without a prescription), decreased numbers of baths, and the use of a cool-mist humidifier in the house (and especially the child's room) to reduce the dryness of the air. When using a cool-mist humidifier, it is important to clean it out daily to prevent the buildup of molds and fungus. A weak solution of water and bleach, followed by a careful rinsing with water, should suffice. More severe cases of dry skin may be treated with a mild hydrocortisone or steroid cream. Some of these steroid creams are available without a prescription at your drugstore; other, stronger ointments do require a physician's prescription. Xerosis is an annoying but easily treated skin problem that resolves with proper care and the end of winter.

[See Excema]

X RAYS

X rays are among the most common medical tests ordered by physicians. X rays of the chest, for example, are very helpful in diagnosing a case of pneumonia *[see Pneumonia]*. Specific X rays of the kidney and urinary tract are often used to find out the cause of a urinary tract infection in a child *[see Urinary Tract Problems]*. Similarly, problems such as sinusitis, broken bones, and traumatic injuries are often diagnosed with the aid of X rays.

Should I worry about my child's exposure to X rays?

For the child who undergoes an occasional X ray examination (once every other year or so), the answer is no. You can measure the exposure to the X rays received during such an examination in milliseconds (one thousandth of a second). This represents a minimal exposure and is harmless. There are tests, such as cardiac catheterization (used to diagnose birth defects of the heart in children) and radiation therapies for cancer, that yield far greater exposure to radiation and X rays. If your child is undergoing one of these medical procedures, you should feel free to discuss any concerns you may have about these procedures with your physician and inquire about the safety precautions employed by those performing the X ray tests or treatments.

YEAST INFECTIONS *[See Thrush]*

YOUTH

When speaking of the joys of youth with both parents and colleagues, we often quote the great American poet Henry Wadsworth Longfellow (from "Morituri Salutamus," 1875).

> *How beautiful is youth! How bright it gleams*
> *With its illusions, aspirations, dreams!*
> *Book of beginnings, story without end,*
> *Each maid a heroine, and each man a friend!*

ZOSTER (Shingles)

Zoster infections are caused by the chicken pox virus (*Varicella zoster*). Unlike chicken pox, zoster is not contagious. These infections occur in children who have already had chicken pox. The virus lies dormant in the nerve cells of a child's body and, for a variety of reasons that remain unclear, reactivates itself to cause the rash of "shingles." For the overwhelming majority of children who experience shingles, the rash is self-limiting, without other ill effects or serious complications.

 ### What are the recognizable features of shingles?

• *A red rash, typically on one side of the body and appearing in a linear fashion (these infections follow nerve paths, which trail along the body).*

• *The rash begins as a collection of red, raised bumps, but quickly progresses to tiny, fluid-filled blisters. These break open and scabs result.*

• *The most common sites for the rash are the back, chest, and belly. For children, the shingles rash is typically not painful or itchy. (Adults, on the other hand, commonly complain of intense burning and itching when experiencing a bout of shingles.)*

• *The rash progresses, with new bumps and blisters forming for several days. By day seven to ten, all of the blisters should be scabbed over. Only 5 percent of all people who experience one episode of shingles ever have another.*

When should I call the doctor?

For most cases, you can simply handle things with telephone communication and a great deal of patience. Most children with shingles do not experience pain or significant problems. Make these children feel as comfortable as possible. Plenty of fluids, comfort foods, and acetaminophen for mild pain or fevers (under 100°F) are a good way to begin. Ointments and lotions are not needed and will only mess up your child's pajamas and sheets. Aspirin should be avoided because of the association of aspirin and varicella-zoster with Reye's Syndrome, a poorly understood metabolic disorder associated with brain damage and death.

You should call your physician if:

- *Your child is complaining of an intense itchiness or burning at the site of the rash.*
- *The rash is near the eye.*
- *The rash appears infected (red, sore, tender) and is oozing a honey-yellow fluid or pus [see Impetigo].*
- *The rash lasts longer than fourteen days, or your child appears to be ill.*

Do I need to keep my child home from school?

Yes. Even though shingles is not infectious, the child with shingles can transmit the chicken pox virus to others. Those children who have not yet contracted chicken pox can potentially get it from exposure to a child with shingles. Typically, the child with shingles should stay home for about seven to ten days, or until all of the blisters have scabbed over. Adults and other friends or family members who have not yet had chicken pox should avoid close contact with the child with shingles until all of the blisters have scabbed.

INDEX

Page numbers in *italics* indicate illustrations.